DISENTANGLING JIHAD, POLITICAL VIOLENCE AND MEDIA

DISENTANGLING JIHAD, POLITICAL VIOLENCE AND MEDIA

Edited by Simone Pfeifer, Christoph Günther and Robert Dörre

EDINBURGH
University Press

Edinburgh University Press is one of the leading university presses in the UK. We publish academic books and journals in our selected subject areas across the humanities and social sciences, combining cutting-edge scholarship with high editorial and production values to produce academic works of lasting importance. For more information visit our website: edinburghuniversitypress.com

Edinburgh University Press Ltd
13 Infirmary Street,
Edinburgh, EH1 1LT

First published in hardback by Edinburgh University Press 2023

Typeset in 11/15 Adobe Garamond by
IDSUK (DataConnection) Ltd

A CIP record for this book is available from the British Library

ISBN 978 1 3995 2379 0 (hardback)
ISBN 978 1 3995 2380 6 (paperback)
ISBN 978 1 3995 2381 3 (webready PDF)
ISBN 978 1 3995 2382 0 (epub)

CONTENTS

FIGURES

NOTES ON CONTRIBUTORS

Ahmed Al-Rawi is an Associate Professor of News, Social Media and Public Communication at the School of Communication at Simon Fraser University, Canada. He is the Director of the Disinformation Project that empirically examines fake news discourses in Canada. His research expertise is related to social media, global communication and news with a focus on Canada and the Middle East. He has authored five books and over 100 peer reviewed book chapters and articles published in a variety of journals.

Enrico De Angelis holds a PhD in Political Communication. He mainly works on new media and public sphere in Syria and Egypt, but also on grassroots media, political communication and journalism in the MENA region. He did a postdoctoral fellowship at Cedej, Cairo, between 2012 and 2014 analysing the networked public sphere in Egypt. He is one of the co-founders of the media platform SyriaUntold and of the Italian version of Orient XXI. He currently works as a researcher consultant for organisations such as Free Press Unlimited, UNESCO, International Media Support, Hivos, Deutsche Welle and Canal France International. He has held teaching positions at the American University of Cairo, Roberto Ruffilli Faculty and the Political Science Faculty at University of Bologna. He has published a monograph on media and conflict and several articles on media in the MENA region. He is particularly interested in critical approaches to Internet studies and the networked public sphere in the Arab world.

Yazan Badran is a visiting professor in the Department of Communication Sciences and an FWO postdoctoral fellow at the Echo and imec-SMIT research centers at the Vrije Universiteit Brussel, Belgium. He was a PhD fellow of the Research Foundation Flanders (FWO) and obtained a PhD in Media and Communication Studies from the Vrije Universiteit Brussel in 2021. His research interests lie at the intersection of new journalism and political activism in the post-2011 Middle East and North Africa region (MENA) and the political economy and journalistic practices of emerging media organisations.

Aïcha Bounaga is a PhD Candidate in Sociology at the LISST (Interdisciplinary Laboratory on Solidarities, Societies and Territories) at the University of Toulouse-Jean Jaurès. Her thesis explores the normative transformations occurring in France from the prevention of 'radicalization' paradigm (2015–20) to the fight against 'separatism' paradigm (2020–2), with a special focus on matters of gender and race.

Robert Dörre is a media scholar with a focus on social media and digital culture. He studied media culture studies, film studies and sociology in Mainz and Cologne and subsequently completed his PhD as part of the DFG-funded research training group Documentary Practices: Excess and Privation at the Ruhr University Bochum. The dissertation, which deals with audio-visual self-documentation in social media, has been awarded the Young Talent Award of the Büchner-Verlag. He is currently a Postdoctoral Researcher of Media Cultural Studies at Ruhr-University Bochum and an Associated Scholar at the Collaborative Research Centre Virtual Lifeworlds.

Hamza Esmili is a postdoctoral researcher within the 'Deradicalizing the City' project at KU Leuven. He defended his PhD in Sociology at Ecole des hautes études en sciences sociales in 2021. His work is focused on religious reaffiliation among immigrants and their children in Europe as well as on the various politico-theological forms of life that emerge from the contemporary reinvestment of the Islamic discursive tradition. Simultaneously, his work questions how such a religious form of life can be received within the liberal society.

Kurstin Gatt is a resident academic in the Department of Middle Eastern and Asian Languages and Cultures at the University of Malta. He lectures on courses about classical and modern Arabic literature, and media Arabic. His main area of interest is the analysis of political discourse in the Arab world, with particular focus on Salafi-Jihadi leaders and mainstream Arab politicians. Gatt is the author of *Decoding DĀ'ISH: An Analysis of Poetic Exemplars and Discursive Strategies of Domination in the Jihadist Milie* (2020). He is currently co-authoring a manuscript about contemporary Arabic political discourse, which investigates the persuasive techniques used by Arab politicians to legitimate their political agenda, discredit their opponents and strengthen in-group cohesion.

Christiane Gruber is Professor of Islamic Art and Visual Culture in the History of Art Department at the University of Michigan, Ann Arbor; she is also Founding Director of Khamseen: Islamic Art History Online. Her scholarly work explores medieval to modern Islamic art and visual culture, in particular figural representation, book arts, modern art and contemporary materiality, and global extremist iconographies. Her most recent publications include her single authored book *The Praiseworthy One: The Prophet Muhammad in Islamic Texts and Images* and her edited volume *The Image Debate: Figural Representation in Islam and Across the World*, both published in 2019.

Christoph Günther holds the Heisenberg position for Islamic Studies in the Department of Religious Studies at the University of Erfurt. Having a background in Islamic Studies, his research interests include religio-political movements in the modern Middle East, visual cultures and iconography, and the sociology of religion. He is the author of *Entrepreneurs of Identity: The Islamic State's Symbolic Repertoire* (2022) and has co-edited *Jihadi Audiovisuality and its Entanglements: Meanings, Aesthetics, Appropriations* (Edinburgh University Press, 2020) with Simone Pfeifer.

Farid Hafez is currently Class of 1955 Visiting Professor of International Studies at Williams College. He is also Senior Researcher at Georgetown University's The Bridge Initiative. In 2017, he was Fulbright Visiting Professor at University of California, Berkeley and in 2014, he was a visiting scholar at Columbia University, New York. He is also Associate Faculty of Rutgers University's Center for Security, Race and Rights. Since 2010, Hafez has been editor of the *Islamophobia Studies Yearbook*, and since 2015 co-editor of the annual *European Islamophobia Report*. He has received the Bruno Kreisky Award for the political book of the year, for his anthology *Islamophobia in Austria* (2009, co-edited with John Bunzl) and has published more than 140 books and articles, including in high-ranking academic journals. Moreover, Hafez regularly publishes op-eds and is frequently interviewed by media outlets.

Jaan S. Islam is a PhD candidate of Islamic Studies and an AHRC Doctoral Fellow at the University of Edinburgh. He has multiple publications in comparative political thought and currently studies Jihadi-Salafism and comparative political theory. Jaan is a co-author of a book on the political thought of Ibn Taymiyya, entitled *Islam and the State in Ibn Taymiyya: Translation and Analysis* (2022).

Martijn de Koning is an anthropologist and teaches at the Department of Islam, Politics and Society at Radboud University, Nijmegen. He has been working on themes related to identity construction of Moroccan-Dutch youth, Salafism, Radicalisation, Islamophobia and racialisation and activism among Muslims in the Netherlands, Germany and Belgium. Together with Nadia Fadil and Francesco Ragazzi, he edited the volume *Radicalization in Belgium and the Netherlands – Critical Perspectives on Violence and Security* (2019). With Carmen Becker and Ineke Roex he wrote *Islamic Militant Activism in Belgium, The Netherlands and Germany – 'Islands in a Sea of Disbelief'* (2020). He maintains his own weblog CLOSER: https://religion-research.org/closer.

Sebastian Köthe studied Screenwriting at the German Film and Television Academy Berlin (dffb) as well as Cultural History and Theory and Philosophy at Humboldt University Berlin. He was a member of the DFG Research Training Group 'Knowledge in the Arts' at Berlin University of the Arts where he finished his PhD thesis 'Witnessing Guantánamo'. Today he is a research associate at the Research Focus in Aesthetics at Zurich University of the Arts (ZHdK). His new project centres on aesthetics of solace and inconsolability. Besides his academic work, he works as freelance editor and educator for different theatre projects and is author at the performance collective copy & waste.

Anja Kublitz is an Associate Professor at the Department of Politics and Society, Aalborg University, Denmark. She holds a PhD in Anthropology from University of Copenhagen and has conducted fieldwork in the Occupied Palestinian Territories and since 2005 among Muslim immigrants in Denmark. Her research concerns how conflicts reconfigure space and time and forge political subjects. Currently she is studying the emergence of Danish jihadists. Her publications include 'Omar is Dead: Aphasia and the Escalating Anti-radicalization Business', *History and Anthropology* 32: 1 (2021); 'The Rhythm of Rupture: Attunement among Danish Jihadists', in *Ruptures: Anthropologies of Discontinuity in Times of Turmoil*, M. Holbraad, B. Kapferer and J. Sauma (eds) (2019), pp. 174–92; and (with Højer, Puri and Bandak) 'Escalations: Theorizing Sudden Accelerating Change', *Anthropological Theory* 18: 1 (2018).

Kevin B. Lee is a US-born filmmaker and educator based in Berlin and Lugano. He has produced nearly 400 video essays exploring film and media. His award-winning *Transformers: The Premake* introduced the 'desktop documentary' format and was named one of the best documentaries of 2014 by *Sight & Sound*. In 2017 he was the first-ever Artist in Residence of the Harun Farocki Institut in Berlin. He is the Locarno Film Festival Professor for the Future of Cinema and the Audiovisual Arts at Università della Svizzera italiana (USI). Previously he was Professor in Crossmedia Publishing at the Merz Akademie, Stuttgart. His video work can be found at https://www.alsolikelife.com.

Darryl Li is Associate Professor of Anthropology and Associate Member of the Law School at the University of Chicago. He is the author of *The*

Universal Enemy: Jihad, Empire, and the Challenge of Solidarity (2020) and has participated in litigation arising out of the Forever War, including the defense of captives held by the US government at Guantánamo Bay.

Nicole Nguyen is Associate Professor of Criminology, Law and Justice at the University of Illinois Chicago. She is author of *Suspect Communities: Anti-Muslim Racism and the Domestic War on Terror* (2019) and *A Curriculum of Fear: Homeland Security in US Public Schools* (2016).

Simone Pfeifer is a postdoctoral researcher at the Research Training Group *Connecting–Excluding: Cultural Dynamics Beyond Globalized Networks* at the University of Cologne. She is a social and cultural anthropologist with a focus on visual, digital and media anthropology. Her research interests include transnational migration and mobility in postmigrant contexts, political violence, religion, and artistic practices, and ethics in (digital) ethnographic research. Her recent publications include *Social Media im transnationalen Alltag* (2020), the co-edited special section *Dark Ethnographies?* (2021) and the co-edited volume *Jihadi Audiovisuality and its Entanglements: Meanings, Aesthetics, Appropriations* (Edinburgh University Press, 2020) with Christoph Günther.

Sindyan Qasem is a doctoral researcher at Freie Universität Berlin. His main focus lies on a hegemony-critical examination of current preventive measures against so-called Islamist extremism. Qasem has obtained a Master's degree from the University of Leipzig in the field of Linguistics and Cultural Studies.

S. Sayyid is a Professor of Social Theory and Decolonial Thought and the Head of the School of Sociology and Social Policy at the University of Leeds. Professor Sayyid is a political theorist. His research interests explore the constitutive interplay between rhetoric and social structures, such as the part played by racism in the formation of modern societies or investigations of alternative worlds signalled by the various Islamist projects. His approach is informed by the intersections between decolonial thought and discourse theory. His substantive work has ranged from Islamophobia, diasporas to political Islam and epistemic decolonisation. Sayyid's recent research has been around organising the Critical Muslim Studies project as a means of understanding Islamicate societies, histories and cultures outside Eurocentric framings. Sayyid's writings have been translated into numerous languages. His major publications include *A Fundamental Fear* (despite being banned by the Malaysian government, now in its third edition, 2015) and *Recalling the Caliphate* (2014). He is the founding editor of *ReOrient: The Journal of Critical Muslim Studies* and an editor of the Pluto Press series: 'Decolonial Studies, Postcolonial Horizons'.

Wendy M. K. Shaw researches post-colonial art historiography and decolonial art history of the Islamic world and the modern Middle East. She is author of *Possesors and Possessed: Museums, Archaeology, and the Visualization of History in the Late Ottoman Empire* (2003), *Ottoman Painting: Reflections of Western Art from the Ottoman Empire to the Turkish Republic* (2011), *What is 'Islamic' Art? Between Religion and Perception* (2019, awarded the Honorable Mention for the 2020 Albert Hourani Book Award of the Middle East Studies Association and the 2021 Iran Book Award) and *Loving Writing* (2021).

ACKNOWLEDGEMENTS

This book reflects critical perspectives and insights that developed from conversations and encounters over the period of the five-year research project entitled 'Jihadism on the Internet: Images and Videos, their Appropriation and Dissemination', generously funded by the Federal Ministry of Education and Research. Not all the people who contributed to these debates and who we were thinking with and along over this time, are represented in this edited volume. Especially during the Symposium on 'Notions of Jihad Reconsidered' in Mannheim and Mainz, that included a joint visit to the special exhibition Mindbombs – Visual Cultures of Political Violence, curated by Sebastian Baden and Larissa-Diana Fuhrmann, we further advanced the themes that convolute in this volume in lively discussions.

For their continuous interest in our research and support of our work, we would therefore first like to thank all faculty and staff at the Department of Anthropology and African Studies at Johannes Gutenberg University Mainz. Matthias Krings drafted the project and guided us as a mentor throughout its entire duration, and we owe him a great debt of gratitude for this. We would also like to thank all members of our team for their involvement in this process: Yorck Beese, Alexandra Dick, Larissa-Diana Fuhrmann, Mirko Scherf and Bernd Zywietz. Many other friends and colleagues have followed our work with keen interest, suggestions and fruitful criticism. They have thus contributed significantly to the success of our work. By way of example, Robert Dörre owes thanks to Yorck Beese, Alexandra Dick, Larissa-Diana Fuhrmann, Katja Grashöfer, Kevin B. Lee, Stephan Packard and Mary Shnayien for their fruitful and astute comments on the ideas underlying his own paper in this volume. Christoph Günther is much obliged to the insights, comments and thoughts provided by Thomas Demmelhuber, Kerstin Eppert, Michael Krona, Dominik Müller, Hanna Pfeifer, and Joram Tarusarira. Simone Pfeifer thanks Cathrine Bublatzky, Heike Drotbohm, Larissa-Diana Fuhrmann, Kevin B. Lee and Morehshin Allahyari for their perspectives, support and insightful comments, and together we thank many others that we cannot list here by name.

At Edinburgh University Press, we are indebted to our editors Isobel Birks, Emma House and Louise Hutton who welcomed our proposal and kindly guided us through a production process that could not have been smoother.

We thank the two anonymous reviewers of our proposal for their valuable suggestions and comments which helped to enhance the quality of the whole volume. For being so generous with their time and for providing thoughtful and constructively critical feedback on prior iterations of our introduction we are grateful to Tom Kaden and Stephan Packard. Rob Glaser, Pip Hare and Dan Ruppel we thank for their support in proofreading the manuscript, and the student assistants Muna Ahmad, Lea Fernengel and Marlene Ziegelmayer for aiding us with the typescript and mark-up.

Last, but not least, our appreciation and deepest gratitude go to the contributors who made this volume possible, and who not only took part in lively conversations about the themes in this book but were also hugely responsible in keeping to the time frame of the publication process. We are thrilled to have worked with them on this project.

FOREWORD

In 2021, a community radio station in Sheffield, UK (Link FM) was sanctioned by the British state's broadcast regulatory authority (Ofcom) for breaching its code by playing a Jihadi nasheed entitled 'JundAllah'. Nasheed is a popular vocal musical form found throughout the Islamosphere. The praise of the Prophet, celebration of faith and struggle in the venture of Islam tend to characterise the lyrical content of a nasheed. While Ofcom conceded that the specific nasheed did not contain any 'explicit or direct calls to carry out a specific criminal action', they nevertheless ruled that the 'cumulative effect of its lyrics and imagery was to condone, promote and actively encourage others to participate in violent acts as a form of devout religious expression . . . thus considered it to contain material that would incite criminal acts or disorder.'[1] The radio station was fined, and its presenter apologised profusely for broadcasting the nasheed in question.

In 1976, Bob Marley and the Wailers released a song from their album, *Rastaman Vibration*, titled 'War'. The song declares that unless the philosophy of racism is discarded, class divisions overcome, fundamental human

---

[1] The news report on the decision can be found at: <https://www.bbc.co.uk/news/uk-england-south-yorkshire-58162579> (last accessed 27 January 2023). The full decision by Ofcom can be found at: <https://www.ofcom.org.uk/__data/assets/pdf_file/0029/233678/sanction-decision-link-fm.pdf> (last accessed 27 January 2023). The quotes are taken from the full decision.

rights guaranteed, and colonial regimes of Angola and Mozambique and apartheid South Africa destroyed, war will continue. The final part of the song's final verse announces: 'We Africans will fight, we find it necessary / And we know we shall win / As we are confident / In the victory / Of good over evil.' The lyrics of this song are a virtual transcription of the speech delivered by Emperor Haile Selassie I before the United Nations General Assembly in 1963 in New York. The song and the album were a tremendous commercial success and continued to be played on radio stations worldwide, including those lands which fall within the bailiwick of Ofcom. To date, Ofcom does not seem to have taken any action against Bob Marley and the Wailers' song 'War', or indicated to radio stations or other media outlets that playing the song while not in itself likely to lead to criminal behaviour and public disorder the cumulative effect of its imagery and lyrics would be to promote acts of violence as a form of religious devotion. It seems clear that the difference between a nasheed and a reggae song is that the former is part of a religiously saturated form of expression. The difference between religion and politics is, of course, one of the critical elements of the liberal-secular matrix, which seeks to regulate Muslimness.[2] It would be understandable that reggae and nasheed are considered distinct on the basis that one is secular and the other is religious, and this would help explain the difference in treatment between the two songs; after all, it is the religious motivation for violence that is the real problem with jihadi nasheeds.

This, however, is where things get a bit less clear-cut. It is important to remember that Bob Marley firmly believed in Rastafarianism. For many Rastafarians, Haile Selassie was not just the emperor of a country that famously resisted becoming part of the spoils of Europe's 'Scramble for Africa', but he was also – depending on the specific community of interpretation – either divine (the incarnation of God) or a semi-divine messianic figure. There-fore, transcription of Haile Selassie's speech into a reggae song is not just the privileging of the exercise of African sovereignty in a racialised world order. It

---

[2] The liberal-secular matrix of integration is described by Schirin Amir-Moazami (2022) as specific dynamic mode of inclusion and exclusion which orders majorities and minorities in state-civil societies that describe themselves as secular and liberal. Amir-Moazami's primary concern is with integration of Muslims in Germany, but the liberal-secular matrix has a wider scope. It is in this wider sense that I am using it.

also carries theological (religious) weight, which is corrosive of the secularist mandated split between the political and religious.[3]

An argument can be made that both these examples of reggae and nasheed share with Franz Fanon the insight that anti-colonialism is a violent phenomenon because it entails the replacement of those who have power with those who have been powerless (2001: 27). In 'War', destruction of colonialism and apartheid is explicitly stated. In 'JundAllah', there is a direct reference to the liberation of al-Aqsa. Both songs describe an ethos of struggle against geopolitical injustices; in other words, they reflect on the uses of political violence to fight a system of violent oppression sustained by a colonial-racial ethos.

It is the retrospective reconstruction of anti-colonialism as the gift of Western liberalism that enables the celebration of a 'War' reprised in 1976, rather than its initial occurrence in 1963. The attempt by Islamists from Maududi to Khomeini, from Sayyid Qutb to Shariati (to cite the most iconic exemplars of Islamism) to re-describe jihad as part of a decolonising imperative is interdicted by Eurocentric claims that the struggle for justice has to operate via an imitation of the Western telos. The insistence that jihad must be read through the articulation of jihadism reproduces the dialectic of extreme and moderate Muslims. It violates Muslim subject positions that reject a reading of jihad through the Westernised and Westernising epistemic template. Themes of political violence, the proper division between religion and politics, and how this political/religious/lyrical content is transmitted through telematic means; all are present in both these cases. One could easily conduct a thought experiment in which the word war in Bob Marley's song was replaced by the word jihad and speculate on the reaction of Ofcom or other state agents and sections of civil society.

The decision by Ofcom to sanction a local radio station for playing what was considered jihadi nasheed is a valuable metaphor for some of the issues *Disentangling Jihad* sets out to explore. One way of describing the innovative and remarkable collection of essays presented in *Disentangling Jihad*

---

[3] The relationship between reggae and Rastafarianism is not isomorphic. One sees an emergence of tension between the ways many early reggae outputs that were beholden to Rastafarian theology, and how the international appeal of the music led to its secularisation; see King (1998).

is to see them as explorations of terrain which excludes jihad from being a metaphorical substitute for war, not only in the context of anti-colonial, anti-racist liberation struggles, but also more broadly as a legitimate form of political violence.

We know from Weber that a state is an organisation with a monopoly of legitimate violence over a given territory. The legitimacy afforded to political violence is not entirely internal to the state because states do not exist separately from other states or forms of social relations that transcend state boundaries. For example, the discourse on human rights, rights to protect, international criminal courts, and other institutions of global civil society are involved in conferring or contesting the legitimacy of political violence.[4] The European empire projects had, by the end of the nineteenth century, established a world system in which the legitimacy of political violence was distributed according to the norms of a racial-colonial order. At the centre of these empires, projects were aspirational nation states, where political legitimacy and rights rested; in the periphery there were communities where political rights were absent.[5] This divide between centre and the periphery was racialised. Part of the racialisation process was the denial of political legitimacy to populations considered to be part of lesser 'races'. This racial barrier was constitutive of the European colonial enterprise, which bequeathed the organisation of the world that we continue to inhabit. Anti-colonial resistances, national liberation wars and projects of epistemic delinking are all in their different contexts struggles against that colonial-racial order. That struggle means contesting claims for conventional distribution of violence and legitimacy.

Disentangling jihad would mean explaining how one type of musical output describing political violence associated with a religious-inflected

---

[4] The contrast between the representation of Ukrainian resistance to occupation with the Palestinian or Kashmiri resistance is instructive in this regard.

[5] John Darwin describes the British Empire as a world system based around a range of political, economic, commercial, diplomatic and cultural relationships. It contained settler colonies, directly governed imperial possessions, treaty ports and clients. I have extended the concept of empire projects to refer to other iterations of the European colonial-racial enterprise to capture the complex ensemble of institutions, ideas and individuals that substantiated these imperial entities.

vocabulary is considered to be worth sanctioning, compared to another type of fusion of political violence and religious vocabularies. The question of what jihad is becomes difficult to address, not because there is a dearth of voices declaring what jihad is. As the pages of this volume show so eloquently, US marine generals, securocrats and politicians have joined the ranks of academics of Islamic studies and members of the ʿulamāʾ in attempting to authoritatively fix the meaning of jihad. Jihad is not an understudied concept. There is no gap in the literature with regard to that definition which this volume attempts to fill. Jihad as an object of study can be found across many disciplines. Anthropologists, criminologists, psychologists, historians and political scientists have all contributed to an expanding body of case studies, policy analyses and psychological profiles of specific jihadists and jihadi groups. There have been studies on the ideology of jihad, theoretical interventions on jihadism and its spread, and predictive models funded to map its future occurrences. What this book does is reflect on the terms of how jihad and jihadism are analysed. This collection stands in opposition to much of the literature on the problematics of jihad. It does so even though it could be argued that some chapters use disciplinary approaches similar to those found in the broader literature on jihad. It does so because this volume's collective voice understands that disentangling jihad requires not only sorting out the various imbrications of jihad and clarifying the conditions for its appropriate applications, but also a sustained critique of some of the current literature on jihad. Disentangling jihad is not only an empirical or ethnographic endeavour; it is also epistemological.

This epistemological impulse of the book arises not only from a common understanding commensurate with a sociology of knowledge which affirms that the production and organisation of academic knowledge is not independent of geopolitical world-making. This sociology of knowledge approach to the study of matters Islamicate can be found in Edward Said's *Orientalism* (and more decisively in his subsequent *Covering Islam*). It is an approach that seeks to unmask the forces behind knowledge production by showing the institutional or economic motivations at work. As some of the essays in the book make clear, research funding is aligned to address specific perceived knowledge deficits in understanding jihad and Muslimness in general. This

type of critique of Orientalism is what I have called 'weak Orientalism'.[6]
Critical to this approach is a belief in the existence of an objective 'Orient'
which is misrecognised due to poor scholarship tainted by individual bias.
The apparent solution is to produce unbiased knowledge, which can supposedly be done via the true spirit of academia. Weak Orientalism works within
the parameters of the dominant paradigm, dealing with epistemological challenges as anomalies. Such studies would enumerate cases of jihad and could
provide valuable taxonomy of armed groups of Muslims engaging in the
struggle in the name of jihad but operate without addressing their relationship with jihad and its meaning except through reference to dictionary-like
definitions. There is, however, another form of the critique of Orientalism
contained in Edward Said's work, which I describe as 'strong Orientalism'.
This approach is characterised by an understanding that the Orient is not an
independent object but rather a construction of Orientalism. In this case,
the real Orient cannot be used to check the basis of knowledge produced by
Orientalism. Strong Orientalism is not about correcting but rather clearing
away Oriental studies. The necessity of abandoning Orientalism as the primary means of understanding jihad is affirmed in various essays in this collection. Liberalism's complicity with imperialism and racism is well established.
Liberalism's complicity with Orientalism, while obvious, has been the subject
of less attention. The essays in this collection highlight how the very idea of
jihad, jihadism and its cognates become the centrepiece of Kafkaesque violent extremism policies undertaken not only by authoritarian governments
but also established liberal-democratic regimes. Organisations dedicated
to monitoring incidents of racism and Islamophobia have been banned in
France. The liberal-democratic conceit that only in liberal-democracies is it
possible to exercise academic freedom and speak truth to power is shown
to be not just hypocritical (the existence of liberal-democratic rule at home
and authoritarian rules over colonies already did that for countries such as
Britain, France and the Netherlands, to name the most obvious examples),
but also Orwellian. Farid Hafez's chapter stands out as a representation of

---

[6] See Sayyid (2015: 31–5) for a discussion of differences between weak and strong Orientalism
and what that means for the development of a method that takes the critique of Orientalism
to its heart.

this Orwellian turn, not just in Austria but more generally among the members of the liberal order. Counter violent extremism programmes and other similar policies have an epistemic as well as kinetic dimension. This volume alerts us to the way Muslim demands for civil rights are deferred by asserting isomorphic links between Muslimness and jihadism. In a world order where Islamophobia has been institutionalised globally, the circulation of the signifier of jihad is significant in the perpetuation of a racialised governmentality that targets expressions of Muslimness and interdicts the ability of Muslims to exercise their collective agency. For established liberal-democratic regimes, the focus on jihadism has a tendency to become a gateway to hollowing out democracies, initially for their Muslim populations but ultimately for societies at large. Orientalism is not only dedicated to investigating what was considered beyond the West, but it also involved policing the frontier between the Western and non-Western.

There is a need for an epistemological shift in how we understand matters Islamicate. One way to describe this epistemological shift is as Critical Muslim Studies. Critical Muslim Studies attempts to understand Muslimness in the context of recognition that the epistemological framework developed in the wake of geopolitical and socio-economic Eurocentrism is no longer adequate in the emerging post-Western world order. Such a shift can only be a collective undertaking which accepts that hegemonic ways to produce knowledge about Islam and Muslims are not fit for purpose. These do not advance understanding of the current conjuncture. The multiple mobilisations around the world which have seen students demanding an epistemic decolonisation have produced conditions that are conducive to an epistemological shift in the way we seek to comprehend Islam and the Islamicate. Contestations over the significance of the idea of jihad, the multiple ways it can be articulated, how themes of violence and political legitimacy are played out, and whether religion is a universal category; these questions are skilfully woven throughout the text of *Disentangling Jihad*, signalling how this book is part of the epistemological shift in the study of Muslimness. The project of Critical Muslim Studies seeks to improve upon the range of examples by which we understand the world and the place of Muslimness in it. The chapters presented here extend examples of how jihad and jihadism continue to shape Muslimness and, in the process, transform relations between the state and civil society. The appearance of books like *Disentangling Jihad* adds not only to the stock of our knowledge of Muslimness but also helps interrogate the ways in which the academy produces knowledge in contested fields.

S. Sayyid, University of Leeds

References

Amir, M. S. (2022), *Interrogating Muslims*, London: Bloomsbury Academic.

Darwin, J. (2011), *The Empire Project*, Cambridge: Cambridge University Press.

Fanon, F. ([1961] 2001), *The Wretched of the Earth*, Preface by J.-P. Sartre, trans. C. Farrington, London: Penguin Group.

King, S. A. (1998), 'International Reggae, Democratic Socialism, and the Secularization of the Rastafarian Movement, 1972–1980', *Popular Music and Society*, 22: 3, 39–60, DOI: 10.1080/03007769808591713.

Sayyid, S. (2015), *A Fundamental Fear*, London: Zed Press.

INTRODUCTION
DISENTANGLING JIHAD, POLITICAL VIOLENCE AND MEDIA

Christoph Günther, Robert Dörre and Simone Pfeifer

This edited volume is one of the outputs of the interdisciplinary junior research group 'Jihadism on the Internet: Images and Videos, their Dissemination and Appropriation'. From 2017 to 2022, the project facilitated collaborative work by six researchers with backgrounds in film and media studies, Islamic studies, social and cultural anthropology, and information sciences. The project sought to explore the ways in which groups fighting in the name of jihad communicate their cause through audiovisual media and how people engage with these communicative endeavours. These key questions reflect the field of tension in which our research operated: between our ambitions to explore the dynamics of our research field from our different disciplinary backgrounds and the structural conditions set by the logics of third party-funded research as part of a civil security funding initiative. This provoked us to critically reflect on the designations 'jihadism' and 'jihadist(s)' in our research and consider how they inflect our interlocutors and research more broadly (see Günther and Pfeifer 2020: 3; Fuhrmann and Pfeifer 2020: 179–81). Controversy developed within our group over whether we might better approach the topic by conceiving of individuals or social collectives as jihadist(s), understanding jihadism as an ideology or global movement, or by critically reflecting on the notion as an analytical framework and dismissing it as a useful category. As notions like jihadism or jihadists serve as catch-all terms employed to describe a range of quite different social and political conflict situations, as well as historical and contemporary groups and individuals, the terminology hardly provides useful categories (see also Li 2015; Li 2020: 24).

Rendering these terms themselves objects of critical debate also reflects our experiences in field research online and on site. Many of our interlocutors reject the terminology, not least because it is seen as integral to a political, academic, security and popular racialised discourse that establishes potentially harmful epistemic associations between Islam, violence and national security interests (Fuhrmann and Pfeifer 2020; see also Damir-Geilsdorf and Menzfeld 2020). Moreover, the prominence of the label in research, security agencies and popular discourses has arguably fostered a narrow understanding of the Arabic word jihad as synonymous with violent attacks in the name of Islam, even though it basically denotes any endeavour towards a praiseworthy goal. Especially in the US and Europe, this multifaceted concept tends to be connotated solely with (unrestrained) political violence and associated with a rather narrow canon of iconography. The notion of the 'Muslim Other' as a figure of unbridled violence has long shaped the history of how European societies have understood and engaged with the South west Asian and North African (SWANA) region. Yet, since the attacks of 11 September 2001, 'jihadism' seems to fulfil an intensified dual function: it identifies 'the evil Other' as the ultimate enemy of democratic civilisation – and thereby justifies the suspension of ethics and the inviolability of human rights to rationalise the War on Terror with its drone wars, their mediations and civil casualties, as well as the long-term extrajudicial detention of prisoners in Abu Ghraib and Guantánamo. Under these circumstances, discourses on Islam, Muslim religiosity and belonging in Europe and the US have become increasingly shaped by a notion of jihadism that adds to and perpetuates Orientalist attitudes and anti-Muslim racism that affects Muslims worldwide (Zine 2022; Bakali and Hafez 2022). Certain characteristics have been attributed to Muslims that intrinsically question their compatibility with European or American notions of social order and mark them as the object of national security strategies (Bayat 2007: 5; Cesari 2012; Cesari 2021; Fox and Akbaba 2015).

It is against this background that the term 'jihadism' all too often serves to gloss over a number of contextual factors that must be recognised in order to understand the ideas and actions of distinct groups and individuals in their specific social, political and economic contexts – and instead emphasises issues of security. This discursive framework of securitisation links issues in a selective way that reflects the underlying political rationale (Gledhill 2008), for example, by delegitimising rightful political claims or denigrating the citizens' rights of those labelled 'jihadists' or 'terrorists' (Fadil et al. 2022). It leads to a narrow and one-sided perspective on complex systems of power, violence, fear and domination and presents societal problems not as the results of policy and capitalist economic developments, for example, but as effects brought about by a threatening 'Other'. With the term 'jihadism' at the center of the title of our research project, we were forced to critically reflect on it in our publications, acknowledging that our own research was associated with processes of securitisation of Islam and could be perceived as being part of a discourse in which Muslims might appear as potential sources of radicalisation and terror.

Unravelling the layers of political violence and their transformation and mediation is one of the central axes of analysis in this book. In this introduction, political violence is understood to encompass all forms of violence enacted with the aim of bringing about fundamental societal transformations. It is used as a term that includes violence perpetrated by states as well as by non-state actors, beyond the normative notions of 'terrorism' or 'resistance' (Bosi and Malthaner 2015: 439; also Poynting and Whyte 2012; Hilal 2021: 23–8), and it refers to the entangled institutional, structural, colonial, physical, gendered and symbolic forms of violence at play in the contexts examined in this book. In this sense, looking at the socioculturally embedded forms of violence (and their mediations) of the so-called Islamic State, or Daesh,[1] for example, necessitates seeing these patterns of violence as resisting colonial and imperialist forms of domination (Fuhrmann 2021:

[1] Daesh is an acronym for *al-Dawla al-Islāmiya fī 'l-ʿIraq wa-l-Shām*. The sound is reminiscent of the Arabic term for trampling down (*daʿsa*) and accordingly marks the destructive intentions of the group that calls itself 'Islamic State'. The designation is intended to signal a distancing from this self-proclaimed aspiration to be 'the' Islamic state.

145) at the same time as they enact similar forms of violent oppression in the SWANA region. These patterns of violence can be seen as rooted 'in the logic of violence of Western modernity/coloniality' (Majozi 2018: 179).

Media technologies and media representations – of political violence or jihad, for example – are both symptoms and agents of violent conflict. While Kittler had understood communication technologies as the 'abuse of military equipment' (Kittler 1999: 97), current conflicts reveal how the media are increasingly becoming a key part of military equipment. Wazhmah Osman has, for example, recently emphasised how well the coverage of the War on Terror serves to obscure the means by which this war is being waged and the costs it entails (Osman 2022: 369–75). However, this discursive dimension is only one aspect of the broad understanding of media that underlies this volume. We do not use 'medium' to address exclusively representational or journalistic functions, nor do we limit the term to technological issues. We seek to analyse media in their processual role as mediators in their aesthetic, discursive, social and, not least, political dimensions.

The aim of this edited volume, therefore, is to disentangle the nexus of jihad, political violence and media, by examining some of the constellations in which this nexus is reproduced, perpetuated or disputed in European and Anglo-American contexts. The contributions shed light on the effects of this nexus in different configurations of knowledge production and reception, social and political controversies, as well as legal procedures and governmental actions. As an introduction, three examples will illustrate the wide spectrum of ways in which jihad, political violence and media are entangled in the present time. Here, we have chosen not to address imagery produced by groups acting in the name of jihad, but instead to focus on a variety of non-combative interpretations of jihad that have so far received little if any recognition from the wider public. The examples below show some of the ways in which the nexus of jihad, political violence, and media infuses quite distinct media aggregates and informs the interpretation of jihad as a concept that guides action under specific social and political conditions. First, we take a German documentary that frames humanitarian aid as jihad as a starting point for our discussion of the ambiguity of jihad as a notion, also historically. Our second example focuses on one of the ways in which the term jihad has been instrumentalised by right-wing actors. We demonstrate how the 'Jihad Squad' meme deploys jihad as a combative term to discredit and racially vilify political opponents. The third example, of environmental activism self-identified as 'eco-jihad', serves to show how hegemonic or dominant frames of the notion can inspire appropriation, resistance and opposition.

Jihad between Humanitarian Work and Military Violence

The German documentary film titled *Addicted to Jihad* (*Süchtig nach Jihad*) lays out a spectrum of practices of jihad ranging from humanitarian work to military violence.[2] Over 106 minutes, the debut work of the journalist and filmmaker Hubertus Koch portrays his – at times naïve – experiences during a two-week journey to the Turkish–Syrian border region and the Bab al-Salameh refugee camp in 2014. He accompanies Mahmud Dahi, who fled Syria in 1980 and now lives with his family in Germany. In October 2012, Dahi had started to regularly ship relief supplies from Germany to the border region, including ambulances and garbage trucks. He also collected donations to build and maintain an orphanage on the Turkish side of the border.[3] Mahmud Dahi calls this work 'my jihad'. He emphasises that for him, religion and politics must be kept strictly separate, and that he understands his endeavour as the fulfilment of what he sees as his religious duty as a Muslim. 'My jihad is my vision; it is what I do. And if I die on the way, I am a mujahid who has died for something good. After all, I don't have to carry a weapon. That is also jihad.'

Dahi's apparently spontaneous statement not only relates his commitment to helping others to his religious beliefs. It also shows that he is aware of the ambiguity of the term jihad and therefore self-consciously grounds his actions in a demilitarised understanding of it – as an individual's civil duty to their religion or to the Muslim community. As the filmmaker explains in the film's voiceover, Mahmud Dahi draws (albeit indirectly) on earlier interpretations of the concept in Islamic intellectual history, namely the distinction between the 'lesser jihad' (*al-jihād al-aṣghar*) oriented towards military battle and the 'greater jihad' (*al-jihād al-akbar*)[4] that is focused on one's own

---

[2] Available at <https://www.youtube.com/playlist?list=PLpr-NGsAGodH-qLTlmoLIUYS7vl-k7TxB> (last accessed 28 January 2022).

[3] Available at <https://spendahilfe.de/spendahilfe> (last accessed 28 January 2022).

[4] The word combination *jihād akbar* in the Ḥadīth is apocryphal, although the corresponding words of the Prophet are probably quite old. See Morabia 1975: 486.

desires (see Cook 2005: 32–48; Peters 2016: 116–18). The advancement of a 'lesser' jihad, as also propounded by followers of Sufi orders who understood devotional practices and an ascetic lifestyle as jihad of a higher degree,[5] has not merely been an attempt to demilitarise the term. Rather, it is arguably a reconceptualisation that in itself points to the significance of sociopolitical conditions in shaping the ways in which Muslims have been interpreting an endeavour towards a praiseworthy goal – the basic meaning of the Arabic word *jihād*.

Mahmud Dahi's emphasis of a demilitarised understanding of jihad reflects his knowledge that throughout Islamic intellectual history, differing and sometimes competing interpretations of jihad have abided side by side. Both combative and non-combative interpretations rest on exegeses of the Qur'an, in which jihad and other derivatives of the root *j-h-d* occur forty-one times.[6] Most relevant passages in the Qur'anic text date to the time after the emigration (*hijra*)[7] of the Prophet Muḥammad and the nascent Muslim community in 622 CE from Mecca to Medina – an oasis city with limited resources. In the context of their vulnerable position in a new settlement, jihad appears as a worldly practice and as a means to ensure the survival of the emerging community by undertaking raids to capture livestock, food and trade goods from neighbouring tribes. The Qur'anic text, however, largely vilifies the antagonists of the early Muslims as unbelievers (*kuffār*) or idolators (*mushrikūn*) rather than portraying them as competitors for resources, hence the militant activism of Muḥammad's community may seem to have been an ideological war in the first place (see Donner 2010: 85). In any case, fighting in this period was essential for the endurance of the emergent Muslim community. It may seem surprising, then, that the Qur'an does not provide a theory of jihad (Noth 1966: 13) nor does it imply that those who

---

[5] Van Ess (2001: 401) describes this development as the 'birth of mysticism from the spirit of Jihad'.

[6] Five of these denote the swearing of an oath, which is irrelevant to the context of this book. See *Encyclopaedia of the Qur'an*, Vol. 3, s.v. 'Jihād'. Afsaruddin (2013: 2–3) also notes that derivatives of the root *j-h-d* in most cases occur in conjunction with other Qur'anic terms that change their connotation.

[7] For a detailed discussion of the range of meanings of the term, see *EQ*, Vol. 2, s.v. 'Emigration'.

strive 'on the path of God' (*fi-sabīl allāh*), that is, the *mujāhidūn*, will acquire religious sanctity. Moreover, even among later scholars, jihad has rarely been understood as an individual duty (*farḍ ʿayn*) that every Muslim must observe, hence it has not been established as the sixth pillar (*rukn*, pl. *arkān*) of Islam.

Yet, as Asma Afsaruddin (2013; 2021) cogently demonstrates, a combative interpretation of the term was by no means the rule in early Qur'an commentaries, *faḍāʾil* works, and beyond Islamic legal texts. She also shows that, under specific sociopolitical conditions, an emerging class of jurists from the second/third century AH (Anno Hegirae) onwards emphasised combative aspects over other interpretations in rendering the meaning of jihad in the Qur'an. Thus, the diversity of readings of jihad and other derivatives of the root *j-h-d* that is found in the early exegeses of the Qur'anic text had diminished significantly in favour of combative interpretations by the fourth century AH. In later exegeses of the Qur'anic text and the Prophetic traditions, as well as in the administrative and juridical literature where it had a broad scope of application, jihad thus predominantly appears in contexts of armed conflict. Furthermore, as Mourad and Lindsay (2012) show, this notion gained even greater prominence in the wake of the Crusades and the Reconquista. This development can be traced grosso modo to the present day, with those Muslim scholars who offer nuanced perspectives on the concept and its diverse interpretations over the course of Muslim intellectual history tending to get less recognition – particularly outside the SWANA region.

Emphasising a demilitarised understanding of jihad, the protagonist Mahmud Dahi not only indicates his awareness of the ambiguity of the concept as well as its differing interpretations throughout Islamic intellectual history. He also explicitly challenges the identification of jihad with political violence advanced by actors including, among others, violent movements that characterise it as an individually binding military struggle, governments in the SWANA region – not least Bashar al-Assad's regime, whose political rhetoric equates jihad with terrorism – as well as politicians, academics and journalists in Europe and the US. The filmmaker not only identifies jihad in groups such as the Free Syrian Army, in the sense of fighting for self-defence, but also tries to offer a more nuanced understanding of the notion. The protagonist Mahmud Dahi underlines the situatedness of notions of jihad with his assertion that humanitarian aid is 'his' jihad, while at the same time his explanation implicitly points to how any specific understanding of the term always relates to other, simultaneously existing interpretations, which other actors, especially those in positions of power, may claim to be definitive.

Not only does the film address questions about the concept of jihad and about political violence; it also foregrounds a media dimension. The film's distribution programme included public screenings in cinemas, schools and universities, as well as its release on the YouTube channel *zqnce* in December 2014. Accordingly, the film finds itself caught in the tension between traditional media such as film, from which it borrows its plot structure, for example, and newer media such as social media, which inspire many of its aesthetic and narratological techniques. The latter are particularly reminiscent of the self-documenting practices typical of influencers that have become popular on YouTube and other video platforms (see Dörre 2022) and allude to a media logic that is inspired by the attention economy and clickbait strategies that the title *Addicted to Jihad* seems to suggest. Even if the film potentially allows viewers to interpret Dahi's motivation as a simply irrepressible will to help, the pathologising formulation seems exaggerated. Additionally, the film's release on YouTube in serial form, cut into several parts, indicates its orientation towards the holy grail of social media: higher viewer numbers.

Similarly, filmmaker Hubertus Koch's direct addressing of viewers invites them into his supposed world of thought through his positionality as a White young man, apparently seeking to establish an intimate relationship with a similar audience. He overtly calls upon viewers to continue watching, for example, by repeatedly stating that the truly horrific footage will not be seen until the fourth part, and at the same time identifies himself as an expert who knows more than the addressed viewers. This dramaturgical build-up of suspense is both a warning and a promise. The uncertainty about what the horrific footage might reveal creates dramatic tension and curiosity and works with the affordances of the platform, which, as each clip ends, immediately offers the next. In this way, the film not only inscribes itself into those spheres of social media where representations of the self dominate, but also calls into question the documentary mode. In the course of this constant breaking of the fourth wall, Koch repeatedly creates ambivalent, reflexive moments and presents his film as a documentary account of his personal experiences and his own evaluation. In the third part, for example, he characterises Mahmud

Dahi's humanitarian commitment as an addiction, and then turns to challenge the audience: 'Too contrived, you say? Fine, but you have no idea anyway!' In other parts of the film, he points out that certain depictions have been exaggerated for dramatic effect, or references the post-production process by editing a glimpse of the editing suite into the ongoing narrative. These and other supposedly self-reflexive scenes create a strange tension between concealing and revealing the film's mediality.

The film reflects a tendency that has been increasingly observed in documentary forms in recent years. Hito Steyerl, for example, notes a 'shift from documentary seeing to documentary feeling, from the distancing gaze to the intense experience' (Steyerl 2008: 13). *Addicted To Jihad* explicitly promises 'participation in strong and above all authentic feelings' (ibid.). The filmmaker describes his approach in the prologue: 'Knowledge is gained from books, media, or stories. But certainty is gained through experience.' Instead of journalistic research and a carefully prepared audiovisual argument, the filmmaker's strategy relies, in line with Steyerl's observation, on 'compressed messages and affects . . . enmeshed in the events themselves' (ibid.: 13). At the same time, the experience-based mode is intended to authenticate the documentation, alongside the filmmaker as he attempts to understand the violent conflict in Syria and Mahmud Dahi's engagement on the ground. This is underscored by the cinematographic style, which favours seemingly improvised shaky GoPro shots, mobile phone footage and selfie-like camera angles; the sometimes poorly lit or unfocused images and variable sound quality create an aesthetic that suggests a risky endeavour of do-it-yourself, if not guerrilla, filmmaking. In a softened form, the effect of the 'documentary uncertainty principle', which Steyerl also introduced and which she developed in relation to images from war zones, is recognisable in this context. She describes the phenomenon whereby images become all the more blurred 'the closer they seem to come to reality' (ibid.: 7) and are attributed authenticity precisely because of their aesthetic lack, which is seen to testify to the context of their own production (see ibid.: 7–9).

Despite its claim to see humanitarian aid as a practice of jihad, the film remains bound on many levels to the polarisations that are generally characteristic of the discourse. Yet the relationships between jihad, political violence and their mediations prove to be far more intricate than such polarisations allow. Indeed, humanitarian aid and militant activism are not strictly separate spheres. Even if their overlappings are not explicitly addressed in the documentary, there are scenes that point to them. When, during lunch in the refugee camp, a child-soldier says that instead of going to school he would rather 'fuck Bashar al-Assad's sister and beat him up', and that car bombings like those undertaken by ISIS are also part of everyday life for children in the camp, the scene illustrates that political violence cannot be easily separated into neat categories of structure, institution or gender. Polarisations can be used to legitimise violence, but they fail to acknowledge the living conditions experienced by those in war-torn environments. Their discursive potency, however, is evidenced by the comments posted on YouTube. While there are many remarks evaluating the documentary, they do not express aesthetic or ethical judgements, nor do they discuss whether it constitutes good journalism. Opinions regarding the film are based primarily on commentators' own assessments of who is responsible for the circumstances of political violence and whether the film's interpretation is consistent with that. Once again, opinions are polarised, reducing the complex historical and political responsibilities that shape the situation in the Turkish–Syrian border region to simplistic designations of perpetrators and victims. The more nuanced perspectives that the film tries to show are thus not reflected in these comments.

Jihad and the (Re-)presentation of Racism in Right-wing Contexts: Jihad Squad

In July 2019, a pastiche of the poster for the film *Gangster Squad* was published on the Facebook page of a regional group of the Republican Party in the US. Titled 'The Jihad Squad', it shows four female Democratic Party representatives in the US Congress who had labeled themselves a squad after their election: Alexandria Ocasio-Cortez (AOC), Rashida Tlaib, Ilhan Omar and Ayanna Pressley.[8] In the manipulated poster, the latter two hold firearms, a fireball explodes beneath the red evening gown of the figure on which AOC's head has been pasted in a montage, and Rashida Tlaib appears to be screaming in rage. In contrast to the more differentiated perspectives mentioned in

---

[8] Available at <https://www.instagram.com/p/BqGTlEPBXXD/?utm_source=ig_embed&utm_medium=loading> (last accessed 28 January 2022).

our first example, the 'Jihad Squad' poster only references hegemonic and violent significations of the term. The figures are thus incorporated into a visual representation of the particular conceptualisation of jihad put forward by the disseminators of the poster, with its subtitles proclaiming that 'Political Jihad is their Game' and 'If you don't agree with their socialist ideology, you're racist' (Brito 2019). While it is not entirely clear whether 'political Jihad' is a reference to the idea of political Islam, relating it to socialism and a twisted misconception of racism illustrates how different forms of stereotyping and implied negative attributions are combined as a strategic defamation.

The visual and rhetorical (il)logic of the poster is strongly reminiscent of Internet memes. Memes condense meanings and invoke a much broader semantic horizon than the simple allusion to a film poster might imply. Thus, with a single image, not only can a whole complex of stereotypes be called up to serve political mobilisation, in this case by the New Right, but it is also possible to generate a high affective potential at the same time (see Strick 2021).[9] Simon Strick classifies the use of such memes as 'meta-politics' (ibid.: 74–83) because they are not concerned with a democratic majority and opinion formation, yet they shape discourses on parties and politicians (see ibid.: 80). In the spheres of the New Right that Strick examines, memes such as the 'Jihad Squad' poster are a common means of discrediting legitimate criticism of racism, for example, and inverting it so that it appears to undermine itself (see ibid.: 75). The fact that such meta-politics are also practised by political organisations is a reflection of the affective climate change that Strick describes in his book on the New Right. In this sense, the poster serves the same function as political campaign posters on the streets, but in an online setting (see Lee and Campbell 2016), by maintaining a relationship with supporters through visibility and the occupation of digital public space.

Despite its swift deletion from the original Facebook page and leading Republicans' efforts to distance themselves from it by dismissing it as 'unauthorised', the 'Jihad Squad' meme has continued to spread across a number of neo-conservative and right-wing websites, thus remaining a discursively operative media artefact. The rhetorical frame that the image provided was

[9] A glimpse of this affective potential can be gained from the heated discussions that have occured on Twitter around the meme (#JihadSquad).

eagerly received and has endured in US political discourse to this day (see, for example, Cole 2021; Arora 2021). The visual representation as well as the discursive formation in which it is embedded reveal at least two aspects relevant to this volume: first, the significance of sociopolitical circumstances in shaping the ways in which people establish and perpetuate a nexus between jihad and political violence, and second, the importance of media, especially visual mediations and their circulation, in manifesting this nexus and entangling it with other forms of violent domination like racism and misogyny.

The poster and its manifold iterations thus visually manifest a specific understanding of jihad that is based upon the nexus of Islam and irrational violence, and attribute this trope to specific individuals. It situates the depiction of the female politicians in the tradition of a particular genre of Hollywood cinema, which itself has a long history of stereotypical portrayal of the enemy and the narrative exploitation of foreign policy conflict situations to perpetuate an Other while patriotically valorising its own. The depiction emphasises a racist trope that dismisses critique voiced by black women as unfounded affect and emotional expression of 'Muslim rage' (see Hilal 2021: 34–8). At the same time, the figure of Angry Black Women reveals the discriminatory power of the discourse around religion and violence, reducing their diversity of experiences and voices to essentialising stereotypes (hooks 2014: 45). Regardless of the congresswomen's own political positioning or religious beliefs, the poster combines a number of stereotypes that form a racist amalgam also cultivated in Hollywood (see Gelado Marcos and Sangro Colón 2016; Shaheen 2001). In the tradition of 1980s action cinema, the poster presents the allegedly Muslim politicians as 'savage criminals' (Kellner 1995: 86). However, certain signs have been reversed. For a long time, Muslim women were only seen as background characters on the screen, but in this poster, stereotypes that would have formerly been male have been inverted (see Shaheen 2001: 13–24). Even in films like *Hell Squad* (1986), in which women played action-packed leading roles, their aim was to fight against (racist stereotypes of) Arab men (see ibid.: 263–4). In this pastiche of a film poster, the stereotypes are not only transferred to the congresswomen, but propose the possibility of an infernal union, which is all the more plausible since film plots always seem larger and therefore more dangerous than life. Furthermore, the poster renders visible a specific vision of (political) jihad, namely in the form of four angry armed women of colour who cannot be trusted to act responsibly in the democratic decision-making process, but who are instead expected to deploy irrational violence to achieve their political goals.

As the meanings that social actors ascribe to the polysemous concept jihad always emerge in relation to specific sociopolitical conditions, the 'Jihad Squad' poster should therefore be considered in the context that in the aftermath of 9/11 the Arabic term jihad became associated, as Cook (2005: 1) writes, '(by most non-Muslims) with unrestrained, unreasoning, total warfare'. This interpretation, narrowing the notion of jihad to 'extreme' combat, attained prominence in the discursive processing and sociopolitical analysis of the attacks on New York and Washington, DC and the subsequently proclaimed War on Terror (see Jackson 2005). Accusations of anti-Americanism, socialism and supposed militancy inscribed in the poster are thus tied to a catchword that directly references the motivations ascribed to 9/11, invoking the idea of Muslims as dangerous fatalists that Salman Sayyid (2014: 4) traces to 'the deep-rootedness of Orientalism in European society' and evidently also in the US context (Hilal 2021: 11–12). Part of this Orientalist stance is the insinuated continuity of a jihad ideology among Muslim communities that, on the contrary, had been by and large absent until the nineteenth century.[10] It became, however, quite prevalent in the 'Western imaginary' (ibid.), not least through the sometimes richly illustrated reports in newspapers and magazines of nineteenth-century Europe that depicted local (Muslim) populations resisting the colonisation of their homeland as

---

[10] Al-Sulāmī's (d. 1106) *Kitāb al-jihād*, Ibn ʿAsākir's (d. 1176) *al-Arbaʿūn ḥadīthan li-ḥathth ʿalā-l-jihād*, and the poetry of Aḥmad ibn Abū Bakr al-Ḥanafī (d. after 1180), for instance, were significant for preaching jihad in favour of Nūr al-Dīn Zangī's and Saladdin's recruitment efforts against the Franks (and other Muslims) and provided foundations for later manifestations of jihad ideology (see Mourad and Lindsay 2012; Goudie 2019). Originating in the wake of the Crusades and the Reconquista, at a time of profound crisis in the self-image of the Muslim community, it is important to interpret these works in relation to their specific sociopolitical circumstances. It thus remains open to debate whether such works were the exception in Islamic intellectual history rather than the rule, or whether this period marked the onset – at least for the Sunni mainstream – of an intensification and reorientation of the jihad concept that, as Mourad and Lindsay argue, became normative in Sunni religious thought.

the counterpart of a bourgeoise *'mission civilisatrice'* in the Global South. The 'Jihad Squad' poster forcefully exemplifies the continuities of these racist and gendered depictions and epistemologies, as here too, people who are supposedly hostile to civilisation are not only marked as different in appearance and violent in a daunting way, but are also shown, as it were, as epitomes of a militant jihad ideology.

Re-claiming Jihad for the Protection of the Environment

Notwithstanding – or perhaps because of – the potency of the association of jihad with political violence in Europe and the US today, many Muslims are trying to counter this discourse, as has already been clearly shown in the section about *Addicted to Jihad*. A very prominent example of reclaiming and resignification of the term is the call for an 'eco-jihad'. In September 2007, the 'Clean Medina Campaign' was launched in Birmingham, UK, by the Islamic Foundation for Ecology and Environmental Sciences (IFEES). Adopting the slogan 'Inner city Muslims show the true jihad' (Clean Medina Campaign Press Release 2007), local Muslim activists cleaned the streets of neighbourhoods of the city that were predominantly inhabited by Muslims.[11] The campaign's efforts were partly directed towards fellow residents, drawing their attention to the problem of littering. The endeavour was also a response to sentiments expressed by the wider city community that attributed the litter problem to the origin or religion of the residents. Designating this campaign as jihad, however, even going so far as to define it as 'true' jihad, was – against the background of what non-Muslim majority societies in Birmingham, the UK and wider Europe generally think the term means – a brave and confident gesture to reappropriate jihad as a positive force and highlight its positive connotations.

The campaign also launched the community film *Clean Medina*.[12] The film plays self-reflexively with notions of jihad that frame it as an act of war. Adopting the logic of a friend/foe distinction, they declare rubbish to be

---

[11] Zbidi (2013) writes that the IFEES is 'regarded as the mother of all Islamic environmental organisations'.

[12] Available at <https://www.youtube.com/watch?v=VZdNqJ9WGFg> (last accessed 8 October 2022).

the enemy and those helping in the fight for clean streets to be righteous believers. In doing so, they ridicule the reductive iconography of jihad that has been disseminated by both militant groups and political epistemologies such as the 'War on Terror'. For example, when someone in the film dressed as Osama bin Laden declares 'international jihad on trash', the film mocks the mainstream media's visualisations of jihad. Beyond the stylistic device of irony, the film also undertakes a serious approach to reconceptualising jihad by confronting viewers with all-too-familiar representations, such as when a preacher on the street calls a group of teenagers mujahidin and asks them to perform jihad 'on the path of God' by picking up litter. When the youth, some of whom are hooded, answer this call by shouting 'Allahu akbar' and raise their litter-pickers in the air, the film clearly alludes to the iconography of videos distributed by violent groups fighting in the name of jihad. But here the participants appropriate and resignify these gestures – deadly rifles are replaced by tools useful to the community. This re-appropriation works not least by disturbing the preconceptions of bystanders and of the video's viewers. In this sense, the video appears as a deconstructive act that undermines both the discursive linkage of jihad and violence (picking up rubbish is obviously a non-violent act) as propagated by militant groups and the intrinsic connection between religion and violence conveyed in security discourses. By ironising militant interpretations, a re-appropriation of the term is simultaneously undertaken through its association with other discursive elements (peacefulness, cleanliness, virtue, community, neighbourliness). Nevertheless, debates about the use of the term on the campaign blog demonstrate that members of the local Muslim community were divided over whether invoking jihad would do a disservice to the campaign's goal in the wider public perception (Ahwal 2008).

Expanding the perspective beyond the local context, the IFEES campaign represents a continuation of a series of environmental protection activities grounded in religious beliefs, values and norms. It is thus situated within an Islamic environmental theology that focuses on the preservation of divine creation and is steadily gaining relevance across the globe (see, among others, Zbidi 2013; Gade 2019; Amirpur 2021; Koehrsen 2021). It is in recognition of this that the term eco-jihad has been coined, which in Muslim-majority countries is also used by major organisations of Muslim scholars and their followers to stress the urgency of the cause and the serious need for individual commitment (Amri 2013). Also, an emerging generation of young Muslim environmental activists in Europe and North America self-confidently frame their ideas and actions as eco-jihad.[13] They use the internet and social media as a means to cast the term in a positive light, foregrounding – albeit indirectly – its demilitarised interpretation and at the same time playing on the often limited knowledge about jihad prevalent in European societies and the specific contexts of its (re)production in politics, academia and the media. Indeed, the invocation of the lesser jihad as the 'true' jihad seems to be primarily (but not exclusively) an assertion directed at non-Muslim majority societies in an attempt to demonstrate that their interpretation of the term is a misapprehension.[14] In political and public debates that invoke an ill-defined notion of Euro-American culture and its supposedly universal values and then assess the extent to which Muslims can (or ought to) conform to this, claiming that the 'lesser' jihad is the 'true' jihad could be seen as apologetic or even as defensive (see van Ess 2012: 126–7). Yet instances of reconceptualising jihad and reappropriating the concept to counter hegemonic discourse formations are also acts of epistemic resistance.

Premise and Structure of the Edited Volume

Our reflections above already point to the contingency and relativity of the significations attributed to the term jihad both historically and across the variations of its current usage, above all in Anglo-European contexts. This edited volume thus foregrounds the situatedness of interpretations and uses of the term jihad in that the selected chapters point to how, over the past twenty years, it has mainly been non-Muslim actors outside the SWANA region who have been shaping globally dominant discourses on the topic of jihad and related word formations such as jihadism – in politics, academia, journalism and wider society. Currently, in Europe and the US, jihad is rarely

---

[13] See, for example, <https://www.theecomuslim.co.uk/p/about-eco-muslim.html> (last accessed 8 February 2022); also Janmohamed 2016, Ch. 15.

[14] Other examples include the 2013 #MyJihad advertising campaign in larger US cities (see Fahim 2013; Yaccino and Si 2013) and the romantic comedy *My Jihad* that was broadcast by the BBC in 2014 (see Janmohamed 2016, Ch. 2).

used to reference the extent or nature of an individual's endeavour for the sake of their religion or the Muslim community. Rather, the meaning of the term has become increasingly narrowed down to denote acts of political violence by Muslim non-state actors, as well as their supposed ideology. This volume aims to transcend such a limited focus. The contributions explore a number of contemporary contexts in which different people employ or reject the use of jihad to describe, categorise and appraise their own or others' ideas and actions. In doing so, the authors contrast globally hegemonic discourse formations with the polysemy of the concept and different actors', at times very distinct, interpretations of it. In particular, we want to draw attention to the significant impact of temporal, spatial, economic and social conditions and their hegemonic entanglements in shaping the ways in which people negotiate the meanings of jihad, including whether and to what extent they consider it a relevant concept for their own lives and the lifeworlds of others.

The first thematic field centres on the production of knowledge and highlights different trajectories of and perspectives on knowledge production relating to the notion of jihad – often countering hegemonic ecologies of knowledge. The second section brings to the fore how mediated and audiovisual dimensions contribute to the discursive entanglement of political violence and jihad. The third section, on ethnographic perspectives, decentres dominant discourses on so-called jihadist actors and deradicalisation processes to offer more nuanced understandings of those actors' political and sociocultural contexts. The fourth and final section critically examines how the archiving of media, particularly in politically violent contexts, is in itself a political act that contributes to and shapes the entanglements of jihad and political violence.

Part I: Notions of Jihad and the Production of Knowledge

The five case studies assembled in the section 'Notions of Jihad and the Production of Knowledge' indicate that in Europe and the US many people's understandings of jihad are predominantly shaped by stakeholders who primarily engage with the ideas and actions of violent Muslim groups. The authors revisit some of the ways in which the term jihad has been deployed, studied, covered and resisted. The contributions provide critical perspectives on the hegemony of non-Muslim actors who interpret and apply the term jihad and its derivatives as categories and taxonomies to evaluate Muslim individuals and groups in relation to notions of security or assess the extent of their conformity to a particular conduct of life or a set of norms, values and beliefs; actors who, moreover, claim that their interpretations are universal.

The contributions draw attention to dichotomous epistemes in political, legal, academic and wider social discourses that locate jihad and the people associated with it in relation to binaries of good or evil, dangerous or benevolent, violent or non-violent, state or non-state, and so forth. In this vein, Jaan Islam engages with the history of the term 'Jihadi-Salafi' as a category applied in order to assess ideas and actions in terms of their propensity to political violence and the (in)compatibility of their proponents to 'Western' norms and values.[15] This categorisation has fostered the taxonomic persistence and reproduction of the notion of a 'global jihad movement' as if it were a largely homeostatic and self-contained entity, regardless of the specific contexts in which individuals and groups have been rendering jihad a central element of their ideas, motivations and actions. This includes claiming that a fascination with nihilism and apocalyptic ideology distinguishes these individuals and groups from 'usual' social-revolutionary movements (as suggested by, for example, Robinson 2021). In such ways, 'Jihadi-Salafi' has not only shaped the perception of Islam across the globe, but more importantly the subjectification of Muslims themselves, and the subjectivities of those identified with the term.

The use of the term jihad also affects concrete institutional contexts, as Nicole Nguyen's article shows. She examines how notions of jihad have guided counterterrorism legal procedures in the US, and demonstrates how strongly the interpretation of the term influences the respective judgements. Darryl Li's article is also devoted to the interpretations of the term and its use as a political weapon in the US context. He points out that jihadism as a concept is not analytically helpful but materially harmful. He further argues that this category is driven by an anti-Muslim animus. Through his careful debunking of common commentaries on jihadism and his critique of expert culture, Li shows how the concept serves as the exercise of secular power.

---

[15] These epistemologies, conventions and bodies of knowledge also feed into popular discourses in the SWANA region where they are reproduced and appropriated in, for example, satellite TV programmes. See Al Jazeera 2019; Alaraby TV 2021.

Taking Austria as an example, Farid Hafez also explores the power relations that shape the contexts of such discourses. He shows how knowledge is produced by institutions and how this knowledge can be used to legitimise state action against Muslims. Especially when it comes to the inversion of the concept of Islamophobia, which gets stripped of its critical dimension and instead re-signified as a weapon of political Islam, Hafez shows how important it is to understand the epistemic dimension of such concepts. With a hegemony-critical intervention, Sindyan Qasem applies the 'oppositional gaze' proposed by bell hooks to analyse two counternarrative video series that deploy the concept of jihad to counter 'Islamism' in the German-speaking context. Through his analysis of two videos, one produced and disseminated by the Federal Office for the Protection of the Constitution (Bundesamt für Verfassungsschutz; BfV) of the German federal state North Rhine Westphalia, and another authored by the violence and extremism prevention organisation 'Turn!' in collaboration with the national centre for political education (bpb), Qasem shows how the main characters and narratives of both contribute to the reproduction of racialised and securitised forms of inequality.

Part II: Audiovisual Mediations and Formations of Jihad

Notions of jihad and their entanglements with political violence are in many respects conditioned by the ways in which they are conveyed. Aesthetic means that appeal to the full spectrum of human senses play a central role in this. Textual, auditory and visual media of dissemination, as well as the ways in which actors use language, sound and visuals, shape our perceptions of what jihad is (or is not) in a certain context or time, what defines those whose activities are described as jihad, and what their actions look or sound like. Whether in films, songs, election posters or apps, in visual art and popular culture – different understandings of the term are expressed through specific mediatised forms, for example, in the iconisation of Osama bin Laden's portrait (Behrend and Wendl 2015). The second section of this book, 'Audiovisual Mediations and Formations of Jihad', approaches this phenomenon through four case studies. Common to all of them is an exploration of the extent to which such aesthetic formations can themselves become socio-political media – expressing ideas and also becoming the subject of political debate. Ahmed Al-Rawi uses the example of educational mobile apps to demonstrate how aesthetic transmission of content can be used to naturalise certain religio-political ideas for children, thereby fostering the formation of subjects loyal to Daesh. Al-Rawi shows how the aesthetics of such apps help create imaginations of an 'Islamic state' and establish a symbolic repertoire (through logos, currency, flags, weapons, diction, conduct, clothes, and many more) that potentially shapes the social identities of the app's users. That a certain aesthetic is not linked exclusively to certain political ideologies, but can transcend or interconnect them to others, is the subject of Christiane Gruber's text. Using a comparative art-historical approach, Gruber compares the symbolic repertoire of Daesh with that of various right-wing groups. She argues that the election posters of right-wing parties such as the Alternative für Deutschland (AfD) in Germany become media of political discourse, which propagate their identity politics by defaming the Other and deploying a visual rhetoric of violence that, perhaps surprisingly, does not stand in contrast to the visual language of Daesh, but rather shares certain elements. In Kurstin Gatt's contribution, aesthetics is examined not in the visual but in the aural dimension. By combining sound and meaning, jihadist chants become platforms of the political. They combine traditional and modern elements and attain a certain popularity and persuasiveness through their aesthetic qualities. Films also have a key function in the discussions that this volume traces. Sebastian Köthe examines a film by the Kurdish documentary filmmaker Hogir Hirori to explore how films negotiate the consequences of the Daesh regime. Köthe comparatively analyses the film in relation to the literary memoir of a survivor of the genocide, and to the Murad Code, which establishes protocols for working with survivors, to derive an ethical perspective from these media artefacts. In his view, films and other documents of testimony not only become platforms of the political; they themselves become the subject of political debates that touch on questions of visibility, ethics and agency.

Part III: Ethnographic Perspectives on Imaginations and Materialities

Contributions in this section address the social, religious and political dimensions of violent hierarchies as well as of forms of (transnational) support networks operating in the name of jihad that have often been neglected in research on 'radicalisation' or political violence (De Koning et al. 2020: 37).

The four texts in this section show how discourses of radicalisation circulate within security, political and media institutions and have affected Muslim institutions, individuals and research in sometimes violent ways (Fadil et al. 2019: 4–6). All the contributions in this section are based on long-term ethnographic fieldwork conducted with individuals and groups involved with counter-radicalisation policies, or with families of European emigrants to wartime Syria. They offer nuanced perspectives on the lives, experiences and perspectives of those who have been categorised as demonised figures such as that of the 'foreign fighter', 'radical', or 'jihadist'. The authors rethink questions of race, nationality, 'whiteness' and the connection between Islam and political violence (see Li 2020; Kublitz 2019; Navest et al. 2016). Such concepts are linked to a variety of attributions that have an impact on the subjectification of people who are labelled as such. The section shows that such attributions also open up semantic spaces that can be interpreted and appropriated by the people and institutions to whom they are ascribed. Through their examination of such semantic spaces, the contributions make it clear that the discriminatory intentions often associated with such attributions are contested, for example, with optimistic and utopian counter-concepts. In this dual perspective, Martijn de Koning examines, on the one hand, the functions that the label 'jihadism' has for the racialised surveillance system in the Netherlands. On the other hand, he also asks how the associated attributions of legal and moral deviance are received by those addressed by it. He reveals the ways in which such people carve out opportunities for themselves to speak up and 'talk back' with counter conduct in video messages or social media posts. Another widespread attribution, which Anja Kublitz explores in her field research, is the alleged nihilistic worldview and apocalyptic telos of jihadist practices. In contrast to this assumption, Kublitz finds that her interlocutors do not long for death, but rather enter into an optimistic relationship with their own temporality on earth, whereby they do not distinguish between political worldly and divine events. This points to a subjective plurality of interpretations, that also comes to bear in Hamza Esmili's contribution. His work enquires into people's motives for emigrating to war-torn Syria. Rather than conceiving his study as a search for 'radicalisation' associated with 'jihad', he demonstrates how the term stimulates a wide variety of fragmented religious utopias. Taking a different approach, Aïcha Bounaga reflects on attributions of radicalisation in the name of jihad. She examines the concept of 'counter-jihad' in France, which indicates a recent shift in how radicalisation is dealt with. It is no longer just a matter of opposing certain behaviours and values, but more importantly of standing up for certain values. The semantic space that opens up in the wake of this is, as Bounaga makes clear, organised along French normative assumptions about what constitutes a good life.

Part IV: Affective Archives – Enduring Sounds and Images

Knowledge assets, aesthetic formations and imaginations of jihad do not simply circulate at any given moment; they are stored and documented in archives. Significantly, in the course of archiving they once again undergo processes of knowledge formation, aestheticisation and imagination. What seems to unite the disparate archives created in relation to or in the name of jihad is the observation that they are affectively charged. The contributions to the fourth section 'Affective Archives – Enduring Sounds and Images' explore such archives and archival practices. They focus on the afterlives of sounds and images that are connected in one way or another to the history of the concept of jihad and seek to trace the complex connections between visibility and violence. Taking Syria as an example, Enrico de Angelis and Yazan Badran examine how the status and meaning of images of violence are constantly (re-)negotiated. With their concept of the 'controversial archive', they draw attention to how such images are repeatedly appropriated and remediated, how they migrate between different contexts and change their meanings in the process. The archival work that such images stimulate is thus an unfinishable process. Robert Dörre's article focuses more strongly on aesthetics as he explores the afterlives, in media theory and digital archives, of images of violence created in the name of jihad. Rather than mystifying the aesthetics of such images – as some media theorists are wont to do – he argues for their re-politicisation, grounded in his rereading of Roland Barthes's theory of myth. He also turns to archives that preserve material from the so-called Islamic State and examines the extent to which they are aesthetically involved in processes of mystification or politicisation of the material. Last but not least, in the final chapter of this volume, Kevin B. Lee reflects on the relationship between visibility and (post-colonial) violence in various artistic works.

The starting point for his reflections is the formative experiences he himself made in encountering the works of Morehshin Allahyari and Harun Farocki. In an essayistic manner, Lee draws on the insights gained from these experiences to reflect critically on violent care in his own artistic projects and to speculate about potential ways to escape the vicious cycle of the mediated reproduction of violence.

References

Afsaruddin, A. (2013), *Striving in the Path of God: Jihād and Martyrdom in Islamic Thought*, Oxford: Oxford University Press.

Afsaruddin, A. (2021), *Jihad: What Everyone Needs to Know*, Oxford: Oxford University Press.

Ahwal, A. (2008), 'The Jihad Word and ITV', <https://cleanmedina.blogspot.com/2008/06/jihad-word-and-itv-by-ayman-ahwal.html> (last accessed 8 February 2022).

Alaraby TV (2021), *Al-salafiya al-jihādiya . . . kayfa tafhamuhā*, <https://www.youtube.com/watch?v=jlyYu1Lu9bg> (last accessed 1 February 2022).

Al Jazeera (2019), *Li-l-qiṣṣa baqīya: ʿal-salafiya al-jihādiya' min ḥarakāṭ iqlīmīya ilā-l-ʿālamīya*, <https://www.youtube.com/watch?v=ASnIa3XkAG0> (last accessed 1 February 2022).

Amirpur, K. (2021), 'And We Shall Save the Earth: Muslim Environmental Stewards', in E. Ehlers and K. Amirpur (eds), *Middle East and North Africa: Climate, culture, and conflicts*, Leiden and Boston: Brill, pp. 39–58.

Amri, U. (2013), 'From Theology to a Praxis of "Eco-Jihad": The Role of Religious Civil Society Organizsations in Combating Climate Change in Indonesia', in R. Globus Veldman, A. Szasz and R. Haluza-DeLay (eds), *How the World's Religions Are Responding to Climate Change*, Hoboken: Taylor and Francis, pp. 75–93.

Arora, M. (2021), 'Rep. Boebert Labels Rep. Omar a Jihadist. Why Don't GOP Leaders Condemn the Slur?', *The Washington Post*, 6 December, <https://www.washingtonpost.com/politics/2021/12/06/boebert-omar-jihad-racism/> (last accessed 18 January 2022).

Bakali, N. and F. Hafez (2022), *The Rise of Global Islamophobia in the War on Terror: Coloniality, Race, and Islam*, Manchester: Manchester University Press.

Bayat, A. (2007), *Islam and Democracy: What Is the Real Question?* Vol. 8, Leiden: Amsterdam University Press.

Behrend, H. and T. Wendl (eds) (2015), *9/11 and Its Remediations in Popular Culture and Arts in Africa*, Berlin and Münster: LIT.

Bosi, L. and S. Malthaner (2015), 'Political Violence', in D. Della Porta and M. Diani (eds), *The Oxford Handbook of Social Movements*, Oxford: Oxford University Press, pp. 439–51.

Brito, C. (2019), 'GOP Group Shares Meme Calling 4 Progressive Democrats the "Jihad Squad"', *CBS News*, 22 July, <https://www.cbsnews.com/news/jihad-squad-illinois-republican-party-meme-poster-alexandria-ocasio-cortez-rashida-tlaib-ilhan-omar-ayanna-pressley/> (last accessed 18 January 2022).

Cesari, J. (2012), 'Securitization of Islam in Europe', *Die Welt des Islams*, 52: 3–4, 430–49.

Cesari, J. (2021), 'Securitization of Islam: The Lethal Combination of Threat and Identity Politics', *Brown Journal of World Affairs*, 28: 1, <https://bjwa.brown.edu/28-1/securitization-of-islam-the-lethal-combination-of-threat-and-identity-politics/> (last accessed 19 August 2022).

Clean Medina (2007), 'Clean Medina Campaign Press Release', 5 September, <https://cleanmedina.blogspot.com/2007/09/clean-medina-campaign-press-release-for.html> (last accessed 7 February 2022).

Cole, B. (2021), 'Marjorie Taylor Greene Doubles Down on "Jihad Squad" Remarks', *Newsweek*, 2 December, <https://www.newsweek.com/marjorie-taylor-greene-jihad-squad-abortion-ocasio-cortez-1655313> (last accessed 18 January 2022).

Cook, D. (2005), *Understanding Jihad*, Berkeley, CA: University of California Press.

Damir-Geilsdorf, S. and M. Menzfeld (2020), 'Methodological and Ethical Challenges in Empirical Approaches to Salafism: Introduction', *Journal of Muslims in Europe*, 9: 2, 135–49.

De Koning, M., C. Becker and I. Roex (2020), *Islamic Militant Activism in Belgium, the Netherlands and Germany: 'Islands in a Sea of Disbelief'*, Cham: Palgrave Macmillan.

Donner, F. M. (2010), *Muhammad and the Believers: At the Origins of Islam*, Cambridge, MA, and London: The Belknap Press of Harvard University Press.

Dörre, R. (2022), *Mediale Entwürfe des Selbst*, Marburg: Büchner-Verlag.

Fadil, N., M. van Buggenhout and E. Dumortier (2022), 'Virtual Innocence: On the Status of the Children of European Departees in Northeast Syria', *Ethnic and Racial Studies*, 1–21.

Fadil, N., M. de Koning and F. Ragazzi (2019), 'Radicalization: Tracing the Trajectories of an "Empty Signifier" in the Low Lands', in N. Fadil, F. Ragazzi and M. de Koning (eds), *Radicalization in Belgium and the Netherlands: Critical Perspectives on Violence and Security*, London: Bloomsbury Publishing, pp. 3–27.

Fahim, S. (2013), '#MyJihad – The "Struggle" to Reclaim Islam', 11 March, <https://muslimmatters.org/2013/03/11/myjihad-the-struggle-to-reclaim-islam/> (last accessed 28 March 2022).

Fox, J. and Y. Akbaba (2015), 'Securitization of Islam and Religious Discrimination: Religious Minorities in Western Democracies, 1990–2008', *Comparative European Politics*, 13: 2, 175–97.

Fuhrmann, L.-D. (2021), 'Contestations of the "War on Terror" and the So-called Islamic State in Art', in S. Baden, L. D. Fuhrmann, K. Jörder and J. Holten (eds), *Mindbombs: Visual Cultures of Political Violence*, Bielefeld and Berlin: Kerber Verlag, pp. 145–52.

Fuhrmann, L.-D. and S. Pfeifer (2020), 'Challenges in Digital Ethnography: Research Ethics Relating to the Securitisation of Islam', *Journal of Muslims in Europe*, 9: 2, 175–95.

Gade, A. M. (2019), *Muslim Environmentalisms: Religious and Social Foundations*, New York: Columbia University Press.

Gelado Marcos, R. and P. Sangro Colón (2016), 'Hollywood and the Representation of the Otherness: A Historical Analysis of the Role Played by Movies in Spotting Enemies to Vilify', *index.comunicación*, 6: 1, 11–25.

Gledhill, J. (2008), 'Anthropology in the Age of Securitization: Annual Joel S. Kahn Lecture', La Trobe University.

Goudie, K. A. (2019), *Reinventing Jihad: Jihad Ideology from the Conquest of Jerusalem to the End of the Ayyubids (c. 492/1099–647/1249)*, Leiden: Koninklijke Brill NV.

Günther, C. and S. Pfeifer (2020), 'Jihadi Audiovisuality and its Entanglements: A Conceptual Framework', in C. Günther and S. Pfeifer (eds), *Jihadi Audiovisuality and its Entanglements: Meanings, Aesthetics, Appropriations*, Edinburgh: Edinburgh University Press, pp. 1–24.

Hilal, M. (2021), *Innocent Until Proven Muslim: Islamophobia, the War on Terror, and the Muslim Experience since 9/11*, an imprint of 1517 Media, Minneapolis: Broadleaf Books.

hooks, b. (2014), *Black Looks: Race and Representation*, London and New York: Routledge.

Jackson, R. (2005), *Writing the War on Terrorism: Language, Politics and Counter-terrorism*, Manchester: Manchester University Press.

Janmohamed, S. Z. (2016), *Generation M: Young Muslims Changing the World*, London: I. B. Tauris.

Kellner, D. (1995), *Media Culture: Cultural Studies, Identity and Politics between the Modern and the Post-modern*, London and New York: Routledge.

Kittler, F. A. (1999), *Gramophone, Film, Typewriter*, Stanford: Stanford University Press.

Koehrsen, J. (2021), 'Muslims and Climate Change: How Islam, Muslim Organizations, and Religious Leaders Influence Climate Change Perceptions and Mitigation Activities', *WIREs Climate Change*, 12: 3.

Kublitz, A. (2019), 'The Rhythm of Rupture: Attunement among Danish Jihadists', in M. Holbraad, B. Kapferer and J. F. Sauma (eds), *Ruptures: Anthropologies of Discontinuity in Times of Turmoil*, London: UCL Press, pp. 174–92.

Lee, B. and V. Campbell (2016), 'Looking Out or Turning In? Organizational Ramifications of Online Political Posters on Facebook', *The International Journal of Press/Politics*, 21: 3, 313–37.

Li, D. (2015), 'A Jihadism Anti-Primer', *Middle East Report*, 276, <https://merip.org/2015/12/a-jihadism-anti-primer/> (last accessed 25 August 2022).

Li, D. (2020), *The Universal Enemy: Jihad, Empire, and the Challenge of Solidarity*, Stanford: Stanford University Press.

Majozi, N. (2018), 'Theorising the Islamic State: A Decolonial Perspective', *ReOrient*, 3: 2, 163–84.

Morabia, A. (1975), *La notion de Gihad dans l'Islam medieval: Des origines a al-Gazali*, Paris: Universite de Paris V.

Mourad, S. A. and J. E. Lindsay (2012), *The Intensification and Reorientation of Sunni Jihad Ideology in the Crusader Period: Ibn ʿAsākir of Damascus (1105–1176) and His Age, with an Edition and Translation of Ibn ʿAsākir's The Forty Hadiths for Inciting Jihad*, Leiden: Brill.

Navest, A., M. de Koning and A. Moors (2016), 'Chatting About Marriage with Female Migrants to Syria', *Anthropology Today*, 32: 2, 22–5.

Noth, A. (1966), *Heiliger Krieg und Heiliger Kampf in Islam und Christentum*, Bonn: Röhrscheid.

Osman, Wazhmah (2022), 'Building Spectatorial Solidarity against the "War on Terror" Media-military Gaze', *International Journal of Middle East Studies*, 54: 2, 369–75.

Peters, R. (2016), *Jihad: A History in Documents*, Princeton: Markus Wiener Publishers.

Poynting, S. and D. Whyte (eds) (2012), *Counter-terrorism and State Political Violence: The 'War on Terror' as Terror*, London: Routledge.

Robinson, G. E. (2021), *Global Jihad: A Brief History*, Stanford: Stanford University Press.

Sayyid, S. (2014), *Recalling the Caliphate: Decolonisation and World Rrder*, London: Hurst.

Shaheen, J. (2001), *Reel Bad Arabs – How Hollywood Vilifies a People*, New York: Olive Branch Press.

Steyerl, H. (2008), *Die Farbe der Wahrheit: Dokumentarismen im Kunstfeld*, Vienna: Turia + Kant.

Strick, S. (2021), *Rechte Gefühle: Affekte und Strategien des digitalen Faschismus*, Bielefeld: Transcript Verlag.

van Ess, J. (2001), *Der Fehltritt des Gelehrten: Die 'Pest von Emmaus' und ihre theologischen Nachspiele*, Heidelberg: Winter.

van Ess, J. (2012), *Dschihad gestern und heute*, Heft 3, Berlin and Boston: De Gruyter.

Yaccino, S. and P. Si (2013), 'Using Billboards to Stake Claim Over "Jihad"', *The New York Times*, 6 March, <https://www.nytimes.com/2013/03/07/us/ad-campaigns-fight-it-out-over-meaning-of-jihad.html> (last accessed 28 March 2022).

Zbidi, M. (2013), 'Islamic Environmentalism: The Call to Eco-jihad', 14 November, <https://en.qantara.de/content/islamic-environmentalism-the-call-to-eco-jihad> (last accessed 21 January 2022).

Zine, J. (2022), *Under Siege: Islamophobia and the 9/11 Generation*, Montreal, Kingston, London and Chicago: McGill-Queen's University Press.

PART I

NOTIONS OF JIHAD AND THE PRODUCTION OF KNOWLEDGE

1

THE PORTRAYAL OF JIHADI-SALAFISM: THE ROLE OF KNOWLEDGE PRODUCTION IN FABRICATING A GLOBAL ENEMY

Jaan S. Islam

Introduction

The academic study of Jihad is shaped by the wider aims of the academy, and the larger geopolitical context of a post-9/11 and post-ISIS world. Following the securitisation of the study of Islam and debates surrounding the nature of Islam and Muslim identity, the question of jihad has and continues to be central in both popular and academic conceptions of Islam. In studying the narratives surrounding jihad in relation to the production of knowledge, it could be said that the academic study of jihad tells us more about hegemonic discourses than it does about the subject in question. As proven by the valuable contributions in this volume, we can see that the image of the 'jihadi' or 'jihadist' occupies a specific image in the mind of the reader or listener, and is inseparable from Islamophobic conceptions of Muslims as the quintessential 'Other' (Mohamedou 2017). In the words of William Scheuerman, the image of the jihadi/-ist represents 'the embodiment of all Western anxieties (and misunderstandings) concerning the nature of religion, politics (liberal or conservative), progress, and the nation-state' (Scheuerman 2006: 111).

The scholars in this volume have been central in laying out the theoretical framework in which we can study and critique the typologies, characterisations and assumptions made in the study of modern jihad(s) (see the contributions in this volume by Sayyid, Nguyen and Hafez). In this chapter, I will address the way in which a specific movement, one that came to be known as 'Jihadi-Salafism', is the product of a specific narrative imposed on Muslims with origins in hegemonic discourses. I show how what has been prided as the 'neutral' and 'value-free' position of the academy hinders our understanding of a complex plethora of social phenomena, and further, unique Muslim articulations of human purpose through one's relationship to the Divine through jihad.

There are two important points of clarification that are first necessary to specify with regard to the portrayal of Jihadi-Salafism. The first is that it is quintessential to understand that the concept of jihad, which I explain below, has always been fundamental to the articulation of Islam and Muslim identity for more than 1,400 years. This spans a great number of traditions, and is by no means confined within the limited historiographical category of 'Salafism' or 'Muslim fundamentalism'.[1] As shown by contributions in this volume and elsewhere, the notion of 'jihad' (as war) being the physical culmination and perfection of spiritual attainment is a motif of various Islamic traditions, ranging from the Ottoman Sufi notion of the 'Ghazi' (warrior) to the image of the mujahid in the 'jihad movement' of Shah Walī-Allah al-Dahlawī (d. 1762) and Syed Aḥmad Barelwī in Mughal India (d. 1831) (Imber 2010; Tareen 2020).

The second point of clarification concerns the nature of Jihadi-Salafism. As I discuss below, it is important to keep in mind the different ways that meaning is constructed through the interpretation of foundational texts. This also applies to the individual terms 'salafi' and 'jihadi'. Building on Asad's (1993) critique of the study of Islam in traditional anthropology, I approach the study of Islamic terms by studying the way Muslims interpret foundational texts. The definitions – and therefore conceptions – of these categories are articulated and understood very differently from the perspective of Muslims engaged in the Islamic hermeneutical tradition. For instance, in the academy, the term 'Salafi' has been associated with 'Islamism', in addition to 'radicalism' and 'fundamentalism' (Hegghammer 2009, cited in Lav 2012). In both

---

[1] As I discuss below, Salafism here refers to a historical hermeneutical movement which interprets Muslim authoritative scriptures – the Qur'an and Prophetic sunna – literally ('alā ẓawāhirihā) and is most pronounced in their insistence on affirming.

cases of comparison and dichotomy, the features chosen to define these terms are reflective of the principles of the characteris-*er*, as opposed to the way a Salafi Muslim for instance may define the term. Many Salafis object to the use of the term 'Islamism' to characterise the path of the *salaf* (the Muslim ancestors) because for them, political Islam – specifically, the type of political Islam that even conditionally or marginally accepts the nation state as a locus of valid political activity – is a horrendous innovation (*bidʿa*) that must be utterly condemned.[2] On the other hand, even the attempt to contrast Salafism with a movement like Islamism reflects an attempt to typologise Islam using modern political divisions that are only useful for an audience seeking to classify Muslims by their level (or modality) of harmfulness to the aims of Western universalism.[3]

We do not find Salafis (or those who associate with the term), on the other hand, articulating their identity as being opposed to 'Islamists' (*islāmiyyūn*), even if Islamists might be on the opposing end of their doctrinal polemics. With Salafism in particular, we almost always observe criticisms of 'Islamists' are not on the basis of their 'Islamism' per se, but rather their affinity with beliefs – and specific scriptural interpretations – that would render them 'innovators' (*mubtadiʿa*) or disbelievers. In the latter case, the concern is not with the category 'Islamist' as such, but rather that certain Islamists fall under a categorisation because of specific beliefs or actions which may or may not be related to their political affiliation.[4] Importantly, the purpose of this study is not to make semantic or terminological objections, but rather to refocus attention to the important role of emic epistemological assumptions in

[2] The pro-Saudi state movement known as Madkhalism, for instance, is extremely critical of figures like Ḥassan al-Bannā, Sayyid Quṭb, Muḥammad Quṭb and others traditionally associated with the Muslim Brotherhood, and routinely practises different forms of excommunication against religious clerics deemed to be sympathetic to their political worldview (Meijer 2011).

[3] Thomas Hegghammer, for instance, makes a list of groups under his analysis of Jihadi-Salafism and divides them by their objectives, regional aims and method of resistance or war, leaving out Saudi Arabia from the classification entirely (Hegghammer 2014).

[4] Al-Madkhalī, for instance, is highly critical of the 'polytheistic' practices of 'grave worship', including praying to the dead pious people, and the deification of Sufi shaykhs (Meijer 2011). Al-Ẓawāhirī similarly expresses shock that some members of the Muslim Brotherhood would seek to justify prayer to the dead (*istighātha*) as a legitimate Muslim practice not condemned by the Qurʾan (al-Ẓawāhirī 1988).

Muslims' articulation of concepts like jihad and what it means to be a 'jihadi' or 'salafi'.

Insofar as this chapter is a study of the term Jihadi-Salafism in the Western academy, I will study figures who are associated with this broadly conceived 'movement' in the academy, even if they deny association with these terms. The three figures chosen for this study include Abū Muḥammad al-Maqdisī (b. 1959), a highly influential figure in the contemporary articulation of Jihadi-Salafism, Abū Ḥamza al-Maṣrī (b. 1958), the figure credited with having coined the term, and Abū Baṣīr al-Ṭarṭūsī (b. 1959), one of the most prominent Syrian jurists behind the Syrian opposition, and not affiliated with any specific militant group. These figures, who can in different ways be considered a part of the 'old guard' – having all participated in the anti-Soviet war in Afghanistan with ʿAbdullāh ʿAzzām (d. 1989), Osama bin Laden (d. 2011) and Ayman al-Ẓawāhirī (d. 2022) – were all active jurists, preachers, scholars and practitioners in the late 1990s when the term would first be used. In this chapter, I explore the use of this term by these figures and their own historiographical accounts of its use, including their willingness to be associated with the term.

Significantly, this study analyses the way in which the term and its synonyms had origins in the Western academy, later being propagated by mass media after 9/11, as opposed to being a term formulated by 'Salafi-Jihadists' themselves. Considering the foreign origin of the term as a classification, I analyse how the figures above responded to its use in defining their own identity with respect to jihad. In all cases, the thinkers acknowledge the foreign nature of the term, and they differ in their willingness to be associated with it. Some, like Abū Baṣīr al-Ṭarṭūsī, refuse to identity either as 'Salafi' or 'Jihadi' despite acknowledging the history of the term in the 1990s, while others, like Abū Muḥammad al-Maqdisī, are explicit in the foreign imposition of the term but express their willingness in this classification.

Furthermore, I argue that for thinkers like al-Maqdisī, although they accept the use of the term, this should not be interpreted as an acceptance of the assumptions behind the academy's use of the term. This includes both the splitting of 'Salafism' into three distinct types (Wiktorowicz 2006), and the distinction of Salafi 'groups' as 'jihadi' on the basis, for instance, of their willingness to excommunicate 'Muslim' rulers. Rather, I show that, as is the case with al-Maqdisī, their acceptance of the term is not their primary marker of identity but rather their willingness to be associated with the Islamic connotations of each term individually. In other words, while al-Maqdisī does not know of the tripartite conception of Salafism – nor does he consider pro-state Salafis to be Salafis to begin with – he is willing to be identified with the term due to the positive connotations of the terms 'Salafism' and 'jihad' in the Islamic tradition. In all cases, al-Maqdisī, al-Ṭarṭūsī, and others are not accepting or rejecting the term on the basis of its academic objectivity in categorising groups, but rather the functionality of the term as an Islamic expression of the centrality of jihad and the role of the pious ancestors (al-salaf al-ṣāliḥ) in the Islamic tradition.

Jihadi-Salafism: A Brief History

It is important to first understand the current historiography of Jihadi-Salafism, and the current state of the literature. In nearly all studies of the concept, whether in the academy or commissioned by the state security apparatuses, Jihadi-Salafism is a unified movement: it has clear, traceable origins, and can be neatly confined within a number of dichotomies we are told defined the Muslim world from the very beginning: between radical, fundamentalist and violent Muslims on the one hand, and 'moderate' Muslims on the other (Devji 2017; Mohamedou 2017; Siddiqui 2020). The genealogy, furthermore, of 'fundamental', 'radical', 'literalist', 'jihadist' and 'Salafi' Islam, we are told, is also simple and has a single origin. Although many of the concepts associated with this division of Muslims can be traced to the first generation of Muslims, such as the significance of jihad and political rule in Islam (Maher 2016: 31–40, 71–5, 111–14), we would wait for nearly 700 years after hijra (1300 CE) for a systematic exposition of Salafi Islam.

Here, we observe that Ibn Taymiyya (d. 1328) features perhaps the strongest of all figures in all studies of Jihadi-Salafism, and is often said to be the 'father or [sic] modern Muslim terrorism' (Jansen 1997: 33) the 'medieval mind' behind political Islam, or the man credited with the common expression of Muslim jurists requiring the death penalty in the absence of repentance, especially of rulers who refuse to implement the sharī'a (Habeck 2007). We are told that Ibn Taymiyya, writing in Mamluk Syria, would also gain notoriety for his extreme views and willingness to pronounce excommunication on the enemies of the

Mamluk ruling elite for not implementing the shariʿa but instead substituting it for Genghis Khan's military code, the *yāsa* (Arabic: *yāsa* or *yāsiq*) (Lahoud 2010: 124; Jansen 1997: 34). Ibn Taymiyya, along with the many students he would produce in Egypt, would then lay the intellectual foundation for Salafism after his death (Bunzel 2016; Halverson 2010).

After Ibn Taymiyya, the next figure in the genealogy of Jihadi-Salafism is Muḥammad ibn ʿAbd al-Wahhāb (d. 1792) and the Najdī school of Ḥanbalism. In a partnership with the nascent Saudi state, Ibn ʿAbd al-Wahhāb would have the opportunity to 'forcefully implement' the imperatives of his interpretation of Ibn Taymiyya's Islam in the country: he would destroy shrines built by the Ottomans over holy graves, kill worshippers deemed to be apostates, and implement their version of shariʿa over the country (Abou El Fadl 2005: 44–74; Halverson 2010: 48; Kepel 2002: 50–2). This would prove to be a crucial step in the development of the violent component of Salafi Islam because Ibn ʿAbd al-Wahhāb was supposedly the only one to violently implement religious orthodoxy in society, and this is an aim shared by the Jihadi-Salafists today (Abou El Fadl 2005: 44–74; Halverson 2010: 48; Kepel 2002: 50–2). 'Wahhābīs' are also credited with having established concepts fundamental to the movement, including the concept of *al-walāʾ wa-l-barāʾ*, which establishes one's faith on the basis of their political affiliation with the Islamic state.[5]

After nearly two centuries, the ideological basis of the movement would be completed with Sayyid Quṭb and 'jihadists' influenced by his ideology, such as ʿAbdullah ʿAzzām and Abū Muḥammad al-Maqdisī. These thinkers would combine the imperatives of Ibn Taymiyya's Islam with the political theology of Sayyid Quṭb which (supposedly) advocated for the establishment of a global totalitarian Islamic state where the shariʿa is forcefully imposed on all of its subjects and remains in a state of constant violent jihad (Maher 2016; Wagemakers 2012).

It is important to note that this narrative is not comprehensive, and deliberately simplifies many of the nuances offered by different researchers as space

---

[5] Wagemakers (2012: 183) is convinced to the extent that he remarks, regarding Ayman al-Ẓawāhirī's treatise on *al-walāʾ wa-l-barāʾ*, that he 'does not quote a single Wahhabi scholar. This is odd, since – as we have seen – Wahhābī scholars have been instrumental in the development of *al-walāʾ wa-l-barāʾ*.

only allows for this very cursory review. I am aware that many studies of Jihadi-Salafism are much more nuanced, and only very few studies make all of the claims above. Furthermore, it is important to note that not all of these claims are false per se, but they often offer a far less complete picture than an analysis that looks beyond Ḥanbalism and Wahhābism as repositories for information. For instance, some have claimed the *al-walā' wa-l-barā'* is exclusive to or more important for Wahhābism than other Muslim traditions. A more in-depth review would reveal that it is rather an essential component of all schools of Islamic law and creed – including Zaydī and Twelver Shī'ism – and that 'Salafi-Jihadists' have drawn influence from these traditions in addition to Wahhābism (and in fact, sometimes exclusively from non-Wahhābī sources).[6]

Elsewhere, I have argued that this simplified historical narrative is really an attempt to capture a foreign phenomena in comprehensible terms: if a movement is extreme, small and marginal, it is easy to understand and identify, and if it is easy to identify, it is easy to eliminate in the form of a litmus test. At the same time, as I have alluded to above, it should not come as a surprise that many studies of Jihadi-Salafism and its history reify the modern, Western dichotomy of the 'good' and 'bad' Muslim, especially in areas where 'Salafi' Islam is contrasted with 'Sufi' or 'folk' Islam which is deemed to be far more moderate and less violent (although by no means historically true).

It is not fair to characterise all studies of Jihadi-Salafism on the same level, and I do not attempt to do such a thing. Rather, I hope to point out two major observations regarding the study of Jihadi-Salafism and connect these to what can only be regarded as the implicit (and sometimes explicit) material objectives of the academy, especially in the study of this subject. First, I show that there is a significant level of misinformation resulting from an oversimplification of complex narratives. Once again, while the studies cited above do not all make the fatal mistakes, there is a strong tendency in the literature to oversimplify the complexity of the tradition deemed to be 'Salafi-Jihadi'. There is, for instance, no interest in any study over the influence of the four Sunni schools of law on thinkers like 'Azzām, al-Ṭarṭūsī or al-Sharīf, although it is certain that Shāfi'ism and Ḥanafism had – depending on the

---

[6] This is the case in al-Ẓawāhirī's treatise on *al-walā' wa-l-barā'*, for instance, as discussed above.

thinker – a moderate to strong influence on their views pertaining to jihad and divine sovereignty. It makes sense that these narratives are overlooked because it is assumed that Wahhābism is responsible for these doctrines. One corollary of this oversight is that we often miss crucial connections in identifying the origins of concepts, such as the importance of divine sovereignty in non-Salafi political thought and its influence on Salafi thinkers.

Second, I argue that the oversimplification and misidentification associated with the study of Jihadi-Salafism is connected to the material objectives of the academy. The study of jihad(-ism) in the post-9/11 era has been highly subsidised by the US Government in addition to virtually every nation state. While many of these studies are commissioned by the security apparatuses themselves, a number of academic grants and general research interest peaked after 9/11 and once again after the rise of ISIS in 2014.[7] In studying jihad, there is a clear incentive and objective of the study, and this is often explicitly stated in both funded and unfunded studies of jihadism: the physical elimination of the enemy. It has become fashionable to start grant proposals and academic articles or books with a phrase resembling the following: 'In order to fight jihadism, we first must understand it'.[8] There is, of course, no inherent reason why an explicit aim of this sort would necessarily lead to unobjective analysis. Based on the available historiography surrounding Jihadi-Salafism, however, I argue that it is clear that certain simplifications both exist but also result from the academy's desire to pinpoint a specific enemy such as to facilitate physical elimination. If Jihadi-Salafism, in order words, is an identifiable, marginal movement easily separated from popular Muslim society, it becomes easy to identify and eliminate its followers. I make this point to say that any attempt to analyse the study of Jihadi-Salafism, or even Islam in general, requires contextualisation of the material incentives that serve as an impetus for research in the academy.

---

[7] This is clear from the large number of funded studies published by various government bodies and thinktanks (for example, Johnston et al. 2019; Byman and Williams 2015).

[8] The examples of these are far too many to count and are often implied or included in the titles of reports, journal articles, and even books. Consider Mary Habeck's (2007) *Knowing the Enemy: Jihadist Ideology and the War on Terror*.

Jihadi-Salafism: Normative Assumptions Revealed

In this section, I will very briefly survey the term Jihadi-Salafism and problems with usage of the term. I also argue that the normative assumptions that underpin the study of terrorism are abundantly clear in the academic study of Jihadi-Salafism.

The term Jihadi-Salafism is a compound of two words, as is the synonymous term Salafi-Jihadism, which is more popular but less accurate in capturing the movement as in a theological and doctrinal context.[9] Salafism, I argue, best denotes a hermeneutical movement within Sunni Islam that would advocate for the 'literal' (*ẓāhir*) interpretation of text in the absence of prevailing indications (*qarīna*). Although many scholars have provided a range of definitions for Salafism, most if not all focus on specific issues pertaining to their doctrine, or even outward appearance, as opposed to approach or interaction with scripture that would define it as a movement (Lauzière 2015: 242; Wiktorowicz 2006; Wagemakers 2016). This includes defining Salafism as a movement that emphasises such concerns as Divine unity (*tawḥīd*), Loyalty and Disassociation (*al-walāʾ wa-l-barāʾ*), jihad and opposition to religious innovations (*bidʿa*) (Maher 2016: 13). The many definitions that formulate Salafism in this manner fall short in answering the question of why Salafism would emphasise these concepts (among others) more than Ashʿarites and Maturidites, for instance. In any case, while this is the theoretical definition of the term in the literature, it is, to my knowledge, generally accepted that Salafism is understood as a doctrinal movement with historical origins in Aḥmad ibn Ḥanbal (d. 855), and would be popularised by Ibn Taymiyya, and Ibn ʿAbd al-Wahhāb several centuries later.

The second component of the term, Jihadi (Jihad-ist), refers to someone who advocates that Islam obligates Muslims to undertake jihad against disbelieving enemies. Some have defined 'jihadism' within Jihadi-Salafism specifically as the movement within Salafism that considers rulers of secular

---

[9] This is because the term Jihadi-Salafism identifies Jihadism as a type within the doctrinal school of Salafism, and thus attempts to understand a distinct branch or school within the creedal doctrine of Salafism and Sunni Islam in general. Salafi-Jihadism, on the other hand, seeks to contextualise 'Salafism' within the phenomenon of a type of armed conflict.

countries to be apostates and which require their forceful removal through violence.[10] There is in the literature significant variation in defining the term, and also a great number of logical inconsistencies. For instance, nobody, to my knowledge, includes the Kingdom of Saudi Arabia, the state in which the official clergy still belongs to the al-Wahhāb family, and is considered the single largest historical state funder of Muslim militia groups in the world, among the lists of Jihadi-Salafi groups or states (Byman 2020: 7). This is despite the fact that at least before its alliance with the US during the Gulf War, state-sanctioned scholars (who historically held great sway over both society and state decisions) had no problem identifying secular rulers as infidels and the act of legislating outside of the divine law as disbelief (*kufr*) (Mimouni 2016: 128–54). In studying the term Jihadi-Salafism in the literature, then, it seems that there is a conscious attempt to associate the movement of Jihadi-Salafism with parochiality, extremism and peripheral-ity. As with the study of 'Terrorism' in the academy generally, scholars have observed a pattern of, first, implicitly defining terrorism as acts committed by non-state actors, even though by far the most deaths caused for political or religious purposes (on both civilian and military targets) are caused by state actors (Silke 2018).

More importantly, there is an implicit connection drawn between 'terror-ism' and peripherality, extremism and parochiality. This connection is framed in such a way that given an assumed terrorism–war binary, state actors are viewed as the status quo or default form of rule, and therefore possess an inherent legitimacy over non-state actors. Regardless of the field or type of 'terrorism' (again, non-state terrorism), studies are framed in a distinct normative fashion where the legitimacy of the state itself is not called into question. While in the Western academy, this is abundantly clear in the study of Muslim and far-left militias (including the fact they are often studied together), while similarly, in other countries, studies of terrorism are framed in a way that opposing militias are identified as 'terrorists' in need of eradica-tion (Roy 2007; Kanji 2018). This is also reflected in criticisms of attempts to

---

[10] Darryl Li (2020: 106) notes that '[d]octrinal approaches in search of a coherent canon have tended to focus on texts endorsing violence against Muslim rulers deemed apostates, arguably the most controversial definition of jihad from a fiqh perspective'.

critically study state terrorism, which are often viewed as polemical attempts to oppose well-established binaries and normative values.

The Historiography of Jihadi-Salafism: 1990–2015

Upon examining the origins of the term Jihadi-Salafism, we find very different results concerning the usage and origin of this flexible and fluid term, and its use both within the Muslim tradition and outside of it. For the purpose of this study, any narrative that articulates an explicit, normative, conception of jihad – while building on foundational Islamic texts – by proponents of its application in violent struggle will be considered for the purpose of this study. However, insofar as this is a study of the Western academic portrayal of Jihadi-Salafism, I look at thinkers who are widely considered in the literature to be Jihadi-Salafists, and not those who necessarily identify with the term.

Jihadi-Salafism: Origins of the Term

The term Jihadi-Salafism and its synonyms would first be used in the mid-to-late 1990s and became widely popular in both the academic literature and the popular media, first used in an academic context by Gilles Kepel in his book *Jihad: The Trail of Political Islam*, originally published in 2000, and in an article in 1998 (Kepel 1998; Kepel 2002: 403). In both works, he attributes the coining of the term to Abū Ḥamza al-Maṣrī, the Egyptian national and former imam of Finnsbury Park Mosque, currently serving a life sentence in the US on terrorism charges (Kepel 1998; Kepel 2002: 403). Kepel identifies al-Maṣrī as a 'representative' of the movement and refers to a tape by al-Maṣrī where he apparently uses the term 'Jihadi-Salafism' to indicate this mysterious branch of Salafism we are assured existed since its conception (al-Maṣrī [1997] 2018).

What is very interesting about the al-Maṣrī tape is his definition of Salafism, as well as 'Jihadi-Salafism' (which he in fact does not say in the tape). Contrary to Kepel's claims of the existence of a loosely affiliated movement with a defined term and name, al-Maṣrī follows the definition of Salafism I proposed in the previous section. Instead of identifying Salafism as a specific movement with defined beliefs and traceable history, he adopts a definition which is as inclusive as possible and synonymous with the term Sunni Muslim. For al-Maṣrī, Salafism is a reference to *ahl al-sunna*, or simply 'followers of the *ṣaḥāba*'

(Prophetic companions). Al-Maṣrī defines Salafism, as discussed above, as the default Islamic orthodoxy, and mentions the irony behind Western definitions of Salafism as 'followers of the righteous ancestors', as it implies that the West, enemies of Islam, are in fact willing to admit that Salafis like him are true Muslims, whereas it would otherwise seem to be within the West's interest not to admit that 'true' or pristine Islam of the *salaf* is the one being practised by true Salafis. In the beginning of the lecture, which is in English, al-Maṣrī makes these remarks:[11]

> What does it mean, Salafism? In the definitions of the Salafi brothers who put that definition for them, they mean by it that the group of people who they are trying to follow the *ṣaḥāba* [Prophetic companions]. Without realising that they did give it a title, and they gave that title to a certain group, and without realising, they start pulling out themselves from the majority *ahl al-sunna wa-l-jamāʻa*, labelling the others with other names, which is contradicting their own policy! When the Salafism is coming – I have to call it Salafism, I have to call it something, but I will explain, why this term is not legal in Islam. When the Salafism came, it came to the people who are labelling themselves different to the Muslims of Sunni Muslims: it came to denounce the *madhhabism*, it came to denounce the blind following, it came to denounce nationalism, it came to denounce every *-ism* [. . .]
>
> Is that title, [an] Islamic title? Yes, there is a *salaf*, the *salaf* are the people of the Prophet, upon him be peace and blessings, or the best generations and those who are following the *iḥsan*, following with righteousness, these are called [. . .] the Salafi people. But for us to be related to them, it's a very beautiful creation from what Allah wanted us to have. Allah Almighty called us Muslims [. . .] [he] said in *Sūrat* [Chapter] al-Hajj, 'strive in the cause of Allah – Almighty – as you should do, and Allah has made ease for you in the religion, and he selected you amongst nations to become the best', and not only that, 'this is the religion of Ibrahim (peace be upon him), and he's the one who called you Muslims before' [Q.22:78], so Allah wanted us to be Muslims . . . and deviation from this title, any extra title, is not allowed in Islam. (al-Maṣrī [1997] 2018: 1:30–4:49)

As it would turn out, academics would continue to define Salafism, besides identifying its characteristics, as 'followers of the *salaf*' up until 2021, when

---

[11] I have omitted notifying the errors in the quote '[*sic*]' due to the large number of errors.

Emad Hamdeh would object that surely, this definition would not suffice, since all non-Shīʿī Muslims claim to followers of the Prophet's companions.[12] More importantly, al-Maṣrī, back in 1997, stressed the importance of defining this orthodox Islam on its own terms without qualifying the term. The corollary is that from an Islamic perspective, any argument or sect must be analysed within the context of the Qurʾan and sunna, and any polemic against sects seeking to claim the title 'Muslim' must defend them on these grounds.

Another important factor to be considered is that in the 1990s, the word Salafism (salafiyya) would come to denote the brand of Salafism sponsored by the Saudi state, the significant difference with al-Maṣrī being the requirement of subservience to the state. To this extent, especially in the UK, it is possible to find references to Salafism strictly in this definition, hence the famous tape released by Abdullah al-Faisal entitled 'The Devil's Deception of the Saudi Salafis', and would trigger a debate with Abū Qatāda (Palestinian al-Qaʿida ideologue) who would warn al-Faisal against excommunicating Saudi clerics (Faisal [1999] 2011; Abū Qatāda, 2011). In the tape, he frequently refers to 'Salafism' and 'Salafis' in reference to the Saudi Salafis.

What is significant for the purpose of this study is the fact 'Salafism' would specifically denote the Saudi strand of Salafism. Thus was the case such that saying the phrase 'I am not a Salafi' could mean that one is a believer in Salafi doctrine but merely not a supporter of the Saudi state. In fact, Abū Ḥamza al-Maṣrī, in the tape referenced by Kepel implies this, where he says, 'I was a salafi before, and I agree with them that everybody should believe in the names and attributes of Allah . . . I learned a lot from them', before proceeding to criticise Saudi Salafis for their abstinence from jihad (al-Maṣrī [1997] 2018: 16:55–17:16). In fact, this definition of Salafism is indicated even in the title of the recording ('Salafism or Shaykhism'). That Salafism would continue to be used in this sense at least until 1999 (with Faisal's tape published in this year), suggests that the term 'Jihadi-Salafism' and 'Jihadi Salafism' would only be used as a normative eponym after the significant increase in the term's use in media outlets following 9/11.

---

[12] He says, quoting Ibn Taymiyya, when asked which group he belongs to: 'He should say, I am not of this, I am not of that, I am a Muslim who is trying to follow the Qurʾan and the Sunna of the Messenger of Allah (may peace and blessings be upon him) [and that's it]' (al-Maṣrī [1997] 2018: 8:40–8:55).

This is significant and entirely contrary to the so-called Salafi-Jihadi account which connects themselves directly to the Qur'an and sunna, the pious ancestors, and not to any group or sect that developed later on. While this account is debated among Muslim sects, what is significant here is that al-Maṣrī rejects the use of the term, and the term Jihadi-Salafism, or Jihadi Salafism, as a sect was, historically, an external imposition on a religious group of people regardless of its basis in reality. Regarding the use of the term, 'Jihadi', al-Maṣrī uses this only once in the recording, where he reprimands Muslims precisely for this classification: 'it is ḥarām [forbidden] . . . [to say] we are salafis, and because we are salafis, this one is jihadi, and this one is ikhwānī, and this one is [whatever] and they start pointing fingers [at each other]' (al-Maṣrī [1997] 2018: 7:20–7:40). Al-Maṣrī states that even if we were to use the term, a Salafi is not just someone who imitates the companions' outward appearance but adheres to the entire religion (al-Maṣrī [1997] 2018: 11–11:46). This is supported by the fact that the term is notably absent from those later associated with the term, including 'Abdullah 'Azzām, the symbolic father of the Arab Afghans fighting the Soviets in the 1980s, and a founding member of al-Qa'ida. Only this would explain its glaring absence in the peak of Jihadi-Salafism, in 1980s Afghanistan, and more importantly, why none of its ideologues, from Sayyid Imām al-Sharīf (b. 1950), to Ayman al- Ẓawāhirī, Osama bin Laden or 'Abdullah 'Azzām, would use such a term, let alone adopt it as an eponym.[13] As we will see, it would only be after the media's popularisation of the term after 9/11 that people would begin to identify with it.

Abū Muḥammad al-Maqdisī: An Account of Positive Reception

One of the foremost thinkers who identifies with the term, Abū Muḥammad al-Maqdisī, offers his own interpretation and historical account. Al-Maqdisī

---

[13] I have not been able to find any references to the term 'Salafi-Jihadi' or 'Jihadi-Salafi' referring to a movement (as opposed to a strategic categorisation of militia groups) in the CIA Abbottabad Archive predating 2001, the earliest being the script of an interview with Abū Muḥammad al-Maqdisī in 2002 (1423 AH) where he describes 'Jihadi Salafism' as a movement 'that combines between calling to complete divine unity (tawḥīd) and jihad with this objective'. See al-Maqdisī (2002).

is a Saudi-educated, Palestinian theorist and one of the most famous jurists or ideologues associated with al-Qaʿida. More recently, he is known for his criticisms of Hayʾat Tahrir al-Sham (HTS), where he advised fighters to refrain from fighting for Abū Moḥammad al-Julani (b. 1982). Importantly, he is the founder of the highly influential jihadist website, *Minbar al-Tawhid wa-l-Jihad* ('The platform of monotheism and jihad') and is likely the first thinker to actively associate himself with the term 'Jihadi-Salafist'. He is currently based in Jordan and his background as the flagbearer of jihad makes him a popular figure for the media, including channels on Jordanian television, Al Jazeera, and others, and remains a controversial and significant thinker, one of the first associated with Jihadi-Salafism (Wagemakers 2012). Al-Maqdisī, in a fatwa on the now-defunct latest version of the *Minbar*, Ilmway.com (Islam 2021), discusses the term Jihadi-Salafism upon being posed with a question regarding its permissibility (to use, identify with, and so on). He first mentions that from within an Islamic perspective, the title does not make sense. After all, how could someone be a Salafi – a follower of the first three generations of Muslims – or even a Muslim, if he does not believe in jihad? Despite the imposed nature of the eponym, al-Maqdisī states, 'Even though we don't oppose it, we never gave ourselves this title' (Islam 2021). For al-Maqdisī, even though he does not refuse to identify the term, or have it imposed on him by the media, he acknowledges that the term itself is not found within the Islamic tradition, and it would not make sense for a Muslim to use this term outside of this context.

Abū Baṣīr al-Ṭarṭūsī: An Account of Rejection

One potential concern of the term 'Jihadi-Salafism' is that instead of focusing on the Islamic character of the movement, it is subjected to the categorisations and dichotomisations imposed by the West. Abū Baṣīr is a Syrian Muslim scholar, and currently resides in London, making occasional trips to Istanbul and Syria since 2013. He is, furthermore, often included in lists of 'Salafi-Jihadi jurists' in academic literature and think tank databases (Hegghammer 2006). Although Abū Baṣīr's influence is not a comparable to that of al-Maqdisī, he is one of the few figures associated with jihadism from the 1980s, earning him the title *shaykh al-mujāhidīn* (Al-Hiwar TV 2013). Importantly, he is a major critic of al-Qaʿida despite his intellectual influence as a theorist. One of the foremost theorists of the Syrian revolution, Abū Baṣīr al-Ṭarṭūsī, was asked a similar question. Al-Ṭarṭūsī had a short TV segment on the London-based Arabic channel Al-Hiwar TV, entitled 'The Jurisprudence of the Revolution' (*fiqh al-thawra*), where he offers Islamic legal responsa and scriptural guidance on the motives, rules, restrictions and goals of the Syrian revolution. Al-Ṭarṭūsī has and continued to be critical of al-Qaʿida's and other groups' tactics which he saw as both as a violation of Islamic law and ultimately destructive to the aims of the opposition (Arabi21 News 2015). In one of the episodes of this show, al-Ṭarṭūsī was asked why he generally refrained from using the terms salafi and jihadi. In response, he said:

> Look, we turned a blind eye to these terms a long time ago. They used to have positive connotations in the past, in the mind of the reader and listener. Unfortunately, today, these terms have become confusing and unclear . . . and they invoke negative connotations in the mind of the hearer or listener . . . often connotations that oppose Islamic ethics and morality. For us, the Islamic legal terms will suffice: God called us Muslims, that's it, I'm Muslim . . . The Prophet (peace and blessings be upon him) unites, and all these other names divide. (al-Ṭarṭūsī 2016a)

In another programme, entitled 'Revisions' (*al-murājaʿāt*) al-Ṭarṭūsī is asked: 'Many people write about you and ascribe things to you, that you are a theoretician of what is called Jihadi-Salafism? . . . Do you accept these classifications?' (ibid.).

In his response, we observe a similar response to that above, amounting to an affirmation of the importance of the *salaf* for any orthodox Muslim, and the significance of jihad as an act which the Qurʾan defines as a criterion for hypocrisy – but not its use as a category defined by their beliefs and political goals:

> I do not ascribe these terms to myself, but regardless, it is a great honour to have others associate me with jihad and the mujahideen [. . .] likewise, it is an honour to be associated with the Salafi path, meaning the Sunni [one], in reference to following the Book and the sunna [. . .] I do not use these terms, names and divisions, however, unfortunately, as they lead to unwanted consequences, including divisions . . . for example, Salafism: if I say, I am

Salafi, you'll ask, what kind of Salafi? [. . .] likewise, if I say, I am *jihadi*, people will not understand: are you a *jihadi*, as in a follower of al-Qāʿida or another group, do you accept this or that tactic [of war], explosions, suicide bombings [and the like]? The term has causedconfusion for the people [. . .] and all of this arises from a lack of understanding Islam in its true nature. (Al-Hiwar TV 2013: 2:40–6:00)

For Abū Baṣīr, these terms are foreign to Islamic scripture and the larger Islamic tradition. For him, the terms detract from an understanding of Islam that can be considered pristine, traditional and orthodox. Jihadi-Salafism is a term that would become used in the 1990s, while the true Islam lived and personified the eternal truths of the Qurʾan and the tradition of the Messenger of God. Here, Abū Baṣīr resembles Abū Ḥamza al-Maṣrī in attempting to confine the theological and political polemics to conformance to the original texts of Islam. Importantly, it would not be the minor juristic disagreements that would define a true Muslim from a hypocrite (*munāfiq*, Qurʾanic term) but pillars considered fundamental to Islamic praxis: jihad and independence from rulers in their mission of implementing a state-conformant, secularised Islam.[14]

Abū Baṣīr's and al-Maṣrī's views on the use of the term, furthermore, can be seen as an attempt to reduce the infighting ('pointing fingers' in al-Maṣrī's words) between Salafis, and even between Sunni doctrinal polemics generally. It is an attempt to capture and continue the practice of the Prophet as practised by his companions. For them, the people of jihad are the flag-bearers of Islam: intellectually independent from political interference, politically independent under the divine law, and the bearers of the banners of jihad 'until the day of judgement'[15] as prophesied by the Prophet Muḥammad 1,400 years ago (al-Ṭarṭūsī 2013).

---

[14] Abū Ḥamza al-Maṣrī [1997] (2018) in his tape 'Is it Salafism or Sheikhism', identifies jihad as the main distinguisher between true believers and hypocrites in the time of the Prophet (see Q.3:154–6, 33:13–20, 9:24, 42–25, 81–96, 120). See also al-Ṭarṭūsī, *Qawāʾid fī al-Takfīr* (n.d.: 26–30); al-Ṭarṭūsī, 'al-Ṣafḥa al-Rasmiyya li-l-Shaykh Abī Baṣīr al-Ṭarṭūsī' [Social Media Channel], Telegram (10 December 2017).

[15] This is part of a Prophetic tradition reported in 'Ṣaḥīḥ Muslim' frequently quoted by the figures discussed above. The text of the ḥadīth states: 'A party among my nation will continue to fight [*yuqātilūn*] upon the truth outwardly [*ẓāhirīn*] until the Day of Judgement' (al-Ṭarṭūsī, 2013).

We could add to these motives a caution behind the serious theological imprecision in labelling groups of people with non-Qur'anic terms. Abū Muḥammad al-Maqdisī, for instance, does not label ISIS – which he opposed since their claim to have established a righteous and legitimate caliphate – as truly 'Salafi', because the adjective Salafi implies orthodoxy and compliance with the Qur'an and sunna. Similarly, both he and al-Ṭarṭūsī label ISIS's jihad as legally impermissible, thus rendering them non-jihadis in the true sense of the term, in reference to someone who undertakes jihad in the path of God.[16] From an Islamic perspective, then, the term is both theologically (for lack of use of a better term) problematic and, I would argue, factually imprecise.

Conclusion: Reconsidering Jihadi-Salafism

In this chapter, I explored the history of the term Jihadi-Salafism in addition to the ways it has been received by those said to be its primary theoreticians. This study examined the narrative that the term Jihadi-Salafism (or Salafi-Jihadism) was coined by Abū Ḥamza al- Maṣrī and that the term denoted a specific religio-political group with a unified agenda and a traceable origin. I have shown that as far as the term is concerned, there is no evidence to suggest the term was used in any Muslim source prior to Kepel's coining of the term in 1998. It was only after its spread in the media that Abū Muḥammad al-Maqdisī and others would use the term. While the terms Salafi and Jihadi were both used prior to the use of the compound term, they did not feature prominently as an eponym and only functioned as secondary descriptors to more common terms, such as *ahl al-sunna* (that is, Sunni Islam). Here, I showed how the term Salafi in the 1990s was not the preferred term of Muslims who adopted the Salafi doctrine but rejected the political quietist connotations of the term.

Significantly, this study showed how even with the gradual adoption by some of the term, it possesses entirely different meanings from the perspective of the

---

[16] Al-Ṭarṭūsī has a book specifically dedicated to criticising ISIS, identifying it as a state 'of extremist kharajites' in direct opposition to the Qur'an and sunna, while al-Maqdisī refrains from the term 'kharajites' but declares the illegitimacy of their caliphate and jihad (al-Ṭarṭūsī, 2016; Abū Muḥammad al-Maqdisī, n.d. [c. 2016]).

theorists themselves. As the cases of al-Maqdisī and al-Ṭarṭūsī have shown, the significance of the term lies in its claim to orthodox Islam and the centrality of jihad in Islamic doctrine and jurisprudence. In contrast, the use of the term in the academy and popular media often portray it as an independent religio-political sect and an identity different from other Salafis and political movements, such as the Muslim Brotherhood. The fact that the so-called founding figures of Jihadi-Salafism, like ʿAbdullah ʿAzzām, never used the term, and frequently blurred the lines between these divisions – ʿAzzām was a senior Muslim Brotherhood figure and had positive relationships with Saudi ʿulamāʾ – shows they are unhelpful in offering a classification of Muslim movements.

It is difficult to suggest concrete steps for improving the study of jihad in the field. As others have suggested in this volume, what matters is the meanings indicated in the use of terms, and not the terms themselves. Even in the absence of using terms like Jihadi-Salafism, the problem remains that the material incentives that shape studies on jihad reinforce the legitimacy of the nation state, which has an active interest in categorising and subjugating Muslim identity in the name of national security. Any attempt to study and understand Islam, especially a subject like jihad, requires a significant reconsideration of the normative and ontological assumptions made in the process of research.

References

Abou El Fadl, K. (2005), *The Great Theft: Wrestling Islam from the Extremists*, New York: HarperOne.

Abū Qatāda, Umar b. Mahmud. (2011), 'Debate', 4 July <https://archive.org/details/iarchive_qatada> (last accessed 5 May 2022).

Al-Hiwar TV (2013), 'Murājaʿāt maʿa al-Shaykh Abū Baṣīr al-Ṭarṭūsī', <https://www.youtube.com/watch?v=WnbNnhSAVvU> (last accessed 5 May 2022).

Al-Maqdisī, A. (n.d.), 'Abū Muḥammad al-Maqdisī: Limādhā lam Usammihim ḥattā al-Ān Khawārij', *Islamion*, 8 April, <http://islamion.com/news/أبو-محمد-المقدسي-لماذا-لم-أسمهم-حتى-الآن-خوارج/> (last accessed 5 May 2022).

Al-Maṣrī, A. ([1997] 2018), 'Is it Salafism or Sheikhism', 11 July, <https://archive.org/details/LiberateKashmirShaykhAbuHamzaAnjemChoudary/Is+it+Salafism+or+Shaykhism+-+Shaykh+Abu+Hamza+Al+Masri.mp3> (last accessed 5 May 2022).

Al-Ṭarṭūsī, A. (2013), 'Qudrat al-Umma ʿalā al-Jihād', 31 July, Tartosi.blogspot.com, <https://tartosi.blogspot.com/2013/07/> (last accessed 5 May 2022).

Al-Ṭarṭūsī, A. (2016a), 'Al-Thawra #2 Fiqh Limādhā Yataḥaffaẓ al-Shaykh Abū Baṣīr ʿalā Lafẓf Jihādī wa-Salafī', <https://www.youtube.com/watch?v=7gwA8UQGNu4> (last accessed 5 May 2022).

Al-Ṭarṭūsī, A. (2016b), *Hādhihī hiya Khiṣāl al-Khawārij: fa-Ḥdharūhā*, Istanbul: GurabaYayinlari.

Al-Ṭarṭūsī, A. (n.d.), *Qawāʿid fī al-Takfīr*.

Al-Ẓawāhirī, A. (1988), *Al-Ḥaṣād al-Murr: al-Ikhwān al-Muslimīn fī Sittīn ʿĀmā*, Markaz al-Fajr li-l-Iʿlām.

Arabi21 News (2015), '"Al-Ṭarṭūsī" Yuḥadhdhir min al-Inḍimām ilā Jabhat al-Nuṣra', 12 April, <https://arabi21.com/story/823755/النصرة-جبهة-إلى-الانضمام-من-يحذر-الطرطوسي> (last accessed 5 May 2022).

Asad, T. (1993), *Genealogies of Religion: Discipline and Reasons of Power in Christianity and Islam*, Baltimore: Johns Hopkins University Press.

Bunzel, C. (2016), *The Kingdom and the Caliphate: Duel of the Islamic States*, Washington, DC: Carnegie Endowment.

Byman, D. (2020), 'Understanding, and Misunderstanding, State Sponsorship of Terrorism', *Studies in Conflict & Terrorism*, 1–19.

Byman, D. and J. Williams (2015), 'ISIS vs. Al Qaeda: Jihadism's Global Civil War', *Brookings Institute*, 24 February, <www.brookings.edu/articles/isis-vs-al-qaeda-jihadisms-global-civil-war/> (last accessed 5 May 2022).

Central Intelligence Agency (2017), 'Minbar al-Tawḥid wa-l-Jihad. "Ḥiwar maʿa al-Shaykh Abu Muhammad al-Maqdisi"', <https://www.cia.gov/library/abbottabad-compound/index.html> (last accessed 5 May 2022).

Devji, F. (2017), *Landscapes of the Jihad*, Ithaca: Cornell University Press.

Faisal, A. ([1999] 2011), 'Devils Deception Of The Saudi Salafis (07.3.11) – By Shaikh Abdullah Faisal', 13 July, <https://archive.org/details/DevilsDeceptionOfTheSaudiSalafis07.13.11> (last accessed 5 May 2022).

Habeck, M. (2007), *Knowing the Enemy: Jihadist Ideology and the War on Terror*, London and New Haven: Yale University Press.

Halverson, J. (2010), *Theology and Creed in Sunni Islam: The Muslim Brotherhood, Ashʿarism, and Political Sunnism*, Berlin: Springer Nature.

Hegghammer, T. (2006), 'Global Jihadism after the Iraq War', *The Middle East Journal*, 60: 1, 11–32.

Hegghammer, T. (2009), 'The Ideological Hybridization of Jihadi Groups', *Current Trends in Islamist Ideology* 9, 26–45.

Hegghammer, T. (2014), 'Jihadi Salafis or Revolutionaries? On Religion and Politics in the Study of Militant Islamism', in R. Meijer (ed.), *Global Salafism: Islam's New Religious Movement*, Oxford: Oxford University Press, pp. 245–66.

Imber, C. (2010), 'What Does Ghazi Actually Mean', in C. Balim-Harding and C. Imber (eds), *The Balance of Truth: Essays in Honour of Professor Geoffrey Lewis*, Piscataway: Gorgias Press, pp. 165–178.

Islam, J. (2021), '"Salafi-Jihadism": Frightening Menace or Scapegoat for the War on Terror?', *Cage*, 15 July, <https://www.cage.ngo/salafi-jihadism-frightening-menace-or-scapegoat-for-the-war-on-terror> (last accessed 5 May 2022).

Jansen, J. (1997), *The Dual Nature of Islamic Fundamentalism*, Ithaca: Cornell University Press.

Johnston, P., M. Alami and C. Clarke (2019), *Return and Expand? The Finances and Prospects of the Islamic State After the Caliphate*, Santa Monica: Rand Corporation.

Kanji, A. (2018), 'Framing Muslims in the "War on Terror": Representations of Ideological Violence by Muslim versus Non-Muslim Perpetrators in Canadian National News Media', *Religions*, 9: 9, 274.

Kepel, G. (1998), 'Le GIA a travers ses publications', *Pouvoirs*, 67–84.

Kepel, G. (2002), *Jihad: The Trail of Political Islam*, Cambridge, MA: Harvard University Press.

Lahoud, N. (2010), *The Jihadis' Path to Self-Destruction*, London: Hurst.

Lauzière, H. (2015), *The Making of Salafism*, New York: Columbia University Press.

Lav, D. (2012), *Radical Islam and the Revival of Medieval Theology*, Cambridge: Cambridge University Press.

Li, D. (2020), *The Universal Enemy*, Redwood City: Stanford University Press.

Maher, S. (2016), *Jihadi-Salafism: The History of an Idea*, London: Hurst.

Meijer, R. (2011), 'Politicising al-Jarḥ wa-l-Taʿdīl: Rabīʿ b. Hādī al-Madkhalī and the Transnational Battle for Religious Authority', in N. Boekhoff-van der Voort, K. Versteegh and J. Wagemakers (eds), *The Transmission and Dynamics of the Textual Sources of Islam*, Leiden: Brill, pp. 375–99.

Mimouni, A. (2016), *Debating al-Hakimiyya and Takfir in Salafism: The Genesis of Intra-Salafi Schism in the 1990s*, PhD thesis, Exeter: University of Exeter.

Mohamedou, M. (2017), *A Theory of ISIS: Political Violence and the Transformation of the Global Order*, London: Pluto Press.

Roy, O. (2007), 'Islamic Terrorist Radicalisation in Europe', in S. Amghar, A. Boubekeur and M. Emerson (eds), *European Islam: Challenges for Public Policy and Society*, Brussels: Centre for European Policy Studies, pp. 52–60.

Scheuerman, W. (2006), 'Carl Schmitt and the Road to Abu Ghraib', *Constellations* 13: 1, 108–24.

Siddiqui, S. (2020), 'Good Scholarship/Bad Scholarship: Consequences of the Heuristic of Intersectional Islamic Studies', *Journal of the American Academy of Religion*, 88: 1, 142–74.

Silke, A. (2018), 'State Terrorism', in A. Silke (ed.), *Routledge Handbook of Terrorism and Counterterrorism*, London: Routledge, pp. 66–73.

Tareen, S. (2020), *Defending Muhammad in Modernity*, Notre Dame: University of Notre Dame Press.

Wagemakers, J. (2012), *A Quietist Jihadi: The Ideology and Influence of Abu Muhammad al-Maqdisi*, Cambridge: Cambridge University Press.

Wagemakers, J. (2016), *Salafism in Jordan: Political Islam in a Quietist Community*, Cambridge: Cambridge University Press.

Wiktorowicz, Q. (2006), 'Anatomy of the Salafi Movement', *Studies in Conflict & Terrorism*, 29: 3, 207–39

2

JIHAD GOES TO COURT: THE INVOCATION OF ISLAMIC IDIOMS IN TERRORISM PROSECUTIONS

Nicole Nguyen

Introduction: When Jihad Goes to Court

On 4 October 2014, nineteen-year-old Mohammad Hamzah Khan and his two younger siblings tried to travel from the US to Syria to join the Islamic State of Iraq and Syria (ISIS). Federal authorities arrested Khan at the airport and charged him with 'knowingly attempting to provide material support and resources, namely personnel, to a foreign terrorist organization' (United States v. Khan 2014: 14). At sentencing, US District Judge John Tharp Jr determined, 'Mr Khan set off to join and aid a terrorist organization that believes it's appropriate and believes it's indeed holy to kill anyone who disagrees with its religious dogma' (United States v. Khan 2016: 24).[1] Rejecting the defence's description of Khan as a 'naïve' and 'foolish' teenager 'seduced by online recruiters', Judge Tharp observed:

> To want to join the Caliphate is to want to join jihad, which is war . . . The war being fought by ISIL is jihad, and that can't be separated from the purpose

[1] In the US, the federal judiciary is comprised of three main levels: district courts (the trial court), circuit courts (first level of appeal) and the Supreme Court (final level of appeal in the federal system). Unlike state courts, the federal judiciary only hears cases arising under federal statutes, treaties or the constitution. US District Court judges are appointed by the president and confirmed by the Senate for a life term.

of the organization . . . This is one organization with one objective, and that objective is jihad. (United States v. Khan 2016: 13–14)

While Khan never wielded a weapon or committed an act of violence, Judge Tharp sentenced Khan to forty months in prison, followed by twenty years of supervised release. Judge Tharp's understanding of jihad as war – and its tethering of violence to Islam – informed how he interpreted the case's factual evidence and how he sentenced Khan.

In the case against Babar Ahmad, prosecutors similarly depicted the defendant's 2001 online publication of two articles in support of the Taliban as reflective of his 'definition of jihad focus[ed] on violent jihad and taking up arms' (United States v. Ahmad 2014a: 9).[2] Refuting the premise that his publications had 'somehow something to do with jihad', Ahmad explained that, given the imminent US invasion, Afghanistan 'was a Muslim land and it was under attack' (United States v. Ahmad 2014b: 91). This anti-Muslim aggression resonated with Ahmad's personal experiences in Bosnia and Kosovo, where he fought in defence of besieged Muslims. In sentencing Ahmad, US District Judge Janet Hall refused to adopt popular interpretations of jihad, reasoning, 'the concept of jihad in Islam is struggle, and it's both an internal and a defensive struggle, but it's never what happened on 9/11' (ibid.: 40–1). Rather than reduce armed struggles to sensationalised notions of jihad, Judge Hall explained that, to understand the defendant's actions, she needed to consider the anti-Muslim geopolitical conditions organising Ahmad's publications, such as the Russian invasion of Chechnya and 'the struggle in Bosnia by Muslims against the Serbs and their efforts to ethnically cleanse Bosnia of Muslims'.[3] As Ahmad explained, 'By the end of the 2000, Muslim clerics began to issue appeals to support the Taliban', which he did by using his website to 'solicit support for

---

[2] Ahmad published the first article before al-Qaʿida's 9/11 attacks. The second publication came after the US believed the Taliban agreed to harbour Osama bin Laden in Afghanistan.

[3] Even in her refusal, however, Judge Hall's reasoning articulated with popular 'culture talk' that reifies the 'good Muslim/bad Muslim' trope, whereby some Muslims correctly interpret and invoke (non-violent) jihad while others use the term to justify their maligned interests (Mamdani 2004: 18). In the absence of other conceptual tools, the mere refusal to equate jihad with 'what happened on 9/11' does not necessarily open alternative analyses, including how jihad is used to organise political violence in pursuit of different geopolitical goals.

the Taliban regime', on the presumption that, like Muslims in Bosnia, Kosovo and Chechnya, the Taliban was 'being victimized by the international community' (ibid.: 88). In weighing these different understandings of jihad and the geopolitical contexts in which Ahmad acted, Judge Hall sentenced Ahmad to 150 months in prison, half of the prosecution's request for a twenty-five-year sentence.[4] *Khan* and *Ahmad* illustrate how the courts have engaged in epistemic, political and legal struggles over what constitutes jihad, key conceptual work that has shaped the outcomes of terrorism-related prosecutions and the role of the criminal-legal system in the global war on terror.

While federal communications have celebrated such convictions as global war on terror victories and reinforced the image of the courts as a 'counterterrorism tool' (Office of Public Affairs 2010), the criminal-legal system is an embodied institution composed of legal actors, like Judge Tharp and Judge Hall, who differently understand the role of the courts, the concept of jihad and the geopolitical contexts defining the terrorism cases before them.[5] Such variances have produced uneven outcomes for those who have the most at stake in these proceedings: defendants and their families. In fact, a case-level analysis of terrorism prosecutions illustrates how judicial power and human agency – in the context of institutional, public and professional pressures – drive the uneven interpretation and enforcement of the law in times of war. Drawing on document analysis of court transcripts, observation of court proceedings and interviews with terrorism lawyers, I explore how legal actors have invoked the concept of jihad to secure convictions and mobilise the courts as a counterterrorism tool. I examine how such 'concept-work' has used Islamic principles and Arabic vocabularies as organising guides to interpret terrorism-related cases; as a courtroom strategy, such concept-work intentionally occludes 'the relations of force in which concepts are embedded' and obscures the material conditions in which defendants acted (Stoler 2016: 17).

---

[4] Judge Hall credited the 110 months Ahmad already served while awaiting trial, meaning he only spent another forty months in prison.

[5] Terrorism prosecutions 'have factored prominently in America's unconventional war with al-Qaeda and its affiliated extremist networks' as, in a 'rather unprecedented way, the executive branch has enlisted the third branch – the judiciary – to pursue its war aims' (Skinner 2013: 309).

While legal actors also invoked additional Islamic idioms like *tawḥīd*, *anṣār* and *hijra*, I specifically focus on the concept of jihad using selected court cases to illustrate the epistemic politics at work in the courts. The concept of 'Salafi-Jihadi', after all, has served as a 'categorical tool used by western academics of Islam to identify "the enemy" in need of destruction following the instability brought by the neo-colonization of the Muslim World (Iraq and Afghanistan being the most prominent)' (Islam 2021: para. 16). Through my analysis of terrorism prosecutions, I focus on the uneven mobilisation of this categorical tool in the courts. As we will see, the strategic invocation of jihad as holy war leaves judges and jurors with few conceptual tools to understand the relationship between power, piety, politics and violence, and empowers the courts to function as a 'counterterrorism tool' and, as the government argued, to 'send a clear message to any would-be jihadists that such conduct is not tolerated by the US government' (United States v. Guled Omar 2016a: 50). The selected cases, however, also demonstrate the uneven ways legal actors have invoked, mobilised and challenged the concept of jihad, as in *Khan* and *Ahmad*. Through this analysis, this article does not intend to condemn or condone certain acts of violence; instead, it merely meditates on the conceptual work legal actors have called on jihad to undertake in the courtroom and how such invocations have informed judicial decision-making.

Framing Financial Donations as Material Support: Legal Contestations over Jihad

In 2002, Adham Hassoun was arrested on terrorism-related charges, alongside alleged co-conspirators Mohamed Youssef, Kifah Jayyousi, Kassem Daher and Jose Padilla.[6] Hassoun's arrest came after six years of financial donations made to charities such as the Canadian Islamic Association, the American Worldwide Relief Organization and the Global Relief Foundation. Hassoun testified that these donations intended to support besieged Muslims in places like Bosnia, Kosovo and Chechnya. In fact, as a part of his charitable

---

[6] While legal scholars and popular media have focused on US citizen Jose Padilla's initial arrest as a material witness, transfer to a military prison for detention, subsequent habeas petition, jury trial and sentencing, the tying of Padilla to Jayyousi and Hassoun made the material support charge against Padilla possible.

giving, Hassoun wrote cheques between 1994 and 2001 with memo lines such as 'Kosovo', 'Chechnya' and 'Afghan relief'. The prosecution, however, alleged that Hassoun's wiretapped conversations revealed that his donations supported the 'global jihad movement'. In this case, legal actors used the concept of jihad to interpret the criminality of Hassoun's donations.

In the superseding indictment, the prosecution explained that it used the terms 'jihad' and 'violent jihad' interchangeably to denote the 'planning, preparing for, and engaging in, acts of physical violence, including murder, maiming, kidnapping and hostage taking' (United States v. Adham Hassoun et al. 2005, 2). In this view, Hassoun 'operated and participated in a North American support cell that sent money, physical assets and mujahideen recruits to overseas conflicts for the purpose of fighting violent jihad' (ibid.: 3). By offering the grand jury the concept of violent jihad to interpret the factual evidence in this case, the prosecution effectively framed Hassoun's stated intention to buy new sports equipment for soccer teams in Somalia as coded language referring to arming foreign fighters preparing for or engaged in 'violent jihad activities', although the FBI never intervened to interrupt this financial flow (ibid.: 8). The superseding indictment concluded that Hassoun and his alleged co-conspirators participated in a 'North American support cell [that] supported and coordinated with other support networks and mujahideen groups waging violent jihad' (ibid.: 3). Indicting 'Salafist philosophy or theology', the putative 'politico-religion engine driving "violent jihad"', the superseding indictment identified Hassoun's conduct as a part of a broader mission to support roving foreign fighters seeking to establish 'a pure Islamic state ("Caliphate") governed by strict Islamic law ("Sharia")' across continents (ibid.: 2).

Unlike previous indictments charging defendants for their participation in or support of specific designated foreign terrorist organisations like al-Qa'ida, this case invoked an allegedly unified global jihad movement to successfully charge, prosecute and convict Hassoun and his co-conspirators for their 'informal "membership" in the jihad movement itself', ultimately attaching criminal liability to highly inchoate activities (Chesney 2008: 10). Invoking jihad expanded the preventive capacity of federal criminal law by identifying the entire alleged 'global jihad movement' as a single violent criminal conspiracy, even if prosecutors could not tie defendants to a specific plot or act of violence (see also Margulies 2007). As in *Ahmad*, the concept of jihad featured centrally in the adjudication of *Hassoun*.

To substantiate this theory of the case at trial, the prosecution first defined 'jihad', 'mujahedeen' and 'radical Salafist ideology', key terms to frame Hassoun's actions as terroristic rather than humanitarian. For example, the prosecution's witness, FBI agent John Kavanaugh, testified that 'to go to a jihad' meant to travel to the frontlines of a military battle, transforming jihad from a general struggle to a place to engage violence (United States v. Adham Hassoun et al. 2008: 46). 'Jihad areas' therefore referred to sites of military engagement, ultimately collapsing the variable geopolitical and historical contexts organising vastly different armed struggles, as with Bosnian Muslims resisting genocidal violence inflicted by Bosnian Serbs and 'Afghan Arabs' fighting alongside US soldiers to expel Soviet forces from Afghanistan (ibid.: 26–7).

Hassoun, however, challenged the government's characterisation of jihad in court filings. For example, in his objections to the prosecution's Presentence Investigation Report, Hassoun contested the government's 'description of the so-called "wider theological, ideological, and geopolitical context"' and its 'sweeping over generalization, based upon an exaggerated, distorted, and one-sided, biased view of the Islamic religion' (United States v. Adham Hassoun et al. 2007: 2–3). While prosecutors condemned the 'violent jihad' waged in Afghanistan, Hassoun explained how the US, 'together with Muslim countries, poured millions of dollars into the training and arming of the Arab mujahedeen who fought in the jihad against the Soviet Union' (ibid.: 3–4). The deeply localised struggle in Afghanistan could not be categorically denounced as a criminal expression of 'global Salafi-jihad' simply because pious transnational fighters participated in the US-backed anti-Soviet resistance; this imprecise category collapsed different armed groups and denied the different political dimensions organising each armed struggle. There is little use in an 'all-encompassing explanation' as 'there is no compelling conceptual reason to group all kinds of violence claiming the label of jihad and to separate them from all the others' (Li 2020: 24).

After challenging the problematic invocation of jihad to condemn violence waged by Muslim fighters – including militia responses to the 1995 Srebrenica massacre and dissident resistance to repressive regimes in North Africa – Hassoun also noted that the prosecution failed to introduce evidence that any of the checks [he] wrote, or funds or other items he discussed in various calls, were ever transmitted to any location overseas for the purpose of 'establishing Islamic states' or for the purpose of 'intimidating [or] coercing' governments through 'violent jihad' or through other means. (United States v. Adham Hassoun et al. 2007: 6)

For Hassoun, he sent money and other goods to sites where 'atrocities were being committed against Muslims in those places and/or relief operations were underway to aid Muslim victims and refugees in those places' (ibid.: 6–7). The criminal prosecution of Hassoun 'effectively criminalized the transmission of aid by religious Muslims wishing to alleviate the plight of their religious brethren suffering under objectively dire conditions of violent oppression, even when the groups receiving aid have not been designated as terrorists' (Said 2015: 110). Pivoting on the condemnation of an entire alleged 'global jihad movement', this broad criminal conspiracy theory of the case allowed the government to 'elide the humanitarian/political solidarity element by highlighting shared doctrinal or political similarities between the defendants and members of al-Qa 'ida with respect to a given conflict' (ibid.). Hassoun therefore rejected the inferred premise that he supported 'violent jihad' because he supported 'mujahadeen' in Bosnia, again noting that such mujahids 'were a recognized part of the Bosnian government's armed forces' (United States v. Adham Hassoun et al. 2007: 8). For Hassoun, participation in or support of a specific armed conflict could not imply allegiance to all other political conflicts claiming the label of jihad. Ultimately, Hassoun challenged the reductive analysis that his alleged subscription to 'Salafist philosophy' offered a way to interpret his charitable contributions as funding the 'global Salafist movement' that murders, kidnaps and maims to achieve its 'politico-religious' agenda, rather than as financial support for survivors of anti-Muslim aggression.

At sentencing, US District Judge Marcia Cooke observed that the jury verdict found that Hassoun's efforts to support 'people sited in various conflicts involving Muslims around Eastern Europe, the Middle East and North Africa' was 'criminal' (United States v. Adham Hassoun et al. 2008: 6). Judge Cooke, however, also determined that 'there is no evidence that [Hassoun and his co-conspirators] personally maimed, killed or kidnapped anyone in the United States or elsewhere'; that they 'did not seek to damage the United States infrastructure, shipping interests, power plants, or government buildings'; and that there 'was never a plot to harm individuals inside the United States or to kill government or political officials' (ibid.: 5–6). In fact, Judge Cooke recognised that the 'plight of Muslims throughout the world pained and moved [Hassoun]' and, ultimately, motivated him to 'violate the statutes in this case', including providing material support to terrorists, as he understood, first-hand, 'what it was like to live through armed conflict and religious persecution' (ibid.: 7).[7] Despite these observations, Judge Cooke sentenced Hassoun to 188 months in prison, followed by twenty years of supervised release. Since Hassoun was not a US citizen, his conviction also meant he would likely face deportation after completing his sentence.

Even after Hassoun served his sentence, the invocation of jihad justified further punishment, even though Judge Cooke concluded that Hassoun did not 'pose . . . a danger to the community' that would require a life sentence (ibid.: 8). After his 2017 release, Hassoun entered Immigration Customs and Enforcement (ICE) custody to determine if he should be 'subject to continued detention as an alien whose release presents a significant threat to the national security or a significant risk of terrorism'. Hassoun's status as a Lebanese-born Palestinian rendered him stateless; since Israel and Lebanon refused to accept Hassoun, his deportation was impossible. Unable to deport Hassoun, ICE Executive Director Matthew Albence determined that Hassoun met the criteria justifying continued detention, on the premise that he had 'assumed a leadership role in a criminal conspiracy to recruit fighters and provide material support to terrorist groups overseas engaging in "jihads" in Chechnya, Bosnia, Kosovo, Algeria, Afghanistan, Pakistan, Somalia, Eritrea, and Libya', and 'remained a continuing threat of recruiting, planning, and providing material support for terrorist activity'.[8] In this detention determination, the US government once again invoked jihad – and the global jihad movement more specifically – as the pretext to continue Hassoun's confinement.

---

[7] Hassoun was convicted of violating 18 U.S.C. § 956(a)(1) – conspiracy to murder, kidnap, and maim persons in a foreign country – 18 U.S.C. § 371 – conspiracy to provide material support for terrorism – and 18 U.S.C. § 2339A(a) – providing material support to terrorists.

[8] Albence's letter to Hassoun was included in publicly available court filings.

When a court ordered Hassoun's release in 2019, the government alleged that the Uniting and Strengthening America by Providing Appropriate Tools Required to Intercept and Obstruct Terrorism (USA PATRIOT) Act imbued the executive branch with the authority to indefinitely detain Hassoun since he posed a threat to national security. An FBI memo fortified the portrayal of Hassoun as a dangerous jihadist by claiming that other incarcerated men reported that Hassoun self-identified as a 'follower of ISIS leader al-Baghdadi', tried to recruit them 'in support of ISIS', and told them how to 'make explosives and plan attacks' (as cited in Adham Hassoun v. Jeffrey Searls 2020: 20). Responding to a habeas petition Hassoun filed to challenge his detention in 2019, US District Judge Elizabeth Wolford ordered Hassoun's release, dismissing the FBI memo as unreliable and rejecting Acting Assistant Field Office Director Jeffrey Seals's logic 'that he should be able to detain [Hassoun] indefinitely based on the executive branch's say-so, and that decision is insulated from meaningful review by the judiciary' (Adham Hassoun v. Jeffrey Searls 2020: 15).

The broad criminal conspiracy established by prosecutors in the original 2007 jury trial enabled the continued portrayal of Hassoun as a national security threat given his commitment to the 'global jihad movement', evident in the FBI's ability to allege that Hassoun recruited for and supported ISIS and therefore posed a continuing security risk. By collapsing different armed political groups into a single category – the global jihad movement – the government positioned armed militias like ISIS and al-Qaʿida as interchangeable organisations given their putatively shared commitment to a unifying 'global-Salafi jihad ideology', irrespective of the different geopolitical contexts and material conditions in which people acted to achieve different political goals. Hassoun's conviction and continued detention illustrate that there is

> no need to make out a link to an act of violence, or even a particular group, as long as the government can allege a kind of theoretical framework to tie all individuals, dangerous or otherwise, with the belief system in question. (Said 2015: 110)

In Hassoun's case, the theory of an alleged global jihad movement served as that link. It was only after a lengthy legal battle that Hassoun was released from detention in 2020 and immediately deported to Rwanda.

Hassoun's case shows how federal prosecutors have invoked an alleged 'global jihad movement' to argue their cases. The conceptual work legal actors have called on the term 'global jihad movement' to undertake in the court corresponds to academic and professional classifications of armed struggles waged by pious non-state actors. For example, a Federal Bureau of Investigation (FBI) report, 'Terrorism 2002–2005', categorised 'terrorists affiliated with the violent global jihadist movement' to account for attacks allegedly conducted by 'loosely affiliated groups devoted to violent international jihad', including al-Qaʿida, al-Qaʿida in the Arabian Peninsula, al-Jamaʿa al-Islamiyya, 'Arab-Afghan *mujahadeen*' and 'homegrown jihadists' in London (Federal Bureau of Investigation 2006: 43). The New America think tank similarly examined 'jihadist terrorism', noting the alleged increase in 'jihadist terrorists' born or raised in the US (Bergen and Sterman 2021). Former FBI agent Ali Soufan referred to a 'jihadi movement', placing 'al-Qaeda aligned jihadi groups', the Egyptian Islamic Jihad and ISIS in the same conceptual category – jihadists – even while recognising such groups often 'rival' each other (Soufan 2019: 2–3). Even critics of terrorism studies have mobilised jihad as a conceptual category by defining terrorism as 'any serious violent or property crime committed to advance a particular ideology (such as, for example, jihadi, left-wing or right-wing ideology)' (Norris and Grol-Prokopczyk 2017: 615). Using the concept of 'jihadi ideology' for definitional purposes effectively collapses different armed struggles into a single category based on a seemingly shared ideology that can be condemned and disavowed without taking seriously the politics and power organising such conflicts. As Li contends, 'Even when jihad is more narrowly defined as armed activity sanctioned by Islam and grounded in its various norms . . . it is [still] a label that has been applied to very different types of conflicts', such as 'fighting against non-Muslims in situations of occupation or civil war', 'revolting against Muslim rulers' and 'warring against the United States in an attempt to force a military withdrawal from Muslim-majority countries and end its support for repressive regimes' (Li 2020: 23).

When mobilised in the courts, these academic theorisations of jihad have anchored criminal conspiracy theories and informed judicial decision-making. How judges and jurors understand jihad and apply the concept to the factual evidence before them has material outcomes for defendants. In *Hassoun*, the prosecution's legal invocation of jihad expanded criminal liability, such that federal prosecutors did not need to connect the defendant's financial donations to a specific designated foreign terrorist organisation or violent plot.

'Mujahidin Orphans and Mujahidin Widows': Humanitarian Aid as Violent Jihad

In July 2010, Amina Farah Ali and her friend Hawo Mohamed Hassan were arrested on terrorism-related charges after they collected and sent donations to Somalia during the 2006–9 Ethiopian invasion and occupation. The grand jury indictment alleged that Ali's donations funded al-Shabaab, defined as 'a terrorist organization based in Somalia, whose primary objective was the violent overthrow of the Somali Transitional Federal Government (TFG)' (United States v. Amina Ali and Hawo Hassan 2010: 3). The indictment also explained that jihad 'is an Arabic word which means, among other things, "holy war"' and, in this case, referred to 'al-Shabaab's and other militias' efforts to topple the TFG through violence' (ibid.). Furthermore, mujahidin 'is an Arabic word which means "holy warriors"' and mujahid 'is the singular form of mujahidin' (ibid.). At sentencing, federal prosecutors used these concepts to frame Ali's conduct as criminal: the provision 'so-called humanitarian aid with clothing' to 'mujahidin orphans and mujahidin widows' provided a 'benefit to al-Shabaab' because 'it makes it a lot easier to find people who are willing to become suicide bombers if they know that their family is going to be provided for after they're gone' (United States v. Amina Ali and Hawo Hassan 2013: 93–4). After Ali's 2011 conviction, US District Judge Michael Davis determined that Ali 'raised money to be sent to al-Shabaab', that al-Shabaab intended to overthrow the Transitional Federal Government, and that Ali's teleconferences 'extoll[ed] the virtues of violent jihad against infidels and apostates' (ibid.: 4). Judge Davis sentenced her to twenty years in prison, followed by a lifetime of supervised release. Legal actors mobilised concepts like jihad and mujahid to interpret Ali's actions and therefore her criminality.

In this case, the invocation of jihad categorically condemned al-Shabaab as a terrorist organisation and upheld the TFG as the legitimate government of Somalia. Such an ahistorical rendering of al-Shabaab, however, erases the organisation's geopolitical origins, long-standing contestations over borders and territories, and localised struggles over sovereign power, all of which transformed al-Shabaab into a more transnational militant group and intensified armed resistance in the region. Al-Shabaab, for example, originally served as the Islamic Courts Union's (ICU) militia. The Islamic Courts Union first emerged as an informal association of Islamic courts in Somalia to provide security after the fall of Siad Barre's authoritarian regime in 1991. In 2000, 'the courts first united to form what would be called the ICU' and eventually 'evolved from a judicial system to a governing apparatus' that provided social services and enforced shariʿa law (Islamic Courts Union 2019). Led by 'young, disciplined fighters recruited across clan lines – *al-Shabaab*', the Islamic Courts Union expanded its authority across central Somalia (Verhoeven 2009: 415). Rooted in shariʿa law and Islam, the ICU 'became popular among communities in south Somalia, as citizens appreciated the security and peace it brought to the local, street level', as in the reopening of schools, the weakening of warlords, and the strengthening of businesses in a more stable environment (Stremlau 2018: 80). Threatened by the rise of the ICU, Ethiopian forces invaded Somalia, at the invitation of Somalia's Transitional Federal Government, ultimately overthrowing the ICU. The bloody invasion led al-Shabaab to splinter from the ICU, in an effort to expel Ethiopian forces and depose the TFG. The ensuing armed struggles destabilised the region, consolidated al-Shabaab's authority and triggered a humanitarian crisis. Understanding Ali's urgent desire to send donations to Somalia, even if through the hands of al-Shabaab fighters, requires an analysis of the geopolitical contexts and material conditions in which Somalis lived, including the reliance on warlords and armed militias to provide security in the absence of an executive authority like the Islamic Courts Union.

At sentencing, the defense integrated this geopolitical landscape into its arguments, explaining that, at the time Ali sent donations to Somalia,

> al-Shabaab had not yet been found to be a terrorist organization. They were a fundamentalist splinter faction fighting in a long-running civil war and they were the last of the fighters that were left after the Ethiopians routed the Islamic Courts Union and they were not part of the corrupt government. (United States v. Amina Ali and Hawo Hassan 2013: 43)

The defence further argued that, in a

> regular war, the laws of war apply. In an irregular war, it doesn't, everything
> is on the table . . . The Bible has the rape of the Sabine women. Rome killed
> everybody in Carthage and then salted the earth around it so no one would
> ever come back . . . [N]o one's hands are clean. (United States v. Amina Ali
> and Hawo Hassan 2013: 46)

In this view, '[a]pplying violence and supporting violence to [a]ffect the operation of a government is politics', as evidenced in US military operations in
Libya, Syria, Vietnam and Afghanistan (ibid.: 48). When al-Shabaab controlled
southern Somalia in 2011, 'the federal government said, "Well, it's still illegal
for you to provide any food to these starving Somalis [since the aid would be
channeled through al-Shabaab]"' (ibid.: 53). The defence illustrated how the
Transitional Federal Government's ineffective executive authority and endemic
corruption made it impossible to reliably send donations through formal state-
sanctioned channels. Ali's intention to make donations through 'trustworthy'
individuals rather than state institutions reflected these complex contexts. Even
prosecutors acceded that Ali 'began sending money' to Somalia in 2007, a year
before the US designated al-Shabaab a foreign terrorist organisation (ibid.: 98).
Despite millions of Somalis facing starvation, material support statutes criminalise 'delivering aid to people trapped in al-Shabaab territory . . . if doing so is
in any way "coordinated" with the designated group'.[9]

Given these conditions, Ali insisted that she focused on finding trustworthy individuals, regardless of their affiliation, who would reliably deliver her
donations directly to Somalis in need. At sentencing, Ali refused to reduce
al-Shabaab to a terrorist organisation and reinforced her intention to 'find
people who are trustworthy', even as Judge Davis questioned her about al-
Shabaab and its perceived 'Islamist' orientation:

> **Judge Davis:** And let's talk about al-Shabaab. Would you agree that al-
> Shabaab is an Islamist organization that follows a very conservative and
> strict interpretation?

---

[9] 'U.S. Anti-Terror Law Hinders Aid Efforts to Somalia' (Washington, DC, 2011), para. 4,
available at <https://charityandsecurity.org/news/US_law_hinders_aid_efforts_Somalia/>
(last accessed 19 April 2022).

Ali: I do know that they were Islamists in their orientation. Most Somalis are of Islamic faith. As far as their interpretation and how extreme they are, I really cannot get into that . . . I did not ask them to explain to me their beliefs and, you know, their interpretation of Islam. My target and my whole aim was to find people who are trustworthy and, you know, I was told that those were people who could be trusted and that's what motivated me.

. . .

Judge Davis: All right. And the good things that they may have mentioned to you, did they tell you that they believed in suicide bombers?

Ali: Okay. I did not ask them about that. Every person will be asked their deeds. They will have to account at some point. So I was worried about my own actions and deeds. And whatever they do, that's something that's entirely up to them.

Judge Davis: Well, then you knew that they believed in suicide bombers?

Ali: I cannot say one way or the other whether they believed in that or did not believe in that, because that's not my main aim. My main aim was to help those people that needed help.

. . .

Judge Davis: Did you hear that they were the provisional government of Somalia, the TFG?

Ali: Yes, I have heard about that, but this government, from what I could tell, was not a government that would address the needs of the people. They were not a government that was responsive to the need of the people, from what I have heard. When I was younger when I was in Somalia, the government at the time was responsive and helpful to the people who needed help. Similarly, the United States government is responsive and helpful to its people, even were able to help us out. But this government, still I did not hear any help that it was offering to anyone.

. . .

Judge Davis: Did you know about al-Shabaab describing itself as waging jihad against enemies of Islam?

Ali: Maybe they – they may be able to answer that question, but, you know, each person can come up with what they consider an enemy, but that question may be better answered by those people. (United States v. Amina Ali and Hawo Hassan 2013: 65–72)

In this courtroom exchange, Judge Davis evaluated al-Shabaab on the basis of its 'suicide bombers', viewing the formal, albeit ineffective, Transitional Federal Government, as the sovereign authority of Somalia, despite the other governance arrangements that maintained order and provided services in ways the TFG could not (Stremlau 2018). If Ali wanted to alleviate the suffering wrought by decades of war, she should have sent her donations through the TFG or TFG-sponsored organisations. Ali, however, sought to engage trustworthy 'individuals' – not state institutions – given Somalia's history of corruption, turmoil and unrest. For Ali, it made little sense to enquire about the political affiliations or religious beliefs of her collaborators as she wanted to work those who could send aid to 'help the needy' (United States v. Amina Ali and Hawo Hassan 2013: 69). Furthermore, al-Shabaab controlled southern parts of Somalia, including the capital city of Mogadishu, until 2011, such that any humanitarian aid flowing into the region passed through al-Shabaab. Criminalising humanitarian aid under material support statutes has hindered humanitarian efforts in Somalia, such that counterterrorism and other laws 'have increased operating costs, slowed down administrative functions and operational response, curtailed fundings, and undermined humanitarian partnerships' (Pantuliano and Metcalfe 2012: 21). For Judge Davis, al-Shabaab's alleged commitment to 'waging jihad against enemies of Islam', irrespective of the localised struggles for territorial control and regional security, rendered Ali's aid criminal. Even if Ali supported 'waging jihad against enemies of Islam', this framework offered little insight into what al-Shabaab was fighting for and why, particularly given the unique conditions that informed regional politics and shaped governance regimes. As invoked in these legal proceedings, jihad reduced a complex conflict into a barbaric expression of 'Islamist' fanaticism and ignored the on-the-ground geopolitical realities and governance structures defined by al-Shabaab's administrative authority.

Contrary to Judge Davis's assessment of al-Shabaab, Ali understood that 'in [her] country, there's corruption, corruption is endemic' and that 'there's no system to protect the needy and the helpless' as 'even when the UN brings food aid to the country, the people with power and guns usually take the food away' (United States v. Amina Ali and Hawo Hassan 2013: 75). For Ali, this context meant searching for individuals with 'integrity' who would ensure that her donations went directly to those in need, regardless of the recipients' political or religious views (ibid.). A terrorism lawyer attorney not representing Ali similarly described this conduct as 'doing good things' and therefore irreducible to the terrorism label applied to it simply because al-Shabaab controlled the receiving refugee camp:

> [Ali] had lived in a refugee camp that was in Somalia. She came to the United States and, unbeknownst to her, it was illegal to give food and clothing. She was putting it together to send to Somalia and the FBI agent said, 'You can't do it', but unfortunately never told her you can't raise money. So, she turned and raised $35,000 which she then sent to the camp which was headed by al-Shabaab. There's an example of someone who was determined, who was focused, who was fighting, doing good things. (Interview, March 2021)

The simultaneous invocation of jihad and delegitimation of al-Shabaab as a governing authority facilitated the demonisation and thus criminalisation of Ali's humanitarian efforts, which began before the US designated al-Shabaab as a foreign terrorist organisation.

At trial, the state's expert witness, Matthew Bryden, reinforced the image of al-Shabaab as a terrorist organisation and therefore the determination that Ali's donations constituted material support to a terrorist organisation. Bryden first testified that al-Shabaab was a militant group driven by Salafism, which he defined as 'a more puritanical version of Islam' (United States v. Amina Ali and Hawo Hassan 2011a: 145). In this view, al-Shabaab subscribed to 'the most extreme, the most rigid . . . elements of Islamic thought and teaching' which 'haven't existed in Somalia before' with 'regular beheadings' authorised by 'the doctrine of takfir', the alleged authority to 'declare someone else an apostate and therefore to make it legal to kill them' (ibid.: 146). At the judge's request, Bryden further clarified that 'Salafism essentially breaks down into what some would call the Salafi Jihadiyya, the jihadist school of thought, and in Somalia what's referred to as the Salafi Jadiiah, the new Salafis'. According to Bryden, 'The new Salafis [in Saudi Arabia] espouse the spreading of their religion through peaceful means; and the Salafi Jihadiyya espouse imposing their rule essentially through violence' (ibid.: 148–9). Such violence included targeted assassinations to depose political leaders, aid workers, journalists, oppositional civil society Somali leaders and individuals 'exiting a mosque' (ibid.: 154). Bryden's analysis engages what Li describes as 'a major strand of the terrorism expert subculture' that uses 'Salafi jihadism' as a convenient script 'to identify a locus of threat without producing much insight' (Li 2020: 106). For Li, 'taking an allegedly "jihadi" segment of Salafism as the main category of analysis reflects the state's obsession' to determine which Muslims we should fear while ignoring how 'this activity of jihad [could] credibly bring together Muslims of such different backgrounds' (ibid.: 108). Such an approach 'shackles' Islam and violence together (ibid.). In other words, the invocation of Salafi Jihadiyya gives us few conceptual tools to understand the relationship between politics and violence while appearing to identify a terrorist typology that can be understood, managed and contained. The term Salafi-Jihad, however, 'is problematic because it paves the way for false dichotomies, a friend–enemy distinction that has justified extrajudicial murder, unlawful detention and counter-extremism programs', even as scholars and Salafis themselves have not adopted a universally accepted definition of Salafism (Islam 2021: para. 29). While Bryden's distinction between Salafi Jadiiah and Salafi Jihadiyya offers little interpretive insight into Ali's actions, it portrayed Ali's humanitarian aid as driven by and contributing to Salafi Jihadiyya.

More specific to Ali's case, Bryden explained that al-Shabaab's local ambition was 'to expel, dismantle the [Transitional Federal Government], and to replace it with their own rule by force' (United States v. Amina Ali and Hawo Hassan 2011a: 144). Donating clothing and money to al-Shabaab thus supported the overthrow of the Transitional Federal Government, a 'secular but self-appointed, powerless executive whose authority was limited to the small town of Baidoa' (Verhoeven 2009: 411). Although the prosecution argued that the Transitional Federal Government was the proper channel for Ali to funnel humanitarian aid into Somali and Ethiopian refugee camps, Bryden also testified that the TFG – plagued by 'endemic corruption' – failed to stabilise and govern Somalia, making Somalis dependent on 'one group or another' to provide security and services, including al-Shabaab (United States v. Amina Ali and Hawo Hassan 2011b: 117, 87). Bryden further explained:

> Over the years, the Transitional [Federal] Government has received revenues from, say, the port of Mogadishu and perhaps to a much lesser extent taxation and also donor funds, whether from Western donors or donors in the Arab world, and these funds have disappeared. (ibid.: 117)

In this view, the Transitional Federal Government's failures, not opposition groups like al-Shabaab, caused 'instability' in Somalia and, 'in the absence of an effective political authority, [al-Shabaab] had free reign of southern Somali territory' (ibid.: 123). Given the TFG's 'endemic corruption' simultaneous to al-Shabaab's political authority, humanitarian aid agencies struggled to operate neutrally and effectively 'because they just can't confirm where the aid is going' (United States v. Amina Ali and Hawo Hassan 2011a: 129). The invocation of Salafi Jihadiyya, however, effectively flattened these complex realities into a convenient narrative: by sending donations to al-Shabaab, Ali contributed to jihadist violence, even incentivising suicide bombers by allegedly directing donations to 'mujahidin orphans and mujahidin widows'. As the prosecution concluded, Ali 'repeatedly called the United States her enemy . . . because they stood in her way of fundraising for al-Shabaab, a group that Mr Bryden testified not only wanted to topple the government in Somalia, but had ambitions for global jihad' (United States v. Amina Ali and Hawo Hassan 2013: 101).

Given these findings, Judge Davis sentenced Ali to twenty years in prison, followed by a lifetime of supervised release, exceeding the statutory maximum of fifteen years, by structuring the sentences for each count consecutively rather than concurrently. Despite this harsh sentence, in 2021, Judge Davis granted Ali's motion for compassionate release during the global pandemic, recognising both that Ali's health declined after contracting COVID-19 and that the material support she provided – approximately $15,000 and shipments of clothing – 'pale[d] in comparison to other terrorist financing cases in which defendants have been released due to the pandemic' (United States v. Amina Ali and Hawo Hassan 2021: 7). Contrary to his reasoning at Ali's sentencing hearing, Judge Davis observed that Ali 'did not pose a danger to the community if released' (ibid.: 6). Judicial discretion can lead to uneven legal outcomes for defendants, such that terrorism lawyers have sought to 'contextualize' their clients' actions in the broader geopolitical contexts in which they operated.[10]

As Ali's case illustrates, legal actors mobilised jihad as an explanatory framework judges and jurors could use to make sense of the cases and defendants

[10] Interview, October 2020.

before them. Although judges and jurors unevenly have interpreted and applied this explanatory framework, the invocation of jihad often has disavowed the geopolitical contexts and material conditions organising defendants' actions, as in Ali's charitable donations made to alleviate the suffering wrought by war. Occluding more than clarifying, the invocation of jihad in courts illustrates the relationship between the law and racial power (Murakawa and Beckett 2010: 698). In other words, legal actors have mobilised the concept of jihad to reinforce anti-Muslim tropes that can return guilty verdicts and justify harsh sentences. Such degradations, however, are not aberrations in an otherwise objective criminal-legal system; they demonstrate the role of the law in 'perpetuating the racial divide' and executing the global war on terror (Dayan 2005: 46).

Conclusion: Rethinking Jihad, Retheorising Political Violence

In 2010, the Department of Justice celebrated the 'continuing value of federal courts in combatting terrorism', particularly by 'incapacitating terrorists' through long prison terms (Office of Public Affairs 2010: para. 4). Although federal authorities have insisted that the criminal-legal system functions as a 'counterterrorism tool', judges have varied in their understandings of the role of the judiciary in the global war on terror, which has led to uneven outcomes in terrorism prosecutions. In a tax case framed by federal prosecutors as 'economic jihad', US District Judge Saylor observed:

> The role of this court, at least in this context, is necessarily narrow. It is not to help – or, for that matter, to hinder – American foreign policy. It is not to help or hinder American law enforcement priorities. It is not to make broad 'statements', 'send messages', or bestow symbolic 'victories' or 'defeats'. (United States v. Muhamed Mubayyid et al. 2008: 4)

Judge Saylor therefore sentenced the defendant, Muhamed Mubayyid, to just eleven months in prison. US District Judge Davis, however, described a group of young Somali boys who discussed travelling to Syria to fight President Bashar al-Assad's brutal regime as 'committed jihadists' who 'believed in and may still believe in the extremist, violent and deadly Jihadist ideology of ISIL and the Islamic State, period'. Even though the defendants never committed an act of violence, Judge Davis handed down harsh sentences, including a thirty-five-year prison term followed by a lifetime of supervised release for Guled Omar. This ruling aligned with the prosecution's claim that only 'actual custodial arrest' effectively 'deterred' Omar from engaging in terrorist violence, necessitating a long prison term to incapacitate him (United States v. Guled Omar 2016b: 9). Cases like *Ahmad, Hassoun, Hassan, Mubayyid* and *Omar* illustrate how legal actors have debated the role of the criminal-legal system in the global war on terror and mobilised Islamic principles and Arabic vocabularies as conceptual frameworks to interpret defendants' actions and intent.

Despite judicial discretion, the criminal-legal system has 'found itself swept up in the geopolitical direction and strategy of the US government'.[11] While some terrorism lawyers worked to 'contextualise' their cases in a way that 'broaden[ed] the scope beyond just this horrible criminal act or conspiracy' and challenged 'the monolithic concept of terrorism',[12] the invocation of jihad in legal proceedings often promoted a 'generalized fear of menacing Islam' (Monaghan 2014: 498), engaged in racial thinking that marks Muslims 'as belonging to the realm of culture and religion as opposed to the realm of law' (Razack 2012: 221), and reduced defendants to caricatures of the Islamist terrorist, whose cultural, psychological and theological perversions drove their support of violence.

Pathologising political violence obscures the material conditions in which people live and thus forecloses alternative approaches to understand and then respond to political violence. By addressing political violence at the scale of the individual actors – the so-called jihadist – this global war on terror approach erases the relationship between the law and racial power, the role of US empire in the making of political violence, and the political demands of armed militants. When political violence is posed as an ideological problem, mobilising the courts to 'incapacitate terrorists' seems like a pragmatic approach to ensuring national security and public safety. The invocation of jihad reinforces this approach by erasing the geopolitical contexts that give rise to political violence and by refusing to take seriously the relationship between power, piety,

[11] Interview, March 2021.
[12] Interview, October 2020.

politics and violence. The criminalisation and punishment of Ali, however, illustrates how damaging and dangerous such conceptual frames can be when set to work in court.

References

Adham Hassoun v. Jeffrey Searls , *decision and order* (No. 1:19-cv-00370 (S. D. Fla. 2020)).

Bergen, P. and D. Sterman (2021), 'Terrorism in America After 9/11', *New America*, 10 September, <https://www.newamerica.org/international-security/reports/terrorism-in-america/> (last accessed 19 April 2022).

Charity and Security Network (2011), 'U.S. Anti-Terror Law Hinders Aid Efforts to Somalia', 18 July, <https://charityandsecurity.org/news/US_law_hinders_aid_efforts_Somalia/> (last accessed 19 April 2022).

Chesney, R. M. (2008), 'Optimizing Criminal Prosecution as a Counterterrorism Tool: A Working Paper of the Series on Counterterrorism and American Statutory Law', Washington, DC: Brookings Institution, https://www.brookings.edu/wp-content/uploads/2016/06/1219_prosecution_chesney.pdf (last accessed 2 February 2023).

Dayan, C. (2005), 'Legal Terrors', *Representations*, 92: 1, 42–80.

Federal Bureau of Investigation (2006), 'Terrorism 2002–2005', <https://www.fbi.gov/file-repository/stats-services-publications-terrorism-2002-2005-terror02_05.pdf/view> (last accessed 19 April 2022).

Islam, Jaan (2021), '"Salafi-Jihadism": Frightening Menace or Scapegoat for the War on Terror?', *Cage*, 15 July, <https://www.cage.ngo/salafi-jihadism-frightening-menace-or-scapegoat-for-the-war-on-terror> (last accessed 19 April 2022).

Li, D. (2020), *The Universal Enemy: Jihad, Empire, and the Challenge of Solidarity*, Palo Alto, CA: Stanford University Press.

Mamdani, M. (2004), *Good Muslim, Bad Muslim: America, the Cold War, and the Roots of Terror*, New York: Three Leaves Press.

Margulies, P. (2007), 'Guantanamo by Other Means: Conspiracy Prosecutions and Law Enforcement Dilemmas after September 11', *Gonzaga Law Review*, 43: 3, 513–57.

Monaghan, J. (2014), 'Security Traps and Discourses of Radicalization: Examining Surveillance Practices Targeting Muslims in Canada', *Surveillance & Society*, 12: 4, 485–501.

Murakawa, N. and K. Beckett (2010), 'The Penology of Racial Innocence: The Erasure of Racism in the Study and Practice of Punishment', *Law & Society Review*, 44: 3/4, 695–730.

Norris, J. J. and H. Grol-Prokopczyk (2017), 'Estimating the Prevalence of Entrapment in Post-9/11 Terrorism Cases', *Journal of Criminal Law and Criminology*, 105: 3, 609–78.

Office of Public Affairs (2010), 'The Criminal Justice System as a Counterterrorism Tool: A Fact Sheet', 26 January, <https://www.justice.gov/archives/opa/blog/criminal-justice-system-counterterrorism-tool-fact-sheet> (last accessed 19 April 2022).

Pantuliano, S. and V. Metcalfe (2012), 'Neutrality Undermined: The Impact of Counter-Terrorism Legislation on Humanitarian Action in Somalia', *Humanitarian Exchange*, 53, 21–3.

Razack, S. H. (2012), '"We Didn't Kill 'em, We Didn't Cut Their Head Off": Abu Ghraib Revisited', in D. Martinez HoSang, O. LaBennett and L. Pulido (eds), *Racial Formation in the Twenty-First Century*, Berkeley, CA: University of California Press, pp. 217–45.

Said, W. E. (2015), *Crimes of Terror: The Legal and Political Implications of Federal Terrorism Prosecutions*, New York: Oxford University Press.

Skinner, C. P. (2013), 'Punishing Crimes of Terror in Article III Courts', *Yale Law & Policy Review*, 31: 2, 309–76.

Soufan, A. (2019), 'Next in Line to Lead al-Qaeda: A Profile of Abu Muhammad al-Masri', *CTC Sentinel*, 12: 10, 1–8.

Stanford University (2019), 'Mapping Militant Organizations: "Islamic Courts Union"', <https://cisac.fsi.stanford.edu/mappingmilitants/profiles/islamic-courts-union> (last accessed 19 April 2022).

Stoler, A. L. (2016), *Duress: Imperial Durabilities in Our Times*, Durham, NC: Duke University Press.

Stremlau, N. (2018). 'Governance without Government in Somali Territories', *Journal of International Affairs*, 71: 2, 73–89.

United States v. A. Hassoun et al. (2005), *superseding indictment* (No. 0:04-cr-60001 (S. D. Fla 2005)).

United States v. A. Hassoun et al. (2007), *defendant Hassoun's objections to revised Presentence Investigation Report* (No. 0:04-cr-60001 (S. D. Fla 2007)).

United States v. A. Hassoun et al. (2008), *jury trial proceedings day 32* (No. 0:04-cr-60001 (S. D. Fla 2008)).

United States v. A. Ali and H. Hassan (2010), *indictment* (No. 0:10-CR-00187 (D. Minn 2010)).

United States v. A. Ali and H. Hassan (2011a), *jury trial volume 3* (No. 0:10-CR-00187 (D. Minn 2011a)).

United States v. A. Ali and H. Hassan (2011b), *jury trial volume 4* (No. 0:10-CR-00187 (D. Minn 2011b)).

United States v. A. Ali and H. Hassan (2013), *sentencing hearing* (No. 0:10-CR-00187 (D. Minn 2013)).

United States v. A. Ali and H. Hassan (2021), *memorandum and order* (No. 0:10-CR-00187 (D. Minn 2021)).

United States v. B. Ahmad (2014a), *government's reply to defendant's sentencing memorandum* (No. 3:04-cr-00301(D. Conn 2014a)).

United States v. B. Ahmad (2014b), *sentencing hearing* (No. 3:04-cr-00301 (D. Conn 2014b)).

United States v. G. Omar (2016a), *government's position on sentencing* (No. 0:15-cr-00049 (D. Minn 2016a)).

United States v. G. Omar (2016b), *sentencing hearing* (No. 0:15-cr-00049 (D. Minn 2016b)).

United States v. M. H. Khan (2014), *criminal complaint* (No.1:14-cr-00564 (N. D. Ill 2014)).

United States v. M. H. Khan (2016), *sentencing hearing* (No.1:14-cr-00564 (N. D. Ill 2016)).

United States v. M. Mubayyid et al. (2008), *memorandum and order on defendants' motions for judgment of acquittal under Rule 29 and government's motion for reconsideration* (No. 4:05-cr-40026 (D. Mass 2008)).

Verhoeven, H. (2009), 'The Self-fulfilling Prophecy of Failed States: Somalia, State Collapse and the Global War on Terror', *Journal of Eastern African Studies*, 3: 3, 405–25.

3

'LOOK A CERTAIN WAY IN ORDER TO RESIST': AN ANALYSIS OF GERMAN SHORT VIDEOS AGAINST ISLAMISM

Sindyan Qasem

Introduction: Counternarratives as a Means of German Hegemonic Knowledge Production

The field of preventing Islamist extremism[1] has been strongly developed in Germany for several years, often in the guise of political education or promotion of democracy. After the 9/11 attacks, and particularly after discovering the involvement of an Islamist terror cell from the German city of Hamburg, Islamist extremism has been identified as the greatest threat to the security of the Federal Republic of Germany by German security agencies. In the early 2000s, preventative approaches to counter Islamist extremism initially manifested themselves almost exclusively in the expansion of criminal law, as well as in the expansion of pre-emptive security authority powers. Subsequently, the first counselling centres to prevent and to counter Islamist radicalisation were established in the Federal Office for Migration and Refugees, and the Federal Office for the Protection of the Constitution.

---

[1] I use the controversial terms Islamism or Islamist extremism here and hereafter in order to highlight the generality and vagueness of the phenomena designated by this term, which is often rightly criticised and, at the same time, to emphasise the addressing and marking of Muslims, in particular with regard to a pronounced danger therefore assumed.

Only from 2014 onwards, with a massive provision of state funding, did a differentiated group of measures to prevent Islamist extremism develop, involving numerous civil society organisations with political-educational, socio-pedagogical, and migration-pedagogical approaches (cf. Figlestahler and Schau 2022: 15–19).

As an essential part of the struggle for the hearts and minds of Muslims in Germany, there have been repeated calls in recent years for an increased production and distribution of powerful narratives against so-called Islamism, especially in the form of short videos, often as part of larger educational programmes. These counternarratives are generally regarded as attractive and convincing means of communication opposing Islamist propaganda. In recent studies and evaluations, counternarratives have already been examined for their effectiveness in preventing Islamist radicalisation (for example, Frischlich et al. 2017). However, critical reflection on the stigmatisation and exclusion (re-)produced by counternarratives has so far been timid, at least in German-speaking countries. In the following, I will, therefore, use a close analysis of narrative structures of two German short videos against Islamism to refine the previously common, effect-oriented view of counternarratives. My aim is to conceptualise counternarratives as hegemonic attempts to order political frontiers. I will particularly take into account how understandings of jihad are appropriated to fit into this order. I have selected the two videos because both have been hailed as parts of exemplary German counternarrative campaigns with different approaches, one produced by a federal state office of the German domestic intelligence service as a disciplinary and instructional effort, and the other financed by the federal agency for civic education and produced by a social work institution with a more sensitive, pedagogical, and even non-conformist, conception. I will pay particular attention to describing the way in which my viewing and analysis of the videos discerns the two as different formations of the same hegemonic order.

Looking at Counternarratives with an Oppositional Gaze

My viewing of short videos opposing Islamism, and analysis of the counternarratives packaged within them, is guided by bell hooks' concept of the 'oppositional gaze' (hooks 1992). In her reflections on the development of an oppositional gaze, hooks describes how socially subordinated persons look back at the roles ascribed to them, and the power mechanisms emerging within these ascriptions, and how they then develop a critical distance to the roles portrayed (ibid.). For hooks it is clear that this looking back is resistant; the critical, questioning, documenting, oppositional view of the dominated's representations even creates agency (hooks 1992: 116). However, this resistant gaze does not follow essentialistically from the power relationship between superior and subordinate roles. Rather, hooks emphasises that the gaze must first be learned: 'one learns to look a certain way in order to resist' (hooks 1992: 116). Hooks reconstructs the development of oppositional views exemplarily from her own critical viewing of the representation of black women in US-American films and TV productions, as well as from interviewing other black women. She states that an oppositional gaze only emerges when black women individually 'resist the imposition of dominant ways of knowing and looking' (hooks 1992: 128).

When I now look at two short videos opposing Islamism as examples, I do so from the perspective of a Muslim scholar. Considering my age only, I am frequently still counted among the target groups of counternarrative campaigns. For my work on anti-Muslim racism, and my criticism of German policies in the face of Islamist extremism, I amsometimes suspected of being apolegetic for Islamism, or even a sympathiser in disguise. In a certain way, I pose a good example of someone who is adressed by German counternarrative campaigns, who is expected to identify with the roles of Muslim men represented therein. The actual opposition, the 'politicization' (hooks 1992: 128) of my gaze, however, like every gaze that wants to be critically directed at hegemonic representations, must first be formed through consistent questioning, through resistant viewing. In the following, I document this process of forming, of resisting.

Using the trenchant description of the British cultural historian Annette Kuhn, to whom hooks also refers in her remarks, the goal of my critique undertaken here can be defined even more pointedly:

> The acts of analysis, of deconstruction and reading 'against the grain' offer an additional pleasure – the pleasure of resistance, of saying 'no': not to 'unsophisticated' enjoyment, by ourselves and others, of culturally dominant images, but to the structures of power which ask us to consume them uncritically and in highly circumscribed ways. (Kuhn 1985: 8)

Following the line of Kuhn's argument, the fact that two YouTube videos are the focus of my critical gaze in the following is not a plea against the consumption of videos as an amusing pastime per se, but rather an expression of a desire to resist the structures and formations of power that want to impose an uncritical viewing of these seemingly banal media products on me.

Undercover Operation: Looking at a Video by the Office for the Protection of the Constitution.

In the YouTube video 'Legal and Islamist?',[2] a conversation between Muslims about the limits of religious activity in Germany is depicted through the use of stylised still photographs. At the beginning of the seven-minute film, which is sober and almost documentary-like, the protagonist, Jamil, is introduced by a narrator: dressed in white robes and wearing a beard and prayer cap, the young adult is portrayed as being active in a Muslim congregation. Jamil recently has been helping organise an ecumenical service, and the narrator further explains that other members of the congregation are also active in city society, one member of the congregation 'even sits on the city council'.[3]

The narration then relates how Jamil learns that security agencies and media reports call his congregation 'extremist', and he wants to find out how this claim, which is incomprehensible to him, has been determined. In the first few minutes of the video, Jamil is shown talking to the imam of the mosque, and the narrator gives a brief summary of the theological basis of the work of the congregation: the imam sees their community as a 'community of the middle', the imam is aware of and accepts that in Germany a life that is exclusively 'shariʿa-compliant' is not possible and encourages Jamil to implement the 'rules of Allah' 'wherever possible' and to try to create more opportunities for Muslims to implement religious practices 'by peaceful and democratic means'.

Since Jamil cannot recognise any 'extremism' in this, the Islamic scholar Naima is introduced by the narrator from the third minute onwards. Naima

---

[2] YouTube video 'Legal und Islamistisch?', 3 December 2020. Available at <https://youtu.be/ozWXQu4MAhY> (last accessed 13 June 2022).

[3] Quotations from the YouTube video 'Legal und Islamistisch?', 3 December 2020, have been translated by the author. Available at <https://youtu.be/ozWXQu4MAhY> (last accessed 13 June 2022).

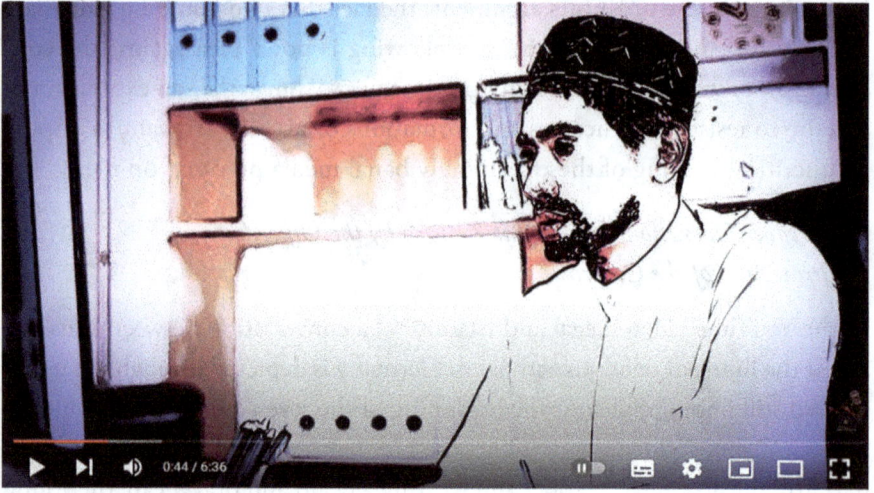

Figure 3.1 Legal and Islamist?
Source: https://youtu.be/ozWXQu4MAhY.

is Jamil's childhood friend and is presented as a 'modernist'. Jamil turns to Naima for an explanation of the view that his congregation is extremist. From the fourth minute until the end of the film, Naima then explains the problem with the congregation from her point of view: the imam does not want to separate state and religion . . .', although this separation is laid down in the *Grundgesetz*, the German constitution. Naima also explains to Jamil that an attitude like that of the imam's, who describes a fully shariʿa-compliant life here in Germany as impossible, makes Muslims who hear this argument feel 'that they are never quite at home in Germany'. Naima further remarks on the concept of 'religious freedom', and emphasises the equality of men and women in Germany. She also says that 'legalists' – like the imam – deliberately use Quranic rhetoric in their argumentation in order to be 'the mouthpiece of all Muslims'. After a plea for freedom of expression in Germany, Naima concludes with an appeal addressed directly to Jamil: 'It's called faith, because we have to believe in it, each for themselves, each as they can.'

Assumptions of Danger and Approaches to Danger

When watching the short video, my gaze first and foremost is caught by the role of Jamil. He is the only one of the three protagonists who does not speak himself; his answers and arguments are always given in indirect speech by the video's narrator. Furthermore, it seems as if numerous arguments that are expressed as counterarguments to the entire counternarrative offered by Naima do not refer to actual statements by Jamil. Instead, it seems as if unspoken assumptions about Jamil's mindset and behaviour, not only as a representative of the congregation, but as a representative of a certain type of Muslim, are already established, and require no explanation, no mention. The role of Jamil is the role of a Muslim young man who is talked about, about whom assumptions are made. It is such stereotyping assumptions of danger (Hohnstein and Glaser 2017: 260–1) regarding the target group of the videos that produce the role of Jamil, who was apparently scripted as an identification figure for the target audience. In this regard, counternarratives opposing so-called Islamism focus primarily on an Islamist ideology, often only vaguely defined, which is sometimes claimed to be attractive to an entire generation of Muslims, and to have broad appeal (for example, Mansour 2015).

In this sense, Jamil is the real 'Jihadi Fool', after whom the satirical YouTube channel on which the video appeared, as part of a larger counternarrative campaign, is named. The young Muslim man is foolish in two ways: on the one hand, he refuses to understand why he is part of an extremist congregation, and why his behaviour is considered dangerous by security agencies. On the other hand, he falls for the arguments of the extremists, he is fooled in exactly the same sense as a whole generation of young Muslims in Germany, who allegedly fall for the promises of Islamists and are ideologically seduced. While many other videos of the satire channel tend to focus on mockery and contempt for the fools, in this particular video Jamil's foolishness is portrayed with the aim of setting the stage for his ultimate enlightenment. He is freed from his foolishness by the arguments of Naima, the Islamic scholar, before he goes further down the road of radicalisation, eventually leading away from so-called legalist Islamism to openly violent militancy. The hashtag 'prevention', with which the YouTube video is labelled, echoes this call for action in response to an implied suspicion: young Muslims such as Jamil, and such as myself, must be dissuaded from their inherent urge towards extremism and hostility to democracy in order to ultimately defend the German order against terrorist violence.

The YouTube channel *Jihadi Fool*, on which the video appeared in December 2020, had been created a year earlier with the aim of 'preventing Salafism' by the Office for the Protection of the Constitution of North Rhine-West-phalia, a federal branch of German domestic intelligence service (Land NRW 2019). In the YouTube video itself, as in the other videos on the channel, there are no references to the affiliation of the channel with the Office for the Protection of the Constitution of North Rhine-Westphalia. It is only on the profile page of general channel information, which can be reached after several clicks, where the connection to the Office for the Protection of the Constitution can be indirectly deduced from the contact e-mail address.[4] The actions of the state itself, and of the security authorities in particular, are thus superficially veiled, and deliberately kept untransparent.[5] The clandes-tine entry of a discursive arena, such as the YouTube platform, by the Office for the Protection of the Constitution even suggests an apparent equality of producer and recipient (cf. Castells 2007). At the same time, addressing the target group in such a way, even if covertly, is already a measure in itself: the observer shows himself to the person being observed, the mere existence of a portrayal of the target group is an announcement that observation is tak-ing place, and it is communicated that the security authorities 'know' the target group. In this regard, the YouTube video fulfils similar functions to the German police practice of *Gefährderansprache*, where police officers approach persons who are deemed to be dangerous at their homes or workplaces, and openly announce their ongoing observation. Instead of taking place at a doorstep, the video constitutes a virtual address.

Per Jean-Paul Sartre, it can be stated that this mere constellation of observer and observed already is powerful. For Sartre, in relation to surveillance and monitoring, the decisive factor is that the monitored are presented with a sign that they are actually being observed (Sartre 1969: 252–302; quoted in Crossley 1993: 408). Moreover, according to Sartre, to experience this

---

[4] The channel thus also undermines a requirement of the YouTube platform, according to which videos of state broadcasters are marked. While, for example, under YouTube videos of the ARD, the notice automatically appears that the ARD is part of the public broadcaster, a marking is completely missing under the *Jihadi Fool* videos.

[5] The obfuscation of state communication through the harnessing of civil society organisa-tions (some of which were founded solely for this purpose) has already been critically docu-mented in the UK, for example, cf. Hayes and Quraishi 2016.

surveilling gaze is to no longer perceive oneself as belonging to oneself, but as belonging to someone else, as being an object in the project of the observer (ibid.). Surveillance in this sense therefore also means that the target group, that I, as soon as the surveillance becomes apparent from this video as well, see myself forced into a relationship with the observer. Then again, as stated by hooks, the development of the oppositional gaze can be understood as a developing gaze that seeks to overcome this imposed relationship between viewer and viewed (hooks 1992: 128). Thus, the surveillance directed at the audience, at me, provokes the critical questioning of the underlying mechanisms, and the countering of this surveilling gaze.

Countering the Securitised Gaze

The criticism of the concealment of the role of the Office for the Protection of the Constitution cannot only be related to the concealment of the YouTube channel's affiliation with the NRW Office for the Protection of the Constitution but can also be made with regard to the narrative of the video itself. For even in the narrative of the video, there is no mention of who is responsible for the classification of Jamil's congregation as 'extremist'. Only an apparently real excerpt from the German daily newspaper *Süddeutsche Zeitung*, inserted for a few seconds displaying the headline '*Verfassungsschutz beobachtet 109 Moscheen in NRW*' (Federal Office for the Protection of the Constitution observes 109 mosques in North Rhine-Westphalia), suggests that it is the practice of the Federal Office for the Protection of the Constitution itself which subsumes Jamil's congregation under the label of 'extremism'.

German cultural theorist and ethnologist Werner Schiffauer coined the term 'security knowledge' to describe this categorising and mapping practice of security agencies, especially the Office for the Protection of the Constitution (Schiffauer 2015). He points out that the assessment of Muslim organisations or persons exclusively according to danger potential and risk assessment creates powerful categories, and orders reality along these categories (ibid.). In a study by the European Network against Racism regarding German policies to counter Islamist extremism,[6] it is pointed out that the knowledge of

---

[6] I was personally involved in conducting the study and formulating the results.

the Office for the Protection of the Constitution about Muslims is also considered expert knowledge outside of security agency contexts. This knowledge is often critically unquestioned and readily adopted by mainstream media outlets, researchers and other public institutions. This adaptation might then lead to public defamation, criminalisation, even job losses, refusal of residence permit extensions and refusals of naturalisation (European Network Against Racism 2021: 6f.). In the video, while it is indeed portrayed that one newspaper seems to have uncritically adopted the constitutional protection agency's assessment of the congregation as extremist, the consequences to which Jamil may have been subjected due to this assessment are not mentioned at all. In this sense, the video not only obscures the practice of the office of constitutional protection itself, but also its far-reaching impact on Muslim communities.

Furthermore, the adaption and diffusion of securitised logics is exemplified in the video when Naima, the Islamic scholar,[7] accuses the imam of contributing to the alienation of Muslims in Germany, and their feeling of not being at home. This statement by the protagonist crystallises a logic of the Office for the Protection of the Constitution, according to which so-called parallel societies provide a breeding ground for Islamism. Such a creation of causality between perceived non-integration and the potential for Islamism must, at the same time, be seen as an expression and driving force for empirically unproven attributions in relation to Muslims in Germany (cf. Qasem 2019a).

In any case, the video does not seem to directly address actual Islamist narratives, or narratives perceived as Islamist. Rather, the video represents the position of the Office for the Protection of the Constitution in the debate surrounding the term 'political Islam', or the security authorities' construction of the term 'legalistic Islam', which was attracting a great deal of attention at the time of the video's release in 2020. Both terms are rejected by critics, primarily because they contribute to the consolidation of a general suspicion of Muslims, especially when used by the security authorities, and because they mark the conformist behaviour of Muslims and Muslim

---

[7] Cf. Amir-Moazami 2018 for detailed accounts of the involvement of Islamic Studies as a scientific discipline in the securitising cartography of Muslims.

organisations as suspicious (Hafez and Qasem 2020: 8). When both the speaker and Naima emphasise several times in the video that members of the congregation are involved in civil society, but that they are nevertheless extremist, it is concealed that, in the logic of the Office for the Protection of the Constitution, it is precisely the civil society and 'legal' activities of the congregation members that are considered particularly dangerous. Jamil, though not portrayed as a militant fighter or a follower of jihadi ideology, is a could-be terrorist. There is a thread lurking between the scripted lines and the still photographs: militancy and terrorism are not named explicitly, but the suspicion of it is present everywhere. As Sara Ahmed puts it so pointedly, the fear of terrorism, of extremist jihad against the present German order, 'sticks' to everything Jamil is portrayed as doing or saying (Ahmed 2014: 79).

In addition, the division made in the video between 'fundamentalists', 'traditionalists' and 'modernists' is another example of the reproduction of the security viewpoint: 'modernists', or Muslims described as liberal, are tolerated and desired 'others', whose role is supposed to be primarily to counter the extremism of the 'fundamentalists'. Internal Islamic controversies, and the diversity of Islamic theological attitudes beyond these debates about extremism and Islamism are, however, ignored by such categorisations by the security authorities. Thus, even the individual figures in the video are little more than securitised silhouettes; they have no history or defined characteristics but are merely products of the heavily cropped and narrowed gaze of the perspective of security agencies. Even more so, the division used, and the upholding of moderate Islamic positions, also reveal the global character of the narrative reproduced in the video: the division into 'fundamentalists', 'traditionalists' and 'modernists', as well as strategic guidance on the instrumentalisation of the respective groups in the fight against a 'radical Islam', are prominently represented by the think tank RAND Corporation, which advises the US armed forces (RAND 2004). The narrative that moderate and modern Muslims in Europe also have a special role to play in reforming the discourse in the Islamic world (for example, Agai et al. 2014: 10), for example, has led to concrete cooperation between theologians teaching in Germany and the Egyptian religious authority under the regime of the military dictator al-Sisi (WWU Münster 2019). In the video itself, by contrast, the theocracy in Iran and 'extremist groups abroad', such as the Muslim Brotherhood and Milli Görüş,[8] are directly associated with the allegedly extremist imam of the congregation. The silhouettes we see in the video are extensions of these presumed axes of good and evil, of liberal and moderate Muslims on the one hand, and fundamentalists on the other. Security knowledge orders reality along these securitised categories – not only in Germany but all over the world.

Interim Conclusion

What exactly does the oppositional gaze, my oppositional gaze, explain that another gaze of this video would not see? It is above all the recognition of the sender of the video, and their intention, that differs from a view only of the roles presented. With knowledge of the problematic categorisations of the Office for the Protection of the Constitution, my understanding of the video changes. I see the video now as an explanation and justification of the security agency's own securitised practice, an explanation and justification of an agency that has often come under criticism in recent years, especially for its ignoring of right-wing extremist terror, such as the NSU, and for its dubious methods and assessments.

My gaze, caught by the role of Jamil at the beginning, also produces an interplay of association and dissociation with this representation of a young Muslim man: on the one hand, I share Jamil's criticism of the assessment of his congregation as extremist, but at the same time I resist having the Office for the Protection of the Constitution explain to him, and to me, why this assessment is justified, despite and against our knowledge. I now see the video itself as the dominant assertion of the agency's own claim of expertise, and their claim to interpretative sovereignty over Muslim life in Germany. The video is not only a counternarrative against terrorists but, above all, a counternarrative against all those who criticise the securitising practice of the Office for the Protection of the Constitution.

---

[8] The classification of the two groups mentioned as extremist by German security agencies is highly controversial, and has also been legally challenged in Germany, for example by Milli Görüş (cf. Peter and Ortega 2014).

At the end of the video, Jamil is shown perplexed and pensive after having listened to the instruction by the Islamic scholar. My own oppositional view precedes Jamil's here; my criticism is fixed and already formulated. And I wish for Jamil, for us all, to also be able to recognise and question the disguised practice of the security agency.

Resistance 'Light': Orderly Protest in a Video Funded by the Federal Agency for Civic Education

In the second video,[9] also just under seven minutes long, the young Muslim man, Jamal al-Khatib, talks about his ideas of coming to terms with injustice and resistance. This video, which is overall reverent and sombre, is part of the second season of a web video series produced by the Austrian social work association Turn Verein fuer Gewalt- und Extremismuspraevention e.V., financed by the German Federal Agency for Civic Education. The web video series is accompanied by both an information leaflet on the theoretical background of Jihadism, Islamism and counternarratives, as well as pedagogical material with educational methods and questions on every video in the series. According to the project information on the Federal Agency for Civic Education's web page, the video series is supposed to distribute 'alternative narratives' to jihadist and Islamist extremist online propaganda to a young target audience (Bundeszentrale für politische Bildung 2020).

As narrator, the protagonist Jamal first recounts his radicalisation in retrospect, and identifies police violence and injustice as triggers for his turning to criminal and militant Islamist groups. He then describes his time in detention, and explains how he began to think, read and write – especially in solitary confinement – with the aim of learning about ways to act against injustice. The question of how to resist 'when injustice happens to you'[10] is presented as the leading question of the video.

---

[9] YouTube-Video 'Widerstand & BESA – Mein Weg: Jamal al-Khatib (Staffel 2, Folge 5)', 4 July 2019. Available at <https://youtu.be/hO-2M_HdzA4> (last accessed 13 June 2022).

[10] Quotations from the YouTube video 'Widerstand & BESA – Mein Weg: Jamal al-Khatib (Staffel 2, Folge 5)', 4 July 2019, have been translated by the author. Available at <https://youtu.be/hO-2M_HdzA4> (last accessed 13 June 2022).

In the third minute of the video, the real action of a Nuremberg school class, which collectively resisted the deportation of a fellow student to Afghanistan, is presented as a positive example of resistance. The police violence that followed the protest is also mentioned, as well as the fact that the deportation of the youth was not prevented by the protest, but rather postponed for the time being due to a bomb explosion in Kabul.

Then, in the fourth minute of the video, racist practices of the Vienna police are shown. The protest by a group of young black men against racial profiling is also presented as a successful example of resistant practice. A hashtag campaign, in particular, is praised in this context: 'This is solidarity', because in order to counter racism and injustice, young people must 'be attentive and open their mouths'.

Jamal al-Khatib then also describes his own commitment to fight injustice: 'That's why my friends and I do it like this: we sit down together and discuss current issues and ask each other questions.' The explanation of the concept of 'Besa', a 'moral code of honour' 'to keep one's promise', and the invocation of this code by Albanians who hid and protected refugees during the Nazi regime, leads to Jamal's appeal to all viewers at the end of the video:

Figure 3.2 Jamal al-Khatib.
Source: https://youtu.be/hO-2M_HdzA4.

'Let's not be persuaded that a new history is impossible. I want to open my mouth and I want you to help me do it.'

Regulative Visibility, Regulated Resistance

In fact, the criticism of concealing state authorship could also be used for this short video that appeared on the YouTube platform. The fact that the Federal Agency for Civic Education commissioned the production of the video as part of a multi-part campaign can only be ascertained indirectly from a remark at the end of the video description. In my consideration of the video, however, I direct my gaze at this point to a different context, expanding on the critique already undertaken regarding the first video, and taking a closer look at the particular relationship between the experience of racism and resistance shown here.

An analysis of the simultaneity of regulatory visibility and discursive erasure of resistant racialised subject positions lends itself to this. The art historian and cultural scientist Johanna Schaffer draws on the remarks of the gender researcher Eve Kosofky Sedgwick on the 'regulatory visibility' and 'discursive erasure' of 'gay men' in intersectionally entangled LGBTQ-hostile, classist, sexist and racist discourses (Sedgwick 1990: 6 FN8). Building on this, Schaffer outlines how the representation and visibility of non-white people must also be considered beyond the mere causality of visibility and empowerment (Schaffer 2008: 102). Based on her analysis of the visual material of anti-racist campaigns, Schaffer then explains how racialised subject positions are, indeed, provided a place in the course of these campaigns as a 'spectacle', but in other social contexts the struggles of those thus exhibited for recognition and equality are discursively erased (ibid.).

This simultaneity is also reflected in the role of Jamal al-Khatib: his Muslim, male voice is heard here, in contrast to Jamil's lack of a voice in the other video, but only because it is staged as part of the prevention of radicalisation. The purpose of the role of Jamal al-Khatib is to be a role model and projection surface for the young target audience (Bundeszentrale für politische Bildung 2020). Though fictitious and exaggerated, Jamal al-Khatib is presented as an authentic character with a contradictory biography who regrets past errors and reflects on his shortcomings. This is not least due to the autobiographical narrative method by which different narrative building blocks from actual youngsters have been merged into the fictious role of Jamal al-Khatib. The social workers from Turn Verein für Gewalt- und Extremismuspraevention emphasise this rootedness of Jamal al-Khatib when giving examples of actual quotes from youngsters in dialogue workshops, the most meaningful being used as the introduction to one of the supplementary materials, where a young man is quoted as having said, 'I want to write a book to keep other youths from going to Syria to join the Islamic State' (Turn Verein für Gewalt- und Extremismuspraevention 2019a: 2). The purpose of Jamal al-Khatib is clearly formulated herein: he tells his story to counter so-called jihadism. Jamal's turn away from jihadi ideology is the spectacle put on stage through the entire web series.

In doing so, the fundamentally problematic nexus of being visibly Muslim and extremist radicalisation remains, and the Muslim everyman, Jamal al-Khatib, is portrayed as a former 'fragile subject with a penchant for terrorism' (Marquardt 2020: 131). Beyond that, he, as the only voice indicated as Muslim in the video, is assigned a place as a purified figure, willingly surrendering to the given hegemonic structures. Jamal al-Khatib is even allowed to call for dissent in the context of preventing radicalisation, and to explore the possibilities of a resistant stance as part of the hegemonic order.

In particular, Jamal al-Khatib's commitment against racism, and his concrete calls to action, appear to be purely functional in this context, as they are primarily intended to convey to the target group that they are not in a passive role, and are, thus, empowered against the victim ideology imputed to them, which automatically makes them susceptible to anti-Semitic and Islamist views (cf. Qasem 2019b). In application-oriented texts for educators active in the prevention of radicalisation, this alleged victim role of young Muslims is often referred to in a similar argumentation. For example, a handout by the German Federal Working Group on Religiously Based Extremism recommends taking the experiences of racism of Muslim youth seriously (Bundesarbeitsgemeinschaft religiös begründeter Extremismus 2017: 14). However, in view of the imminent danger of instrumentalising these experiences for the 'victim ideology' of the 'neo-Salafists', it is immediately argued that young people must learn to deal with 'contradictions' and 'conflicts' (ibid.; cf. Qasem 2019b). The video on Jamal al-Khatib follows this logic of action, according to which those affected by racism must themselves bear the responsibility for dealing with racism, and although it establishes regulatory visibility it, thus, omits the view of the systemic structures, the perpetrators and the beneficiaries (cf. Schaffer 2008). Even though Jamal al-Khatib's video, in contrast to the video of the Office for the Protection of the Constitution, clearly names racism and injustice, there is a fundamental contradiction between the anti-racist gestures in the video and their simultaneous embedding in a campaign designed to prevent Islamist extremism. This is because a purely preventative approach, in which young people's experiences of racism are merely taken as an opportunity to ensure that these experiences of racism do not pose a threat to the existing order, is fundamentally different from work that is actually critical of racism.[11] In this context, powerful categories such as religious affiliation and migration background would be questioned and revealed; furthermore, the aim would be to change existing orders (cf. Qasem 2019b).

Looking at the video from this angle, it becomes apparent to me that the self-optimisation offered in Jamal al-Khatib's video as resistance to racism cannot be an answer to the power of racist discourses. This is especially true if groups that are already perceived as 'dangerous, threatening, too loud' in racist discourses were to display their self-confidence and self-empowerment offensively, as Jamal al-Khatib demands, then 'aggression' against them and 'lack of understanding' from the outside would possibly increase (Sow 2016). Here, too, it becomes clear that such self-empowerment would only be desired and tolerated if it was accompanied, as in the case of Jamal al-Khatib, by the much-demanded distancing from Islamism. However, an acceptance of self-confident behaviour shown by Muslims outside of this framework of prevention work seems unlikely. In the context of preventing Islamist extremism, addressing racism is, therefore, always linked to the condition of openly distancing oneself from Islamism and, thus, to the constant reassociation of Muslim youths as potential threats.

When looking more closely at the supplementary educational materials accompanying the web video series, this contradiction of apparent empowering rhetoric and actual self-subjugation to hegemony becomes even more

---

[11] Critique of racism (in German: *Rassismuskritik*) should be understood in this context as the art of not allowing oneself to be so governed by racist forms of action, experience and thought; the concept of critique of racism includes power- and self-reflexive perspectives on actions, institutions, discourses and structures (Mecheril and Melter 2014: 14).

evident. In the materials it is suggested to discuss, among other things, one quote from Jamal al-Khatib uttered during the video when referring to his reflection on facing injustice: 'I felt helpless and powerless, this is why I began to write. My writing pad and pen became my best friends. It is like therapy. This is my jihad al-nafs, my struggle against bad thoughts, wishes, and against my rage' (Turn Verein für Gewalt- und Extremismuspraevention 2019b: 16). Then, a question to be used in discussing this quote is suggested:

> What do you think Jamal meant when mentioning bad thoughts/wishes/feelings? Jamal is not forbidding himself to have such bad feelings, he is doing something with it: he is writing about it. What do you think would happen if he would forbid himself such bad thoughts? (ibid.)

From everything the videos of the web series and the educational material offers, it is clear what this last suggestive question hints at – Jamal, were he not to write about his feelings, would become more and more enraged, he would radicalise, and he would go back to being a jihadist fighter. When he mentions his writing as his *jihad-al-nafs*, he is portrayed as fighting against the 'bad' within him. However, all he does is a cathartic exercise, his writing is self-therapeutic – and he is offered as a role model to the target audience because he has found a way to manage his rage. The multi-faceted theological concept of *jihad-al-nafs* is appropriated here only to mean self-containment and loyalty to the given hegemonic order. In this there is a crucial similarity to the video from the *Jihadi Fool* web series: theological debate and variability are being abridged in order to make Islamic ideas fit into the present order, be it the promotion of moderate Islam in general, or the call for self-therapeutic jihad in this video in particular.

It is no surprise then that the video lacks a serious call to fight injustice. The example of the school class protesting against the deportation of a fellow pupil, which is presented in the video as a positive example of resistant behaviour against racism and injustice, shows the extent to which the narrative, staged in this way, conceals an essential aspect that is absolutely necessary for a consistent analysis critical of racism. The video tells us that resistance against deportation is possible, but at the same time it hides the fact that the action of the school class was ineffective in itself, and that in a radical struggle for an actual end to deportations by German authorities, the structural character of deportation practice, racist jurisdiction and the effects of a dehumanising biopolitics would need to be addressed first and foremost. From this omission, I detect another principal truth: the acts of 'solidarity', as portrayed throughout the video, and as often hailed as acts of humanity and hope, are always confined by power and hegemony.

After all, under the pretext of countering an Islamist extremist narrative, the video conveys that a fundamentally different life – specifically, a fundamentally different form of society outside the structures that produce injustice in the here and now – is not conceivable in Germany. Unsurprisingly, the Federal Agency for Civic Education, in its function as a German state authority *qua natura*, would not fund a video which promotes the idea that a radically different world is possible. The postulated resistance, consequently, takes place strictly within the framework of the given order, and is only given space if the given overall conditions are accepted and tolerated. That this staging of resistance also happens by appropriating the symbolism, aesthetics and iconography of countercultural, left-wing and radical left-wing groups – books about the communist revolutionary and anti-imperialist guerrilla fighter Ernesto Che Guevara and the German anti-fascist resistance group White Rose are inserted; Jamal al-Khatib and his friends appear in black hoodies and balaclavas; stickers are stuck on wildly, and graffiti is sprayed – should not obscure the fact that such videos are actually intended to categorically deny and prevent any form of radicalism. More so, radicality is discursively erased, as long as it does not appear as an attitude of former Islamists that has been overcome by their (re-)integration inIhe hegemonic order.

Finally: The 'Oppositional Gaze' as a Radically Critical Gaze of Hegemony

My reflections on the two videos, and the roles of Jamil and Jamal, show that there is a parallelism far beyond the probably coincidental, but nonetheless significant, similarity of the two names of the protagonists: these are similar roles, and there are similar assumptions and logics shaping these roles, and there are similar careers that are retrospectively enacted, or speculatively anticipated, for these roles. This parallelism is no coincidence, since both the

Office for Protection of the Constitution and the Federal Agency for Civic Education are ultimately similar authorities, both subordinate to their respective ministries of the interior. Both institutions use the roles of young Muslim men with different creative means, but with similar goals in the course of their own counternarrative campaigns. While civic education measures in the context of preventing Islamist extremism have often been characterised as being far more open, critical and emancipatory than the more repressive measures by security agencies, in looking at these two videos I found them to be part of the same phalanx to defend German democracy and all of its contradictions and injustices.

My gazing back at the roles portrayed in the videos, therefore, confirms that state narratives are never innocent, but always 'powerful and tricky' (Maan 2015: 1), and part of a hegemonic game. The narratives packaged within these two short videos need to be understood as political devices. This understanding needs to be further linked to a conception of society as a space continuously determined by ordering practices. Counternarratives are part of an ongoing hegemonic game in which political–ideological boundaries are constantly being redrawn through the weaving of new narrative strands, and a dichotomisation of the social field is striven for (Laclau 2000): who are 'we'? What do we stand for? What do we stand for when the 'others' are against us? The oppositional view of the power constellations resonating in these questions then becomes a critical view of hegemony that must go far beyond a critical examination of the (in-)adequacy of representations of racialised or religiousised subject positions. The very act of narrating against Islamism is an ordering and powerful practice that produces exclusions, and must, thus, become the focus of a hegemony-critical analysis. It is necessary to question the apparent truths that are depicted in the narratives. So, when I looked specifically at the assumptions about Muslims crystallising in two short videos, and the mode of dealing with Muslims represented within them, I gazed back; I stared back at instruments and structures of power by means of which Muslims – and I as part of them – are measured and mapped, disciplined, dominated.

Of course, a critique of German hegemonic policies vis-à-vis Islamist extremism is by no means fully formulated with the documentation of the development of a single oppositional gaze undertaken here. Much more needs to be analysed, with many different perspectives, not only on the representations of Muslims in counternarratives but, more fundamentally, on the interweaving of these representations in existing relations of domination, on the relationship between the prevention of Islamism and colonialism, on the domineering conception of neutrality, and also on the staging of Muslim women in particular, and the respective structures behind it. I dare say that a foundation stone for this further critique of hegemony has been laid here, as it has become comprehensible how an oppositional view produces resistance not only against representation as such, but against the underlying power mechanisms.

This resistance is inherently radical. For the oppositional gaze creates agency precisely when a non-identification with the roles offered in the videos is achieved. This non-identification is even an escape from a double-consciousness (Du Bois [1903] 2007: 8) in the sense that overcoming the formation of a desirable and conforming identity of the ruled according to the expectations of the ruled takes place. At the same time, looking back at the concrete practice of erasing radicality in the counternarratives affords the possibility of reforming an identity of the radical. For it is precisely during this looking, that the fundamental nature of hegemonic relations is called into question in a radical way.

One question, of course, remains: is this exertion of developing an oppositional gaze, of developing a critique of hegemonic policies, different than the self-therapeutic exercise of Jamal al-Khatib, who only writes to manage his rage? The answer is not easy. But yes, this exertion, this struggle to politicise, this effort to recognise injustice, could unfold into something bigger than self-containment, as long as the writing inspires an actual endeavour to change the injustice. Although I have not made any advances in formulating ideas on how to overcome injustice concretely, I have at least pointed to one significant truth regarding the way forward: that is that we will not learn how to change the world for the better from state-sponsored counternarrative campaigns.

References

Agai, B., M. Bassiouni, A. Başol, J. Ben Abdeljelil, M. C. Bodenstein, N. Çakır, S. Güneş, A. Omerika, F. Rahmati, Ö. Özsoy, E. Şahin and U. Simon (2014), 'Islamische Theologie in Deutschland: Herausforderungen im Spannungsfeld divergierender Erwartungen', *Uni Frankfurt*, <https://www.uni-frankfurt.de/58246066/Positionspapier.pdf> (last accessed 13 June 2022).

Ahmed, S. (2014), *The Cultural Politics of fear*, 2nd edn, Edinburgh: Edinburgh University Press.

Amir-Moazami, S. (ed.) (2018), *Der inspizierte Muslim: Zur Politisierung der Islamforschung in Deutschland*, Bielefeld: Transcript.

Bundesarbeitsgemeinschaft religiös begründeter Extremismus (2017), 'Zivilgesellschaftliche Präventionsarbeit im Themenfeld religiös begründeter Extremismus', <www.bag-relex.de/wp-content/uploads/2018/11/BAG_RelEx_Publikation_pdf.pdf> (last accessed 13 June 2022).

Bundszentrale für politische Bildung (2020), 'Jamal al-Khatib X NISA: Eine Projektvorstellung', 6 August, <https://www.bpb.de/lernen/digitale-bildung/bewegtbild-und-politische-bildung/jamal/290934/eine-projektvorstellung> (last accessed 13 June 2022).

Castells, M. (2007), 'Communication, Power and Counter-power in the Network Society', *International Journal of Communication*, 1, 238–66.

Crossley, N. (1993), 'The Politics of the Gaze: Between Foucault and Merleau-Ponty', *Human Studies*, 16: 4, 399–419.

Du Bois, W. E. B. ([1903] 2007), *The Souls of Black Folk*, New York: Oxford University Press.

European Network Against Racism (2021), 'GERMANY – Suspicion, Discrimination and Surveillance: The Impact of Counter-Terrorism Law and Policy on Racialised Groups at Risk of Racism in Europe', <https://www.enar-eu.org/IMG/pdf/suspicion_discrimination_surveillance_factsheet-germany.pdf> (last accessed 13 June 2022).

Figlestahler, C. and K. Schau (2022), 'Prävention und Sicherheit. Ein (Rück-) Blick auf die Präventions- und Distanzierungslandschaft in Deutschland', in Bundesarbeitsgemeinschaft religiös begründeter Extremismus (ed), *Zur Sicherheit: Prävention? Sicherheit im Kontext der Präventionsarbeit gegen religiös begründeten Extremismus*, pp. 13–22, <https://www.bag-relex.de/wp-content/uploads/2022/01/220120-Ligante4-BPDF.pdf> (last accessed 13 June 2022).

Frischlich, L., D. Rieger, A. Morten and G. Bente (eds) (2017), 'Videos gegen Extremismus? Counter-Narrative auf dem Prüfstand', *Polizei + Forschung*, 51, Wiesbaden: Bundeskriminalamt.

Hafez, F. and S. Qasem (2020), 'Muslims under General Suspicion: Perspectives on the Prevention of So-called Islamist Extremism', *Islamophobia Studies Yearbook/Jahrbuch für Islamophobieforschung*, 11, 7–14.

Hayes, B. and A. Qureshi (2016), 'We are Completely Independent: The Home Office, Breakthrough Media and the PREVENT Counter Narrative Industry', CAGE, <https://www.cage.ngo/product/we-are-completely-independent-report> (last accessed 13 June 2022).

Hohnstein, S. and M. Glaser (2017), 'Wie tragen digitale Medien zu politisch-weltanschaulichem Extremismus im Jugendalter bei und was kann pädagogische Arbeit dagegen tun? Ein Überblick über Forschungsstand, präventive und intervenierende Praxis im Themenfeld', in S. Hohnstein and M. Herding (eds), *Digitale Medien und politisch-weltanschaulicher Extremismus im Jugendalter: Erkenntnisse aus Wissenschaft und Praxis*, pp. 243–81, <https://www.dji.de/fileadmin/user_upload/bibs2017/Digitale_Medien.AFS.Band.13.pdf> (last accessed 13 June 2022).

hooks, b. (1992), 'The Oppositional Gaze: Black Female Spectators', in b. hooks (ed.), *Black Looks: Race and Representation*, Boston: South End Press, pp. 115–31.

Kuhn, A. (1985), *The Power of the Image: Essays on Representation and Sexuality*, London and New York: Routledge.

Laclau, E. (2020), 'Foreword', in D. Howart, A. J. Norval and Y. Stavrakakis (eds), *Discourse Theory and Political Analysis: Identities, Hegemonies and Social Change,*Manchester: Manchester University Press, pp. x–xi.

Land NRW (2019), 'Verfassungsschutz startet YouTube-Kanäle zur Salafismus-Prävention', *Pressemitteilung*, 22 August, <https://www.land.nrw/de/pressemitteilung/verfassungsschutz-startet-youtube-kanaele-zur-salafismus-praevention> (last accessed 13 June 2022).

Maan, A. (2015), *Counter-terrorism: Narrative Strategies*, New York: University Press of America.

Mansour, A. (2015), *Generation Allah: Warum wir im Kampf gegen religiösen Extremismus umdenken müssen*, Frankfurt: Fischer.

Marquardt, P. A. (2020), 'Junge MuslimInnen als fragile Subjekte mit dem Hang zum Terrorismus? Kritik der dominierenden Erzählung und pädagogischen Prävention von Radikalisierung', *Islamophobia Studies Yearbook/Jahrbuch für Islamophobieforschung*, 11, 131–51.

Mecheril, P. and C. Melter (2014), 'Rassismustheorie und –forschung in Deutschland: Konturen eines wissenschaftlichen Feldes', in C. Melter and P. Mecherli (eds), *Rassismuskritik. Band 1: Rassismustheorie und –forschung*, Schwalbach: Wochenschau.

Peter, F. and R. Ortega (eds) (2014), *Islamic Movements of Europe*, London and New York: I. B. Tauris.

Qasem, S. (2019a), '"Gute Arbeit, gute Bildung, Integration und Teilhabe" – Islamismusprävention als Universalschlüssel für die (Post-)Migrationsgesellschaft? Debattenbeiträge des Präventionsnetzwerks gegen religiös begründeten Extremismus. Türkische Gemeinde in Deutschland', *Debattenbeitrag*, <https://praeventionsnetzwerk.org/wpcontent/uploads/2020/03/Debattenbeitrag-S.-Qasem-Islamismuspr%C3%A4ventions-als-Universalschl%C3%BCssel.pdf> (last accessed 13 June 2022).

Qasem, S. (2019b), 'Erfahrungen von Rassismus als Radikalisierungsfaktor: Ein (Gegen-)Beispiel', *Bundeszentrale für politische Bildung*, 30 August, <https://www.bpb.de/politik/extremismus/radikalisierungspraevention/295169/erfahrungenvon-rassismus-als-radikalisierungsfaktor-ein-gegen-beispiel> (last accessed 13 June 2022).

RAND (2004), 'RAND Study Describes How West Can Counter Radical Islam', 18 March, <https://www.rand.org/news/press/2004/03/18.html> (last accessed 13 June 2022).

Sartre, J.-P. (1969), *Being and Nothingness*, London: Routledge.

Sedgwick, E. K. (1990), *Epistemology of the Closet*, Berkeley: University of California Press.

Schaffer, J. (2008), *Ambivalenzen der Sichtbarkeit: Über die visuellen Strukturen der Anerkennung*, Bielefeld: Transcript.

Schiffauer, W. (2015), 'Sicherheitswissen und Deradikalisierung', in D. Molthagen (ed.), *Handlungsempfehlungen zur Auseinandersetzung mit islamistischem Extremismus und Islamfeindlichkeit*, Berlin: Friedrich-Ebert-Stiftung, pp. 217–44.

Sow, N. (2016), 'Vorsicht bei Empowerment für Kinder und Jugendliche: "Mit Selbstbewusstsein Rassismus entgegentreten . . ." (aka: "Hör nicht auf die. Sei stark.")', *Noah Sow Blog*, 3 February, <https://www.noahsow.de/blog/en/mit-selbstbewusstsein-rassismus-entgegentreten-aka-hoer-nicht-auf-die-sei-stark/> (last accessed 13 June 2022).

Turn Verein für Gewalt- und Extremismusprävention e.V. (2019a), *Das pädagogische Paket 2*, <https://www.turnprevention.com/_files/ugd/0cc6d7_b22650c129c74deabac6f411cfc28406.pdf> (last accessed 13 June 2022).

Turn Verein für Gewalt- und Extremismusprävention e.V. (2019b), *Das pädagogische Paket 2. Pädagogische Materialien*, <https://www.turnprevention.com/_files/ugd/0cc6d7_371ad9553817455d828d5b069082aa65.pdf> (last accessed 13 June 2022).

WWU Münster (2019), 'Zentrum für Islamische Theologiue stärkt Beziehungen zu Ägypten', 29 January <https://www.uni-muenster.de/news/view.php?cmdid=10057> (last accessed 13 June 2022).

4

CRIMINALISING CRITICAL SCHOLARSHIP: AUSTRIA'S INTELLIGENCE SERVICE AND ISLAMOPHOBIA STUDIES

Farid Hafez

Introduction

The War on Terror led to the invention of a series of programmes that build on the imagination of threatening Muslim masculinity prone to violence and threatening the social and political order of Western states from the inside. In the wake of the infamous so-called War on Terror, the securitisation of Islam and Muslims became formally institutionalised in several countries around the globe. Following the UK and the Netherlands, several United Nations resolutions (2178, 2354 and 2396) were introduced to implement so-called Countering Violent Extremism (CVE) projects in the member states (Kundnani and Hayes 2018). With this, the notion of 'radicalisation' has become so normalised and found its way into everyday language. While these measures were presented to counteract the harsh forms of military hard power, what followed was a minimisation of human rights and a weakening of civil society. Many scholars argue that CVE programmes have not been an alternative to the securitisation, but rather the opposite: they have turned CVE into a means of securitisation and oppression (Ragazzi 2022; Naji and Schildknecht 2021; Fadil et al. 2019; Walker 2021).

Junaid Rana introduced his concept of the terror-industrial complex to understand the subsequent expansion of this machinery. He draws on James

Risen, who spoke about the formation of the Homeland Security-industrial complex to reference how companies tried to receive military contracts and thus built the infrastructure of the Global War on Terrorism, which for Risen is 'made up of a web of intelligence agencies and their contractors, companies that mostly provide secret services rather than large weapons systems and equipment' (Rana 2016). Since this complex has to reconfirm the threat to sustain itself, Rana speaks of a form of endless war that perpetuates a system of racial capitalism. Rana calls this the 'racial infrastructure', which for him is 'a spatial formation in which the social, political, and economic relationships of racial systems operate through dominance and discursive power' (ibid.). Rana identifies what he calls the terror-industrial complex that is an expansion of security and surveillance measures by the nation state (ibid.: 114), which for him is a form of 'structural violence' (ibid.: 115). Most important for our discussion is that 'the power of governance by the counter-terror state is based in pre-emption and a conditional logic of a threat of terror as excess' (ibid.: 121).

The expansion of countering violent extremism programmes to countering non-violent extremism has to be seen in the light of this terror-industrial complex. The latter does not target violence but thought. Not militancy, but ideas. Not actions, but indeed the minds of people. The trend of expanding the notion of 'countering violent extremism' to 'countering non-violent extremism' (Hafez 2019a) has ultimately widened the field of intervention by the state.

As we have seen throughout the last years, some European countries like Austria and France have introduced measures and legislation to combat or even outlaw what has become known as 'political Islam' or 'Islamist separatism'. These notions, which are legally not defined, but which are central to political debates in both countries, do not refer to violent forms of political action, but rather to social groups that are problematised by the power structures (Hafez 2022).

This chapter is dealing with the case of Austria, where recently a law was introduced making 'political Islam' a criminal offence, a measure that was harshly criticised by human rights organisations (Ranftler 2021). The case of France, where several Muslim NGOs including one of the most active anti-racist monitoring bodies, the Collective Against Islamophobia in France (CCIF) were even dissolved, shows that it was not violent groups that were targeted, but Muslim civil society that was connected to the contested concept of 'political Islam' or 'Islamist Separatism'. I see these measures as a strategy of the governments in place to restrict religious freedom for Muslims, narrowing down their visibility as well as their agency of self-organisation. Drawing on Salman Sayyid's understanding of Islamophobia as referring to the attempt to prevent the Muslim subject from being given a place in the world as a Muslim, the non-existence of an epistemological and political space (Sayyid 2014: 8) forms the heart of the problem, which I identify in these measures.

These recent repressive measures have led to a reaction on behalf of NGO activists as well as academics like me, who have dedicated part of their lives to thinking and talking about as well as criticising and countering Islamophobia. As a consequence, Islamophobia Studies in itself became criminalised and was reframed as an Islamist tool of war, a manifestation of 'political Islam'. This happened along similar lines, where mundane action would be reframed to become a part of a threatening strategy, a form of 'jihad', as the examples of love jihad in India (Rao 2011) or legal jihad in Western countries (Goldstein and Meyer 2008: 395).

In this article, I want to trace back the knowledge production that framed 'political Islam' to become a more dangerous evil than militant political action by drawing on think tanks and state institutions with their pivotal scholars, who shaped the public understanding as well as the policy-making processes. As a first step, I will demonstrate how 'political Islam' was generally framed by think tanks, scholars, politicians, government officials and intelligence agencies as a problem. In a second step, I will show how different governments in Austria used the battle against 'political Islam' to legitimise different policies. This will especially reveal the extent to which 'political Islam' was used to curtail religious freedom and free speech. Finally, I will especially elaborate how the problematisation of agency criticising Islamophobia was interpreted as a form of 'political Islam'. This will draw on the files of the intelligence agency that started an investigation against alleged proponents of 'political Islam', in which more than 100 people were taken as suspects of terrorist organisation, state enemy and criminal organisation. This was done based on the allegation that these quite diverse groups and people were allegedly part of the Muslim Brotherhood or Hamas, although the Muslim Brotherhood is not designated as a terrorist organisation in Austria. My home was also brutally raided by the intelligence agency and special troops. As a critical voice in the Austrian public, who has been criticising Austrian governments for their policies towards Muslims for years, this shows how they problematise my critique of state-institutionalised Islamophobia.

Politicising 'Political Islam'

The introduction of the notion of so-called 'political Islam' in political debates in Austria is very much connected to the coming of power of Sebastain Kurz of the Christian-Democratic Austrian People's Party (Österreichische Volkspartei; ÖVP), who became Integration State Secretary in the Ministry of Interior in 2011, then Minister of Foreign and Integration Affairs in 2013 and Chancellor of two subsequent coalition governments in 2017 (first with the far-right FPÖ and in 2020 again with the Greens), before he had to resign amid a corruption inquiry in October 2021. A near-state institution, the Austrian Integration Fund (Österreichischer Integrationsfonds; ÖIF), played a crucial role in creating a discourse around the notion of 'political Islam'. Legally a fund of the Republic of Austria, the ÖIF sets the agenda of Austria's integration policy on a federal level. By regularly inviting leading anti-Muslim voices, especially from Germany, Switzerland and the US, it has shaped the discourse on Islam in the public, legitimising many of the anti-Muslim policies of ÖVP-led policies regarding Islam.[1] Panels were organised on topics such as 'The Influence of Political Islam' (Österreichischer Integrationsfonds 2018a) and speakers were invited to tour Austria to talk about the threat of 'Political Islam in Austria' (Österreichischer Integrationsfonds 2018b). Later, the Documentation Centre for Political Islam was established to consolidate several experts and the efforts to criminalise Muslim civil society activism and critics of the government's policies.

With the existing 'knowledge' on 'political Islam', several politicians of the ÖVP repeatedly framed 'political Islam' as the greatest threat to Austrian society. The ÖVP's General Secretary argued: 'The poison of political Islam must not endanger our society . . . Violent clashes, territorial conflicts, and parallel justice are on the agenda according to the executive officials and

---

[1] See the country reports covering Austria in the European Islamophobia Report: Hafez 2018; Hafez 2019b; Hafez 2020a; Hafez 2021a.

judges' (*Kronen Zeitung* 2018a). By using terminologies like 'poison', those who are framed as proponents of 'political Islam' are dehumanised, which justifies any extraordinary means against them. This discourse, reminiscent of the anti-Semitic discourse that dehumanised Jews (Musolff 2007), in which Muslims are framed as 'carriers of poison', implies that every thinkable measure can be taken to protect oneself from this 'poison'. It allows political leaders to justify political measures to be taken against this allegedly dangerous group of people.[2]

In the government's coalition programme of the ÖVP and FPÖ in 2017, 'political Islam' for the first time becomes a focal point of security policies (*Wiener Zeitung*, n.d.). The coalition programme requires that essential sources of faith such as the Qur'an be submitted in an authorised translation by the Islamic Religious Society, mirroring the Catholic Church as a strictly hierarchical institution. This clearly shows how much politicians are interested in managing an otherised religion that is seen as a potential threat. Beyond that, the programme reiterates a 'ban on foreign financing' and a 'criminal law against political Islam'. Subsequently, some state administrations also started implementing the notion of 'political Islam' (for example, the Ministry of Education, Science and Research, n.d.). Most importantly, it was the intelligence agency that adopted this vocabulary.

While Austria's domestic intelligence service, the Federal Office for the Protection of the Constitution (Bundesamt für Verfassungsschutz und Terrorismusbekämpfung; BVT) had in the past used the terminology Islamism and jihadism in its annual report dating back as far as 1997, the notion of 'political Islam' was only used in the 2019 title. Moreover, the content of the report deviated from other previous reports as well as following reports. For the first time, the legally recognised Islamic Religious Community (IGGÖ) was presented not as an ally against so-called 'extremism', but as an organisation from which risks emanate (Hafez 2023). The report presents three types

---

[2] Armin Langer (2020) has shown in his research that religiously observant Jews were depicted by Enlightenment philosophers as people who would strive for a political separation from the rest of society. Jewish religious practice was seen as a sign of a separatist, political cult which forms a 'state within a state', similar to today's assumption of Muslims forming a so-called 'parallel society'.

of problematic manifestations: while the first two speak of jihadist and thus violent expressions of so-called 'Islamic extremism', the third speaks explicitly of non-violent Islamic movements. According to the report, while these movements denounce the democratic constitutional state, they cooperate with parties, associations and NGOs to have a social and political impact. This could lead to a 'strategic infiltration with the aim of shaping and regulating the society according to social beliefs of the *caliphate* and *shari'a*' (Hafez 2019c: 3). Here, political participation is framed as potential infiltration. According to the report published in 2019, Islamists use education, social welfare services and the organisation of cultural life in order to create a 'counter-society' (*Parallelgesellschaft*). The goal is to prevent 'assimilation' (Bundesministerium für Inneres 2019: 15), which then becomes the very goal of the intelligence service itself. While many Austrian Muslims would argue that integration is often nothing but a euphemism for assimilation, never has any state agency made this so explicit in an official document. Saying this, the BVT clearly goes beyond its own scope, discussing not only security threats in society but also laying down a social agenda. While it alleges Islamists have an agenda of creating an alternative society, it appears this state agency itself follows a clear agenda of making Muslims invisible. This major shift in the administration suggests that the discourse started by the ÖVP has found its way into the state bureaucracy.

This tendency found its peak in the proclamation to create a monitoring centre that tracks so-called religious extremism, conducts research, documents and archives it (Österreichischer Rundfunk 2019a), a move which was only achieved when the Greens joined a coalition with the ÖVP as the junior partner in 2020. Stating that the battle against 'political Islam' was a 'top priority', the Greens and ÖVP agreed to introduce a documentation centre to target religious extremism (which was originally presented and finally implemented as the Documentation Centre for Political Islam) (Bock et al. 2020). This centre was established on 15 July 2020, and presented by the Minister of Interior, Susanne Raab, alongside two academics, the German theologian Mouhanad Khorchide and the US-based researcher Lorenzo Vidino (Bridge Initiative Team 2020a). The Documentation Centre has been presented as 'part of the national strategy of extremism prevention and deradicalisation' (*Wiener Zeitung* 2020). With an annual budget of €1,700,000, Minister Raab, says the Documentation

Centre allows 'for the first time in Austria . . . to independently and scientifically deal with the dangerous ideology of political Islam and offer insights into the previously hidden networks' (*Kronen Zeitung* 2020). The board includes some of the most well-known authors that have supported the anti-Muslim policies of the ÖVP, such as Lorenzo Vidino (Bridge Initiative Team 2020a) and Heiko Heinisch (Bridge Initiative Team 2020b). During the presentation, the minister argued: 'Because political Islam is poison for our social coexistence and must be fought with all means', and claimed that with the establishment of the Documentation Centre for Political Islam, 'Austria thus becomes a pioneer in Europe' (Bridge Initiative Team 2020b). And indeed, this initiative has been taken as an example to copy for German politicians of the Christian Democratic CDU/CSU (Hafez 2021b).

As these examples reveal, institutions and initiatives around Sebastian Kurz's ÖVP have succeeded in the problematisation of the notion of 'political Islam', arguing that it would represent a secret form of subversion of Western societies. And this discourse showed its political effects.

Fighting 'Political Islam' in Practice

On one hand, the image of the enemy of 'political Islam' has been used to campaign against political opponents. For Sebastian Kurz's ÖVP, the most important opponent was the Social Democratic Party of Austria (Sozialdemokratische Partei Österreichs; SPÖ), which has been governing in the capital city of Vienna since 1945 (Hafez 2020b). Sebastian Kurz rallied against the SPÖ, which was represented as a safe haven for 'political Islam', a discourse reminiscent of the *völkisch*-nationalist discourse against the Socialists in interwar Austria, where the Socialists were framed as a Jewish-led party that was 'jewisising' the country (*Verjudung*) (Hafez 2019d). As Chancellor Kurz declared, fighting 'political Islam' means monitoring Islamist associations, Islamist ideology on social media, and segregation i n the realm of education (Renner 2019).

Numerous legislations were implemented to battle 'political Islam', especially following the inception of the new coalition of ÖVP and FPÖ in 2017. FPÖ Party whip Johann Gudenus announced a new act in mid-2019 that forbids the promotion of so-called 'political Islam' (*Der Standard* 2018), but this did not happen under their legislation period, since the coalition broke in mid-2019. This was reiterated following the murder of four people in Vienna by a former ISIS sympathiser. The Greens pushed against this move and watered the bill down to ban 'religiously motivated extremism', while Integration Minister Raab still declared during the presentation of the law that this is directed against 'political Islam' (Gaigg and Schmidt 2020). Until now, there has been no definition of 'political Islam' offered by the government, while at the same time, one could deduce from the implemented policies, what the government means when they accuse Muslims of following 'political Islam'.

But we can clearly understand from the government's actions what they mean when speaking about 'political Islam'. In total, the laws, institutions and measures that were introduced by various ÖVP-led governments reveal the extent to which 'political Islam' did not only become a means for political campaigning against the opposition, but a way to regulate and manage a religious minority that they do not see as equal, but rather as a societal threat that has to be kept in a marginalised position. The lack of a legal definition, it seems, is a strength rather than a weakness, since it allows the Austrian government to go against every kind of Muslimness, from religious practice to organised communities to critical opposition, as the next section will show.

To give just a few examples: when the ÖVP–FPÖ-led coalition government announced to close eight mosques to fight 'political Islam' (*The Local* 2018), the Chancellor framed the government's initiative as a means to protect common Muslims from 'political Islam' (Gigler and Jungwirth 2018). Following a complaint by the mosques, the Viennese Court of Administration ruled half a year later that this initiative was unlawful (*Österreichischer Rundfunk* 2019b). Another initiative was the ban of the hijab, first for pre-school in 2018 and then for elementary school in 2019. According to Vice Chancellor Strache (FPÖ), the ban was designed to assure integration, as for him, the hijab 'plays into the hands of political Islam, which has already created dangerous parallel societies in diverse structures of associations' (Pándi 2018). Also, Chancellor Sebastian Kurz argued this would protect Muslim girls from 'political Islam' (*Kronen Zeitung* 2018b). The hijab ban for pupils in elementary school was contested by several Muslim parents and the Constitutional Court finally repealed the law in December 2020 (Verfassungsgerichtshof Österreich 2020). Following the militant attack in November 2020, the Minister of Integration (ÖVP) announced to close a mosque to fight 'Islamist extremism', although there was no criminal offence (Bundeskanzleramt 2020). Half a year later, the mosque was reopened after it contested the measure and won at the Viennese regional court (Rachbauer 2021).

Only the Documentation Centre for Political Islam has suggested a still rather vague definition six months after its inception, where it suggested to speak of political Islam as a

> Gesellschafts- and Herrschaftsideologie that seeks to transform or influence society, culture, the state or politics on the basis of values and norms that are regarded by their proponents as Islamic, but which contradict the principles of the democratic constitutional state and human rights. (Wolf 2020: 3)

As Professor of religious studies Franz Winter argued, the suggested definition 'leaves many questions unanswered and is thus again subject to a possibly arbitrary assessment' (Winter 2021). Even more so, it is not legally binding and thus more relevant for the public discourse and irrelevant for the governmental politics.

Criminalising Scholarly Dissent: The Case of Islamophobia Studies

Some of the academics who regularly supported the anti-Muslim measures and laws of the ÖVP-led governments also promoted a view that speaking about Islamophobia would be a way to silence critics against Islam. During panel discussions of the ÖIF, panelists argued that Islamophobia was a means for 'political Islam' to prevent reforms of Islam by liberal Muslims, saying: 'Political Islam strives to take over the Muslim community in Europe. In the process, ideas for reform or justified criticism are immediately dismissed wholesale as "Islamophobic"' (Österreichischer Integrationsfonds 2020). One of the academics of the advisory board of the Documentation Centre for Political Islam, the US-based Lorenzo Vidino, said in an interview in the German Frankfurter Allgemeine Zeitung, when asked if he thinks that 'jihadism or so-called political Islam was more dangerous, the militants or those who try to implement their views through politics', the following: 'It is difficult to compare the two. Because they are two different forms of threats. But if I had to choose, I would say that "political Islam", which is also called "legalistic Islamism", is the greater threat' (Meier 2021).

The same Lorenzo Vidino had authored a report titled 'The Muslim Brotherhood in Austria' that was commissioned by the ÖIF and co-sponsored by the Austrian intelligence service (BVT) in August 2017. There, he connected the study of Islamophobia with 'political Islam' and identified Islamophobia as a 'problematic element of the Brotherhood's discourse' due to 'its narrative of victimhood'. He explains:

> Drawing on some anti-Muslim incidents and attitudes that unquestionably exist, European Brotherhood organisations, in a similar fashion to their counterparts throughout the West, have purposely exaggerated them and tried to foster a siege mentality within local Muslim communities, arguing that the government and Western societies are hostile to them and to Islam in general. This dynamic has been particularly evident in Austria over the last few years, as Brotherhood-linked entities have used the charge of 'Islamophobia' with abundance, leveraging it at times with good reason (as the problem does exist in Austria), but in many cases without much foundation and for calculated strategic reasons. The combination of these two elements can potentially be explosive. If Muslims in Gaza have the right to defend themselves, and their use of violence is actually a divinely sanctioned jihad (as a preacher of the Austrian Brotherhood milieu like Adnan Ibrahim states) one can argue, why not also in the West, where, according to what the Brothers say, they are also under attack? (Vidino 2017: 36)

Vidino then continues to state that the Muslim Brotherhood has never openly called to violence, but that a mental form of violence is potentially construed. By arguing this way, he is still able to hold his academic credentials by not exaggerating and sticking to the facts, but he also insinuates the violent potential of an alleged Muslim Brotherhood-discourse on Islamophobia. In a way, he problematises any discussion on Islamophobia, as he does not elaborate on how talking about Islamophobia could look like without feeding into a 'siege-mentality'. Hence, the allegation remains with all who speak about Islamophobia. For Vidino, the critique of Islamophobia

> has become an extremely effective tool to silence critics and force policymakers to work with Brotherhood organisations. The charge of Islamophobia is brought not just against those that criticise Islam, but, rather, against those that criticise the Brothers. Any criticism of a Western Brotherhood leader or

organisation is met with an accusation of racism and Islamophobia. In some cases, the Brothers, always aware of what chords to strike, tailor their charges according to the country in which they operate. Therefore, in the United States those who criticise them are guilty of McCarthyism, in Italy of fascism and, in most others, of post-colonial mentality. The use of the Islamophobia weapon has unquestionably silenced many critics of the New Brothers and led many policymakers to engage them out of fear of being tarnished as a racist or Islamo-phobe. These labels, whether deserved or not, are hardly claims that any public figure and, in particular, any politician would take lightly. (Vidino 2017: 47)

While Vidino's argument that politicians would not want to be called out as racist might sound appealing to anti-racist scholars, it is indeed not representative of a political landscape like Austria – and indeed many other European countries – where quite blatant racist statements are the rule rather than the exception or at least pass unchallenged.

One week after a militant attack in Vienna by an alleged jihadist, a raid against thirty people, that included myself, took place (Siddiqui 2021). Interior Minister Karl Nehammer argued on 9 November 2020 that this was aimed at 'cutting off the roots of political Islam' (*The Local* 2020). When the defendants, who up until today are accused of being part of a terrorist organisation, a criminal organisation and a state enemy, were interrogated immediately following the raids, they were asked questions that had little to do with violence and militancy, but a lot to do with an Orientalist perspective on Islam, being Muslim and political views: how many non-Muslim friends do you have? Do you visit a mosque and if yes, which mosque? What do you think about the caliphate? What do you think about peace with Israel? Should kids raised in Austria be educated to become martyrs? Do you want to introduce shari'a? Do you know the Protocols of the Elders of Zion? What do you understand by the term 'Islamophobia'? In your opinion, is this term justified? If so, please explain why and what do you understand by this term? Are Muslims suppressed in Austria? Is Islamist global terrorism possibly the reason for fears emanating from Islam or is it the oppression, especially of women or people of other faiths, by the norms of the shari'a? May your son marry a Christian, unbeliever or a Jew? Do you designate your son's spouse? What does the term *Kuffare* [sic] mean for you? Are Christians for you *Kuffar*? Is one allowed to kill in the name of God? Do you and your wife and your kids observe the prayer times?[3] These are just a few of the hundreds of questions that the terrorism suspects were asked.

Without going into detail, the fact that suspected terrorists were asked what they think of the term 'Islamophobia' and if that term by itself was justified, if Muslims are suppressed in Austria and if 'Islamist global terrorism' or rather 'the oppression, especially of women or people of other faiths, by the norms of the shariʿa might be 'the reason for fears emanating from Islam', reveals, how the intelligence service has become to view these issues. While in 2009, the annual report of the domestic intelligence service, BVT, defined Islamophobia as a 'discrimination or stigmatisation of Islam and Muslims that can lead to radicalisation' (Bundesamt für Verfassungsschutz und Terrorismusbekämpfung 2010: 56), with the shift in Islam-related politics between 2010 and 2017 (Hafez and Heinisch 2018), the BVT promoted rather contrasting ideas. Meanwhile, people like Vidino have become central to the knowledge production for the secret service. A German translation of his report was included as part of the investigation files against alleged terrorists. Vidino was also invited by the intelligence service as a witness and presented himself as an advisor for 'law enforcement agencies around the world', saying he was 'appointed by Italian Prime Minister Matteo Renzi as coordinator of the "National Commission on Jihadist Radicalisation"' (16 St 52/19t, ON32, 41), thus being not only a mouthpiece for the government's actions, but also an aid in the law enforcement.

After six months of investigation, a report by the Styrian branch of the domestic intelligence service was dedicated to the analysis of my publications in foreign news outlets (LVT ST 2409/2019, 8 April 2021). Based on the investigation of a USB stick from another person who became a suspect later on, which had a Power Point presentation of an European Muslim umbrella organisation with one slide saying 'We have to create awareness towards Islamophobia', my writings on different English-speaking news media from

---

[3] The questions are taken from the files of the investigation. Some of them can also be accessed online via Facebook, 'Arabischer Palästina-Club, Politisch motivierte Razzia und Gesinnungsfragen bei BVT-Vernahmen', 15 November 2020. Available at <https://www.facebook.com/permalink.php?story_fbid=1760584047452617&id=1060883244089371> (last accessed 2 February 2023).

Al Jazeera to Haaaretz to Anadolu Agency were reframed as part of the 'strategy in the creation of a parallel state' (16 St 52/19t, ON 1144, 19 May 2021, 731–999). As the report argued, the 'Islamophobia file in Europe . . . is an essential part in the establishment of an Islamic political vision in Europe' (ibid.: 111). The report further continues: 'This way, the term "Islamophobia" becomes a strategic instrument for the Muslim Brotherhood. A main representor in the usage of this strategic term "Islamophobia" is the suspect Dr Farid Hafez' (ibid.). The report continues:

> In the strategy papers for the establishment of a parallel state or caliphate . . . it is defined that a public discourse must take place by means of the term 'Islamophobia'. For this reason, representatives of political Islam and the Muslim Brotherhood frequently use the term 'Islamophobia' in the media. The experts Heiko HEINISCH and Nina SCHOLZ have already pointed out in their book 'Alles für Allah' (Everything for Allah) that the word 'Islamophobia' is used by members of the Muslim Brotherhood as a combat term (*Kampfbegriff*) in order to cast Muslims in the role of victims and thus influence public opinion. Muslims are deliberately portrayed as victims, and the broad masses are thus led to believe that they are constantly disadvantaged and discriminated against. Especially these victim narratives around the term 'Islamophobia' in combination with the propagation of values, which are understood as superior and Islamic, lead specifically to a divide of the society. HAFEZ permanently uses the word 'Islamophobia' in his articles and also frequently draws the comparison of Muslims today with the Jews at the time of the Nazi regime. (16 St 52/19t, ON 1144, 19 May 2021, 121)

Heiko Heinisch, who is a member of the scientific board of the Documentation Centre for Political Islam as well as an author of several studies that have been commissioned by the latter as well as by the ÖIF to support the policy claims of Sebastian Kurz's anti-Islam policies (Hafez 2020b), becomes the source of the secret agency's assessment. Their publications serve as evidence for the policy claims to argue that 'the word "Islamophobia" is used by members of the Muslim Brotherhood as a combat term (*Kampfbegriff*) in order to cast Muslims in the role of victims and thus influence public opinion' (Hafez 2020b). Rather than viewing the critique of Islamophobia as a means of public deliberation and part of a political debate in the public sphere, criticising

Islamophobia becomes a tool to 'divide the society' (ibid.). The file of the intelligence agency further continuous:

> Islamophobia thus turns out to be a combat term that is consistently used to deflect criticism of Islam or of problems and human rights violations within Muslim communities and to label them as 'anti-Muslim racism'. As a result, critics . . . and other serious scholars and journalists are denounced as 'Islamophobic' in the 2016 European Islamophobia Report, putting them in the same corner as right-wing populists, right-wing radicals, and racists. (ibid.)

Although the raid was later deemed illegal by the Higher Court of Graz and thus human rights violations were rather to be located with the Austrian state authorities, the intelligence service depicts those who write about Islamophobia as the enemy that seeks to deflect criticism from Islam as well as from Muslims, who violate human rights. And more than that, the Regional Court of Graz (Landesgericht Graz), which had allowed the raid in the first place, issued a decision that upheld the investigation against me, taking up the arguments of the intelligence service, saying that

> activities in the preparation of the so-called Islamophobia Report and his activity with the Bridge Initiative at Georgetown University is intended to disseminate the fighting term 'Islamophobia' with the goal of preventing any critical engagement with Islam as a religion . . . in order to establish an Islamic state . . . (Landesgericht Graz 2022: 2)

This shows the far-reaching impact of the intelligence service's work, which I read either as a projection of the Austrian government's own violations of human rights onto Muslims or at least as a deliberate ignorance of all the court rulings that have rescinded the many violations of law by the Austrian government in restricting Austrian Muslims' freedom of religion and freedom of association.

Conclusion

In this article, I showed, how 'political Islam' was framed by think tanks, scholars, politicians, government officials and intelligence agencies as a problem, and how several ÖVP-led governments were thus able to restrict the religious freedom of Muslims. Several laws and political measures were implemented to allegedly fight 'political Islam' and were later overturned by regional courts as well as the Constitutional Court for clashing with the constitution. The empirical examples show that the proclaimed fight against 'political Islam' was used to legitimise the constraint of religious freedom, be it the wearing of the hijab or the running of mosques. Finally, not only were Muslim civil societies targeted, but also the critique of the policies described here was criminalised, especially the problematisation of Islamophobia. Especially I, as an outspoken and critical scholar of Islamophobia Studies, have been targeted by the intelligence service, being a suspect of terrorism inter alia for talking about Islamophobia and criticising those who have enabled these measures.

The measures taken by the ÖVP-led governments under Sebastian Kurz reveal an ideological focus against Muslim visibility and religious praxis, as the ban of the hijab and the closing of mosques show. And the Austrian intelligence service's measures reveal the expansion of countering violent extremism programmes to countering non-violent extremism. It is an eminent example of how the terror-industrial complex does not target violence but thought, not militancy, but indeed ideas like the critique of Islamophobia that aims at creating more equality. This is an example of the trend of expanding the notion of 'countering violent extremism' to 'countering non-violent extremism' that has ultimately widened the field of intervention by the state. By curtailing not only religious freedom, but also freedom of speech and academic freedom in the course of criminalising Islamophobia Studies, this reconfirms two observations made by Rana: (1) this War on Terror is so massively expanded that it becomes a war with no end, and (2) this racial capitalism or racial infrastructure reproduces structural violence to pre-empt the threat of terror and constantly reconfirms itself, while in fact questioning several basic human rights to those post-colonial subaltern subjects, who are not seen as fully human and who are thus denied specific rights that are guaranteed for the dominant parts of the society. Critique is interpreted as an act of terrorism. Finally, the Appellate Court of Graz refuted this argument and decided on 4 January 2023 that Islamophobia Studies is no act of terrorism, ending the investigation and closing the case. But still, the state prosecutor and the intelligence agency seem unimpressed by many of the decisions of the Appellate Court and continue with their efforts.

References

16 St 52/19t, Investigation Files of the State Prosecutor of Graz, ON 32, 31 March 2021.

16 St 52/19t, Investigation Files of the State Prosecutor of Graz, ON 1144, 19 May 2021.

Bock, F., G. Heidegger, G. Krammer, T. Sill and C. Smekal (2020), 'Liveticker: Wie sich Kurz und Kogler Präsentieren', *Österreichischer Rundfunk*, 2 January, <https://orf.at/live/5076-Wie-sich-Kurz-und-Kogler-praesentierten-/> (last accessed 29 November 2020).

Bridge Initiative Team (2020a), 'Factsheet: Lorenzo Vidino', *Georgetown University Initiative*, 22 April, <https://bridge.georgetown.edu/research/factsheet-lorenzo-vidino/> (last accessed 29 November 2020).

Bridge Initiative Team (2020b), 'Factsheet: Heiko Heinisch', *Georgetown University Initiative*, 3 March, <https://bridge.georgetown.edu/research/factsheet-heiko-heinisch/> (last accessed 29 November 2020).

Bundesamt für Verfassungsschutz und Terrorismusbekämpfung (2010), <https://www.dsn.gv.at/501/files/VSB/Verfassungsschutzbericht_2010_Berichtszeitraum_2009.pdf> (last accessed 15 April 2022).

Bundeskanzleramt (2020), 'Kultusministerin Raab: Schließung von radikaler Moschee und Verein nach dem islamistischen Terroranschlag in Wien angeordnet', 6 November, <www.bundeskanzleramt.gv.at/bundeskanzleramt/nachrichten-der-bundesregierung/2020/kultusministerin-raab-schliessung-von-radikaler-moschee-und-verein-nach-dem-islamistischen-terroranschlag-in-wien-angeordnet.html> (last accessed 15 April 2021).

Bundesministerium für Inneres (2019), 'Verfassungsschutzbericht 2018', <www.dsn.gv.at/501/files/VSB/Verfassungsschutzbericht_2018.pdf> (last accessed 15 April 2021).

Der Standard (2018), 'Gudenus will Gesetz gegen politischen Islam bis Mitte 2019', 16 December, <https://mobil.derstandard.at/2000094068620/Gudenus-will-Gesetz-gegen-politischen-Islam-bis-Mitte-2019> (last accessed 5 September 2019).

Fadil, N., F. Ragazzi and M. de Koning (eds) (2019), *Radicalization in Belgium and the Netherlands: Critical Perspectives on Violence and Security*, London: Bloomsbury Publishing.

Gaigg, V. and C. Schmidt (2020), 'Antiterrorpaket: Neuer Straftatbestand zielt auf religiöse extremistische Verbindungen ab', *Der Standard*, 16 December, <www.derstandard.at/story/2000122537911/ministerrat-will-umstrittenes-anti-terror-paket-beschliessen> (last accessed 29 December 2020).

Gigler, C. and M. Jungwirth (2018), 'Regierung überprüft 61 Imame und schließt sieben Moscheen', *Kleine Zeitung*, 8 June, <https://www.kleinezeitung.at/politik/

innenpolitik/5442906/Jetzt-live_Regierung-plant-Ausweisung-von-40-Imamen-und> (last accessed 5 September 2019).

Goldstein, B. and A. Meyer (2008), 'Legal Jihad: How Islamist Lawfare Tactics Are Targeting Free Speech', *ILSA Journal of International & Comparative Law*, 15, 395, <https://ikhwaninfowhoswhoen.data.blog/page/4/> (last accessed 5 September 2019).

Hafez, F. (2018), 'Islamophobia in Austria: National Report 2017', in E. Bayraklı and F. Hafez (eds), *European Islamophobia Report 2017*, Istanbul: SETA, pp. 27–66.

Hafez, F. (2019a), 'Muslim Civil Society under Attack: The European Foundation for Democracy's Role in Defaming and Delegitimizing Muslim Civil Society', in J. Esposito and D. Iner (eds), *Islamophobia and Radicalization Breeding Intolerance and Violence*, Basingstoke: Palgrave Macmillan, pp. 117–37.

Hafez, F. (2019b), 'Islamophobia in Austria: National Report 2018', in E. Bayraklı and F. Hafez (eds), *European Islamophobia Report 2018*, Istanbul: SETA, pp. 87–126.

Hafez, F. (2019c), 'Official Islam as a Threat? Paradigm Shift in Austria's Security Politics', *SETA Perspectives*, 56, 1–5.

Hafez, F. (2019d), 'From Jewification to Islamization: Political Anti-Semitism and Islamophobia in Austrian Politics Then and Now', *ReOrient*, 4: 2, 197–220.

Hafez, F. (2020a), 'Islamophobia in Austria: National Report 2019', in E. Bayraklı and F. Hafez (eds), *European Islamophobia Report 2019*, Istanbul: SETA, pp. 79–114.

Hafez, F. (2020b), 'Rassismus im Bildungswesen: Zur Disziplinierung des muslimischen "Anderen" im Bildungswesen am Beispiel des Diskurses zu islamischen Kindergärten in Österreich', in M. Oberlechner, R. Heinisch and P. Duval (eds), *Nationalpopulismus bildet? Lehren für Unterricht und Bildung*, Frankfurt am Main: Wochenschau Verlag, pp. 100–22.

Hafez, F. (2021a), 'Islamophobia in Austria: National Report 2020', in E. Bayraklı and F. Hafez (eds), *European Islamophobia Report 2020*, Istanbul: LWI.

Hafez, F. (2021b), 'Why Is Europe on a Witch Hunt against "Political Islam"?', *Middle East Eye*, 25 May, <https://www.middleeasteye.net/opinion/europe-islamophobia-witch-hunt-against-political-islam> (last accessed 15 April 2021).

Hafez, F. (2022), 'Criminalizing Muslim Agency in Europe: The Case of "Political Islam" in Austria, Germany, and France', *French Cultural Studies*, 34: 3, 1–16.

Hafez, F. (2023), 'Das Dispositiv "Politischer Islam". Eine Fallanalyse aus der österreichischen Politik', *Frankfurter Zeitschrift für islamisch-theologische Studien*, pp. 121–42.

Hafez, F. and R. Heinisch (2018), 'Breaking with Austrian Consociationalism: How the Rise of Rightwing Populism and Party Competition Have Changed Austria's Islam Politics', *Politics and Religion*, 11: 3, 649–78.

Kronen Zeitung (2018a), 'Politischer Islam Darf Bürger Nicht Gefährden', 1 October, <https://www.krone.at/1780687> (last accessed 5 September 2019).

Kronen Zeitung (2018b), 'ÖVP & FPÖ fixieren Kopftuchverbbot in Kindergärten', 4 April, <http://www.krone.at/1684440> (last accessed 5 September 2019).

Kronen Zeitung (2020), 'Dokumentationsstelle nimmt Extremismus ins Visier', 15 July, <https://www.krone.at/2192166> (last accessed 29 November 2020).

Kundnani, A. and B. Hayes (2018), *The Globalisation of Countering Violent Extremism Policies: Undermining Human Rights, Instrumentalising Civil Society*, Amsterdam: The Transnational Institute.

Landesgericht Graz (2022), Beschluss (Decision), 22 HR 44/20x, 6 April 2022.

Langer, A. (2020), '"Judaism Is Not a Religion, but a Political Organization": German Jews under Suspicion in the Age of Enlightenment and Parallels to Contemporary Islamophobic Discourses', in F. Hafez (ed), *Islamophobia Studies Yearbook*, Vol. 11, 91–110.

LVT ST 2409/2019, 8 April 2021.

Meier, C. (2021), 'Projekt gesellschaftliche Umgestaltung', *FAZ*, 11 February, <https://www.faz.net/aktuell/feuilleton/debatten/lorenzo-vidino-ueber-den-politischen-islam-in-deutschland-17183411.html> (last accessed 15 February 2021).

Ministry of Education, Science and Research, 'Rebellion (Neo)Salafismus – Umgang mit Jugendlichen, die mit extremistischen Ideologien sympathisieren', <www.schulpsychologie.at/fileadmin/upload/persoenlichkeit_gemeinschaft/Rebellion_Neo-Salafismus_.pdf> (last accessed 15 February 2021).

Musolff, A. (2007), 'What Role Do Metaphors Play in Racial Prejudice? The Function of Antisemitic Imagery in Hitler's Mein Kampf', *Patterns of Prejudice*, 41: 1, 21–43.

Naji, N. and D. Schildknecht (2021), 'Securing Swiss Futurity: The Gefährder Figure and Switzerland's Counterterrorism Regime', *Social Sciences*, 10: 12, 1–16.

Österreichischer Integrationsfonds (2018a), 'ÖIF-Diskussion zu Islam in Europa: "Muslime müssen in Europa geltende Werte und Gesetze leben"', 23 January, <https://www.ots.at/presseaussendung/OTS_20180123_OTS0166/oeif-diskussion-zu-islam-in-europa-muslime-muessen-in-europa-geltende-werte-und-gesetze-leben> (last accessed 5 September 2019).

Österreichischer Integrationsfonds (2018b), '17. Sitzung des Integrationsbeirats: Schwerpunkt Arbeitsmarktintegration und politischer Politischer Islam in Österreich', 30 November, <https://www.integrationsfonds.at/newsbeitrag/17-sitzung-des-integrationsbeirats-schwerpunkt-arbeitsmarktintegration-und-politischer-islam-in-oesterreich_3857/> (last accessed 5 September 2019).

Österreichischer Integrationsfonds (2020), 'Bruckner: Berechtigte Religionskritik und Antimuslimische Haltungen Nicht Vermischen', 5 February, <https://

www.integrationsfonds.at/newsbeitrag/podiumsgespraech-bruckner-5144>
(last accessed 29 November 2020).

Österreichischer Rundfunk (2019a), 'Offenbar Beobachtungsstelle Gegen Extremismus Geplant', 12 January, <https://orf.at/stories/3107424/> (last accessed 15
November 2020).

Österreichischer Rundfunk (2019b), 'Gericht: Moscheenschließung rechtswidrig',
14 February, <https://wien.orf.at/v2/news/stories/2964549/> (last accessed 15
November 2020).

Pándi, C. (2018), 'Strache will jetzt Kopftuchverbot in Kindergärten', *Kronen Zeitung*,
31 March, <http://www.krone.at/1682481> (last accessed 5 September 2019).

Rachbauer, S. (2021), 'Nach Terroranschlag geschlossene Moschee in Meidling
sperrt wieder auf', *Kurier*, 10 April, <https://kurier.at/chronik/wien/nach-
terroranschlag-geschlossene-moschee-in-meidling-sperrt-wieder-auf/401347205>
(last accessed 15 April 2021).

Ragazzi, F. (2022), 'Counter-radicalization, Islam and Laïcité: Policed Multiculturalism
in France's Banlieues', *Ethnic and Racial Studies*, 42: 9, 1–21.

Rana, J. (2016), 'The Racial Infrastructure of the Terror-industrial Complex', *Social
Text*, 34: 4, 111–38.

Ranftler, J. (2021), 'Plattform für eine menschliche Asylpolitik', <https://www.
parlament.gv.at/PAKT/VHG/XXVII/SNME/SNME_36398/imfname_
879344.pdf> (last accessed 15 April 2021).

Rao, M. (2011), 'Love Jihad and Demographic Fears', *Indian Journal of Gender Studies*,
18: 3, 425–30.

Renner, G. (2019), 'Ein DÖW für Islamisten! Oder: Wie die Regierung schnell
zurück zu ihrem Lieblingsthema kommt', *Kleine Zeitung*, 3 March, <https://
www.kleinezeitung.at/meinung/5588894/Beobachtungsstelle-neu_Ein-DOeW-
fuer-Islamisten-Oder_Wie-die> (last accessed 19 December 2019).

Sayyid, S. (2014), *Recalling the Caliphate: Decolonization and World Order*, London:
Hurst.

Siddiqui, U. (2021), 'Muslim Austrian Academic Shares Tale of Gunpoint Raid', *Al
Jazeera*, 4 March <https://www.aljazeera.com/news/2021/3/4/muslim-professor-
reveals-raid-in-austria> (last accessed 15 April 2021).

The Local (2018), 'Turkey Furious as Austria Plans to Expel up to 60 Imams', 8
June, <https://www.thelocal.at/20180608/austria-will-expel-several-foreign-
funded-imams-and-shut-seven-mosques-chancellor-says/> (last accessed 15
April 2021).

The Local (2020), 'Police in Austria Raid Dozens of "Islamist-linked" Addresses',
9 November, <www.thelocal.at/20201109/police-in-austria-raid-dozens-of-islamist-
linked-addresses/> (last accessed 15 April 2021).

Verfassungsgerichtshof Österreich (2020), 'Verhüllungsverbot an Volksschulen ist verfassungswidrig', 11 December, <https://www.vfgh.gv.at/medien/Verhuellungs-verbot_an_Volksschulen_ist_verfassungswid.de.php> (last accessed 15 April 2021).

Vidino, L. (2017), 'The Muslim Brotherhood in Austria', August 2017, Vienna.

Walker, R. (2021), *The Emergence of 'Extremism' Exposing the Violent Discourse and Language of 'Radicalisation'*, London: Bloomsbury Publishing.

Wiener Zeitung (2020), 'Job Advertisement for the Board of the Documentation Centre for Political Islam', 16 July, <https://www.wienerzeitung.at/amtsblatt/aktuelle_ausgabe/artikel/?id=4409041> (last accessed 29 November 2020).

Wiener Zeitung (n.d.), 'Zusammen. Für unser Österreich. Regierungsprogramm 2017–2022', <https://www.wienerzeitung.at/_em_daten/_wzo/2017/12/16/17 1216_1614_regierungsprogramm.pdf> (last accessed 15 April 2021).

Winter, F. (2021), 'Muslimbrüder, immer und überall? Die Dokumentationsstelle Politischer Islam und eine erste Studie', *Der Standard*, 14 January, <https://www.derstandard.at/story/2000122867610/muslimbrueder-immer-und-ueberall> (last accessed 15 April 2021).

Wolf, F. (2020), 'Vorwort', <https://www.integrationsfonds.at/fileadmin/user_upload/OeIF_Persp2020_PolitischerIslam.pdf> (last accessed 15 April 2021).

5

WILL THE REAL JIHADI PLEASE STAND UP? ON 'JIHADISM' AS A CONCEPTUAL WEAPON

*Darryl Li**

In 2018, the commandant of the US Marine Corps, General Robert Neller, was speaking at a Pentagon press briefing. A reporter asked about the situation in Afghanistan – where the US was locked at the time in both combat and peace talks with the Taliban movement. The conversation was relatively staid until Neller, in a pique of frustration, berated the Taliban for presenting themselves as mujahidin – those engaged in jihad. His remarks are worth considering at length:

> The terrorists call themselves, you know, they're the freedom fighters, they're the *mujadeen* [*sic*]. They're not. They're criminals. I think the Arabic word is *takfiri* [*sic*]. They're apostates. They hide behind Islam. They sell drugs. They kill innocent people. That's not what Islam is. The Afghan army and the American – we're, we're the mujadeen! *We're* the mujadeen. That's the message.[1]

* Portions of this chapter originally appeared in 'A Jihadism Anti-Primer', *Middle East Report*, autumn 2015, and are reprinted courtesy of the Middle East Research and Information Project.
[1] See, 'Marine Corps Commandant: "We Are the Mujahideen" in Afghanistan', C-Span.org. Available at <https://www.c-span.org/video/?c4727755/marine-corps-commandant-we-mujahideen-afghanistan> (last accessed 3 February 2023).

'That's not what Islam is.' Neller's outburst, speaking so presumptuously yet passionately on behalf of Islam, attracted its fair share of derision on social media. One Twitter user, ever mindful of divine omnipotence, declared, 'Only allah [*sic*] could give me this laugh.' Another quipped, 'Daʻwah [Islamic proselytising] by a White Christian you love to see it.' Others of course noticed the resonances with debates over cultural appropriation ('White folk really wanna try every costume'). One simply replied with an image from the ending of the Hollywood film *Rambo III*: the sentence 'THIS FILM IS DEDICATED TO THE BRAVE MUJAHIDEEN FIGHTERS OF AFGHANISTAN' imposed over a desolate war-torn landscape. This was a cheeky reminder of how the term mujahidin gained prominence in Western media discourse through US support and romanticisation of Afghans in their jihad against the Soviet Union in the 1980s.

Neller's comments may have tickled some, but they also provide an excellent occasion to reconsider one of the fundamental terms structuring public debates throughout many parts of the world in recent decades: jihadism. In Islamic jurisprudence (*fiqh*), jihad is a technical term referring to certain forms of armed struggle that are grounded in the strictures of the faith. The term is thus widely glossed as 'holy war' in the West. People who identify as Muslim,

Figure 5.1 General Robert Neller, one of the real mujahidin.
Source: Image in the public domain.

whether believers or not, have always and will always debate the proper under-standings of jihad. These debates are not the topic of this chapter. Instead, we will consider jihad*ism*, a concept that has become more prominent since the 1990s, whose practitioners are often labelled not as mujahidin – the emic term embraced by believers – but rather as jihadis or jihadists.[2]

During the quarter-century when the global power of the US was at its zenith, jihadism was glossed as the primary challenge to that order. From the aftermath of the Soviet defeat in Afghanistan through the 9/11 attacks to the advent of the self-declared Islamic State in Syria and Iraq, or ISIS, the spectre of mobile Muslim multitudes wreaking global havoc gave rise to a vast body of commentary. Much of this work is empirically or conceptually flawed, whether due to anti-Muslim animus, conceptual fealty to the national security state, or both. Many critical challenges to discourses on jihadism, however necessary and salutary, have also unwittingly contributed to the stul-tifying nature of these debates. This chapter provides a brief overview of the most common arguments and their shortcomings, while also drawing atten-tion to underexamined problems inherent in the jihadism concept. While it is undeniable that a very broad swathe of actors in the world understand and describe the violence they enact in terms of jihad, that by itself does not mean that jihad*ism* is a useful category for understanding these phenomena. This chapter argues that the jihadism concept is both analytically unhelpful and materially harmful in its deployments. No analysis of contemporary jihad practices can proceed without also critically interrogating the demands for and demands on such commentary.[3]

Jihadism – again, I am referring here to a concept, rather than any specific movement or set of actors – developed from longer-running discourses around

---

[2] In modern Arabic, *jihādī* serves as a masculine adjective for things pertaining to jihad; as a noun for a person (jihadist), it usually appears either in translation from Western languages or as pejorative. Similarly, the feminine noun *al-jihādiyya*, used for 'jihadism', is a neologism adopted from Western discourses. In other languages that use many Arabic-origin terms, a similar distinction exists. In modern Turkish, for instance, *mücahit* is positive, while *cihatçı* insinuates an instrumental misuse of jihad. My thanks to Ahmet Yusuf Özdemir and Rebecca Bryant for this point.

[3] Most important in this regard is Talal Asad's linking of Western horror and fascination at suicide bombing to deeper assumptions in modern liberal forms of subjectivity (Asad 2007).

'international terrorism' that had been circulating since at least the 1960s.[4] The terrorism concept has been widely criticised as a tool for depoliticising non-state actors, from leftist revolutionary movements onward (Zoller 2021; Erlenbusch-Anderson 2018; Stampnitzky 2013). Jihadism represented a distinctive evolution in terrorism discourse, emerging in a very different context. The collapse of the Soviet Union in the early 1990s had heralded a Western liberal triumphalism celebrating the spread (or, more grandly, the 'globalisation') of neo-liberal capitalism. Whereas international terrorism was largely seen as a by-product of existing interstate dynamics – between Cold War superpowers or Israel and Arab states – this 'end of history' promised the evaporation of any serious alternatives and, consequently, of real political conflicts.

As the most prominent form of violent dissensus to the post-Cold War order, jihadism therefore could only be understood as anti-political fanaticism. This sense of irrationality was further compounded by both liberal and left ideologies of secularism and their respective notions of how politics and religion are (or should be) strictly separated categories. Finally, the transnational character of some jihad mobilisations – with Muslim volunteers travelling to war zones such as Afghanistan, Bosnia, Syria and Somalia without the direction or control of any state – reinforced the notion that jihadists rejected the nation-state form altogether (needless to say, no such assumption is made about Western volunteers fighting in Ukraine these days). In the post-Cold War context, this combination of violence, religion and transnational mobility made jihadism appear as a unique threat to the international order. Such jihadists were imagined as opposed to anything that was not them – especially the liberal world order – and therefore an enemy to all, a universal enemy.[5]

As noted above, the forms of jihad attracting the most notoriety have been those carried out by people operating in reaction to and against the diktats of the US-dominated world order. At the same time, what makes such jihads noteworthy and even terrifying in elite discourse cannot be disentangled from those elites' own assumptions and interests. Any critical assessment of

---

[4] There was, of course, an earlier wave of moral panic over terrorism, usually of the anarchist variety, in the late nineteenth and early twentieth centuries.

[5] At the same time, transnational jihad movements made universalist claims of their own (Li 2020).

jihadism as a concept must keep this interactional context in mind. Thus, this chapter proceeds to excavate the contours of the jihadism concept and the debates it has made possible.

Anything but the Real Jihadi

The most important thing to understand about discourses on jihadism is the extent to which they are driven and shaped by anti-Muslim animus.[6] This animus exerts an immensely powerful gravitational pull on nearly all discourse about contemporary jihad practices. It exceeds individual intent and cannot be ignored or simply bracketed in the belief that objective study of jihadism can be readily separated from racist propaganda. Even many good faith attempts to push back on anti-Muslim animus end up reinforcing some of its basic assumptions. The distortionary effect of anti-Muslim animus is often revealed in the kinds of disclaimers that accompany discourses on jihadism. Such disclaimers can serve as useful red flags for any sceptical or discerning reader.

There are four common ways of discussing jihadism that indirectly reveal the gravitational pull exerted upon them by anti-Muslim animus, some in more obvious ways than others.

Perhaps the most basic level of commentary on jihadism runs on the shock of discovery that jihadists are 'more civilised' or 'less Islamic' than expected. This includes highlighting as a noteworthy discovery the fact that jihadists are organised, care about money, know how to use computers, or play video games. Or, from the other side, that they may not be particularly familiar with Islamic textual traditions, that they fall in love, or consume narcotics. Setting the bar this low reveals far more about the expectations of their presumed audiences – namely, of being backwards fanatics – than about contemporary jihad practices. This banalising narrative serves both the state – which seeks to discredit the jihadists' self-presentation as superhuman idealists – and liberal critics, who point to impiety or lack of religious learning as proving that Islam as such is not the issue.

---

[6] Because Muslimness in different historical contexts has been understood as a confessional category, as nationality, or even as a racial group, formations of anti-Muslim animus – such as Orientalism, Islamophobia, anti-Muslim racism – also have different genealogies, whose mapping is beyond the scope of this chapter (Kumar 2021; Rana 2007; Said 1978).

Moving ever so slightly outward from this most basic level of commentary is another common disclaimer among specialists, namely the reassurance that 'understanding is not endorsing'. There is a curious performance of insisting that study of jihadism or making available media materials produced to support jihad does not make one an apologist or a proponent of 'moral equivalence' between state violence and jihad. The argument often goes that the study of jihadism is necessary because one must understand the enemy to better combat it. This skittishness about overly 'humanising' the enemy partially is a response to draconian laws that can criminalise anyone possessing or distributing jihad media materials. But this concern seems overblown when one speaks, for example, of white terrorism experts who seek to serve the state. Rather, this disclaimer is better understood as a kind of boundary maintenance reinforcing the false idea that the only choices on hand are apology for jihad or joining the fight against it. Needless to say, studies of Western state violence rarely carry such disclaimers – indeed, if there is any disclaimer it leans in the opposite direction of stressing that such violence is merely a deviation from an otherwise legitimate use of force.

A third form of argument especially common among liberal critics of the War on Terror insists that Muslims not be understood as a monolith. The 'not all Muslims are violent' trope animates much of the contemporary commentary on Muslim societies. Discussions of political groups fashioning themselves in Islamic terms, such as the Muslim Brotherhood in Egypt or the Justice and Development Party in Turkey, often include disclaimers that they should not be conflated with jihadism, whatever else one may say about them. There is also scholarship showing that even groups engaging in violence under the banner of jihad cannot all be lumped together – nationalist organisations such as Hamas and Hizbullah are distinguished from transnational groups like al-Qaʿida. In other words, not all Muslims are pious, not all pious Muslims are Islamists, not all Islamists are violent and not all violent Islamists are at war with the West (or other Muslims they dislike). Much of this work is salutary but there is one significant limitation to this approach when it comes to the question of jihadism: telling audiences who is *not* a jihadist is not particularly helpful for understanding jihadism on its own terms. Moreover, the 'not all Muslims' argument can all too easily play into the distinction between 'good' and 'bad' Muslims that states have long employed as an instrument of rule

(Mamdani 2004). It is much better at telling the state *which* Muslims not to torture or bomb than it is at arguing against those practices in the first place.

Fourth, the line of argumentation often taken among the staunchest critics of US imperialism tends to speak of jihadists as little more than as puppets of Washington. A more sophisticated variant of this argument is to highlight the role of US proxies like Saudi Arabia and Pakistan in stirring up jihadist energies. This 'Frankenstein theory of jihad' insists that the US and its allies can manufacture such groups but then somehow always loses control over them without ever really explaining how this happens (an even more conspiratorial argument is that the US continues to control such groups, which at least enjoys the virtue of consistency). Again, there is much truth to this approach: US state violence, to say nothing of the structural violence of global capitalism, is indeed a crucial part of the conditions that give rise to many of the groups demonised in the War on Terror. The House of Saud's role as a leading exporter of counterrevolution and the Pakistani military establishment's ruthlessness in pursuit of domestic and foreign policy goals are a matter of well-established record. But these claims of creation or control of jihadist groups tend to stretch the available evidence and essentially erase any autonomous agency for those groups. They do not challenge the demonisation of jihadism as backward violent fanaticism, but merely try to assign responsibility for it elsewhere. Politically, this narrative can bizarrely turn into a redirection of militarism rather than a rejection of it. If the US (or its proxies) created jihadism, then going to war against those groups (or against the proxy states that sponsor them) is arguably all the more justified to clean up its own mess.[7]

These four tendencies in commentary on jihadism are not all equal: some are more mindful of the problems of anti-Muslim animus than others, and some are more analytically or politically useful than others, but all are distorted by the gravitational pull of the anti-Muslim animus that hangs over all such conversations. Moreover, they all tend to take the concept of jihadism for granted. They may argue over who falls into that category or who is responsible

---

[7] One respected left-wing commentator on the region, Patrick Cockburn, has gone so far as to argue, 'The "war on terror" has failed because it did not target the jihadi movement as a whole and, above all, was not aimed at Saudi Arabia and Pakistan' (Cockburn 2014).

for creating it, but they avoid giving an account of it. That task has fallen to the community of self-described jihadism experts.

Behold the Real Jihadi: On Expert Cultures

Beyond the most common tropes in discussions of jihadism outlined abroad, there is a flourishing ecosystem of expertise on the matter that is fuelled by public interest and seeks to shape it. Even in its earlier Cold War iterations, terrorism expertise suffered from an intimate relationship with the national security state that left it without the autonomy needed to develop into a serious intellectual project.[8] In the War on Terror, the field has become even more complex and fractious, drawing together enterprising bloggers, established think tanks, private companies, state-backed research institutes and traditional universities. Against this backdrop, a more sophisticated, professionalised generation of specialists in jihadism has emerged. This newer cohort is more likely to have at least some relevant linguistic experience and may even dabble in critiques of Islamophobia to bolster its own credibility, although rarely in ways that openly challenge the racist fearmongering that provides much of the fuel for this ecosystem's existence. Indeed, the idea that terrorism expertise can defuse anti-Muslim animus simply through dispensing more enlightened knowledge is akin to trying to tame a voracious monster by feeding it a healthier diet.

At the broadest possible level, there have been two approaches to the study of jihadism as a theoretical puzzle. The first takes on Islam as a locus of explanation, while the second tends to favour other factors instead to the extent we can identify it as the 'not Islam' approach.[9] The terms of debate tend to reinforce the idea of Islam as a problem that one must argue either for or against, which ultimately leads to the trap of toxic authenticity that underlies debates on jihadism.

---

[8] As Lisa Stampnitzky has shown, the field has always been structurally precarious and intensely aware of its shortcomings (Stampnitzky 2013). The influence of such experts as individuals should not be overstated; just as often they feel disrespected by the academy and ignored by policymakers (McMurtrie 2013).

[9] At times, this debate has mapped onto the intellectual rivalry and personal animosity between the two most prominent French scholars on the topic, Gilles Kepel and Olivier Roy (Nossiter 2016; Burgat [2016] 2020: 196–211).

From Jihadi Doctrine to Jihadi Culture

Writing on jihad that traces genealogies of Islamic scholarship often seeks to explain how bad Muslims belong to one particular doctrinal school or pietistic orientation but not others. This type of writing on jihad often strings together names like Ibn Taymiyya, Sayyid Quṭb, ʿAbdallah ʿAzzām and Osama bin Laden to get to 11 September 2001 with all the sophistication of explaining the Holocaust by skipping from Hobbes to Nietzsche to Hitler. The doctrinal category receiving the most attention is the Salafi trend in Islam, which is often described as literalist, puritanical and ultraconservative. The focus on Salafis as bearers of violence is so strong that the terms 'Jihadi-Salafism' or 'Salafi-Jihadism' – with their fungibility being itself an alarming sign of the slipperiness at work – have become key concepts in this expert literature. The jihadism discourse has updated the old racist canard 'not all Muslims are terrorists, but all terrorists are Muslim' by simply substituting the narrower 'Salafi' for 'Muslim'.

The Jihadi-Salafism concept originated among Western security commentators. It was never a term of self-designation before 9/11 and is rarely accepted as such even today (see Jaan Islam's chapter within this volume). The fundamental problem of this approach lies in its unsophisticated attempt to map doctrinal categories onto political ones. Three points are worth considering here. First, at the most obvious level, the historical correlation between doctrinal position and armed jihad seems weak at best. In the nineteenth century, Sufis frequently led anti-colonial jihads – Sufis from the same orders that today are celebrated (often by authoritarian regimes) as pacifist. At the same time, a great many Salafis worldwide are uninterested in organised politics of any kind, let alone armed action. Second, experts of course recognise that many Salafis are non-violent. Perhaps the most widely cited study on the topic introduced a typology of Salafis as quietist, political or violent (Wiktorowicz 2006). But setting up 'politics' and 'violence' as mutually exclusive basically treats (Western) state violence as normal while conflating all forms of non-state violence as deviant. For instance, a Salafi who happens to work as a police officer in a secular state is necessarily engaged in the work of violence but is not a 'violent Salafi' in the sense that the category is meant to convey; and Salafis in Kuwait are 'political' insofar as they participate in electoral politics while also being 'violent' in supporting jihads abroad against non-Muslim aggressors in Afghanistan and Bosnia-Herzegovina (Li 2020: 95). Third, and most important, even when Salafis engage in armed jihad, they do not necessarily share a single approach. Definitions of Salafi-Jihadism tend to highlight violence against Muslim rulers deemed apostates (arguably the most controversial definition of jihad from a *fiqh* perspective) or total rejection of the nation state.[10] Such partial definitions, however, may exclude self-identified Salafis who engaged in jihad such as the 'godfather of jihad', 'Abdallah 'Azzām (Hegghammer 2020, 302–3).[11]

The point is not that these doctrines are unimportant or ideological smokescreens for other social forces. Instead, ideas must be situated with respect to movements, organisations and structures to identify the elective affinities that may make one school or another associated with radicalism at specific points in time. It is impossible to write good intellectual history without good history in general, which is missing for the transregional migratory worlds in which many of these groups emerged.

Another variant of the 'Islam-focused' approach eschews any explanatory role for doctrinal texts and instead leans into practices observed among contemporary jihad groups, placing them under the label of 'jihadi culture'. This school compiles descriptive laundry lists of behaviours, from prayer to poetry. For experts who are primarily concerned with tactical aspects of how armed groups function, jihadi culture acts as a kind of residual category of everything else they cannot readily understand or process. In this sense, work on jihadi culture at its most benign simply acts as a guide to various references one encounters in media materials by jihad groups.

The problem, however, is that many of the practices identified as jihadi culture are not particular to jihad at all and are indeed widespread among Muslims in general. Images from jihad groups' media productions depicting

[10] Daniel Lav defines Salafi-Jihadis as those who support violence against ruling regimes in Muslim-majority countries (Lav 2012: 11); Shiraz Maher glosses Salafi-Jihadis as 'violent rejectionists' opposed to the state in general (Maher 2016: 11–12); Joas Wagemakers understands 'Jihadi-Salafis' as those endorsing violence against Muslim rulers who do not apply shari'a in full (Wagemakers 2016: 57).

[11] Perhaps the most sophisticated account of Salafis writing about jihad thus far, by Nathan French, refers to Salafi-Jihadis without attempting to define the category in political terms. Instead, French focuses on theodicy in Salafi thought that bear on diverse jihad efforts (French 2020).

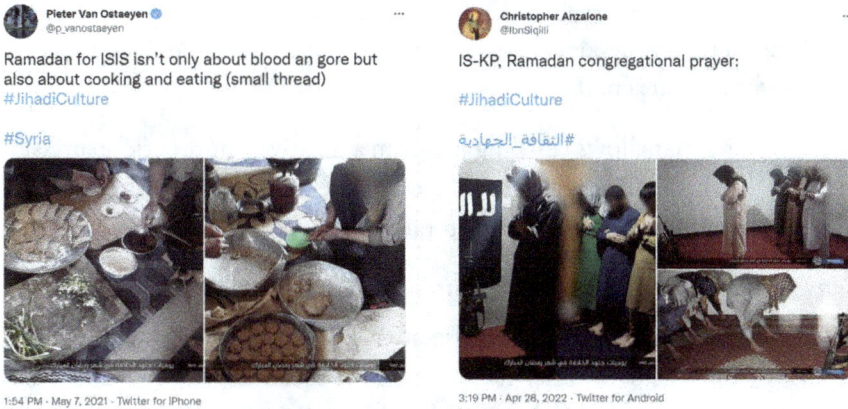

Figure 5.2 Tweets by prominent online jihadism experts presenting cuisine and prayer as instances of 'jihadi culture'.
Source: Image in the public domain.

cooking and even prayer have been reshared by jihadologists with the hashtag #jihadiculture or its variants (see Figure 5.2). While perhaps intended 'only' as tongue-in-cheek, such statements in a context of broader anti-Muslim animus ultimately reinforce the association of everyday Islamic religious and Muslim cultural practices with violence. Thus, jihadi culture not only lacks much conceptual utility – other than debunking caricatures of jihadists as insincere Muslims – it ultimately underwrites state logics of profiling.

As is so often the case, culturalism here ultimately reinscribes stale and harmful notions of Muslim essentialism, in two ways. First, while jihadi culture is defined as everything jihadists do that is not strictly necessary to military endeavours, many common non-military practices, such as playing football, merit barely a mention (Hegghammer 2017a). In other words, 'culture' appears only in things attributable to Islam and that therefore stand for alterity.[12] Second, the concept underwrites claims about Muslim authenticity that reflect unexamined assumptions of whiteness, allowing one progenitor of the concept to conclude, for example:

In the eyes of prospective recruits from a conservative religious background, jihadi groups can appear as culturally relatively authentic. This is in contrast

---

[12] An entirely separate matter, however, is how those engaged in jihad take up or critique notions of culture (*thaqāfa*) in their own praxis (French 2020: 32–3).

to other subcultures, such as the Ku Klux Klan or the skinhead movement, which, culturally speaking, represent complete innovations and sharp breaks from the mainstream. (Hegghammer 2017b, 200)

The reasoning that allows labelling jihadism a 'relatively authentic' expression of Islam but the Ku Klux Klan to be a 'complete innovation' in the history of whiteness is, unsurprisingly, assumed rather than explicated.

From Radicalisation to Radical Solipsism

The second major stream of expertise attempts to displace the pathology of jihadism from Islam to other factors, such as social deprivation and exclusion (Khosrokhavar [2015] 2017; Truong [2017] 2018). This approach has developed largely in the study of subjugated Muslim populations of Middle Eastern and African origin in Western Europe. If the doctrinal and cultural approaches are inheritors of traditions of Orientalist scholarship and colonial anthropology, the radicalisation school hails from sociological traditions originally developed to study the urban poor in the Global North.

The radicalisation approach has occasionally yielded some sound findings, mostly of a negative nature, like the apparent lack of a clear correlation between socio-economic status and jihad activity, or the diversity of motivations from humiliation and disaffection to positive desires to help others. Yet radicalisation, as critics have shown, nonetheless depoliticises jihad activism as consistently as rival Islam-focused approaches (Bounaga and Esmili 2020; Fadil et al. 2019; Sakhi 2018). This is unsurprising insofar as this work largely focuses on populations in the West, where organised jihad formations are smaller and less robust than in majority-Muslim societies. But in a prevailing context where the political goals and logics of certain groups are widely misrecognised or obscured under the label of 'terrorism', such an approach risks methodological atomisation, subsuming politics into the question of recruitment. Radicalisation literature tends to ask why people fight with little if any regard to what they may be fighting for.

Moreover, the factors identified in radicalisation studies are often shared across much broader swathes of the population, so they hardly explain why those specific individuals joined jihads as opposed to other armed groups or even state militaries. Political movements and apparatuses of violence of all stripes have drawn and incorporated atomised and traumatised individuals. Yet just as studying the individual pathways of US army recruits is not a substitute for understanding the politics of the US wars in Iraq and Afghanistan, the same is true of members of jihad formations such as the self-declared Islamic State in Iraq and Syria.

More sophisticated than the radicalisation school are approaches that seek to situate contemporary jihad as an instance of broader social phenomena shared throughout the world. They locate contemporary jihads in a shared world with Western modernity, rejecting any attempting to render such jihads as backwards or exotic, and thereby also reject jihadologists' desire to serve state security agendas. But instead of exoticising Muslim difference, such analysts risk subsuming the political content of contemporary jihads into a kind of Western solipsism: jihad is just a symptom of the same global phenomena 'we' all face. Two works in this vein are worthy of note, because they are among the most insightful theorisations of contemporary jihad but also demonstrate the limits of this approach.

Faisal Devji's *Landscapes of the Jihad* – perhaps the first text that attempted to make sense of al-Qaʿida with reference to social theory outside of the security studies field – argued for understanding contemporary jihad practices as instances of what he calls 'globalisation'. This allowed him to show, helpfully, that contemporary jihad groups often do not respect traditional hierarchies of Islamic authority. But calling al-Qaʿida globalised doesn't necessarily shed much light on al-Qaʿida or on globalisation. This is because globalisation is a loose concept here: it conjures endless chains of 'effects without causes'. The 9/11 attacks, Devji asserts without evidence, were not political because their authors could not possibly have predicted their consequences.[13] Instead, al-Qaʿida's jihad must be understood as 'ethical' action in the sense that it is undertaken purely for its own sake, a kind of nihilistic performance art.[14]

---

[13] Devji does not define ethics or politics, though he refers to 'the politics of control', 'the politics of instrumentality', 'the politics of intentionality' and 'politics' more or less interchangeably (Devji 2005: 2, 3, 7, 12, 14, 20).

[14] '[T]he attacks of 9/11, immaculately planned and executed though they were, lacked intentionality because Al-Qaeda could neither control nor even predict their global repercussions. Hence the actions of this jihad, while they are indeed meant to accomplish certain ends, have become more ethical than political in nature, since they have resigned control over their own effects, thus becoming gestures of duty or risk rather than acts of instrumentality properly speaking' (Devji 2005: 3–4).

The result is to abjure political action and historical context as much as the jihadologist's insistence on doctrine, using 'globalisation' rather than 'Islam' as the all-explaining category.[15]

In a similar vein, Suzanne Schneider's analysis of ISIS updates Devji by insisting that jihadism is a product of neo-liberalism rather than globalisation. Here, ISIS is presented as a mirror image of right-wing populism in the West. While this comparison is not devoid of merit, the invocation of neo-liberalism does not come with any attempt to rigorously situate jihad formations in an analysis of political economy or questions of capitalism. Neo-liberalism is manifested, for instance, in the fact that ISIS publishes reports with charts and graphs – a point that, bizarrely, seems to presume that such practices never existed before neo-liberal capitalism. The argument is made in some jest ('the Islamic State will have you know it is not slacking on its record-keeping') (Schneider 2021: 185), but as with the jihadi culture crowd, humour also reveals the deeper logic at work: concepts like neo-liberalism, capitalism or modernity ultimately blur together in rehashing the truism that ISIS is not medieval. Like Devji, Schneider insists on the modernity of jihadism while positing that modernity as pathological, nihilistic, antipolitical – but with the added twist that the pathology is one shared by the West. One can raise questions about this kind of analytical levelling, but the bigger problem is that the effects of such arguments never fall on both sides with equal weight. To diagnose right-wing populism in the West as pathological for readers who must contend with it as a force in electoral politics in their own societies is altogether different from imposing the same assessment on groups like ISIS, whose pathology was always taken as self-evident.

Reducing jihadism to a symptom of watchwords such as modernity, globalisation and neo-liberalism risks stretching those categories so far as to become virtually meaningless. Without developing some specificity to these concepts by connecting them with rigorous study of the struggles and dilemmas contemporary jihad formations actually face, the arguments remain speculative at best, tautological at worst: jihadism is modern, globalised

[15] The Mauritanian scholar and former diplomat Mohammad-Mahmoud Ould Mohamedou similarly foregrounds questions of globalisation but without jettisoning the analysis of strategic interaction and political commitment (Ould Mohamedou 2007, 2017).

and neo-liberal in a world where everything is. These approaches reject the racialised exceptionalism that drives much of the commentary on jihad, but they share a refusal to understand contemporary jihad formations as political projects on their own terms.

'We're the real mujadeen'; Or, There is No Real Jihadi

At this point, it may be helpful to return to the story that opened this chapter, namely the declaration by an American general that the 'real mujadeen' in Afghanistan were the US military and the forces of Washington's client regime in Kabul. As noted above, the tirade raised eyebrows and elicited belly laughs. But rather than pile on to the mockery, we can use the statement as a diagnostic of how the jihadism concept works as an instrument of secular power.

It is important to note that Neller was speaking as a relatively liberal technocratic warrior on terror. Unlike officers who embrace fully the idea of Islam as the enemy, Neller recognised the Taliban as having politics – he referred to 'their agenda' as a matter of fact, recognising the existence of a political dispute. Note also that the chest-thumping appeal at the end was aimed – however clumsily – at driving a wedge between the Taliban rank and file and their leadership, which he claims is off living in luxury somewhere outside the country. Most likely he was referring to the Taliban political office in Doha, Qatar, which is not too far from the al-'Udeid US military base. This was also not typical War on Terror logic, instead recognising the Taliban as people with interests, both individual and collective.

All this being said, the good general's enthusiasm helpfully reveals the assumptions behind so much of the discussion around jihadism. Conventional wisdom labels the Taliban as jihadists, as if they are the only Afghans engaged in jihad. But that reading would glide over the context of Afghan politics. Let us recall that although the Taliban style themselves as the Islamic Emirate of Afghanistan, the regime they defeated in 2021 was the Islamic Republic of Afghanistan. Both claimed the mantle of fighting for Islam. And this was no mere lip service – the regime included many of the mujahidin warlords who fought against the Soviet Union in the 1980s. A discourse that sets up the Taliban alone as jihadists erases arguably some of the best-known people to claim the title of mujahidin in recent decades.

Neller, to his credit, does not parrot the standard discourse. Indeed, he inverts it and thereby pushes it to its logical limits. In Talal Asad's influential articulation, secularism as an exercise of power does not merely delineate the boundaries of religious categories, but inevitably redefines their content (Asad 2003). Neller does not present himself as a Muslim believer, yet he is comfortable holding forth on which invocations of jihad are authoritative and which are not. And he does so without saying that he is doing so, exercising a power that is taken for granted. In declaring that the Afghan government and their US allies are 'the real mujahdeen [*sic*]', Neller is casting the Afghan government as mujahidin and the Taliban as mere jihadists, or pretenders who distort the faith. Neller even calls the Taliban 'apostates', which he mistakenly renders using the Arabic term *takfiri* (an apostate in the technical sense of someone repudiating Islam is a *murtadd*). *Takfiri* is a pejorative term for those who overzealously or unjustifiably declare others to be unbelievers. As some critics pointed out, if anyone was acting like a *takfiri* here, it was Neller.

The paradoxical exercise of secular power that Neller put on display is the same enacted by the category of jihadism. Among Muslim believers, the term jihad connotes religiously sanctioned forms of struggle, from armed combat to internal purification, and believers vigorously contest its proper usages. But constructing jihadism as an ideology, movement or analytical category perniciously weighs in on debates among believers while claiming the mantle of secular social science. Unless one defines jihadism to mean anything Muslims call jihad, then it inevitably requires making choices about which invocations of jihad count as jihadism. This choice produces a residual category of 'non-jihadist jihads' that can only ever be undertheorised. Depending on one's definition of jihadism, non-jihadist jihads include a great many historically significant episodes, such as the Ottoman Empire's participation in World War I and its call on Muslims in the French and British imperial armies to revolt; the discourse of both sides in the 1980–8 Iran–Iraq war; and even groups seeking to eject foreign occupiers and achieve national self-determination, such as Hamas and Hizbullah.

A boilerplate disclaimer that jihadism is not widely supported among Muslims worldwide does not address this problem, and not only because it is wilfully blind to the fact that most non-Muslim audiences will not take on board such caveats. Rather, what is striking here is that the enormous body of commentary on jihadism necessarily focuses on and elevates the invocations of jihad that are most controversial among Muslims, while putting aside all the forms of jihad that are more widely supported. The logic that purports to distinguish jihad from jihadism – or, by implication, authentic from inauthentic forms of Islam – tends to conveniently map this distinction onto whatever is consistent with Western ruling consensus. It is another version of the trap of toxic authenticity whereby Muslims are subjected to unending and insatiable demands to condemn violence in order to prove their loyalty.

The concept of jihadism thus sheds little light on contemporary jihad practices, but it usefully reveals how empire thinks, how it structures relations of compliance and enmity. And after all, if the US military can decide which forms of jihad count as jihadism, then claiming the label for themselves is only the next logical step. And this is ultimately the logic of universalism at work. It's not simply about declaring who is friend and who is enemy, but about being able to make that decision on behalf of others. This is why the US can construct a concept such as 'foreign fighters' to describe those who travel to Iraq or Afghanistan for jihad against the US (Li 2010) – while unself-consciously coding their own militarised presence in these countries as 'international' rather than 'foreign'.

References

Asad, T. (2003), *Formations of the Secular: Christianity, Islam, Modernity*, Stanford: Stanford University Press.

Asad, T. (2007), *On Suicide Bombing*, New York: Columbia University Press.

Bounaga, A. and H. Esmili (2020), 'War by Other Means: Fighting "Radicalization" in France (2014–2019)', *Islamophobia Studies Journal*, 5: 2, 199–209.

Burgat, F. (2020 [2016]), *Understanding Political Islam*, trans. Thomas Hill, Manchester: Manchester University Press.

Cockburn, P. (2014), 'Al-Qaʿida, the Second Act: Why the Global "War on Terror" Went Wrong', *The Independent*, 18 March.

Devji, F. (2005), *Landscapes of the Jihad: Militancy, Morality, Modernity*, Ithaca, NY: Cornell University Press.

Erlenbusch-Anderson, V. (2018), *Genealogies of Terrorism: Revolution, State Violence, Empire*, New York: Columbia University Press.

Fadil, N., M. de Konig and F. Ragazzi (eds) (2019), *Radicalization in Belgium and the Netherlands – Critical Perspectives on Violence and Security*, London: Bloomsbury.

French, N. S. (2020), *And God Knows the Martyrs: Martyrdom and Violence in Jihadi-Salafism*, New York: Oxford University Press.

Hegghammer, T. (2017a), 'Introduction: What Is Jihadi Culture and Why Should We Study It?', in T. Hegghammer (ed.), *Jihadi Culture: The Art and Social Practices of Militant Islamists*, Cambridge: Cambridge University Press, pp. 1–21.

Hegghammer, T. (2017b), 'Non-military Practices in Jihadi Groups', in T. Hegghammer (ed.), *Jihadi Culture: The Art and Social Practices of Militant Islamists*, Cambridge: Cambridge University Press, pp. 171–201.

Hegghammer, T. (2020), *The Caravan: Abdallah Azzam and the Rise of Global Jihad*, Cambridge: Cambridge University Press.

Khosrokhavar, F. (2017 [2015]), *Radicalization: Why Some People Choose the Path of Violence*, trans. Jane Marie Todd, New York: The New Press.

Kumar, D. (2021), *Islamophobia and the Politics of Empire*, 2nd edn, New York: Verso.

Lav, D. (2012), *Radical Islam and the Revival of Medieval Theology*, Cambridge: Cambridge University Press.

Li, D. (2010), 'A Universal Enemy? "Foreign Fighters" and Legal Regimes of Exclusion and Exemption Under the "Global War on Terror"', *Columbia Human Rights Law Review*, 42: 2, 355–428.

Li, D. (2020), *The Universal Enemy: Jihad, Empire, and the Challenge of Solidarity*, Stanford: Stanford University Press.

Maher, S. (2016), *Salafi-Jihadism: The History of an Idea*, London: Hurst.

Mamdani, M. (2004), *Good Muslim, Bad Muslim: America, the Cold War, and the Roots of Terror*, New York: Pantheon.

McMurtrie, B. (2013), 'Terrorism Experts Are Sought by the Public but Not by Academe', *Chronicle of Higher Education*, 24 June.

Nossiter, A. (2016), '"That Ignoramus": 2 French Scholars of Radical Islam Turn Bitter Rivals', *New York Times*, 13 July.

Ould Mohamedou, M.-M. (2007), *Understanding Al Qaeda: The Transformation of War*, London: Pluto Press.

Ould Mohamedou, M.-M. (2017), *A Theory of ISIS: Political Violence and the Transformation of the Global Order*, London: Pluto Press.

Rana, J. (2007), 'The Story of Islamophobia', *Souls: A Critical Journal of Black Culture, Politics, and Society*, 9: 2, 148–61.

Said, E. (1978), *Orientalism*, New York: Vintage.

Sakhi, M. (2018), 'Terrorisme et radicalisation: Une anthropologie de l'exception politique', *Journal des anthropologues*, 154–5: 3, 161–81.

Schneider, S. (2021), *The Apocalypse and the End of History: Modern Jihad and the Crisis of Liberalism*, New York: Verso.

Stampnitzky, L. (2013), *Disciplining Terror: How Experts Invented 'Terror'*, Cambridge: Cambridge University Press.

Truong, F. (2018 [2017]), *Radicalized Loyalties: Becoming Muslim in the West*, trans. Seth Ackerman, Cambridge: Polity Press.

Wagemakers, J. (2016), *Salafism in Jordan: Political Islam in a Quietist Community*, Cambridge: Cambridge University Press.

Wiktorowicz, Q. (2006), 'Anatomy of the Salafi Movement', *Studies in Conflict & Terrorism*, 29: 3, 207–39.

Zoller, S. (2021), *To Deter and Punish: Global Collaboration Against Terrorism in the 1970s*, New York: Columbia University Press.

PART II

AUDIOVISUAL MEDIATIONS AND FORMATIONS OF JIHAD

6

TERRORISM EDUCATION IN ISIS'S USE OF CHILDREN'S MOBILE APPS

Ahmed Al-Rawi

Introduction

This chapter deals with the Islamic State in Iraq and Syria (ISIS) and its state-building efforts with the assistance of educational apps. Previous media studies on ISIS have not focused on the theoretical concept of state-building in relation to mobile apps, for the terrorist organisation aimed at building an imagined Islamic state with the assistance of media productions. This study fills a major gap in research as there are no previous empirical studies that focused on these educational apps and their jihadist objectives. I argue here that the terrorist group ISIS aimed at providing well-designed and executed apps that do not only offer important language and religious teaching, but also aim at jihadising children into believing in militant jihad, hatred of non-Muslims, and other beliefs that ISIS held. The goal is to use such educational apps that offer standard leaning objectives and language to assist in the nation-state-building efforts of ISIS.

In his seminal study on nation building, Karl Deutsch (1963) argues that several elements contribute to the formation of states including establishing economic production means, trade, education and mass communication especially by offering communicative spaces. Ernest Gellner (2008) focuses on other aspects in state-building like the importance of educational and linguistic homogeneity and standardisation, but he suggests that the role of media cannot be overlooked here since it enhances values and creates co-cultural group or cultural area. ISIS seems to have employed most of these policies in building its state. In this regard, Harris Mylonas (2012: xx) defines nation-building as 'the process through which governing elites make the boundaries of the state and the nation coincide' by employing three main polices: accommodation, assimilation and exclusion. In general, there are violent and non-violent means of state-building; however, accommodation and assimilationist policies are often non-violent though the latter are 'often coercive' (ibid.: 23).

In order to build a state, the elite group must implement certain policies, often with the use of force in order to ensure that the new political system can work. Historically, A. D. Smith states that there are four types of nation-state-formations: the Western, for example European countries; the Immigrant, for example, US, Canada and Australia; the Ethnic, for example, Japan; and the Colonial, for example, many Arab and African states that were formed due to colonial powers (Smith 1986: 241–2). In this chapter, I argue that ISIS has followed standardised and systematic state-building policies which are largely borrowed from the Baʿth's regime strategies especially in the way the latter implemented accommodation and assimilation policies after Iraq annexed Kuwait in 1990. In its utopian objective in creating a caliphate, ISIS attempted to establish another type of an imagined state, especially that its goal was to demolish the Sykes–Picot Agreement (1916). This new envisioned state, which I call 'the jihadist *umma*', represented ISIS's vision of a militant and extremist ideology.

In this regard, Benedict Anderson discusses the notion of states as 'imagined communities' that are often able to impose or create 'prime culture areas'. Nations are in an imagined state because its members must continuously share a collective identity and think that they all belong to the same place. This is mostly done by the elites whose duty it is to unify the members of the nation, and media plays an important role here. Anderson mentions how some South East Asian colonies were formed by making accommodation to and maintaining the impact of some religions like Islam and Buddhism as they 'could rarely do more than to regulate, constrict, count, standardise, and hierarchically subordinate these institutions to its own' (Anderson 2006: 173). In this regard, C. Geertz believes that the state needs to unify its people to better achieve its goals despite their ethnic, racial and linguistic differences

(Geertz 1963), and ISIS attempts to do this by using its own radical version of Islam as a unifier, especially in imposing assimilation policies.

As for the relationship between media and state-building, they are closely connected because media plays a highly important role in disseminating the idea of 'imagined communities', especially in enhancing the national identity of the nation's diverse and scattered members. Whether they are called 'communicative spaces' (Deutsch 1963), 'cultural areas' (Gellner 2008) or 'prime culture areas' (Anderson 2006), assimilation policies intend to shape a given culture through media and in diverse ways. In general, media is used as a unifier or a medium for unity. In this regard, Ross Poole mentions that socialisation, language and mass media play important roles in forming the national identities of most individuals living in a certain nation (Poole 1999: 14). Furthermore, John Postill discusses the third wave of nation-building represented in Malaysia in 1963 and other South East Asian countries and emphasises that the role of media is 'integral to their formation and maintenance' (Postill 2006: 15). In the case of Canada, cultural industries represented in media productions and outlets are regarded as highly significant in unifying the nation because they

> provide an information base around which various communities and other social groups that make up . . . [the Canadian] society can coalesce and interact, at the best of time contributing to social cohesion, and a sense of belonging on the part of all members of society. (Gasher et al. 2008: 74)

Since Canada is the second largest country in the world, policies were issued from the beginning of the twentieth century to emphasise the role of media in enhancing the national identity. For example, the first media policy, which was called the Aird Commission (1929), stressed the following in relation to the role of radio broadcasting: 'In a country of the vast geographical dimensions of Canada, broadcasting will undoubtedly become a great force of fostering a national spirit and interpreting national citizenship' (ibid.: 194–5).

It is important and relevant to note here that one of the main elements that assist media and state-building in shaping national identities is standardisation. In other words, people living in a certain nation need to consume and absorb the same messages, symbols and cultural practices in order to feel a sense of shared values, beliefs and outlook towards life. In this regard, Stein Rakkan argues that there are four main institutional solutions in state-building such as standardisation which incorporates 'conscript armies, compulsory schools, mass media, creating channels for direct contact between the central elite and parochial populations of the peripheries' (Rakkan 1999: 83). As indicated above, standardisation incorporates several aspects such as language, education and media. In relation to the first element, language has always been important in state-building as it is used as 'a salient identity symbol, as well as a political instrument' (Luong 2004: 123). There are numerous examples on how language teaching and imposition has been used to unify the nation, such as the case of enforcing Kazakh and Uzbek languages and vocabulary in Kazakhstan and Uzbekistan, particularly after the break-up of the Soviet Union (Ubiria 2015), or the standardisation of the Romani language of the stateless Roma people in the Baltic states (Daftary and Grin 2003). Other examples of language standardisation include Zimbabwe (Ndhlovu 2009), Bosnia (Kolstø 2016), and other parts of South East Asia such as Indonesia (Sercombe and Tupas 2014). In relation to education, the standardisation of the American educational system and curricula have been regarded as crucial as it led to 'the development of national and state content and performance standards . . . [which] are an instrument of public control of education' (Rapport 2015: 164). In other words, standardisation provides an important centralised tool for the state to control and monitor the overall educational process. Other aspects of standardisation include laws such as the case of Turkey (Aslan 2014: 146) and currency.

In connection to other assimilation practices, special attention is devoted to children because ISIS wants to plant the seeds of jihadism in them. In this regard, an ISIS document written in Arabic contains instructions directed to Syrian schools. It instructs teachers and educators to get rid of all images from the curriculum that do not correspond with Islamic shariʿa as well as removing the phrase 'the Arab Syrian republic' and the words 'home' or 'homeland' wherever they occur by replacing them with the term 'Islamic State'. The document instructs the following: 'Do not teach the concept of nationalism and pan-Arabism but instead teach the idea of belonging to Islam and its followers' (Al Malah 2015). It further instructs educators to remove any references to 'democracy or voting' as well as any images that 'do not align with Islamic Shariah law'. It was estimated that about 50,000 children were living under ISIS's control in early 2016 (Townsend 2016), and they are compelled to attend school where they get military training and jihadist indoctrination; otherwise, their parents would be punished (CNN Arabic 2015). In this respect, mobile apps targeting children have been designed to teach them Arabic language and ISIS's militant ideology (Knox 2016). As a matter of fact, ISIS calls children *ashbāl al-khilāfa* (cubs of the caliphate) (RT 2015) as part of introducing its own militarised vision of childhood. In this regard, the term *ashbāl al-khilāfa* is incidentally similar to the name given to children during Saddam Hussein's rule, especially those enrolled in Uday Saddam Hussein's militia, Fedayeen Saddam. Staring in the 1990s, these military-trained children were called *ashbāl al-qa'id* or *ashbāl ṣaddām* (president's cubs or Saddam's cubs) (Singer 2003). As part of its standardisation policy, between 2014 and 2017 ISIS followed the same educational policies throughout its controlled territories (Arvisais and Guidère 2020: 498; Gadais et al. 2022: 3) using a systematic method of delivering exams throughout the school year with a clear emphasis on teaching Islamic thought, Arabic language, English language starting from grade four and computer literacy starting from the first year in the intermediate level. For example, a student is expected to graduate at the age of fifteen after spending five years in primary school starting from age six, two years in the intermediate level and two other years in secondary school. All school textbooks should stress militant ideology as well as strict Islamic learning and should use the hijra calendar when referencing Islamic holidays as the standard that needs to be followed. ISIS, in other words, wanted to militarise a whole generation of children and the whole society in order to mobilise its members and prepare them to protect the terrorist group. This observation aligns with previous research on the ISIS curriculum, whose goal is to 'further its political and religious agenda, although in very different ways like militarisation, banalisation of violence and the establishment of its complex and extreme but also fragile Islamic doctrine' (Arvisais et al. 2021: 1).

The Diwan al-Ta'lim (Teaching Ministry) was responsible for developing a new curriculum and replacing the older ones introduced by the Syrian and Iraqi governments. Then, the Committee for the Development of Curricula and Textbooks was established in September 2014 to support ISIS's efforts to create its new militant curriculum (Arvisais et al. 2021: 2).

To sum up, almost all the state-building endeavours by ISIS are standardised since they can be observed in the different cities (*wilayāt*) that the group controls, which means that it requires a collective effort. Besides, standardisation gives legitimacy to the group's brand and projects it as a fearful establishment, especially if continuous violence and intimidation are practised. The general goal is to subdue the masses with fear tactics, erase the previous cultural heritage and spaces, and cleanse society from unwanted members. To do so, ISIS used its own hybrid version of Salafist Islam (Hassan 2016) in order to achieve its nation-building goals. Mohammed Saad, a Syrian activist who was once imprisoned and tortured by ISIS, rightly mentions that the group is a 'criminal gang pretending to be a state' (Hendawi 2016). This type of pretence can be linked to Anderson's imagined communities concept (Anderson 2006), and Berman and Shapiro are correct in observing that ISIS is 'a failed state in the making' (Berman and Shapiro 2015).

In terms of media use, ISIS places great importance on media as it is regarded as part of its fight against its enemies. ISIS's media division has its own news agency that is called Amaq (depths) which runs its own Android app, and there is also the monthly *Dabiq* magazine in Arabic and English as well as al-Bayan radio station in Mosul with its mobile app (Callimachi 2016; Shiloach 2015a). In relation to social media, the group uses only a few centralised Twitter accounts that 'tweet official statements and news updates' as well as provincial accounts run from the provinces ISIS controls 'which publish a live feed about [local] Isis operations' (Kingsley 2014). The centralisation of media messages is meant to standardise the message which is part of the state-building effort and branding a unified image. This standardisation has even been seen in the kind of standard emojis ISIS followers often use (Shiloach 2015b). In fact, many of ISIS's media strategies are similar to Saddam Hussein's media policy, including running a centralised Ministry of Information and its Iraqi News Agency (INA) (Al-Rawi 2012). In relation to these educational mobile apps, they are considered mediascapes that function as deterritorialised third spaces (Appadurai 1990; Bhabha 1994), for space and physical presence are secondary, while consumption of mobile apps becomes the primary virtual bridge (Urry 2002) connecting children and ISIS. In other words, mobile educational apps are virtual spaces where culture is transmitted in appealing ways (Al-Rawi 2020).

To sum up, media productions are used for mobilisation and advocacy because they are meant to assist in the state-building efforts of ISIS in order to better achieve its intended objectives. This media vision is similar to that followed by totalitarian states in the Middle East. According to W. Rugh who studied media systems in the Arab world, media is expected to mobilise the public and propagate for the state in Ba'thist Syria and Iraq (during Saddam Hussein's rule), Sudan and Libya during Mu'ammar al-Gaddafi's rule (Rugh 2004: 29–31). In its Jihad 3.0, ISIS seems to view media in a similar way, though the group uses high-production means and various new technologies such as educational apps to increase the appeal of its messages (Al-Rawi 2016).

This chapter attempts to answer the following research question: how does ISIS use educational apps in order to assist in its state-building efforts?

Method

One of the main data sources has been ISIS's publishing agency that is known as al-Himma Library, which has not been well researched in previous studies despite the fact that it ran several educational apps targeting children and published hundreds of books. This study analyses four children's educational mobile apps used by ISIS (Letters in 2 parts, Night and Day Supplications, and Alphabet Teacher) that are produced by al-Himma Library. To run the educational apps, I used Bluestacks software on a desktop computer. In terms of method, I used the Walkthrough method (Light et al. 2018) that discusses the different features of each app, and I provide a description and contextualisation of these apps supported by screenshots. This method examines among many aspects of the apps' 'embedded cultural meanings and implied ideal users and uses' (ibid.: 881) as well as providing some 'interpretative aspects' that are 'underpinned by specific theoretical frameworks' (ibid.: 882). In 2018, I also collected six school textbooks produced by ISIS from the website Archive.org in order to compare the educational apps with these textbooks that were used in the territories controlled by this terrorist group.

Results and Discussion

The majority of the messages found on the educational apps are focused on Arabic language teaching as well as Islamic jurisdiction following the group's strict interpretation of Islam. First, it is important to shed some light on the standard textbooks produced by ISIS. As Figures 6.1 and 6.2 show, there is clear emphasis on military training and militarising children's minds by focusing on warfare training and showcasing weapons, even in mundane subjects like mathematics and science. Second, we can find a very strict application of Islamic teaching by, for example, blurring the faces of all humans and even animals because it could illicit idolatry. On the educational apps, there are no images but only animated pictures.

Regarding these educational apps, they can be downloaded anywhere and can work offline, allowing more users from any part of the world to engage with them, which can ultimately enhance the ISIS brand image. Second,

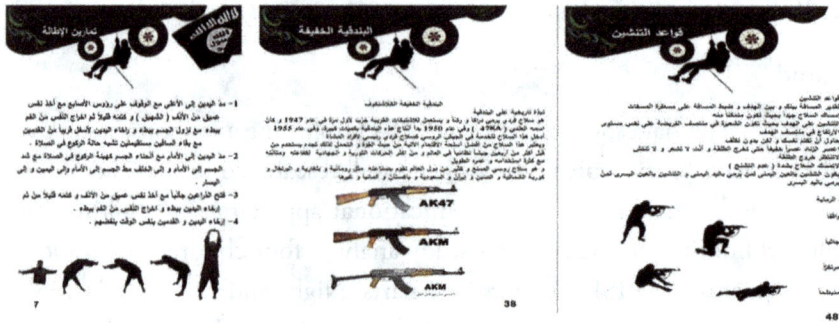

Figure 6.1 ISIS Physical Education textbook for Level 2 secondary and intermediate schools.
Source: Image in the public domain.

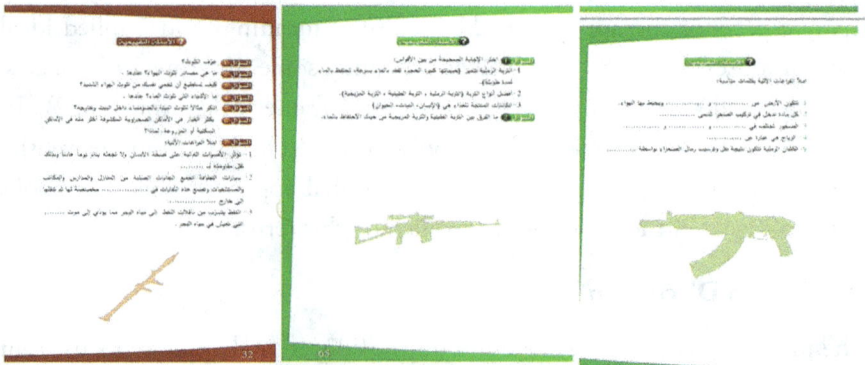

Figure 6.2 ISIS Science textbook for Grade 4.
Source: Image in the public domain.

the apps are fun, interactive and interesting to use due to their audiovisual content, making them more appealing than using textbooks. Third, the apps project a brand image of the terrorist group that is technologically savvy, advanced and versatile, which can be used for promotion.

To answer the research question, the results of the study show that the educational apps are largely meant to teach standardised and strict Islamic jurisdiction as well as Arabic language, both of which can assist in creating a jihadist nation state through standardisation. These apps are also meant to militarise or what I term 'jihadise' children using a variety of strategies. In this respect, jihadise means the process of implanting the concept of jihad and promoting it in the mind of new recruits and, in the scope of this study, it will be related to children. For example, the 'Letters: Teaching the Alphabet to the Cubs' app (see Figure 6.3) is designed in two parts, both for very young children, as it deals with basic Arabic language-learning skills, especially the alphabetical letters.

This indicates that these apps are used for private educational purposes mostly targeting kindergarteners. Using the Walkthrough method, there is a

Figure 6.3 The educational app Letters.
Source: Image in the public domain.

link in the app to al-Bayan radio station, and there is also some background information on al-Himma Library, making the app serve multiple purposes. Though not all the examples contain military words and pictures, they still constitute a sizable sample. For example, Figure 6.4 showcases modern weapons when teaching the alphabet, while Figure 6.5 highlights old weaponry.

Figure 6.4 Showcasing modern weapons in the Letters app.
Source: Image in the public domain.

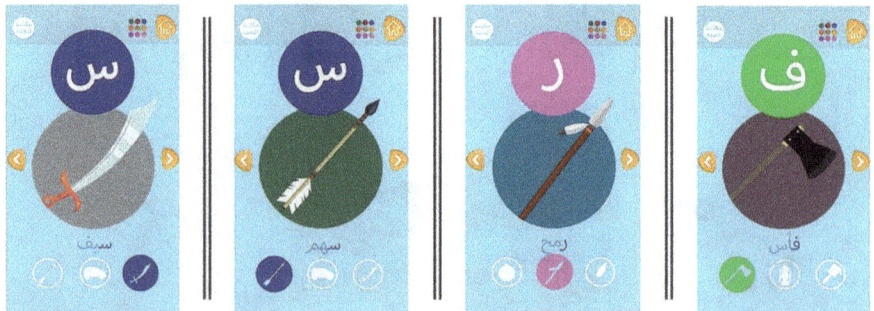

Figure 6.5 Showcasing old weapons in the Letters app.
Source: Image in the public domain.

I argue here that the use of old weapons is meant to provide a nostalgic view of the Islamic caliphate which can invoke positive sentiments amongst young learners. The terrorist group planned on managing an imagined state that was allegedly similar to what appeared in early Islam (Thielman 2014; Shane and Hubbard 2014), particularly in connection to religious rules, duties and obligations, such as alms giving and praying on time. Hence, many messages in these educational apps emphasise following Islamic teachings religiously. There is also emphasis on highlighting the Islamic golden dinar, which is ISIS's standardised currency, giving the perception of a real state. In general, the majority of other audio and visual examples are meant to enhance strict religious beliefs and the idea of the material existence of ISIS, while the militarisation of the curriculum is meant to 'jihadise' the young generation in a way that makes war, fighting and violence normalised in everyday life.

In relation to the second app 'Night and Day Supplications' (See Figure 6.6), it can be described as a very simple app for young children to learn forty-two night- and day-times Islamic supplications and prayers.

Similar to the previous app, its audiovisual interactive goal is to enhance religious beliefs in an engaging way, and two sections include supplications

Figure 6.6 The Night and Day Supplication educational app.
Source: Image in the public domain.

against the enemy and another one to be recited when facing the enemy and those in power. For example, one supplication states: 'Oh God who revealed thy Book, who speeds the judgement, defeat the opponent parties. God defeat them and destabilise them' (Figure 6.7). Figures 6.7 and 6.8 show the

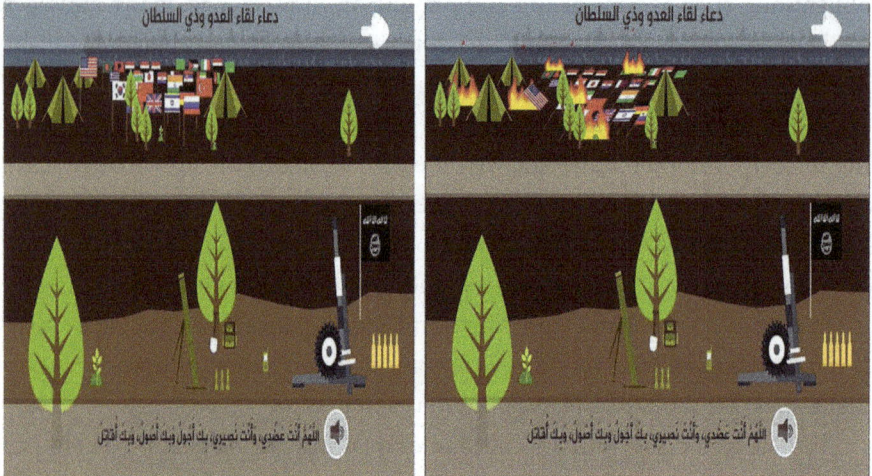

Figure 6.7 Supplication when facing the enemy or those in power in the Night and Day Supplication app.
Source: Image in the public domain.

Figure 6.8 Supplication against the enemy in the Night and Day Supplication app.
Source: Image in the public domain.

interactive feature of the app as the user needs to click on the weapons to activate them in targeting enemy tanks that carry the US flag as well as enemy camps that have the national flags of most coalition forces fighting ISIS. As can be seen, the user attains a simplistic sense of agency and a perceived idea of victory when clicking on the weapons as the tanks, flags and camp tents get easily destroyed.

Finally, the 'Alphabet Teacher' educational app (see Figure 6.9) is similar to the previous two apps as there is once again emphasis on the militarisation of the curriculum and disseminating strict religious beliefs. To enhance the belief in ISIS's brand, the app highlights some common statements such as 'it will remain by God's willing' in reference to the Islamic State.

Similarly, ISIS's currency, which is the Islamic golden dinar, is used to remind the app's users of the perceived legitimacy of the terrorist group. When observing the educational items that are used to teach the Arabic alphabet, we can find that thirteen out of twenty-two are militarised to enhance the sense of warfare and conflict among children. In brief, the goals of these educational apps are to enhance militarisation, weapon training, jihadist thought and extremism.

As stated above, ISIS intended to build a transnational jihadist *umma* state with the use of media due to its importance in shaping a collective identity.

Figure 6.9 The Alphabet Teacher educational app.
Source: Image in the public domain.

ISIS's goal was to create followers who were actively willing to participate in jihad and blindly follow all of ISIS's rules without questioning their superiors. To educate children on the importance of jihad, ISIS introduced their appealing mobile apps as a means to influence them. This jihadist identity was the ideal that ISIS sought to establish in its imagined Islamist state, and children were the ideal target groups who could be easily mobilised from an early age. In reality, ISIS attempted to use its own radical version of Islam as a unifier to militarise and subsequently jihadise younger generations, partly via using these educational apps, for they are vital cultural sites that are also used as branding strategy to show the terrorist group as technologically advanced.

To sum up, ISIS actively sought to create a state by marketing its global brand as a powerful one partly using media productions such as its educational apps. In its state-building efforts, mobile communication techniques are used to target children living under ISIS's control. In global marketing, international brands using standardised advertising need to be available to consumers by their high visibility, unified logo and standard messages (de Mooij 2010), and ISIS achieved something similar with its use of standardised messages in these educational apps in an attempt to create a stronger brand whether it be inside its past territories or outside of them.

References

Al Malah, A. (2015), 'The Complete Story of ISIS Curriculum in Caliphate Land . . . Learn About It', *Huffington Post*, 10 December, <http://www.huffpostarabi.com/2015/12/10/story_n_8767888.html> (last accessed 30 January 2016).

Al-Rawi, A. (2012), *Media Practice in Iraq*, Basingstoke: Palgrave Macmillan.

Al-Rawi, A. (2016), 'Video Games, Terrorism, and ISIS's Jihad 3.0', *Terrorism and Political Violence*, 30: 4, 1–30.

Al-Rawi, A. (2020), 'Mobile News Apps as Sites of Transnational Ethnic Mediascapes', *The Journal of International Communication*, 26: 1, 73–91.

Anderson, B. (2006), *Imagined Communities: Reflections on the Origin and Spread of Nationalism*, New York: Verso Books.

Appadurai, A. (1990), 'Disjuncture and Difference in the Global Cultural Economy', *Theory, Culture & Society*, 7: 2–3, 295–310.

Arvisais, O. and M Guidère (2020), 'Education in Conflict: How Islamic State Established Its Curriculum', *Journal of Curriculum Studies*, 52: 4, 498–515.

Arvisais, O., M. H. Bruyère, C. Chamsine and M. A. Mahhou (2021), 'The Educational Intentions of the Islamic State through Its Textbooks', *International Journal of Educational Development*, 87, DOI: https://doi.org/10.1016/j.ijedudev.2021.102506.

Aslan, S. (2014), *Nation Building in Turkey and Morocco*, Cambridge: Cambridge University Press.

Berman, E. and J. Shapiro (2015), 'Why ISIL Will Fail on Its Own', *Politico magazine*, 29 November, <https://www.politico.com/magazine/story/2015/11/why-isil-will-fail-on-its-own-213401/> (last accessed 30 January 2016).

Bhabha, H. (1994), *The Location of Culture*, London: Routledge.

Callimachi, R. (2016), 'A News Agency with Scoops Directly from ISIS, and a Veneer of Objectivity', *The New York Times*, 14 January, <http://nyti.ms/1lbIyHh> (last accessed 30 January 2016).

CNN Arabic (2015), "داعش"يفرض التعليم الإلزامي"بولاية الخير"ويجلد مدرسين ويرغمهم على تنظيف الشارع' ('ISIS imposes compulsory education in al-Khair province, flogs teachers and forces them to clean streets'), 14 March, <http://arabic.cnn.com/isis-syria-education-teachers-punishment> (last accessed 7 January 2016).

Daftary, F. and F. Grin (2003), *Nation-building, Ethnicity and Language Politics in Transition countries*, Local Government and Public Service Reform Initiative/European Centre for Minority Issues (ECMI).

De Mooij, M. (2010), *Global Marketing and Advertising: Understanding Cultural Paradoxes*, Los Angeles: Sage Publications.

Deutsch, K. (1963), *Nation-building and National Development: Some Issues for Political Research*, New York: Atherton.

Gadais, T., G. Touir, L. Décarpentrie, M. Al-Khatib, A. Daou, C. Chamsine and O. Arvisais (2022), 'Education Under the Islamic State of Iraq and Syria: A Content Analysis of the Physical Education Curriculum', *Frontiers in Education*, 7, DOI: 10.3389/feduc.2022.854413.

Gasher, M., D. Skinner and R. Lorimer (2008), *Mass Communication in Canada*, Don Mills, Ontario: Oxford University Press.

Geertz, C. (ed) (1963), *Old Societies and New States: The Quest for Modernity in Asia and Africa*, New York: The Free Press of Glencoe.

Gellner, E. (2008), *Nations and Nationalism*, Ithaca, NY: Cornell University Press.

Hassan, H. (2016), 'The Sectarianism of the Islamic State: Ideological Roots and Political Context', *Carnegie Endowment for International Peace*, 13 June, <http://carnegieendowment.org/2016/06/13/sectarianism-of-islamic-state-ideological-roots-and-political-context-pub-63746> (last accessed 7 July 2016).

Hendawi, H. (2016), 'Double Standards Fuel Disillusionment with Islamic State', *Associated Press*, 18 January, <https://www.ctvnews.ca/world/double-standards-fuel-disillusionment-with-islamic-state-1.2741253> (last accessed 19 February 2023).

Kingsley, P. (2014), 'Who is Behind ISIS's Terrifying Online Propaganda Operation?', *The Guardian*, 23 June, <http://www.theguardian.com/world/2014/jun/23/who-behind-isis-propaganda-operation-iraq> (last accessed 5 January 2016).

Knox, P. (2016), 'Evil ISIS Using New Smart Phone App to Brainwash Kids into Becoming Jihadi Killers', *The Daily Star*, 11 May, <http://www.dailystar.co.uk/news/latest-news/514590/ISIS-islamic-state-cubs-of-caliphate-smart-phone-Android-app-brainwash-children-Syria-Iraq> (last accessed 16 June 2016).

Kolstø, P. (2016), *Strategies of Symbolic Nation-building in South Eastern Europe*, London: Routledge.

Light, B., J. Burgess and S. Duguay (2018), 'The Walkthrough Method: An Approach to the Study of Apps', *New Media & Society*, 20: 3, 881–900.

Luong, P. J. (2004), *The Transformation of Central Asia: States and Societies from Soviet Rule to Independence*, Ithaca, NY: Cornell University Press.

Mylonas, H. (2012), *The Politics of Nation-Building: Making Co-Nationals, Refugees, and Minorities*, New York: Cambridge University Press.

Ndhlovu, F. (2009), *The Politics of Language and Nation Building in Zimbabwe*, Vol. 2, New York: Peter Lang.

Poole, R. (1999), *Nation and Identity*, London: Routlegde.

Postill, J. (2006), *Media and Nation Building: How the Iban Became Malaysian*, New York: Berghahn Books.

Rapport, A. (2015), 'Facing the Challenge: Obstacles to Global and Global Citizenship Education in US Schools', in J. Zajda (ed), *Nation-Building and History Education in a Global Culture*, New York: Springer, pp. 155–70.

Rokkan, S. (1999), *State Formation, Nation-building, and Mass Politics in Europe: The Theory of Stein Rokkan, Based on His Collected Works*, Oxford: Clarendon Press.

RT (2015), *Caliphate's Cubs Conduct Mass Execution for the First Time*, 29 March, <https://goo.gl/JAOC8Z> (last accessed 7 January 2016).

Rugh, W. A. (2004), *Arab Mass Media: Newspapers, Radio, and Television in Arab Politics*, New York: Greenwood Publishing Group.

Sercombe, P. and R. Tupas (eds) (2014), *Language, Education and Nation-building: Assimilation and Shift in Southeast Asia*, New York: Springer.

Shane, S. and B. Hubbard (2014), 'ISIS Displaying a Deft Command of Varied Media', *The New York Times*, 30 August, <https://www.nytimes.com/2014/08/31/world/middleeast/isis-displaying-a-deft-command-of-varied-media.html> (last accessed 7 January 2016).

Shiloach, G. (2015a), 'This New ISIS App Brings Terror Straight to Your Cell Phone', *Vocativ*, 30 November, <http://www.vocativ.com/255768/this-new-isis-app-brings-terror-straight-to-your-cell-phone/> (last accessed 7 January 2016).

Shiloach, G. (2015b), 'ISIS Loyalists Can Download: A Secret Set of Terrorist Emojis', *Vocativ*, 24 November, <http://www.vocativ.com/254247/isis-loyalists-use-these-bloody-icons-like-emojis/> (last accessed 7 January 2016).

Singer, P. W. (2003), 'Fighting Child Soldiers', *Military Review*, 83 :3, 26.

Smith, A. D. (1986), 'State-making and Nation-building', in J. A. Hall (ed), *States in History*, Oxford: Blackwell, pp. 228–63.

Thielman, S. (2014), 'ISIS' Sinister Media Strategy, and How the West is Fighting Back', *ADWeek*, 10 September, <http://www.adweek.com/news/television/isis-sinister-media-strategy-and-how-west-fighting-back-160021> (last accessed 10 January 2016).

Townsend, Mark (2016), 'How Islamic State is Training Child Killers in Doctrine of Hate', *The Guardian*, 5 March, <https://www.theguardian.com/world/2016/mar/05/islamic-state-trains-purer-child-killers-in-doctrine-of-hate> (last accessed 5 May 2016).

Ubiria, G. (2015), *Soviet Nation-building in Central Asia: The Making of the Kazakh and Uzbek Nations*, Vol. 30, London: Routledge.

Urry, J. (2002), 'Mobility and Proximity', *Sociology*, 36: 2, 255–74.

7

FROM ISIS TO THE AFD: ULTRAIST RHETORIC AND VISUALITY IN ALT-ORIENTALIST CONCURRENCE

Christiane Gruber

In April 2019, the German nationalist and right-wing populist party Alternative für Deutschland (AfD, Alternative for Germany) put up a series of campaign posters in the lead-up to the European Parliamentary elections (Figure 7.1).

The posters appeared in various cities and high-traffic junctures, including parks and bus stops. To further disseminate these political images in the digital sphere, the Berlin-based AfD's Twitter account posted them online, where it lauded such visuals as essential pedagogical tools in its series entitled 'Learning from Europe's History' (*Aus Europas Geschichte lernen*). One of these campaign posters, showing turbaned men inspecting the teeth of a white-fleshed nude woman, was posted on Twitter on April 8, 2019.[1] This image included the hash-tagged statement: 'On the basis of numerous motifs from European art history, our #EUElection campaign is intended to draw attention to the common value that must be defended today more than ever.' This so-called 'common value' (*gemeinsame Wert*) is clarified through the written reference to the 2015–16 New Year's Eve (*Silvesternacht*) in Cologne, at

---

[1] Available at <https://twitter.com/AfDBerlin/status/1115572899115675649> (last accessed 4 June 2022).

Figure 7.1 Campaign poster by Alternative für Deutschland (Alternative for Germany), Germany, April 2019.
Source: Image in the public domain.

which time German women were sexually assaulted by foreign men described as of Arab or North African origins (BBC 2016). The image is thus intended to stoke a fear of lustful, violent foreign interlopers while also stirring the urge to defend white women's honour and their physical integrality.

Other renditions of the AfD's poster using the same painted scene expand the visual's semiotic range through other captions, including the exclamation: 'So that Europe won't become Eurabia' (*Damit aus Europa kein 'Eurabien' wird!*), as in Figure 7.1. The historical lesson that is putatively to be learned goes beyond sexual intimidation and violation to activate a larger geographic reference to 'Eurabia', a portmanteau term embraced by various white nativist groups to describe an Islamist takeover of Europe through migratory invasion (Litmann 2005). The image thus seeks to stoke an existentialist fear of Euro-Christian cultural extinction, whereby the Old Continent is embodied by an exposed odalisque who stands ripe for the taking by a closing circle of dark-skinned and/or Muslim intruders. This Orientalist–Islamophobic cliché, premised on rape- and race-based anxieties, is not new or surprising to scholars who have studied the evolution of the alt-right's xenophobic rhetoric over the years. This rhetoric involves a medley of tropes, above all the terrorisation and racialisation of religion wherein Islam, in particular, is conceptualised as contra-white (Aziz 2021; Yukich and Edgell 2020).

Beyond such verbal stratagems, what is striking in this particular case is the AfD's reliance on a European art historical canon that involves an Orientalist painting, twisted and turned for alternative ends. These recent rhetorical and visual tactics aim to craft a picture of insurmountable alterity above all else. Moreover, the Orientalism of Edward Said from several decades ago (Said 1978) gives way to today's imagistic landscape of romanticised radicalism, which I term 'alt-Orientalism'. This approach to the Other transcends critical theory and post-colonial discourses about imperial power and domination writ large to explore how identitarian movements and ultraist groups wilfully deploy Orientalising imageries to vex opponents, cause dismay, consolidate public opinion and entrench a binary worldview.

These incendiary and polarising efforts gain a new life online, where they spread and speciate in multi-participant platforms and groups: some mainstream and others ultra-conversative, neo-Nazi, or jihadist. On the Internet, images quickly turn into memes: that is, digital visuals engaging shorthand cultural symbols that are then virally transmitted through participatory behaviours (Denisova 2019; Kien 2019; Blackmore 1999). The most widespread among such graphics warn of European and Muslim hybridity: that is, the formation of a new mixed breed that neo-conservative and Islamophobic conspiracy theorists refer to as 'Eurabia', the latter also central to the AfD's alt-Orientalist poster caption. Such mongrelised memes point to a purist discourse on race that is central to white nativist groups, which in turn is reified in a pictorial language that undergoes semiotic cooptation, diversion and reinvestment. Per Nicolas Bourriaud, images that navigate in such conflictual agoras essentially act as social go-betweens and constructed situations whose 'spectacle deals first and foremost with forms of human relations' (Bourriaud 2002: 84–5).

Beyond Orientalist iconographies and memetic admixtures, other images aim to depict Western civilisation on the precipice of death. This portentous scenario instrumentalises end-of-times rhetoric while also depicting the white race as if at the knife's edge of survival. Such iconographies pretend to offer lessons in European art history but in fact circulate online in close symbiotic relationship with ISIS's extremist visuals, most notably its photographs and films of human beheadings. Whether in alt-right European posters or jihadi digital spheres, images of decapitation engage in a looping of Orientalist and self-Orientalising stereotypes, each of which build a polarised yet unified global visual culture of call-and-response extremism.

Before proceeding any further, two questions must be addressed: first, how does one define extremism and, second, how can art history and visual culture, as the allied humanistic disciplines at the centre of this study, potentially provide a tool kit for an 'interventionist' analysis of sorts?

Regarding the former, Peter Coleman and Andrea Bartoli provide several useful definitions for 'extremism', which they posit can be, among others: an incentive-driven ideological construction, a rational strategy in a game of power, an emotional outlet for severe feelings, and an apocalyptical worldview (Coleman and Bartoli 2015). The third premise, which takes a psychological approach, is best left to scholars who study extremists' psychological distress and their black-and-white perception of the world, a kind of cognitive splitting or simplicity that results in ideological dogmatism, the belief in conspiracy theories, and religious intolerance and over-confidence (van Prooijen and Krouwel 2019). Moreover, the fourth possibility – the doomsday mode, especially with regards to ISIS's output – has already been studied extensively (McCants 2015). For the purposes of this study, the first two premises – namely, the constructed 'extreme' position as declaratively anti-middleground along with the calculated use of messages within a larger conflictual landscape – take centre stage. I argue that extremist visuality should be considered a 'rational' endeavour in the visual field: in other words, it is a 'judo politics' (Wintrobe 2006: 7) with two partners engaged in, and benefitting from, ideological sparring in pictured form.

Such battling also quickens a dichotomisation of the global visual lexicon. The emergent binary concepts and motifs that are examined in this study include male v. female, Europe v. Islam, and peace v. violence. Such contrarian copulates are not a stable given, however. They rely on an entrenchment of perceptual realities as well as an acceleration of the viewing process itself. And this is where the methodologies of art history and visual culture can provide a theoretical – and perhaps practical – intervention as both aim to highlight the complexity of visual operations through iconographical analysis, itself a slowing down of the seeing process. Such interpretative deceleration and double-checking, especially along Panofskian lines, can help lay bare an image's constructed nature and hence expose, perhaps even undermine, its tactical foundations.

Female-mania and the Sexually Depraved Other

The pictorial source of the AfD's variously captioned poster is a painting entitled *The Slave Market* (*Le marché d'esclaves*) executed in 1866 by the renowned French Orientalist painter Jean-Léon Gérôme (Figure 7.2) (Lees 2012; Des Cars et al. 2010: 272–4). Known for his academic style and treatment of mythological subjects, Gérôme also produced a wide range of drawings and paintings based on his travels to Egypt and the Near East. These images often include a close attention to details, including facial features and ethnographic types, clothing and headgear, and various objects that the painter collected and used as props in his Paris studio.

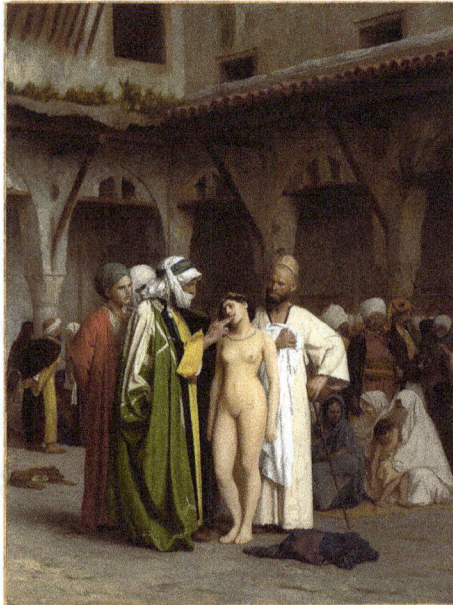

Figure 7.2 Jean-Léon Gérôme, *The Slave Market*, oil on canvas, 1866. Source: The Clark Institute, Williamstown, MA, 1955.53.

To these elements he added others, most especially an emphasis on the idealised female nude, whether represented as relaxing in a Turkish bathhouse or as an object of the slave trade. Scholars such as Linda Nochlin have pointed out that these types of depictions display an 'imaginary Orient' at the height of French colonialism, in which documentary realism is combined with an erotic mystification of the female body put on full display for the European beholder's visual enjoyment and possession (Nochlin 1989). A decade prior, Edward Said examined these types of sexualised tropes within European literature through a post-colonial reading that positioned itself as resistant to facile dichotomies (Şahin, Schleck and Stearns 2021).

For Gérôme himself, however, slavery and the female nude transcended a mere Orientalist fantasy staged in nineteenth-century Cairo, Damascus or Istanbul. Indeed, the auctioning of a female nude formed a central theme in about half a dozen paintings of his, some of which take place in ancient Rome instead (Figure 7.3). The topic of the slave trade offered the French artist an opportunity to explore the statuesque and sensualised

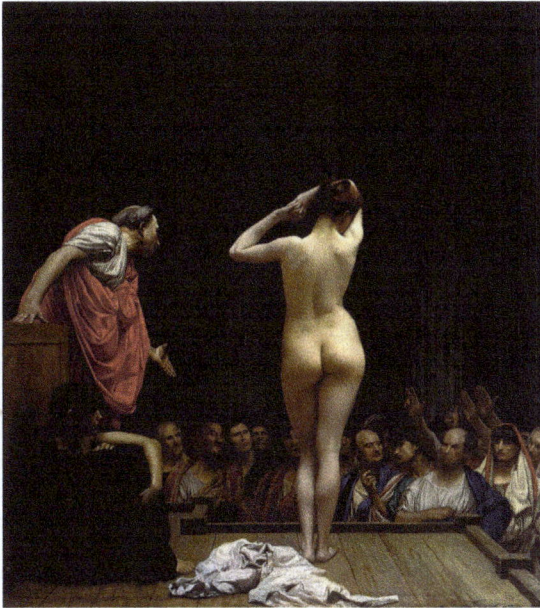

Figure 7.3 Jean-Léon Gérôme, *Slave Market in Ancient Rome*, oil on canvas, c. 1884. Source: The Walters Art Museum, Baltimore, 37.995.

female form as well as an occasion to depict a wide range of body gestures and facial expressions among a crowd of interested male buyers. Beyond physical forms and movements, Gérôme also used the female nude to perfect a chiaroscuro effect, a strong contrast achieved in the painting through a dark background and the ricocheting of light upon the woman's pearlescent backside.

Gérôme's female slave depictions augur their own purchasability in the Paris salons where, despite the overt and rather daring eroticism of their contents, they proved highly desirable items for private acquisition and, eventually, museum ownership and display. In this manner, the artist might be offering an underhanded and self-referential commentary on the allure and marketability of his own paintings rather than scathing commentary about Orientalist notions involving despotism and sexual deprivation. After all, his depictions of female slaves in ancient Rome – depicted as faceless in repoussé or blinded by their own forearms – do not make for the crafting of a grand pictorial narrative about the moral or cultural superiority of Western European civilisation.

And yet, through the AfD's modified visual syntactics, Gérôme's *Slave Market* has achieved this semiotic status. The painting instead presents a moral lesson by reasserting paradigmatic art historical motifs that, we are told, aim to preserve a larger European 'common value'. As suggested by the poster's diversionary textual 'voice-overs' (Bourriaud 2002: 7–11), this 'common value' is twofold: the first consists in protecting European women from Muslim sexual predation and the second is the eugenic notion of miscegenation, wherein the female embodiment of a free and sovereign Europe faces the threat of sexual penetration and hence the birthing of a mixed breed called 'Eurabia'. This pictorial move seems to tip its hat to the mythology of the rape of Europa by Jupiter, who transformed himself into a bull to abduct the beautiful Phoenician princess whose name eventually gave the continent its appellation.

Apparently, AfD entrepreneurs decided not to reassert the Ovidian tale or rely on Titian's famous painting (Pope 1960), as neither is easily overglazed with an anti-Muslim animus.

This Islamophobic availing of an Orientalist image caused consternation both within and beyond Germany. In the United States, Olivier Meslay,

Director of the Clark Art Institute where the original Gérôme painting is held, issued a series of statements on Twitter on 30 April 2019 (that is, three weeks later, so it took some time for the story to gain international traction). In his retort, he noted that: 'We strongly condemn the use of the painting to advance AfD's political stance and have written to them insisting that they cease and desist [from using this painting]' (Hickley 2019). Meslay's statement leverages two responsorial strategies: the first is what Ghassan Hage calls the 'condemnation imperative' (Hage 2003: 67), whereby an individual erects a strong binary between himself and the Other through absolute rhetorical rejection, and the second is his use of the legal doublet 'cease and desist', which warns an individual or organisation of alleged illegal activity, infringing on intellectual property or using an unlicensed product or image.

Meslay then added that 'the Clark Institute owns Gérome's painting and we are strongly opposed to the use of this work to advance any political agenda. We did not supply this image to the AfD Berlin.' Here, the museum director leaves moral censures and legal caveats to the side to stress that the Clark Art Institute is an unwilling participant in the German political poster campaign. Meslay then ends his series of tweets by finally admitting that the high-resolution digital image of the painting is available in the public domain and therefore 'there are no copyrights or permissions that allow us to exert control over how it is used other than to appeal to civility on the part of AfD Berlin' (CBS News 2019). This last comment reveals that our web-based 'Commons' proves a double-edged sword: on the one hand, it allows for the free and open use of images in scholarly talks and articles such as this one, while, on the other, it provides creative fodder for race- and sex-based fearmongering. The battle over this canonical European painting turned alt-right Orientalist clickbait captures this rather uncanny toggling.

The AfD's visual's 'shock-and-awe' approach accelerated its viral spread, thereby amplifying the party's ideological platform, footprint and influence. Indeed, Meslay's public stance gave the party an opening to strike back, with its spokesperson declaring that the museum's 'gag order' is futile and that 'the German public has the right to find out about the truth about the possible consequences of illegal mass immigration' (ibid.). In this instance, as in many others, a well-intentioned condemnation coupled with a legalistic yet unenforceable threat not only did not silence or halt the AfD, but, through a boomerang effect, transformed the poster campaign into a *succès de scandale* covered from one media story to the next. Echoing P. T. Barnum's famous dictum that 'there is no such thing as bad publicity', this poster controversy turned into a global circus for rival position-taking. Within this political theatre, Gérôme's Orientalist painting was diverted, recoded, fought over and reasserted to sharpen ideological divides, especially with regards to the EU's and Germany's immigration policies.

Beyond such issues, Gérôme's painting is thematically linked to another matter of the moment: namely, the emergence of female slavery at the height of ISIS's power in Iraq and Syria in 2014–15. At that time, ISIS militants overtook the Sinjar area, in Iraqi Kurdistan, killing Yazidi men and capturing women and girls. From Sinjar, these and other Middle Eastern non-Muslim females were subsequently transported to registration sites in Iraq and Syria, and from there they were taken to be sold at 'slave markets' (*ṣūq ṣabāyā*) located in the Syrian cities of Raqqa, then de facto capital of ISIS's caliphate, and Tadmur, near the ancient city of Palmyra.

Female bondage and servitude can be traced back to the early Islamic period. However, practices of enslavement – whether European, American or Islamic, and whether during times of war or peace – often rely on a 'superficial and selective enactment of certain provisions from scripture and law' (Ali 2015; also see Ali 2010). While journalists and newsreaders across the globe became perturbed by ISIS's violent form of female enslavement, for the militant group such sorties exceeded sexual desire and conquest. Much more tactically, these subjection operations aimed to clear a swathe of land of its non-Muslim minorities and to unleash a genocidal strategy involving physical extermination and psychological torture – or what ISIS operators call a 'vexation and exhaustion' (*nikāya wa inhāk*) martial manoeuvre (Gruber 2019: 137). These women war captives also were monetised through human trafficking, a hyper-modern practice that cannot be explained away, or sexually Orientalised, as a recrudescent medieval Muslim phenomenon (Nicolaus and Yuce 2017). As several scholars have stressed, ISIS's trade in the female body thus must be understood primarily as a market economy, having generated a pool of funds, much like the militants' seizure of natural resources, agricultural lands, military bases and ancient Near Eastern antiquities.

Documentary photographs revealed that these captured females were chained up and encaged like chattel slaves. And although indeed stripped and inspected prior to being sold, they were not arrayed in the nude in any sexually titillating manner, as is the case for Gérôme's *Slave Market*. Rather, they were often cloaked from head to toe, sometimes their faces fully covered in a black niqab. Such photographic scenes record human exploitation, and not sexual exploits. In the throes of such devastation, the AfD's repackaging of a European painterly tradition adds insult to injury by reframing war crimes as a salacious gawking at the pain of others. These 'pictures of calamity', to borrow Susan Sontag's expression (Sontag 1982: 359), breach ethical lines while enabling viewers mock forms of control and possession.

This, it can be argued, is likewise the case for the AfD poster, which invites its beholders to adopt a voyeuristic position involving the crafting of white moral supremacy. This self-stereotyped ethical register, however, relies on several semiotic diversions of Gérôme's painting. Through such alterations, the poster effectively muddles Orientalism and othering, the latter a painterly style and the former a racialised mode of subjection. This imbroglio tactic is a 'rational' one – a visual 'judo politics' of sorts – that deliberately drags a historical image towards a latter-day reframing by political actors active on the far right. This radicalised gloss and deflection prove central to the AfD's 'alt-Orientalism' brand in both rhetoric and visuality.

In-between Memes: Eurabian Mongrels

The AfD's alt-Orientalist female enslavement concoction is also propelled by, and animating of, European nativist anxieties. Suggestive of a white woman's looming violation by a group of black and brown males, Gérôme's painting is diverted to recall recent sexual assaults in Germany while also foreshadowing the resultant birth of a mixed-race offspring. This hybrid human entity *in potentia* is conjured up via the metaphor of 'Eurabia' – a linguistic creolisation of what right-wing groups consider non-coterminous cultural and religious spheres: that is, Christian Western Europe and Muslim Arab lands. The word 'Eurabia', however, is not new to the AfD and its campaign posters; instead, it has a longer history and context of usage that merit discussion.

The term 'Eurabia' made its debut in earnest in 2005, with the publication of *Eurabia: The Europe-Arab Axis*, published by the British-Swiss Giselle Litmann who writes under the pseudonym of Bat Ye'or, or 'Daughter of the Nile' (Litmann 2005). Although she fashions herself a historian, Litmann propounds various conspiracy theories, chief among them a putative plan for Islam to take over Europe through the secret efforts of members of a global ruling elite. This so-called 'Green Peril' (or 'peril of Islam') – as she and other European and American neo-conservatives argue (Huntington 1996) – has as its ultimate goal the annihilation of Christian heritage and culture through migratory submersion (Bergmann 2018: 123). This fear is sometimes put to picture via digital images showing a green, mosque-silhouetted 'spill' overtaking the European continent (Figure 7.4). In this glum Eurabian scenario, it is claimed that Christians will be reduced to a state of 'dhimmitude': that is, of being classified as dhimmis, or non-Muslim minority groups whose second-class status may devolve into slavery.

Figure 7.4 Digital graphic showing the expansion of Islam in Europe, undated. Source: M-SUR / Alamy Stock Photo.

Related to this fear of religious takeover and fall in status is the correlative issue of demographic decline. Right-wing writers, conspiracy theorists and white nationalists, such as Bat Ye'or, Renaud Camus and Richard Spencer, refer to this process of racial decimation as the so-called 'Great Replacement' (Camus 2011). Within today's alt-right spheres, including among the Proud Boys (Stern 2019) and members of Identity Evropa, the frequently repeated slogan 'You Will Not Replace Us' verbalises such fears, as does the drive to establish a white ethnostate or 'whitopia' (Stern 2019: 51–69). Such calls for a Christian 'crusade' recall the rhetoric of Islamists who similarly use the trope of the 'victorious faction' (al-ṭā'ifa al-manṣura) to claim superiority for themselves through practices of jihad. This 'symmetrical appropriation' (Günther 2022: 92f) creates a rapprochement for these so-called 'strange bedfellows' (Schneider 2021), all of whom trade in the notions of tradition, disenfranchisement and heroism (Brzuszkiewicz 2020; Rogan 2019).

Replacement anxieties need not be immediate or aggressively imposed, however. White nationalists point to a more pernicious and durable underlying condition, which they identify as social, ethnic and racial diversity. They contend that the ethos and practice of multiculturalism, along with its state-sponsored programmatic and financial support, lead to racial mongrelisation, diluting the white race and leading to a white genocide. Moreover, in their estimation, supporters of diversity – which is mocked in Germany with the diminutive expression 'Multi-Kulti' – are guilty of genocide by association (von Laer 2012). Their sheepish tolerance and naïveté provide the last nail in the coffin of Western civilisation – or what Niall Ferguson calls 'impire': that is, an implosion of empire that ushers in a period of post-colony in which Europe itself becomes colonialised (Carr 2006: 5). Ergo, this looming demise requires preemptive Western 'counter-colonization' efforts against Muslim immigration (Camus 2011: 51), a remarkable capsizing of the history of European colonialism per se.

Right-wing proponents of the twinned notions of racial creolisation and civilisational collapse require strong dichotomies to forcefully make their cases and to differentiate between in-groups and out-groups. Beyond relying on emotivist conceptual modes and engaging in cognitive splitting, as psychologists note, this process of thinking also requires a thought-out script for public speech, including the rhetorical leveraging of binaries in which whites and non-whites, Christians and Muslims, are posited against one another as if polar opposites on the ontological spectrum (Tomić 2013). This false dilemma fallacy is the key ingredient of polarised politics as it rejects third-siderism and the middleground – or what ISIS refers to as the 'gray zone' requiring extinction (Anonymous 2015).

European right-wing groups struggle against this zone of cultural complexity and political compromise though a range of visuals, especially Internet memes. These digital images are crafted and manipulated with ease, and they spread quickly and widely across web-based platforms by both political supporters and rivals. Their success is predicated on their free-floating reproducibility and mutability, both of which can catalyse moral panic and mass hysteria (Kien 2019: 78–82). Their persuasive qualities also endow them with a 'mindbomb' quality, especially within ideologically divisive registers (Denisova 2019: 33–5). Last, but not least, as emotional catalysts and replicators, their potential ability to induce anger and anxiety in visual form can lead to a condition that Susan Blackmore terms 'meme-fear', which stokes their viewers' deepest worries and suspicions (Blackmore 1999: 8–9).

In today's European right-wing memeplex, the blazon or flag of Eurabia counts among the most widespread of these politically charged memes (Figure 7.5). Unlike the Gérôme painting, which requires prolonged pictorial and exegetical analysis, this visual cuts to the chase through its logographic minimalism. The visual operation is as follows: the EU's blue field ornamented with a ring of stars is overlaid with the flag of ISIS, which includes the Islamic proclamation of the faith (*shahāda*) inscribed above and in the central medallion. This facile Photoshopping echoes the Eurabian conspiracy, which posits an identitarian admixture and eventual sublimation of 'Western civilisation' under the brunt of Islamic jihadism.

The picture is not as clear as one might presuppose, however. Turning first to the European flag, the EU's official website notes that the twelve stars represent union, solidarity and harmony among the peoples of Europe, while the number twelve stands as a symbol of perfection. It therefore does not represent the number of countries in the EU, which has enlarged its roster of member states over the decades. Additionally, the colours are explained through the metaphor of the firmament, with its golden stars illuminating a blue sky ('European Flag'; 'Graphics Guide to the European Emblem'). No other

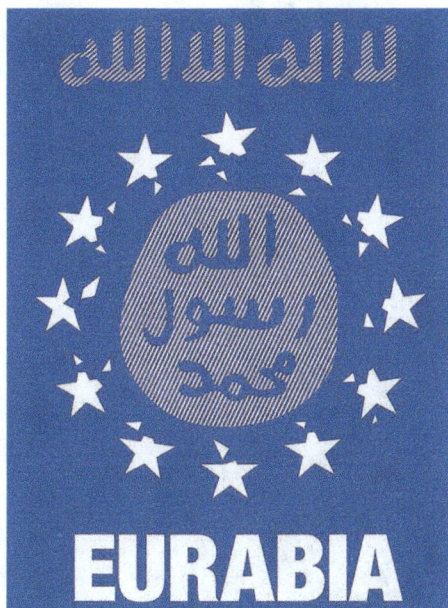

Figure 7.5 'Flag' of Eurabia, showing the EU flag overlaid with the banner of ISIS. Source: Internet meme in the public domain.

indications or explanations of the flag's design history are provided. The relative semiotic barrenness of the flag's graphic elements fosters a larger sense of inclusivity and representation for a continent whose constituencies are highly varied and whose member states are at times in disaccord. It thus appears to function as a graphic equivalent to the 'empty word' in marketing, into which different stakeholders can interject and deduce meaning as they see fit, thus curtailing the image's potential for unlimited semiosis (Potts 2003: 22).

As several journalists and scholars have shown, the EU flag nonetheless tells a different story – one that is not at all devoid of meaning. Rather, the circle of stars is reminiscent of the Virgin Mary's astral crown, especially in depictions that show her as the 'Star of the Sea' (*Stella Maris*) or as illustrating her immaculate heart (Figure 7.6). In such images and sculptures, Mary's head is framed or surmounted by twelve glowing stars, and indeed the EU flag's designer, Arsène Heitz, has admitted that he was inspired by this type of Marian iconography after he experienced an apparition of the Blessed Virgin on the Rue du Bac in Paris ('European Union Flag').

Figure 7.6 The Immaculate Heart of Mary Statue, Roman Catholic Church of Saint Anne, Zegiestow, Poland, undated.
Source: Photograph by Adam Ján Digel, 2019.

Albeit stripped of its religious embodiment and visually abstracted, the EU flag nevertheless preserves a substrate message in both iconographical and religious terms. To those in the know, it can further enable the alt-right and other nativist groups to argue for the purely Christian character of the EU, a stance that has made the inclusion of Muslim majoritarian Turkey a long-standing impasse.

For its part, the ISIS flag combines three major elements (Figure 7.7). The first is the colour black, which represents the Abbasid dynasty (750–1250 CE) that ruled from its imperial capital in Baghdad and whose caliphal mantle was claimed to be inherited by Abū Bakr al-Baghdādī, ISIS's de facto leader until his killing in 2019. Additionally, the colour black is connected to darkness and death, and thus it is likely that ISIS media strategists and designers made a conscientious decision to use this foreboding hue as a quick and effective 'vexation operation'. Some scholars argue that this black banner also points to ISIS's overarching doomsday approach: that is, as a material harbinger of an impending end-of-days battle and moral reckoning (McCants 2015: 19–22).

Figure 7.7 ISIS propaganda photo showing masked militants holding the ISIS banner, undated.
Source: Handout / Alamy Stock Photo.

Besides the overwhelming black field, the second element is the Arabic-script *shahāda*, which declares ISIS an Islamic state labouring under the imprimatur of the Prophet Muḥammad, captured by the jagged seal impression that contains the Prophet's name and honorific title, 'Messenger of God'. However, much like the EU flag, ISIS's logo contains creative complications, particularly in its claims to Islamic history and the sunna (tradition) of the Prophet Muḥammad. Leaving aside the militant group's medley of historical manoeuvres tying their flag to early Islamic war banners and its lapidary script as suggesting antiquity and authenticity (Günther 2022: 96–102; Ostovar 2017: 89–90), I would like to focus on the impression of Muḥammad's signet ring, or *khatam*. Islamic textual sources state that the Prophet had an inscribed ring that he used to seal official letters. While the ring itself has been lost, several letters preserved today in the Topkapı Palace in Istanbul are believed to include the Prophet's seal impression. It is this lapidary impression that ISIS has borrowed from the Ottoman palace's relics chamber, thereby framing their own flag as both a secondary contact relic and as bearing prophetic sanction for their own endeavours.

And yet, like other putatively early Qur'ans and several relics housed in the Ottoman palace, the seal-impressed letters have been shown to be nineteenth-century forgeries, as suggested by misspellings, paleographic unsteadiness and odd spacing (El Shamsy 2021). Another logographic conundrum therefore presents itself: just as the EU flag includes an undertone of Christianity, the ISIS flag is not what it seems. Instead of carrying any authentic Islamic historical value, it is merely a throw-back impression – forged in modern times – coopted and altered by militants through the uncanny visuo-material process of Orientalised self-fashioning.

The Eurabian logo is a 'mindbomb' of a different order. On the one hand, this logographic counter-jihad appropriates motifs in the ISIS flag based on the presumption that they are uncomplicated and pure *ab initio*. And indeed, agents operating on either side of the ideological divide concoct such visuals by adopting both the ring of stars and Muḥammad's seal impression as if autonomous and opposite entities, which are then conjugated into a memetic mixed breed. In accordance with a white nativist and Islamophobic worldview, the Eurabian grapheme therefore acts as a digital surrogate for the human mutt. In other words, it is a Christo-Muslim memetic mongrel, a monstrous compound heralding its own genetic demise.

This emphasis on polar opposites within a larger political landscape emphatically rejects the productive potential of identity hybridity and hyphenation, as articulated by Homi Bhabha (Bhabha 1994: 313); it also mocks various forms of interaction and interlocution that include Islamic cultural registers. Instead, these types of 'mutational signs' (Denisova 2019: 7) reveal the dangers of oppositional self-construal, its concomitant emotional contagion as spread through digital algorithms, and the eventual affective mass confluence that may lead to extremist acts (Barsade et al. 2018) – whether these be ISIS-driven terrorist attacks in Europe and America or the January 2021 storming of the United States' Capitol by a motley of alt-right, nativist and hate groups.

At the Knife's Edge

Along with images of enslaved females and Eurabian memes, a third leitmotif in the ultraist mediatic nexus is the sword. This symbol shuttles back and forth between Islamist and alt-right ideologists, and it abounds in their intertwined visual propaganda. For instance, another digital flag of Eurabia shows the

EU's ring of stars, this time on a background suggestive of the Huntingtonian 'Green Peril' of Islam, with 'Allah' inscribed in Arabic script in the centre and two scimitars perilously leaning in from the margins (Figure 7.8). This visual is clearly reliant on the flag of Saudi Arabia – itself not surprising given Eurabia's linguistic conjugation of 'Europe' with 'Arabia' – but the latter's single sword has been duplicated. In addition, rather than fulfilling an honorific or heraldic purpose, within the Eurabian meme the sword suggests a looming enclosure and double-pronged attack.

Alongside such digital logographs, the sword also played a prominent role in the AfD's 2019 poster campaign entitled 'Learning from Europe's History'. Much like Gérôme's *Slave Market* was diverted in various semantic ways within this same pictorial series, so too was the painting of a beheading overlaid with the exclamation: 'Stop the head-cutter at the EU borders!' (*Kopfabschneider an EU-Grenzen stoppen!*) (Figure 7.9). The general term 'decapitator' is not given a precise name or identity, here. Its coded reference nevertheless hides in plain sight, and it is one to which we will return shortly.

Figure 7.8 'Flag' of Eurabia, inscribed in its centre with 'Allah' and flanked by two scimitars.
Source: Internet meme in the public domain.

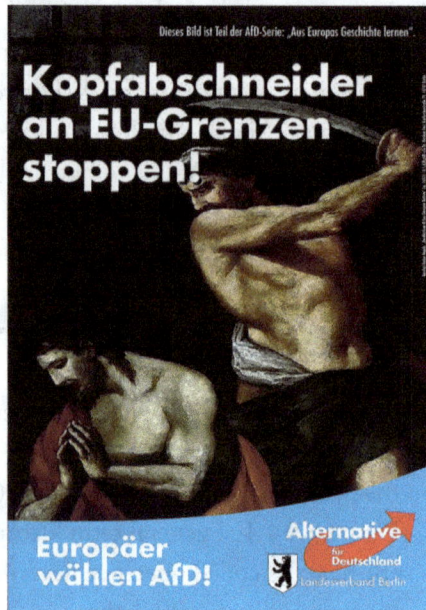

Figure 7.9 AfD poster depicting the decapitation of St John the Baptist and inscribed with the expression 'Stop the head-cutter at the EU borders!' (*Kopfabschneider an EU-Grenzen stoppen!*).
Source: Image in the public domain.

But first, a few words on the painterly source. The AfD poster again reasserts the European artistic tradition, but this time the inspiration is not an Orientalist image but rather a painting of the decapitation of St John the Baptist, attributed to Anton Angelo Bonifazi (1615–82 CE). This rather poorly known artist active in seventeenth-century Italy practised in the Baroque style, using a strong chiaroscuro effect to heighten the bright white skin tone of the genuflecting early Christian saint. His executioner, sent by King Herod, exhibits a darker complexion. Why this specific Baroque painting was chosen remains a bit of a mystery given that numerous other representations of St John's decapitation are well known and available, including by such famous artists as Caravaggio (d. 1610 CE). However, no other painting, to my knowledge, provides such a close-up view of the sweeping sword nor such a sharp focus on a kneeling Christian captive draped in a bright orange cloak.

These iconographic elements hint that this less illustrious European painting of St John's decapitation was purposefully – that is, 'rationally' – selected in order to coopt and divert ISIS's dread-inducing visual culture. Since 2014, ISIS militants have systematically crafted and marketed a particular brand of terror, and they have been so successful in their efforts that viewers quickly recognise its key tropes. These motifs suffuse ISIS's mediatic performances of human decapitation, whose scenes are staged, rehearsed, professionally lit, and shot from various angles to be later stitched into a final product aiming for optimal dramatic effect (Harmanşah 2015; Tugendhaft 2020).

In such horror-reality films, ISIS militants force their lighter-skinned and at times Christian prisoners to wear jailbird orange jumpsuits, in emulative revenge for Muslim hostages clad in these very same vestments while held in America's overseas military prison complex (Gruber 2019: 141–6). Moreover, ISIS's captives are forced to kneel on the ground, while their bodies are beheaded by various blunt weapons, including scimitars (Figure 7.10) that revel in and redirect the European neo-conservative-Orientalist trope of the

Figure 7.10 ISIS fighter beheads an alleged spy in a propaganda video capture released by ISIS, Hama, Syria, 5 April 2016.
Source: Handout / Alamy Stock Photo.

'medieval savage' – an ill-used past on the ascendant in Europe, America, the Middle East, and elsewhere (Albin et al. 2019). As a result, this bait-and-switch combination of motifs choreographs a new genus of pictorial revanchism that is viciously parasitic of Orientalist clichés and whose primary goal consists in spreading optical trauma and psychological mayhem both locally and internationally, both key to ISIS's greater martial strategy of consolidating power on the ground.

The AfD's poster of Bonifazi's painting of St John the Baptist's decapitation – an otherwise poorly known artwork in the Western canon – thus does not truly offer a lesson in European history. Rather, its designer's selection seems primarily propelled by the painting's homicidal thrust, its hunched composition, its spotlight on the sword, and its orange colour symbolism, all syncopated to prompt European viewers' immediate recall of ISIS's vexation tactics. This visual and cognitive tethering is further entrenched thanks to the poster's caption that calls for stopping 'decapitators' at the EU's borders. Such head-cutters are, obviously, not the persecutors of early Christian saints like St John but rather the Muslim immigrants and refugees of today. Within AfD and alt-right Eurabian rhetoric, any Muslim man or boy arriving on or living in the European continent essentially fits the bill as a potential rapist, proto-terrorist or killer-in-waiting. Like other ultraist visuals containing alt-Orientalist iconographies and Islamophobic prosaisms, the AfD poster activates the fustian fear of 'border security' to suggest the impending martyrdom of a saintly Western civilisation. And through its iconographic boomerang effect, the poster paradoxically expands the international footprint of jihadist visual culture.

In their conjoined efforts to spread truculent images, the AfD, ISIS and other would-be antagonists depend on each other. They require a swarm of willing interlocutors, both on the World Wide Web and within the public sphere. Through mirroring and mimicry, ultraist visual 'vexation operations' pandered by the AfD, ISIS, and other hate and extremist groups also may deepen biased emotions and thus further forward the perception of rivalrous worldviews. In these hyper-mediated visual scenarios, both friend and foe come together through their proximity online, where they operate in antagonistic synchronicity and co-mingle in both emotional and rational ways. Sometimes they even come together in the streets as large-scale floats (Figure 7.11).

Figure 7.11 German carnival parade showing an ISIS militant winding up an AfD partisan, Düsseldorf, 27 January 2017.
Source: Photograph by Jochen Tack.

In such carnivalesque performances, third-party actors use the aesthetics of puppetry to lampoon what they see as the parasitic character of partisan politics: in this particular case, ISIS's instrumentalisation of AfD followers as 'our useful idiots' (*unsere nützlichen Idioten*) winding up and screeching out their 'hatred of Muslims' (*Hass auf Muslime*). Actors on both ends of the extremes thus tread on the proverbial knife's edge, revealing how hatred is stoked, and how it cuts both ways.

Art History's 'Interventionist' Method

A close analysis of the rhetorical and visual production of Euro-American alt-right groups reveals not a diametric clash with ISIS's own output but rather a concurrence in symbolic lexica, in which an alternative form of Orientalism – that is, an Islamophobic anathemising of the perceived other – is asserted to craft and entrench a white nativist stance. This polarised position involves perceived identity-based taxonomic purisms as well as calculated efforts to stoke a fear of migration, miscegenation and misogyny.

This competitive conjunction of painting, photography, reprographic and digital arts also reveals how ultraist imageries are never neutral or natural; rather, they are always enmeshed in complex social, political, religious and cultural matrices, in which opposite constructs attract one another and thrive in rivalrous colloquy. This one-upmanship results in a rather circuitous conversation involving a larger algorithmic morass of fake news, conspiracy theories and negative affective spiralling. It also twists and turns images both old and new, such that we witness European actors emerging as semioclasts of the Western painterly tradition and Islamists as exoticising an emic Islamic history along with its visual and material heritage.

Although such collusive operations may seem ironic based on today's taxonomic expectations of world cultures and religions, they expose a larger problematic: namely, the complex, constructed and contextual character of images in themselves. Pictorial operations have long captured the attention of art historians, especially that of Erwin Panofksy, whose iconological method of 'reading' images has influenced scholars' methodological approaches for over seventy years. Key to the practice of iconology – which Adi Efal describes as philology in figural form (Efal 2016) – is the slow and careful investigation of an image. The process begins with close observation to enable observers to uncover the forms, schemes and operations at play. This requires an unhurried form of critical seeing, itself acquired over time through eye-training or what Elizabeth Sears calls 'visual calisthenics' (Sears 2007: 278). Then follows the decoding and classification of an image within a spatio-temporal structure (Panofsky 1957: 6f). The latter analytical system, Panofsky and other art historians argue, must be consistent but elastic, and scholars must be able to identify interpretative pinch points in order to pivot and self-correct during their explicative investigations (ibid.: 10, 17). This control mechanism – itself a critical method of intervention against potentially self-induced errors – is of paramount importance to detect and maintain an artwork's original meaning.

As Adi Efal notes, 'it is by following mistakes and deformations in the representation of artworks that the philological trail is formed' (Efal 2016: 25). Additionally,

> just as a particular word can have changed its meaning because of a change
> in linguistic usage and thus have changed the whole tenor of the linguistic

proposition, so, too, within the total artistic organism any detail at all can be interpreted in the present completely differently from what it was in the past and so have a completely erroneous formal effect upon us. (ibid.: 24)

This pathway for explication, which takes into account erroneous formal effects on viewers, proves fruitful when it comes to understanding the visuals produced by the AfD and ISIS. Indeed, both pictorial corpora depend on obfuscations and diversions – all rationally conjured up and implemented – in order to yank images at the extremes of meaning. Art History's analytical tools, especially those rooted in the iconological tradition, can help expose images' visual structures and subterfuges, in turn offering the possibility of countervailing their overall emotional impact and political influence. Such a method can be considered 'interventionist' in two ways: first, it provides new critical insights on ultraist operations in the pictorial realm and, second, it can enable an undermining of their presumptive stability and earnestness.

The art historian's contribution, then, aims to break the visual stalemate by inducing a neutral exegetical state and by rerouting images towards more accurate historical contexts and meanings. This practice may help reduce visualised tugs-of-war at the edges of the political spectrum and eventually reduce intergroup conflict, also known as etiological escalation within the fields of peace psychology and bystander intervention. As ultraist groups engage in a negative spiralling of images, Art History, for its part, can offer some 'counter-tipping measures' and 'buffering effects', such as those used in behavioural psychology. These include, among others, an un-coupling of antagonists, a de-forming of cliques and a neutral mood induction (Barsade et al. 2018: 144–6).

But psychology does not suffice as an explicative method, so we shift our angle from the emotive domain back to the rational field: to evidence-based thinking, itself one of the greatest assets of the academic modus operandi. We thus ask ourselves in closing: in this loop of reciprocal radicalisation, how can we, as scholars, intervene in order to break the vicious cycle? One possibility, put forth by Julia Ebner in her book entitled *The Rage: The Vicious Circle of Islamist and Far-Right Extremism* (2017), is to de-escalate the extremes that feed off one another. Instead, we can attempt to break the circularity of ultraist image-worlds by shifting our vantage point 'from mythos to logos' (Ebner 2017: 206) in order to capture the productive messiness of a given situation. This methodological stance may provide a deradicalisation solution that Ebner calls 'mobilizing the middle' (ibid.: 200). As many scholars have shown, the best remedy against global forms of extremism is education: that is, critical thought turned into a mood-neutral practice. Within the humanities, Art History as a discipline can provide us with one means among many of cultivating anti-extremist thinking and seeing: that is, an interventionist act that demystifies and disengages the 'crisis-construct' (Strnad and Hynek 2020: 85) of ultraist images whose concurrence is built on but a shaky edifice.

References

Abdelrahim, Y. A. (2019), 'Visual Analysis of ISIS Discourse Strategies and Types in *Dabiq* and *Rumiyah* Online Magazines', *Visual Communication Quarterly*, 26: 2, 63–78.

Albin, A., M. Erler, T. O'Donnell, N. Paul and N. Rowe (eds) (2019), *Whose Middle Ages? Teachable Moments for an Ill-used Past*, New York: Fordham University Press.

Ali, K. (2010), *Marriage and Slavery in Early Islam*, Cambridge, MA: Harvard University Press.

Ali, K. (2015), 'The Truth About Islam and Sex Slavery History Is More Complicated Than You Think', *HuffPost*, 19 August, <https://www.huffpost.com/entry/islam-sex-slavery_b_8004824> (last accessed 13 February 2023).

Anonymous (2015), 'The Extinction of the Gray Zone', *Dabiq*, 7, 54–66.

Aziz, S. (2021), *The Racial Muslim: When Racism Quashes Religious Freedom*, Berkeley: University of California Press.

Barsade, S., C. Coutifaris and J. Pillemer (2018), 'Emotional Contagion in Organizational Life', *Research in Organizational Behavior*, 38, 137–51.

BBC (2016), 'Germany Shocked by Cologne New Year Assaults on Women', *BBC*, 5 January, <https://www.bbc.com/news/world-europe-35231046> (last accessed 13 February 2023).

Bergmann, E. (2018), 'The Eurabia Doctrine', in E. Bergmann (ed.), *Conspiracy & Populism: The Politics of Misinformation*, Cham: Palgrave Macmillan, pp. 123–49.

Bhabha, H. (1994), *The Location of Culture*, London and New York: Routledge.

Blackmore, S. (1999), *The Meme Machine*, Oxford and New York: Oxford University Press.

Bourriaud, N. (2002), *PostProduction: Culture as Screenplay: How Art Reprograms the World*, New York: Lukas & Sternberg.

Bourriaud, N. (2010), *Relational Aesthetics*, trans. S. Pleasance and F. Woods, Dijon: Les Presses du réel.

Brzuszkiewicz, S. (2020), 'Jihadism and Far-Right Extremism: Shared Attributes with Regard to Violence Specacularization', *European View*, 19: 1, 71–9.

Camus, R. (2011), *Le grand remplacement*, Paris : Reinharc.

Carr, M. (2006), 'You Are Now Entering Eurabia', *Institute of Race Relations*, 48: 1, 1–22.

CBS News (2019), 'U.S. Museum Demands German Anti-Islam Party Stop Using 19th-century "Slave Market" Painting', *CBS News*, 30 April, <https://www.cbsnews.com/news/us-museum-germany-far-right-afd-anti-islam-party-slave-market-painting/> (last accessed 13 February 2023).

Coleman, P. and A. Bartoli (2015), 'Addressing Extremism', ICCCR (Columbia University) and ICAR (George Mason University), <https://resolvenet.org/research/publications/addressing-extremism> (last accessed 13 February 2023).

Denisova, A. (2019), *Internet Memes and Society: Social, Cultural, and Political Contexts*, New York: Routledge.

Des Cars, L., D. de Font-Réaulx and É. Papet (2010), *The Spectacular Art of Jean-Léon Gérôme (1824–1904)*, Milan: Skira.

Ebner, J. (2017), *The Rage: The Vicious Circle of Islamist and Far-Right Extremism*, London: I. B. Tauris.

Efal, A. (2016), *Figural Philology: Panofsky and the Science of Things*, London: Bloomsbury Academic.

El Shamsy, A. (2021), 'The Hoax in the ISIS Flag: Claiming to Channel Pure Islam, the Islamic State Fell for a Long-Debunked 19th-Century Hoax', *New Lines Magazine*, 28 October, <https://newlinesmag.com/essays/the-hoax-in-the-isis-flag/> (last accessed 13 February 2023).

'European Flag', official website of the European Union, <https://european-union.europa.eu/principles-countries-history/symbols/european-flag_en> (last accessed 13 February 2023).

'European Union Flag', in *All About Mary*, Marian Library, University of Dayton, <https://udayton.edu/imri/mary/e/european-union-flag.php> (last accessed 13 February 2023).

'Graphics Guide to the European Emblem', Annex A1, *Europa Interinstitutional Style Guide*, <http://publications.europa.eu/code/en/en-5000100.htm> (last accessed 13 February 2023).

Gruber, C. (2019), 'The Visual Culture of ISIS: Truculent Iconophilia as Antagonistic Co-Evolution', in I. Busch, U. Fleckner and J. Walman (eds), *Nähe auf Distanz: Eigendynamik und mobilisierende Kraft politischer Bilder im Internet*, Berlin: de Gruyter, 125–55.

Günther, C. (2020), 'Iconic Socioclasm: Idol-breaking and the Dawn of a New Social Order', *International Journal of Communication*, 14, 1830–48.

Günther, C. (2022), *Entrepreneurs of Identity: The Islamic State's Symbolic Repertoire*, New York and Oxford: Berghahn.

Hage, G. (2003), '"Comes a Time When We Are All Enthusiasm": Understanding Palestinian Suicide Bombers in Times of Exighophobia', *Public Culture*, 15: 1, 65–89.

Harmanşah, Ö. (2015), 'ISIS, Heritage, and the Spectacles of Destruction in the Global Media', *Near Eastern Archaeology*, 78: 3, 170–7.

Hickley, C. (2019), 'US Museum Criticizes use of Gérôme's Slave Market in German Right-wing Campaign', *The Art Newspaper*, 30 April, <https://www.theartnewspaper.com/2019/04/30/us-museum-criticises-use-of-geromes-slave-market-in-german-right-wing-campaign> (last accessed 13 February 2023).

Huntington, S. (1996), *The Clash of Civilization and Remaking the World Order*, New York: Simon & Schuster.

Kien, G. (2019), *Communicating with Memes: Consequences in Post-Truth Civilization*, Lanham: Lexington Books.

Lees, S. (2012), 'Jean-Léon Gérôme: Slave Market', in S. Lees (ed.), *Nineteenth-century European Paintings at the Sterling and Francine Clark Art Institute*, Williamstown, MA: Sterling and Francine Clark Art Institute, pp. 359–63.

Litmann, G. (aka Bat Ye'or) (2005), *Eurabia: The Euro-Arab Axis*, Madison, NJ: Fairleigh Dickinson Press.

Matusitz, J., A. Madrazo and C. Udani (2019), *Online Jihadist Magazines to Promote the Caliphate: Communicative Perspectives*, New York City: Peter Lang.

McCants, W. (2015), *The ISIS Apocalypse: The History, Strategy, and Doomsday Vision of the Islamic State*, New York: St Martin's Press.

Nicolaus, P. and S. Yuce (2017), 'Sex Slavery: One Aspect of the Yezidi Genocide', *Iran and the Caucasus*, 21, 196–229.

Nochlin, L. (1989), 'The Imaginary Orient', in L. Nochlin (ed.), *The Politics of Vision: Essays on Nineteenth-century Art and Society*, New York: Harper & Row, pp. 33–59.

Ostovar, A. (2017), 'The Visual Culture of Jihad', in T. Hegghamer (ed), *Jihadi Culture: The Art and Social Practices of Militant Islamists*, Cambridge: Cambridge University Press, pp. 82–107.

Panofsky, E. (1957), 'The History of Art as a Humanistic Discipline', in E. Panofsky (ed.), *Meaning in the Visual Arts: Papers in and on Art History*, Garden City, NY: Doubleday & Company, pp. 1–25.

Pope, A. (1960), *Titian's Rape of Europa: A Study of the Composition and the Mode of Representation in This and Related Paintings*, Cambridge: Isabella Stewart Gardner Museum.

Potts, A. (2003), 'Sign', in R. Nelson and R. Shiff (eds), *Critical Terms for Art History*, 2nd edn, Chicago and London: University of Chicago Press, pp. 20–34.

Rogan, R. (2019), 'Quest for Immortality: An Analysis of ISIS's *Dabiq*', *International Journal of Communication*, 13, 5080–99.

Şahin, K., J. Schleck and J. Stearns (2021), '*Orientalism* Revisited: A Conversation Across Disciplines', *Exemplaria*, 33: 2, 197–208.

Said, E. (1978), *Orientalism*, New York: Pantheon Books.

Schneider, S. (2021), 'Strange Bedfellows: The American Far-Right and Today's Jihad Do Have Something in Common – Just Not What You Think', *Religion Dispatches*, 10 September, <https://religiondispatches.org/strange-bedfellows-the-american-far-right-and-todays-jihad-do-have-something-in-common-just-not-what-you-think/> (last accessed 13 February 2023).

Sears, E. (2007), 'Eye Training: Goldschmidt/Wölfflin', in G. Brands and H. Dilly (eds), *Adolph Goldschmidt (1863–1944): Normal Art History im 20. Jahrhundert*, Weimar: VDG, pp. 275–94.

Sontag, S. (1982), *A Susan Sontag Reader*, New York: Farrar, Straus, Giroux.

Stern, A. M. (2019), *Proud Boys and the White Ethnostate: How the Alt-Right is Warping the American Imagination*, Boston: Beacon Press.

Strnad, V. and N. Hynek (2020), 'ISIS's Hybrid Identity: A Triangulated Analysis of the *Dabiq* Narrative', *Defence Studies*, 20: 1, 82–100.

Tomić, T. (2013), 'False Dilemma: A Systematic Exposition', *Argumentation*, 27: 4, 1–22.

Tugendhaft, A. (2020), *The Idols of ISIS: From Assyria to the Internet*, Chicago: University of Chicago Press.

Von Laer, H. (2012), *Multi-Kulti am Ende? Perspektiven in einer heterogenen Gesellschaft*, Berlin: Lit.

van Prooijen, J.-W. and A. Krouwel (2019), 'Psychological Features of Extreme Political Ideologies', *Current Directions in Psychological Science*, 28: 2, 159–63.

Welch, T. (2018), 'Theology, Heroism, Justice, and Fear: An Analysis of ISIS Propaganda Magazines *Dabiq* and *Rumiyah*', *Dynamics of Asymmetric Conflict*, 11: 3, 186–98.

Wintrobe, R. (2006), *Rational Extremism: The Political Economy of Radicalism*, Cambridge: Cambridge University Press.

Yukich, G. and P. Edgell (2020), *Religion is Raced: Understanding American Religion in the Twenty-first Century*, New York: New York University Press.

8

THE SOUND AND SENSE OF JIHAD: REVISITING THE NOTION OF JIHAD IN JIHADI-THEMED ARABIC CHANTS

Kurstin Gatt

Introduction

In recent years, Arabic chants have received scholarly attention for their strong presence on the battlefield among Salafi-Jihadi groups. From al-Qaʿida in the Arabian Peninsula to the Islamic State in Syria (henceforth: IS) and Boko Haram in Nigeria, Salafi-Jihadi groups have integrated Arabic chants as part of their psychological warfare to recruit new fighters, to galvanise support for their ideology, to fuel people's sentiments against foreign forces and to undermine the ruling governments. This chapter reconciles sound – the auditory experience of chants – with sense, namely, the meaning and interpretation of a particular text, including the affective dimension attributed to the Arabic chants disseminated by Salafi-Jihadi groups. The objectives of this chapter are twofold. First, this contribution draws parallelism between the notion of jihad as deployed in contemporary Arabic political discourse and in Salafi-Jihadi parlance to assess whether the militant meaning of jihad is part of mainstream Arabic political discourse or exclusive to Salafi-Jihadi propaganda. Second, this chapter examines the sound and sense of jihadi-themed Arabic chants at the nexus of tradition and modernity by suggesting a broader understanding of Arabic chants within the Arabic-speaking environment. From an emic perspective, this study investigates Arabic chants of jihadi nature in light of 'invented traditions', illustrating how secular and religious practices are appropriated at the textual and sound level. In terms of tradition, this study compares the uses and functionality of Arabic chants with other long-standing oral and auditory traditions in the Arabic-Islamic cultures.

The Notion of Jihad in Contemporary Political Discourse

The earliest meaning of jihad that is rendered in the Arabic dictionary *Lisan al-'Arab* is that of 'making an effort or investing one's energy, whether in speech or action'. Associated with it is the meaning of loyalty in war (see also Bengio 1998: 186). Historically speaking, the term jihad is located with the Prophet Muḥammad, who reminded his followers to engage in *jihād al-nafs* or the conscious engagement to bring a positive change, which was regarded as the greater form of jihad (*jihād al-akbar*). On the other hand, jihad of the sword (*jihād al-sayf*), which permitted physical combat with the sword in certain limited situations, was considered as the lesser form of jihad (*jihād al-asghar*) or a 'battle . . . holy war against the infidels as a religious duty' (Wehr and Cowan 2016: 169).

Over the past centuries, the meaning of jihad has migrated from the inner Muslim circle to the political and military realms. The dimension of spiritual exertion as prioritised by the Prophet lost its value among Salafi-Jihadi groups.[1] The notion of jihad has experienced semantic narrowing over time to the extent that it came to be chiefly and irrecoverably linked to violence. According to Ofra Bengio, the principal connotation of jihad, which dates back to the days of the Prophet and is still prevalent today, 'was that of warfare for the sake of Allah against infidels or those who refused to accept Islam.

---

[1] For the lack of a better term, I adopt the fundamentalist dimensions of the term 'Salafi-Jihadi' to refer to extremist groups within Islam that have a transnational outlook, reject electoral politics, are often reluctant to make truces or engage in political compromises, and focus exclusively on armed struggle. While I acknowledge that the newly coined Western collocation of 'Salafi-Jihadi' may contain 'entirely different meanings from an internal Muslim perspective' and may also be 'reminiscent of false dichotomies often applied to distinguish between "good" and "bad" Muslims in the West' as discussed by my colleague Jaan S. Islam in this volume, I cannot find a more befitting term to refer to the groups considered in this study.

The Qur'an itself uses the word frequently in this sense' (Bengio 1998: 186). In the political sphere, jihad is appropriated as an ideological tool, especially in times of war. Politicians use the term jihad as part of their political jargon to give conflicts a sense of historical depth and help to obscure their actual causes. In turn, wars are framed as a religious struggle. Due to its strong religious connotations, the notion of jihad resonates with predominantly Muslim communities. The term deprives the opposite side of legitimacy and discredits the adversaries by depicting them as apostates, heretics or infidels. For instance, the Wahhabi community in the Arabian Peninsula used the term jihad with reference to the internecine war within the Wahhabi community and against non-Wahhabi Muslims (see also ibid.: 186ff.).

Similarly, Bengio reports that in preparation for the Iraq–Iran war, the Ba'th Party had to replace its secular political discourse with an Islamicised form of discourse. The scholar argues that this form of discourse

> drew on themes of historical, above all Islamic, provenance. In some measure, this process was intentional and guided from above; in part it was forced on the regime by specific circumstances; and in part it sprang spontaneously from deep layers of the Iraqi collective experience. (ibid.: 159)

Additionally, Bengio reports that at the beginning of the Iraq–Iran war, Saddam addressed a troop of soldiers with the words, 'This is the day of your jihad' (ibid.: 186). Consequently, Saddam was addressed as *mujāhid* in the list of titles, and the term *mujāhid* replaced its parallel secular term *munāḍil*, the former title which originated from the revolutionary ideology of the Ba'th Party (ibid.).

On a similar note, Nouri al-Maliki, Iraq's first prime minister post-US invasion, realised that he could not communicate his message effectively to a predominantly Muslim audience unless the political discourse with which he came to power also included a kind of public language that borrowed its idiom from the Islamic tradition. A few months before stepping down, al-Maliki intensified the use of Islamic rhetoric as his last discursive tool to calm down the protests that erupted across the country against his leadership, calling upon the Iraqis to unite and fight back against IS. In this particular context, al-Maliki used three terms to describe the act of struggling or fighting in descending order of importance, namely, *jihād, kifāḥ* and *niḍāl*. It is worth noting that the Islamic term *jihād* precedes the two near-synonyms of secular nature *kifāḥ* and *niḍāl* (see also Gatt 2018: 175).

Libya's former leader Colonel Muʿammar Gaddafi exploited the religious associations of jihad during his last years in power to guide and spur aggression against a perceived internal or external enemy. In a speech held in the city of Benghazi on the occasion of the Prophet's birthday in 2010, Gaddafi mobilised Islamic terms in his bid to raise aggression against the perceived external enemy, namely, Switzerland, for banning the construction of new minarets. Libya's former leader also targeted the internal enemy, which consisted of Salafi-Jihadi groups whose competing ideology was gaining currency in the Islamic world in general, specifically in Libya. More subtly, Gaddafi used this occasion to score political points by linking the transnational struggles of the Muslim communities across the globe with Libya's political turmoil. Gaddafi initiated his speech by reminding his audience that jihad is a religious duty (*farḍ*). He then advanced this idea by moving from the religious to the political realm to introduce his own interpretation of jihad. According to the politician, jihad consisted of defending oneself, one's religion, fighting in the path of God (*kifāḥ fī sabīl allāh*), the Prophet, the Qur'an, the mosques and specifically al-Aqsa mosque (Libyan pen 2021: 14:44). At the same time, Gaddafi positioned himself against other interpretations of jihad. He registered his disagreement with the Salafi-Jihadi interpretation of jihad, claiming that the acts of jihad carried out by groups such as al-Qaʿida constitute 'terrorism' (*irhāb*), 'crimes' (*ajrām*) and 'mental illnesses' (*maraḍ nafsī*). Contrarily, Gaddafi expressed his support for the 'sacred Palestinian struggle' (*al-kifāḥ al-filasṭīnī al-muqaddas*), which he considered as a clear example of jihad. Targeting Switzerland as the perceived external adversary, Gaddafi declared that any Muslim worldwide who attempted to engage in any way with Switzerland was an infidel (*kāfir*) working against Islam, Muḥammad, God and the Qur'an. He also accused Switzerland of destroying places of worship and instigated his audience to boycott Switzerland, its products, planes, ships and embassies.

The process of transposing Islamic terminology from the religious realm to the political sphere is one of the most frequent persuasion strategies in Arabic political discourse that extends beyond the speeches of Saddam Hussein, Nouri al-Maliki and Muʿammar Gaddafi. These examples demonstrate that the militant meaning of jihad, which promotes violence against a perceived enemy, is not exclusive to the Salafi-Jihadi paradigm but has been instrumentalised as a persuasion strategy in mainstream Arabic political discourse for many decades.

The Notion of Jihad in Arabic Chants

The notion of jihad is subject to competing interpretations in the religious, political and military realms. In the context of Arabic chants, Salafi-Jihadi groups have adopted a narrow understanding of jihad to the extent that the term appears exclusively in its militant form in modern Salafi-Jihadi propaganda. For example, in a chant attributed to the famous chant singer Abu Mazin and disseminated through al-Qaʿida propaganda channels, the notion of jihad is expressed in terms of its violent and transitional dimensions.

وَنُمَزِّقُ الطَّاغوتِ وَالكُفْـــرا	بِجهادِنا سَنُفَتِّتُ الصَّخْـــرا
وَإرادَةٍ لا تَعْرِفُ القَهْـــرا	بِعَزيْمَةٍ جَبَّارةٍ كُبْـــرى
بِدِمائِنا سَنُلَوّنُ الفَجْـــرا	وَنُجَنِّدُ الوِجدان وَالفِكْـــرا
بِكِفاحِنا سَنُحَوّلُ المَجْـــرَى	وَنَرودُه يا أُمَّتـــي نَصْرا
سَيَزُول لَيْلُ الشِركِ وَالإلْحاد	بِجهادِنـــا بِالمِشْعَلِ الوَقَّاد
وَنَفُلُّ جَوْرَ القَيدِ والأصْفــاد	وَنَخوضُها بِعَزيْمَةٍ وَجَلاد

By means of our jihad, we will crumble the rocks,
    and tear the infidels and apostasy apart.
With great, fierce determination
    and a will that knows no defeat,
We will recruit the hearts and minds
    and we will colour dawn with our blood.
O Muslim polity, we want this to be a victory,
    our fighting will change the path.
Through our jihad and our luminous torch,
    the night of polytheism and apostasy will disappear.
We will fight with strength and determination,
    we will defeat the unjust restrictions of the handcuffs.[2]
(Said 2016: 335)

---

[2] The English translation is my own.

The violent dimension of jihad is amplified through the frequent use of the *fa ʿʿala* verbal form, which indicates an intensive, reiterative or habitual action (Wright 1955: 137). Examples include 'crumbling' (*nufattitu*), 'tearing apart' (*numazziqu*) and 'colouring dawn with blood' (*nulawwinu al-fajrā*). Similarly, the transitional dimension is expressed through the notion of 'changing the path' (*nuḥawwilu l-majrā*). The term jihad is also accompanied by positive-connoting terms such as 'fierce determination' (*ʿazīma jabbāra*), 'victory' (*naṣr*) and 'luminous torch' (*mishʿal al-waqqād*).

In Salafi-Jihadi rhetoric, the act of dying for the group is often depicted in terms of jihad and it is compared to the strength of the lion, which is the ultimate symbol par excellence evoking qualities of bravery, strength and valour in the Islamic tradition. The IS-affiliated chant *Ummati Kānat Lā Tarḍi l-Wahan* ('My Muslim polity was not satisfied with the weakness') calls upon the 'lions of Islam' who are 'the embodiment of jihad' to fight against the Persians who are referred to as non-Arabs (*ʿajam*).

في زَمانٍ قادَ عُرْبَهُم عَجَم   يا أسودَ الدّينِ يا رَمْزَ الجِهاد

O lions of Islam, the embodiment of jihad,
    in the past, the Arabs ruled over the Persians.
(Gatt 2020: 268)

It is worthy to note that in some cases, the militant form of jihad is framed in terms of traditional motifs that have developed from pre-Islamic onto Islamic and modern times. One example is the motif of asceticism (*zuhdiyya*) which deals with 'the binary sets of life and death, the worldly and the outwardly, and the ephemeral and immortality' (ibid.: 198). The verb *zahada* means 'to renounce', 'to withdraw' and 'to forsake'. In the pre-Islamic period, the motif of asceticism dealt with renunciation (*zuhd*) and calling others to lead a life of abstention (*tazahhud*).[3] With the advent of Islam, the concept of asceticism was retooled to encourage and praise those who shun luxury in favour of a simple and pious life. In fact, *zuhd* in the Qur'an conveys the general meaning of 'a life of self-denial and devotional exercises' (Hamori 2008: 265).

---

[3] See Lane (1863); Ibn Manẓūr (1955–6); Wehr and Cowan (2016), *z-h-d*.

The ascetic impulse in jihadi-themed Arabic chants does not only refer to the binary sets of life and death; it also links the call to a life of abstention with the militant meaning of jihad. Militant activists and supporters of IS are reminded that the transfer from a temporal to an everlasting spiritual state can only be realised if they perform jihad and sacrifice themselves for the group. This blended reinterpretation of the ascetic concept and the militant meaning of jihad appears in an IS-affiliated chant known by its incipit *Kun Ma'a Allāh Naqiyyan* ('Be pure with God').

دونَكُمْ خوضوا مَيادينَ القِتالِ   إنْ أَرَدْتُمْ عِزَّةً في كُلّ أَمْــر

فازَ مَنْ لَبَّى وَضَحَّى كُلَّ غالي   ذِرْوَةُ الأمْرِ جِهادٌ فارْتَقوها

يَسْمَعُ الهَمْسَ بِذَرّاتِ الــرّمـــالِ   كُلُّ مَنْ يَدعوهُ يَلْقاهُ قَـريباً

وَعُراةً فَــاكْسُنا ثَــوْبَ المَعالي   يا إلَه الكَوْنِ جِئْنَاكَ حُـــفَـاةً

تَلْقاهُ يُـنْـجيكَ في سودِ الـلَّيالي   رَبُّكَ الحامي فاسْألْهُ خالِصاً

ثُمَّ يَبْقى وَجْـهُ رَبّي ذُو الجَلالِ   كُـــلُّ ما فَوْقَ البَرايا زائِلٌ

If you desire the glory in every matter other than yourselves,
    then embark boldly in the arenas of fighting.
The peak of the matter is jihad, so rise to it,
    for whoever heeds the call and sacrifices everything precious succeeds.
Everyone who calls him meets him soon.
    He hears the whisper in the tiny particles of sand.
O God of the Universe, we have come to you barefooted and naked,
    so clothe us in the garments of excellence.
Your Lord is your patron, so ask him sincerely.
    He will save you [even] in the darkest of times.
All that is above creation is transitory.
    What remains is the face of the Lord of Majesty.
(Gatt 2020: 201–2)

In this excerpt, the notion of jihad takes on a transitional dimension. The recipients of the chant are reminded to abstain from the luxuries of life because anything that is worldly is temporary (*zā'il*), and anything which is outwardly such as God is ephemeral (*yabqā*). The difference between human beings and God is projected through the clothing images. Humankind is described as appearing 'barefooted and naked' (*jiʾnāka ḥufātan wa-ʿurātan*) in front of God, whereas God is depicted as the one who clothes humans. This imagery recalls Islamic teachings about the Day of Resurrection, whereby the people will be gathered 'barefooted, naked and uncircumcised' (*tuḥsharūna ḥufātan ʿurātan ghurlan*).[4] Jihad is also framed in terms of fighting and self-sacrifice, and it is referred to as 'the peak of the matter' (*dhirwatu l-ʿamri jihādun*). The 'peak of the matter' is an intertextual reference to a passage from the Prophetic traditions which states that 'the head of the matter is Islam, its support is prayer, and the top of its hump is jihad' (*raʾsu l-amri al-islāmu, wa-ʿamūduhu l-ṣalātu, wa-dhurwatu sanāmihi al-jihādu*).[5] The orientational metaphor of going 'up' to reach jihad is also reminiscent of Islamic metaphors of ascending to heaven after death, such as Prophet Muḥammad's ascension to heaven known as *miʿrāj*. It is noteworthy to mention that metaphors assigned to Islam in classical Islamic scholarship are appropriated in jihadi-themed Arabic chants to narrow the gap between Islam and the militant interpretation of jihad. This connection is highlighted in the Islamic teachings attributed to ʿAlī b. Abī Ṭālib (d. 661 CE), the son-in-law of the Prophet, who argues that the four pillars of faith consist of forbearance (*al-ṣabr*), conviction (*al-yaqīn*), justice (*al-ʿadl*) and struggle against the evil (*jihād*).[6]

While reminding the recipients about their Islamic teachings, the chant advances by providing its interpretation of jihad, namely, actively fighting on the battlefield (*mayadīn al-qitāl*), heeding the call to jihad and sacrificing everything (*labbā wa-ḍaḥḥā kulla ghālī*). The sequence of the motif of asceticism followed by the militant meaning of jihad demonstrates that while jihadi-themed Arabic chants are replete with motifs of religious nature, their use is made from a vantage point beneath the transcendental status of the Qurʾan and the Prophetic traditions.

---

[4] Available at <https://sunnah.com/bukhari:6527> (last accessed 5 January 2022).

[5] Available at <https://tinyurl.com/dhirwatul-amri> (last accessed January 2022).

[6] 'Faith . . . stands on four pillars: forbearance (*al-sabr*), conviction (*al-yaqin*), justice (*al-ʿadl*), and struggle against the evil (*jihad*)' (Qutbuddin 2013: 132–5).

In a different IS-affiliated chant called *Ḥayātu al-Dhulli Lā, Lā Artaḍīhā* ('I am not satisfied with a life of humiliation'), the notion of jihad is depicted in the contradictory terms of 'life and death' and 'humiliation and honour'.

وَحُبُّ المَوتِ بِـالعِزِّ مَـرامُ	حَيَاةُ الذُلّ لا،لا أَرْتَضيهـــــا
فَما لِلـعَـبْـدِ في الدُنْيـا مَقـامُ	فَـلا وَالله لاَ أَخْشـــــى المَنايا
لَفَضْـلُ اللهِ يُؤْتـي مَنْ يَشاءُ	وَإنَّ المَوْتَ في دَرْبِ الجِهادِ
لِحُـبِّـكَ لا أَكِـلُّ وَلا أَنـامُ	فيا دَرْبَ الجِهادِ هَلُـمَ إنَّـــــي
خُـذِلْتُ مِنَ البَرِيَّةِ أَوْ أَلَـمُ	سَأَبْقى وَافِياً بِالعَهْدِ مَهْمـا
سَأَبْقى ثابِتاً مَـهْمـا أسامـوا	وَمَهْما سامَني الأَعْداءُ قَهْراً

I am not content with a life of humiliation,
   longing for an honourable death is the purpose.
By God, I swear I do not fear my fate,
   for the servant does not reside in the [material] world.
Indeed, death in the path of jihad
   is a gift God gives to whomever He wills.
Come forward O path of jihad,
   for your love, I am neither weary nor can I sleep.
I will remain loyal to the pact
   even if I suffer from setbacks or blame from [other] humans.
Whatever oppression enemies afflict me with,
   I will remain steadfast against whatever they intend to do.[7]
(Gatt 2020: 203–4)

Through text, Salafi-Jihadi groups like IS demand visceral commitment to the group. In this chant, the notion of jihad has a performative dimension and is directly linked to one's readiness to fight and die for the group. The performance of jihad is expressed in terms of several attributes that project how cadres should approach their death through jihad. These attributes include honour (*ʿizz*), fearlessness in the face of death (*lā akhshā al-manāyā*), worldly transience (*fa-mā li-l-ʿabdi fī al-dunyā maqām*), God's gift (*faḍlu allāhi*),

---

[7] This verse echoes the Qur'anic verse which reads: 'And to establish prayer (*aqīmū al-ṣalāla*) and fear Him. And it is He to whom you will be gathered'. See Qur'an, 6:72.

eagerness (*la akillu wa-lā anāmu*), loyalty (*sa-abqā wāfiyan*) and steadfast-ness (*sa-abqā thābitan*). The phrase 'the path of jihad' (*darb al-jihād*), which appears twice in this excerpt, is a loaded term that echoes the phrase 'jihad in the path of God' (*jihād fī sabīl allāh*), explicitly reminding the recipients that jihad is a religious duty ordained by God.

The link between jihad and death is explicitly pronounced in an IS-affiliated chant *Yā Fawza Man Nāla al-Shahāda* ('O victory in obtaining martyrdom'). The listeners are invited to heed the call in the chant and perform jihad. Death by jihad is beautified and the audience is reminded that their blood drops will remove their sins and their corpse will be covered with musk and perfume once they die.

تُمْحى الذُّنوبُ إذا الدِّماءُ تَقَطُرُ	يا فَوْزَ مَنْ نالَ الشَّهادَةَ صادِقاً
مِسْكٌ تَفوحُ جِـراحُـه وَتُعَطُّرُ	وَإذا الزُّهورُ تَعَطَّرَتْ بِعَبيرِهَا
وَتَسَلَّحـوا بالـحَـقِّ لاَ تَتَأَخَّروا	وَتَجَهَّزوا يا إخْوَتـي لِعَدُوّكُمْ
عِـزٌّ إذا ما نَسْتَجيبُ وَمَفْخَرُ	قوموا لِحَيَّ عَلى الـجِـهادِ فَإِنَّهُ

O victory for whoever accepts martyrdom truthfully,
> The dripping of blood washes away the sins.
When the flowers exude fragrance,
> his wounds emit musk and [his wounds] are perfumed.
O brothers of mine, prepare yourselves against your enemy,
> be armed with the truth and do not linger.
Rise to perform jihad,
> because when we respond to it, it becomes genuinely high-ranking and a source of pride.
(ibid.: 264–5)

In some cases, jihad acquires a spatial dimension. In another verse extracted from the same chant, militant fighters are encouraged to fight in 'the arena of jihad'.

وَتَـذَكَّـروا سـاحَ الجِـهادِ تَذَكَّروا	فَامْضـوا بِـجَـدٍّ مِـنْ مُـجِـدٍّ هِـمَّةٌ

Go ahead in all seriousness and vigour from an earnest person,
> and keep in mind the arena of jihad.
(ibid.: 264)

The listeners of the chant are reminded that their companions were ready to leave the comfort of their home and emigrate in order to sacrifice their lives for the sake of jihad.

إخْـوانـكُـمْ شَـدّوا سُـروجَ مَطِيّهِمْ   كابولُ شَدّت والنّجائِب ضمَّروا

وَتَـذَكَّـروا أهْـلَ الجَـزِيـرَةِ إخْـوةً   تَرَكوا النّعِيمَ إلى الـجِـهادِ وَغـادَروا

Your brothers have tightened their horse's saddle,
    Kabul is in dire straits, and the noble warriors dwindle one by one,
Do you remember those who lived in the [Arabian] Peninsula as brothers?
    They left their comfort to join jihad, and departed.
(ibid.: 264)

Through implicit references to the Prophetic traditions, the spatial dimension of jihad is compared to the pilgrimage (*al-ḥajj*) to the city of Mecca.

شُدّوا الرّحالَ إلى الجِهادِ عَسَكُم   أنْ تُـقْـتَـلُوا فِالله أوْ أنْ تُنْـصِـروا

Be ready to travel and perform jihad.
    You may either be killed for the sake of God or be victorious.
(ibid.: 265)

The command 'be ready to travel' (*shuddū l-riḥāl*) in this verse appears in the Book of the Pilgrimage (*Kitāb al-Ḥajj*). According to the Prophetic traditions, ʿAisha narrated that ʿUmar said, 'Be ready to travel for Ḥajj (*shuddū al-riḥāl fī al-ḥajj*), as it is one of the two kinds of jihad.'[8]

Reconciling Sound with Sense

The relationship between music and text has been the subject of scholarly inquiry for the past centuries. The English poet Alexander Pope writes in one of his poems titled 'Sound and Sense' that '[t]he sound must seem an echo to the sense'. In the Arabic poetic tradition, the nearest equivalent of the complementary pair of 'sound and sense' appears in the discussion between form (*lafẓ*) and content (*maʿnā*) (Van Gelder 2012: 3). In the seminal work

---

[8] Available at <https://tinyurl.com/shuddulrihal> (last accessed 5 January 2022).

al-ʿUmda, the Tunisian poet and literary critic Ibn Rashīq al-Qayrawānī (d. 1063 CE) compares the relationship between form (*lafẓ*) and content (*maʿnā*) to the relationship between the body and the soul, arguing that 'the sounds are a body its soul being the sense; they are connected to it as is the soul to a body, which is weak through their weakness and strong through their strength' (Ibn Rashīq 1972: 124).

On a similar note, in the discussion about medieval music compositions, David Wilson argues that 'the music does not attempt "to interpret" the text; rather, it is a vehicle for a poetry that is already highly stylized' (Wilson 1990: 344). Wilson also stresses that '[t]here is no attempt to integrate music and text emotionally. Rather, the melody is a musical element governed by its own rules onto which text is placed' (ibid.: 241). To date, however, there are no universal principles that intimately link the sound of a poetic or musical composition with its sense. For this reason, it is erroneous to argue in favour of a harmonious correlation between the sound and sense in Arabic chants. This chapter argues that the efficacy of the sound and sense is linked to the simultaneous attribution of tradition and modernity.

Tradition and Modernity

From an emic perspective, the dichotomous relationship between tradition and modernity holds the key to the effectiveness of jihadi-themed Arabic chants. This relationship concurs with what Eric Hobsbawm calls 'invented traditions', which include both 'traditions' which are 'actually invented, constructed and formally instituted and those emerging in a less easily traceable manner within a brief and dateable period . . . and establishing themselves with great rapidity' (Hobsbawm and Ranger 2013: 1). The concept of tradition consists of the appropriation of material culture borrowed from the manifold domains of Muslim cultural production. This process selectively reconstructs material culture that is already meaningful to speakers of Arabic and Muslims in a positive way. Effectively, Salafi-Jihadi groups continually engage in a complex process of appropriating, reclaiming, reimagining and recreating traditions belonging to mainstream Arabic-speaking and Islamic communities to push forward the Salafi-Jihadi ideology and derive their legitimacy from traditional practices related to violence, warfare and hegemonic discourses (see also Gatt 2020).

Appropriated Qur'anic citations, formulaic religious expressions, ancient wisdom, allusions to Islamic figures and warriors feature in different forms of written and audiovisual productions, including poetry, chants, speeches, newspaper articles, school books, videos, iconography and nomenclature.[9] IS, for example, appropriates the figure of the Prophet by 'interweaving a range of allusions to the figure of the Prophet and reclaiming the spiritual and worldly inheritance of Muḥammad and the ṣaḥāba' (Günther 2021: 469). Additionally, Salafi-Jihadi groups exploit the 'aura of factuality' created around the figure of the Prophet in mainstream Islamic culture to 'bolster hierarchical power structures' and to incentivise 'authorities to cloak themselves in the aura of the past in order to legitimise their present endeavours' (ibid.: 448–73).

Whether secular or religious, the selective reconstruction of traditions seems to be a fundamental persuasion strategy underlying Salafi-Jihadi messaging and propaganda. Links to historical events are so unprecedented that they need to be invented by 'creating an ancient past beyond effective historical continuity, either by semi-fiction . . . or by forgery' (Hobsbawm and Ranger 2013: 7). The main objective of exploiting different traditions in the case of Salafi-Jihadi cultural products is to establish historical continuity with the Islamic past and to deliver a narrative that raises the level of enthusiasm among the supporters. Given that the Arabic and Islamic traditions span over millennia, Salafi-Jihadi groups have a vast array of references at their disposal. This issue is best explained by the historian Hugh Kennedy, who admits that in the vast historical records, one may find references both to 'an aggressive and fiercely controlling' caliphate as well as a caliphate that is 'generous and open to different ideas' (Kennedy 2016: xvi).

At times, 'invented traditions' not only use 'old materials', but 'may also be forced to invent new languages or devices, or extend the old symbolic vocabulary beyond its established limits' (Hobsbawm and Ranger 2013: 7). The Salafi-Jihadi narrative borrows conflicting elements from tradition, including pre-Islamic or 'un-Islamic' practices. For example, several scholars have noted that the ethos of blood vengeance – an integral part of Salafi-Jihadi ideology

---

[9] The manipulation of tradition in the Salafi-Jihadi milieu is discussed in Boudali et al. (2006); Kendall and Khan (2016); and Hegghammer (2017).

and propaganda – is essentially pre-Islamic and contradicts Qur'anic teachings (Fakhro 2018: 402–22). Names of historical figures are also used to this effect. For example, IS named its all-female morality policing brigade after the seventh-century female poet al-Khansā' even though such brigades have no equivalence in the Islamic tradition (see also Gatt 2020: 89). In the poetic realm, Salafi-Jihadi propaganda includes frequent references to pre-Islamic verses (Kendall and Khan 2016: 228–9).

In Salafi-Jihadi communication, tradition is attributed simultaneously to modernity. The notion of modernity includes the use of twenty-first-century technology. Whereas the Salafi-Jihadi narrative is intricately linked to the Arabic and Islamic traditions, the transmission of Salafi-Jihadi communication, including chants, relies increasingly on modern technological advancements. Militant Islamist groups have embraced chants as a novel art form since the late 1960s and have continually developed it to different extents (Said 2016: 45ff.; Pieslak 2017: 67ff.; Hegghammer 2017: 188). Modern technology is evident in the high-quality production of flashy magazines, videos and audiovisual material such as chants. The production of chants shows the amalgamation of strict conformity to traditional poetic conventions coupled with sound effects from the battlefield, including gunshots, explosions or the sound of marching soldiers.

The dependence of Salafi-Jihadi material on modern means of transmission stems from the increasing need to reach different categories of people transnationally, including Muslims and Arabic-speaking individuals residing in Arab countries as well as others living outside it. The possibility of streaming the events taking place on the battlefield in real-time via social media has created an unprecedented scenario that narrows the gap between individuals across the globe and militants of Salafi-Jihadism.

At the textual level, Arabic chants circulated in the Salafi-Jihadi milieu resonate culturally with the Arabic-speaking communities because of their rigid structure and Islamic rhetoric. At the level of sound, the added effects accompanying modern manifestations of Arabic chants disseminated by IS such as explosions, gunshots and marching may appeal to the global youth because these effects glamorise the life of militant Salafi-Jihadi fighters.

In popular culture, similar sound effects are evident in rap and hip-hop music. A contemporary subgenre of hip-hop music known as 'drill', for instance, engages with similar effects and it is 'often rhythmically rigid – with a snare falling on the third beat of each bar – drill moves to skippy, syncopated hi-hat patterns echoing the rapid fire of a machine gun'. Different to other forms of hip-hop, drill music is characterised by 'its combative energy and its particular concern with gang conflict and murder' (see also Davies 2021). The subliminal sound effects are intended to replicate the soundscape of the human world. In the case of jihadi-themed Arabic chants, the sound effects mirror the noise of the battlefield, whereas in the case of hip-hop music, the sound effects are often linked to the underworld, including attacks between gangs, drug dealing and street crime.

On a sociocultural level, Arabic chants serve as a multi-functional platform that appeals to foreign-based and grassroots recruits. Generally speaking, this means that consumers of music may witness similar experiences to grassroots recruits when listening to Arabic chants. For non-Arab consumers, the sound of Arabic chants may be reminiscent of music. For Arabic speakers or Muslims living in the Arab or Islamic world, the sound of incantation is culturally authentic because it alludes to imaginations of a glorious heritage. To that extent, the sound and sense of Arabic chants function as a potent bridge to transmit the Salafi-Jihadi ideology globally across mainstream Islamic and non-Islamic cultures.

The Uses of Arabic Chants

The different uses of jihadi-themed Arabic chants shed light on the strategic function and practicality of music in the Salafi-Jihadi subculture. Although academic scholarship taking theories from the field of music as its focal point has reaped significant results, this research is hampered by the contradiction of the Salafi-Jihadist ban on music for its sensually arousing potential.[10] Moreover, given the uncompromising stance of Salafi-Jihadism on music, it is implausible to assume that Salafi-Jihadi composers borrow elements from non-Arabic or Arabic music as a blueprint for Arabic chants. Keeping this in mind, this study benefits from a comparative and contrastive analysis of cultural practices in the Arab and Islamic world that may have contributed to the success of Arabic chants in a particular milieu.

---

[10] The Salafi-Jihadi stance against music is well-documented in scholarly literature. See also Said (2016) and (2012: 863–79); and Pieslak (2017: 63ff.).

On a cultural level, Arabic chants derive their authenticity in terms of sound and sense from the Islamic idiom and the poetic style. At the textual level, chants enjoy several intertextual connections with traditional values, the Qur'an and the Prophetic traditions. At the sound level, chants instrumentalise the emotional charge of the oral performance induced by the beautiful chanting voices reminiscent of the Qur'anic recitation (*tajwīd*). In mainstream Islamic cultures, chants are mobilised for educational and religious purposes. Salim 'Abd al-Qadir Zinjir (1953–2013), for instance, composed children's poetry in the form of Islamic chants for education, motivation, good upbringing in the Islamic faith and active participation in one's community. Emotionally laden messages transmitted through sound help transmit different messages subliminally. The oral performance of Qur'anic recitation is 'at the center of Islamic corporate and individual piety' (Denny 1989: 5). In principle, *tajwīd* focuses on clarity of expression, the proper timing of syllables and the phonetic changes to the spoken word, which convey the values of magnanimity and salvation.

Stylistically, the Qur'an and Arabic chants of jihadi nature represent different forms of rhythmic discourse developed from the secular and the sacred traditions respectively, involving an internal sound system that facilitates memorisation. Both stylistic features are birthed in the oral tradition and are aimed at an auditory culture that responds positively to rhythmic discourse. The composition of the Qur'an follows a rhymed prose style (*saj'*), whereas the structure of Arabic chants is based on the classical Arabic ode (*qaṣīda*). The act of memorising verses from the Qur'an is the primary source of identification among the Muslim communities. According to the Quran Academy, those who memorise the Qur'an (*ḥāfiẓ*) are privileged on various levels. Memorisers are elevated in this world and the Hereafter, they are protected from the fire of Hell, they are always in the company of the high angels, their deed of memorisation will intercede for ten members of their family who were destined to go to Hell and, finally, they will be able to recite the Qur'an at all times (Khan 2014).

On the battlefield, the integration of the oral traditions (Qur'an and poetry) narrows the gap between the sacred and the secular spheres. With the advancement of technology, the secular and sacred spheres became interconnected. Depending on the atmosphere, militants would alternate between playing the Qur'anic recitations and chants on their car stereo (see also Hegghammer 2017:

189). This alternation benefits Salafi-Jihadi propagandists who continually seek to influence their followers' judgements and provoke actions. An example of this link is the depiction of pre-Islamic and even 'un-Islamic' values such as blood vengeance as part of the Islamic tradition (see also Gatt 2020). This link is further accentuated in Salafi-Jihadi audiovisual material, whereby recited verses borrowed verbatim from the Qur'an and the Prophetic traditions and Arabic chants are integrated at various stages of Salafi-Jihadi propagandist videos. Violent scenes of beheadings and shooting on the battlefield are equally accompanied by the soothing voices of Qur'an recitation and jihadi-themed Arabic chants.

Salafi-Jihadists strategise Qur'anic recitation on the battlefield to the extent that, as early as the 1980s, a Salafi-Jihadi group made up of pre-dominantly Arabic speakers 'recited the Qur'an on loudspeakers as a form of psychological warfare against the enemy'. Likewise, al-Qaʿida operatives in Somalia 'recited the Qur'an to boost the morale of his own men' (Hegghammer 2017). The IS female poet known by her pseudonym Ahlam al-Nasr argues that through her writing, which consists of text with embedded Qur'anic verses and poetry, she hopes 'to arouse desire and motivate the supporters, enraging and causing them to commit suicide against the disbelievers' (al-Nasr 2018).

Popular Appeal of Arabic Chants

Arabic chants are widespread among Salafi-Jihadi groups due to their popular appeal. Arabic chants are popular on the battlefield because they are culturally authentic and practical. Additionally, chants enjoy a popular appeal due to their links with mainstream Islamic traditions (Gatt 2021). In the Arabic-speaking environment, the appeal of Arabic chants goes beyond the Salafi-Jihadi milieu. Historically informed, chants date back to the tense political atmosphere arising in Egypt and Syria during the 1970s in the period known as 'the Islamic Awakening' (al-ṣaḥwa al-islāmiyya). Chants of Islamic and political nature were instrumentalised as a pivotal part of the counter-culture challenging the status quo during that time, including Muslim rulers (see also Gatt 2020: 124ff.; Said 2016: 45ff.). From this time onwards, chants have featured as a tool to communicate messages of political or religious nature in mainstream Arabic and Islamic cultures.

The practice of incorporating chants as an integral part of a group's culture, its daily rituals and discourse is not only restricted to the Salafi-Jihadi groups. Other Arabic-speaking ideological groups such as Hizbullah and Hamas, and non-Arabic speaking groups such as the Taliban, have equally resorted to chants as an auditory vehicle to communicate their messages. Similarly, mainstream political parties in the Arab world have produced national chants (*anashīd waṭaniyya*) as a musical accompaniment to propagate the pan-Arab nationalist ideology.[11]

Formally, Arabic chants produced by pan-Arab nationalists, Islamic preachers, Islamists and Salafi-jihadists are unified through the shared, rigid structure of the *qaṣīda*, with its end-rhyme and fixed metre.[12] However, the content of the chants differs significantly depending on the affiliation of the chants. For example, chants produced by Salafi-jihadists tend to differ contextually from chants produced by pan-Arab nationalists.[13] For this reason, it is imperative to regard chants in general terms as a 'communicative vehicle' that facilitates the diffusion of particular national, Islamic or ideological values (see also Gatt 2022). This does not mean that there is a clear-cut distinction between different sociopolitical and religious realms such as the Islamic and Salafi-Jihadi spheres. Salafi-Jihadi groups often exploit Islamic chants verbatim or with minor adaptations for their own benefit.[14] IS, for example, made frequent use of Islamic chants to legitimate its discourse and operations and to consolidate its image and identity as part of mainstream Islamic culture (see also Gatt 2020: 82). Thus, the circulation of chants is 'not just about engendering militancy, but also about identity building' (Lahoud 2017: 54). While one may argue that Arabic chants of jihadi nature bear striking resemblances to chants of Islamic nature, the jihadi-themed chants are often identified by their aggressive political activism, which includes a transnational outlook and an exclusive focus on armed struggle (Gatt 2020: 21ff.).

[11] Other examples are found in Gatt (2020: 59–63).

[12] Although chants are based on the classical Arabic ode, structural alterations exist, such as the deviation from the strict monorhyme.

[13] The national anthems in the Arab world follow the structure of the classical Arabic ode, with some alterations. Neo-classical poetry in Arabic is also intrinsically linked to pan-Arab nationalist ideology. See also Gatt (2020: 60ff.).

[14] For examples of ascetic verses of Islamic in nature, see also Gatt (2020: 198ff.).

Shared Functions of Music and Arabic Chants

In our attempt to broaden our understanding of Arabic chants, this section maps out similarities between the various functions of Arabic chants among Salafi-Jihadi groups and music globally. The anthropologist Alan Merriam provides a thorough anthropological investigation of the uses and functions of music across different cultures (Merriam 1964: 209–28). As a reference point, this study adopts and adapts the use and function of music listed in Alan Merriam's work about the functions of sound in Arabic chants of jihadi nature. The uses and functions will be discussed with reference to the projection of the sound and sense of jihad in Arabic chants of jihadi nature.

The Function of Aesthetic Enjoyment and Entertainment

In warfare, music fulfils the functions of aesthetic enjoyment and entertainment. Radical organisations such as the Taliban have exploited the power of chants as 'a source of entertainment' and as 'a key component of the Taliban information and propaganda war' (Johnson and Waheed 2011: 3–31). Similarly, jihadi-themed Arabic chants are identified through their alluring soundscape, which is exploited to entice recruits into the ranks of Salafi-Jihadi groups. Modern facets of Salafi-Jihadi groups like IS borrow sonic effects from the battlefield to create rhythms such as the blast from explosions, the clashing of swords, the marching of soldiers and the stuttering of gunfire (Gatt 2020: 125). Additionally, Arabic chants produced by modern Salafi-Jihadi groups include other technological means of aestheticisation such as pitch correction, the digital reverb effect and delay (see also Dick 2019: 97; Weinrich 2020: 261ff.).

The Function of Expressing Emotions

Chants do not express individual emotions at a specific point in time but are intended to express and evoke emotions collectively for a particular group. Generally, music and Arabic chants of jihadi nature fulfil the general function of stimulating, expressing and sharing collective emotions. The soundscape of music and Arabic chants alike functions 'as a mechanism of emotional release for a large group of people acting together' (Merriam 1964: 222). Through text and music, Arabic chants exploit key emotions such as sorrow, pride, desperation, shame and hope to create sympathy for the Salafi-Jihadi groups and fuel the people's resentments against the adversaries, recruit new fighters and undermine the government of the country. If music can arouse collective emotions within a particular group, then it is precisely this ability which 'makes it a valuable tool in propaganda, recruitment, membership retention, morale, and motivation to action' (Pieslak 2017: 77).

Different types of music may also foster interpersonal bonds and provide 'a communal basis for social relationships, and at the same time [they] also draw demarcation lines between different social agglomerations, whereby "we" are mostly connoted in a positive sense and "the others" in a negative sense' (Barber-Kersovan 2004: 7). In an IS-affiliated video called *Purification of the Souls*, militants appear sitting on the ground holding rifles and chanting verses led by a child (see also Zelin 2017: 14:57). This extract illustrates how Salafi-Jihadi propaganda appropriates ideas and memories related to the poetic tradition to build group rapport. Beyond words, the upbeat melody of Arabic chants imparts the exaltation of the ego, promoting glory, pride and territorial victories, the stirring of new courage and vigour in enlivening chants, grief in the laments to fallen fighters and anger against the adversaries. On the battlefield, Arabic chants help boost the fighters' morale, express solidarity with one another, ease the hardship of the battlefield and build group rapport through collective incantation (see also Gatt 2020: 144). In this context, then, music 'provides a rallying point around which the members of society gather to engage in activities which require the cooperation and coordination of the group' (Merriam 1964: 227).

The Function of Physical Response

The Salafi-Jihadi ideology, which revolted against the image of idlers and replaced it with 'an activist and self-sacrificial ethos', is sounded out in the groups' chants (Lahoud 2017: 55). Salafi-Jihadi groups use the sounds, tones and rhythms of chants to stir up emotions of anger and grief that promote violence and send humans, mainly men, into battle. Gratrud argues that people tend to be less critical of messages that are set to music. This benefits extremist groups because 'it facilitates the delivery of messages that air grievances, glorify violence, and dehumanise the enemy' (Gratrud 2016: 1052). Although physical reactions to music are probably culturally shaped and therefore one cannot assume that a particular type of sound elicits a particular physical reaction, 'physical response seems clearly to be an important function of music' (Merriam 1964: 224). Arabic chants contribute to the political identity of the respective organisations and also operate in tandem with militants in recruitment strategies, engendering a culture of militancy and motivating actions against the perceived enemy. More specifically, music and Arabic chants play a pivotal role in eliciting, exciting and channelling crowd behaviour by encouraging the 'physical reactions of the warrior and the hunter' (Merriam 1964: 224).

The Function of Validation of Social Institutions

Arabic chants are rooted in a war environment (see also Said 2016: 45ff.). In times of political turmoil, where anti-establishment movements seek to obtain political power, different ideological groups exploit the sociopolitical function of music to create an organisational identity and validate their institutions. In the case of Salafi-Jihadi groups, claims of legitimacy are sounded out in the groups' chants because the auditory component signals authority and also serves as a warning against the opponents in a war zone. For example, IS used chants on the battlefield to demarcate the groups' territory (Marshall 2014). It is also a common practice for militant jihadists to play chants on the car stereos while patrolling Salafi-Jihadi compounds, or to play chants on large speakers during social gatherings or while on the battlefield. Chants are also set as ringtones on mobile phones (Marshall 2014; Said 2016: 864; Hegghammer 2017: 189; Seymat 2014). The auditory element also reminds the listeners of 'the proper and improper in society' and tells 'people what to do and how to do it' (Merriam 1964: 224–5). For sympathisers of Salafi-Jihadi groups, the act of memorising Arabic chants signals their affiliation and represents their loyalty to and membership in the group.[15] Engaging in listening to or chanting jihadi-themed Arabic chants shows one's willingness to be identified as part of the group and one's motivation to engage in the group's activities. To sum up, jihadi-themed Arabic chants communicate implicit messages continually, serving multiple functions in the group. These functions demonstrate that the sound and sense of jihadi-themed chants should be appreciated beyond the aesthetical layer made up of words set to rhythm.

---

[15] Music also plays an important role in the process of radicalisation. See also Moeller and Mischler (2020).

Conclusion

This study set out to reconsider the notion of jihad in jihadi-themed Arabic chants and determine the causes of their efficacy among Salafi-Jihadi groups. This research has examined how the meaning of jihad has developed from its spiritual dimension to violent, transitional, spatial and performative dimensions that result in death. The discussion has shown that while it is fair to conclude that the notion of jihad in jihadi-themed Arabic chants appears almost exclusively in its militant form, this tendency is not exclusive to the Salafi-Jihadi groups. Evidence suggests that the militant dimension of jihad had already been broadly circulated and 'legitimated' through mainstream political discourse about warfare. It was also argued that the incantation of jihadi-themed Arabic chants is reminiscent of the oral secular and sacred traditions, mainly the Qurʾanic *tajwīd* and poetic recitations. The participatory auditory practice of chanting appeals to the Arabic-speaking and Muslim cadres because it legitimates and sacralises the message, and restores a sense of pride in the Arabic and Islamic heritage. At the textual level, this chapter has revealed that sound is reinforced through an Islamic repertoire and intertextualities to the Qurʾan and the Prophetic traditions. Additionally, the text is characterised by its simplicity and directness of style, its bipolar worldview between good and evil and its pious militancy-scriptural rhetoric. Authenticity is emphasised through the replication of the main features of the classical Arabic ode, including its fixed metre, end-rhyme and common themes. One of the more significant findings to emerge from this study is that jihadi-themed Arabic chants share similar functions and uses to international music. In terms of modernity, this study has outlined the shared functions and uses of music with the role of Arabic chants in the Salafi-Jihadi milieu and has argued in favour of a broader understanding of this cultural artefact. Taken together, this work has exemplified how the sound and sense of jihadi-themed Arabic chants work in tandem to promote a cultural product that continues to develop dialogically with its globalised sociocultural and political environment.

References

Al-Nasr, A. (2018), 'Akhiran rabbuna kataba al-samaha: bi-qalam shaʿiratu dawlati al-islam ahlam al-nasr', *al-Ghurabaʾ li-l-iʿlam*, <https://bit.ly/2KzBJxo> (last accessed 5 January 2018).

Barber-Kersovan, A. (2004), 'Music as a Parallel Power Structure', in M. Korpe (ed.), *Shoot the Singer! Music Censorship Today*, London: Zed Books, pp. 6–11.

Bengio, O. (1998), *Saddam's Word: Political Discourse in Iraq*, Oxford: Oxford University Press.

Boudali, K. L., O. Afshon and J. Brachman (2006), *Islamic Imagery Project: Visual Motifs in Jihadi Internet Propaganda*, West Point, NY: Combating Terrorism Centre.

Davies, S. (2021), 'The Controversial Music that Is the Sound of Global Youth', *BBC*, 8 June, <https://www.bbc.com/culture/article/20210607-the-controversial-music-that-is-the-sound-of-global-youth> (last accessed 16 April 2022).

Denny, F. M. (1989), 'Qur'an Recitation: A Tradition of Oral Performance and Transmission', *Oral Tradition*, 4: 1–2, 5–26.

Dick, A. (2019), '"The Sounds of the Shuhada": Chants and Chanting in IS Martyrdom Videos', *BEHEMOTH: A Journal on Civilisation*, 12: 1, 89–104.

Fakhro, D. (2018), 'Tracing the Movement of the Blood Vengeance Theme within Arabic Poetry: From the Classical Poetic Tradition to the Present', *British Journal of Middle Eastern Studies*, 47: 3, 402–22.

Gatt, K. (2018), 'Reconciling the Iraqi Nation: A Rhetorical Analysis of Nuri al-Maliki's Political Discourse', in B. Backe, T. Hanstein and K. Stock (eds), *Arabische Sprache im Kontext: Festschrift zu Ehren von Eckehard Schulz*, Leipziger Beiträge zur Orientforschung, Vol. 37, Berlin: Peter Lang, pp. 161–86.

Gatt, K. (2020), *Decoding DA'ISH: An Analysis of Poetic Exemplars and Discursive Strategies of Domination in the Jihadist Milieu*, Litkon, series 45, Wiesbaden: Reichert Verlag.

Gatt, K. (2021), 'Popularising the Political: Jihadi Chants as a Medium for Motivation and Mobilisation', in L. Behzadi, P. Konerding and F. Wiedemann (eds), *Popular Culture in Modern Arabic Art, Music and Literature*, Bamberg: Bamberg University Press, pp. 59–96.

Gatt, K. (2022), 'Poetry as a Communicative Vehicle in the Jihadi Milieu: The Case for Modern Extremist Poetry', *British Journal of Middle Eastern Studies*, 49: 5, 993–1013.

Gratrud, H. (2016), 'Islamic State Nasheeds as Messaging Tools', *Studies in Conflict and Terrorism*, 39: 12, 1050–70.

Günther, C. (2021), 'al-Dawla al-nabawiyya: Appropriating the Prophet's Authority in the Islamic State's Media', in R. Chih, D. Jordan and S. Reichmuth (eds), *The Presence of the Prophet in Early Modern and Contemporary Islam*, Vol. 2, Leiden: Brill, pp. 448–73.

Hamori, A. (2008), 'Ascetic Poetry (*Zuhdiyyat*)', in J. Ashtiany, T. M. Johnstone, J. D. Latham, R. B. Serjeant and G. R. Smith (eds), *The Cambridge History of Arabic literature: 'Abbasid Belles Lettres*, Cambridge: Cambridge Press, pp. 265–74.

Hegghammer, T. (2017), 'Non-Military Practices in Jihadi Groups', in T. Hegghammer (ed.), *Jihadi Culture: The Art and Social Practices of Militants Islamists*, Cambridge: Cambridge University Press, pp. 171–201.

Hobsbawm, E. and T. Ranger (eds) (2013), *The Invention of Tradition*, Cambridge: Cambridge University Press.

Ibn Manẓūr (1955–6), *Lisān al-'Arab*, Beirut: Dar Sadir.

Ibn Rashiq (1972), *al-'Umda fi mahasin al-shi'r wa-adabihi wa-naqdihi*, Vol. 1, Beirut: Dar al-Jil.

Johnson, T. H. and A. Waheed (2011), 'Analyzing Taliban *Taranas* (Chants): An Effective Afghan Propaganda Artifact', *Small Wars & Insurgencies*, 22: 1, 3–31.

Kendall, E. and A. Khan (eds) (2016), *Reclaiming Islamic Tradition: Modern Interpretations of the Classical Heritage*, Edinburgh: Edinburgh University Press.

Kennedy, H. (2016), *Caliphate: The History of an Idea*, New York: Basic Books.

Khan, N. (2014), 'Tasheel ut Tahfeedh: A Guide to Memorising the Qur'an', *Quran Academy*, November, <http://quranacademy.org.uk/wp-content/uploads/2014/11/A-Guide-to-Memorising-the-Quran-by-Shaykh-Nagib-Khan.pdf> (last accessed 6 January 2022).

Lahoud, N. (2017), 'A Cappella Songs (*anashid*) in Jihadi Culture', in T. Hegghammer (ed), *Jihadi Culture: The Art and Social Practices of Militants Islamists*, Cambridge: Cambridge University Press, pp. 42–62.

Lane, E. W. (1863), *An Arabic–English Lexicon: I–VIII*, London and Edinburgh: Williams and Norgate.

Libyan Pen (2021), '*Khitab al-za'im al-libi mu'ammar al-Qadhafi*', YouTube video, 14:44, 19 October, <https://www.youtube.com/watch?v=tqQKPSvc8Ko> (last accessed 5 January 2022).

Marshall, A. (2014), 'How ISIS Got its Anthem', *The Guardian*, 9 November, <https://www.theguardian.com/music/2014/nov/09/nasheed-how-isis-got-its-anthem> (last accessed 12 January 2022).

Merriam, A. P. (1964), *The Anthropology of Music*, Evanston: Northwestern University Press.

Moeller, V. and A. Mischler (2020), 'The Soundtrack of the Extreme: Nasheeds and Right-Wing Extremist Music as a "Gateway Drug" into the Radical Scene?' *International Annals of Criminology*, 58: 2, 291–334.

Pieslak, J. (2017), 'A Musicological Perspective on Jihadi Anashid', in T. Hegghammer (ed.), *Jihadi Culture: The Art and Social Practices of Militants Islamists*, Cambridge: Cambridge University Press, pp. 63–81.

Qutbuddin, T. (trans.) (2013), *A Treasury of Virtues: Sayings, Sermons, and Teachings of 'Ali, with the One Hundred Proverbs, Attributed to al-Jahiz*, New York: New York University Press.

Said, B. (2012), 'Hymns (Nasheeds): A Contribution to the Study of the Jihadist Culture', *Studies in Conflict and Terrorism*, 35: 12, 863–79.

Said B. (2016), *Hymnen des Jihads: Naschids im Kontext Jihadistischer Mobilisierung*, Wuerzburg: Ergon Verlag.

Seymat, T. (2014), 'How Nasheeds became the Soundtrack of Jihad', *Euronews*, 8 October, <https://www.euronews.com/2014/10/08/nasheeds-the-soundtrack-of-jihad> (last accessed 5 January 2022).

Van Gelder, J. G. (2012), *Sound and Sense in Classical Arabic Poetry*, Wiesbaden: Harrassowitz Verlag.

Wehr, H. and J. M. Cowan (2016), *A Dictionary of Modern Written Arabic*, Lavergne, TN: Snowball Publishing.

Weinrich, I. (2020), ' "Nashid" between Islamic Chanting and Jihadi Hymns: Continuities and Transformations', in C. Guenther and S. Pfeifer (eds), *Jihadi Audiovisuality and its Entanglements: Meanings, Aesthetics, Appropriations*, Edinburgh: Edinburgh University Press, pp. 249–72.

Wilson, D. F. (1990), *Music of the Middle Ages: Style and Structure*, New York: Schirmer Books.

Wright, W. (1955), *A Grammar of the Arabic Language*, Vol. 1, 3rd edn, Cambridge: Cambridge University Press.

Zelin, A. Y. (2017), 'Purification of the Souls–Wilayat al-Raqqa', *Jihadology* (blog), 20 June, <http://jihadology.net/2017/06/19/new-video-message-from-the-islamic-state-purification-of-the-souls-wilayat-al-raqqah/> (last accessed 5 January 2022).

9

DOCUMENTING THE YAZIDI SURVIVAL OF GENOCIDE: AESTHETICS AND POLITICS BETWEEN *SABAYA*, THE MURAD CODE AND *THE LAST GIRL*

Sebastian Köthe

On 3 August 2014, the self-proclaimed Islamic State (ISIS) invaded the Sinjar region, a territory disputed between the Kurdish and Iraqi governments in the north-west of Iraq, ancestral and contemporary home of many Yazidi communities. An endogamous, ethnic and religious minority, Yazidis look back to a *longue durée* of defamation, persecution and attacks, leading to the mythical figure of seventy-two *ferman*, a term used to describe the historical massacres and genocides.[1] After terror attacks in August 2007 killed twenty-three Yazidi workers in Bashiqa and more than 500 people in

---

[1] In her analysis of the repeated attacks against the Yazidis, Caroline Schneider emphasises the heterogeneous forms and functions of violence against the Yazidis since the thirteenth century. She enumerates religious, political, economic, social or ideological reasons such as tax collection, religious control and military conscription for the violence that has taken the form of 'massacres, persecutions, torture, imprisonment, displacement, forced conversions, discrimination, suppression, enslavement, sexual violence and prejudice' (Schneider 2021: 416). Schneider is right in being careful not to reduce the Yazidi's role as victims but to describe them as a rich and resistant group of survivors that today needs resources and time to 'define or redefine their identity and find new ways to survive as a group' (ibid.: 417).

the towns of Til Êzêr and Siba Sêx, Yazidis counted the seventy-third *ferman*.[2] When ISIS invaded Sinjar in August 2014, when Sunni neighbours cooperated with the invaders, when the Kurdish Peshmerga withdrew without fight, and when the Iraqi state failed to protect them, Yazidis counted the seventy-fourth *ferman*. More than 5,000 men were killed; around seventy mass graves have been found until today (RASHID 2019: 33). More than 7,000 Yazidi girls and women were enslaved. They were forced to convert to Islam; to work and serve; they were systematically sexually abused, distributed among fighters, sold to other militants or sold abroad (ibid.; El-Masri 2018: 6–8). In contrast to most other forms of modern slavery, ISIS's institutions and media officially acknowledged it and tried to legitimate it as official policy (Revkin and Wood 2021). Yazidi boys were separated from their families, forced to convert to Islam, indoctrinated and enlisted to ISIS's military. Around 250,000 Yazidis fled from Sinjar, another 35,000 from the twin towns of Bashiqa and Bahzani. By destroying more than forty-five religious sites as well as homes, agricultural equipment, livestock and other infrastructures, ISIS intentionally and 'systematically targeted the culture, identity and heritage of Iraqi Yazidis . . . threaten[ing] the unique identity and survival of the community' (RASHID 2019: 30). The landmines and improvised explosive devices left behind by ISIS threaten the returnees until today (ibid.: 34–5). Serhat Ortaç has explicated that this constitutes genocide in the sense of the Convention on the Prevention and Punishment of the Crime of Genocide which was ratified by 147 states, including Syria and Iraq (Ortaç 2016: 10–22). This view was also adopted by political bodies such as the European Parliament (European Parliament 2016) and the United Nations Human Rights Office of the High Commissioner (UN OHCHR 2016).

In December 2014, an alliance of Yazidi and Peshmerga fighters, supported by US airstrikes, fought back against the occupation and liberated the territory north of Sinjar. In November 2015 the Singal Alliance liberated the important town Singal, south of the mountain. Slowed down by conflicts between the Kurdish and Iraqi governments, the southern region

[2] Schmidinger points out that the mythical and non-empirical quality of the count of seventy-two was ignored or forgotten by Yazidis when they continued the count (Schmidinger 2019: 63–6).

was freed only in May 2017 by Yazidi forces together with Iraqi armed forces (Schmidinger 2019: 103–10). With the fall of Baghouz Fawqani in Syria in March 2019, ISIS lost its last territorial enclave. Yet, more than 2,000 Yazidi women and children were still missing (ibid.: 97). Many Yazidis could not or would not return to Sinjar. The war destroyed the region's social and economic infrastructure. There have been no justice or reconciliation initiatives regarding the collaboration of Sunni populations with ISIS. Its political status between Kurdistan and Iraq is still unresolved and it has no form of autonomy. Many Yazidi families are torn apart: due to murder and displacement, due to the traumatic consequences of genocide, due to diaspora movements mainly to Germany and Australia.

In this article, I explore the strategies of survival of the enslaved Yazidi women and their communities by analysing and relating three artefacts: Hogir Hirori's feature documentary *Sabaya*, released in 2021, the 2022 Murad Code on working with survivors or victims of systematic and conflict-related sexual violence, and Nadia Murad's 2017 memoir *The Last Girl*. I investigate aesthetic media such as documentary film and literary memoirs as situated, historic testimonies about the Yazidi genocide. Through their attention to form and their focus on survivor agency these testimonies enable a more nuanced view on the extreme challenges of Yazidi survival. Focusing on their relationality – between filmmakers and protagonists, writers and readers, perpetrators and survivors – and relating them with a broad code of conduct enables the inclusion of an ethical perspective on their aesthetic forms.

Hirori's documentary depicts the rescue of enslaved girls and women from Syria's al-Hol camp by a small organisation called Yazidi Home Center. *Sabaya*[3] is a portrayal of a fractured community after genocide. After the film's release, *The New York Times* accused Hirori of not having obtained informed consent by the participating women. In his defence, Hirori provided messages by the involved women and gestured towards the Murad Code which explicitly links his documentary to international human rights work and the first-person perspective of survivors such as Nadia Murad. While the Murad Code is an abstract guideline debating practical and philosophical questions of survivor autonomy and effective political work,

---

[3] The film's title refers to the Arabic term used by ISIS to describe captives, *ṣabāyā*.

Murad's memoir of her time as a *ṣabiyya* (female captive) enables a different perspective on the women's agency, resistance and survival that affects the Yazidis' self-image and history. Through a close reading and assemblage of a documentary film, a code of conduct and a survivor memoir, I discuss the following questions in the framework of aesthetics in the field of cultural history and theory (*kulturwissenschaftliche Ästhetik*): in what sense is the Yazidi community still surviving the genocide even after the defeat of the self-proclaimed caliphate? How do Hirori's aesthetic and epistemic choices frame the Yazidi survival? What ethical guidelines can be extrapolated from the Murad Code for an aesthetic form such as documentary film? How do survivor testimonies such as Nadia Murad's widen the perspective on the affected women's as well as the broader community's survival and resistance?

Sabaya – Surviving Genocide

Sabaya depicts the work of the Yazidi Home Center in north-east Syria. It begins with a radio announcement on the loss of ISIS's last territory in March 2019 and ends around October 2019 with Turkey's attack against the Kurdish territories in Syria destabilising the region once more. The film's protagonists are Mahmud and Shejk Ziyad, who rescue missing Yazidi girls and women sold into sexual slavery, so-called *ṣabāyā*,[4] from al-Hol refugee camp where ISIS has a strong presence until today, often through the wives of killed or imprisoned male militants.[5] In the course of the film, we witness the frantic behaviour of Mahmud and Shejk Ziyad – always on their phones, smoking, sleepless – and we follow three dangerous rescue missions into the camp and see glimpses of life at the Center. Here, Mahmud's wife Siham and his mother Zahra take care of the survivors, among them seven-year-old

---

[4] For an overview on ISIS and their use of slavery, see Al-Dayal and Mumford 2020. For an analysis of the modern aspects of ISIS's slavery and the archaic fantasies of ISIS slavery by right-wing parties such as the German AfD, see Christiane Gruber's article 'From ISIS to the AFD: Ultraist Rhetoric and Visuality in Alt-Orientalist Concurrence' in this volume.

[5] Al-Hol was established by the UN High Commissioner for Refugees during the 1991 Gulf War. In the course of the US invasion of Iraq it was expanded and served after the fall of ISIS 'to shelter those who had recently lived under ISIS's control or were perceived to be the partners, children and relatives of male ISIS members' (Saad 2020: 1). With around 73,000 refugees – almost all of them women and children – in December 2018 and around 57,000 in September 2021, al-Hol is still far beyond its maximum capacities (see Saad 2020; REACH 2021).

Mitra. They take off and burn their abayas and niqabs, tell fragments of their stories, cry and care for one another. The film closes with some women returning home to their families and so-called infiltrators – former Yazidi ISIS captives – arriving at al-Hol, donning abayas and niqabs, risking their freed lives to free other enslaved Yazidis. While the film's opening suggests a linear historical narrative, beginning with ISIS's defeat and suggesting the liberation of the remaining ṣabāyā, its ending suggests a circular temporality: Turkey's attack enables imprisoned ISIS militants to flee; to free enslaved women, former ṣabāyā must return to al-Hol, camouflaged as Muslims. Hirori's documentary depicts survival in the midst of and after genocide through the focal point of the Yazidi Home Center – its actions, sufferings and ways of engaging with each other.

In *Sabaya* it is not only the abducted women and girls who are not present, but also those who are searching for them. At one point, Mahmud replies to a warning of danger: 'I know, but we are already dead' (22:55). Hirori takes care to show how Mahmud is absorbed by his mission. He calls off his participation in a wedding. Siham bemoans that she hasn't seen him for three days and that he is always hurrying to leave again. In another scene she finds him awake at night. Her question – 'Are you still awake?' – finds a strange answer: 'I don't know what to do. There is no reception' (1:09:45).

The film starts with Mahmud trying to get better mobile phone reception – a problem that will haunt him for the duration of the movie. His relations with his phone seems emblematic for his struggle to re-establish connection. If there is not a cigarette or pistol in his hand, there is his phone. He uses it to exchange numbers, to exchange voice messages, to manage the return of people, to look at images of ISIS's atrocities, to study the characteristics – eyes and hands – of veiled victims. People call to beg him to look for a specific person, to thank him, or to negotiate smuggling operations. Having reception becomes synonymous with re-establishing ethnic survival.

At one point, he and Shejk Ziyad tape hundreds of portrait photos of missing ṣabāyā carefully on cardboard panels until the panels fill the whole room. They literally take up the space of Mahmud's life. He tries to memorise their characteristics. 'One picture before and one picture after ISIS kidnapped her. Such a difference' (48:44). The images not only help in finding the captured girls and women, in this careful arrangement they are given a personal and respectful place, a shrine or archive or memorial, taking over the home of those who stayed back.

Hirori contrasts this obsessive care for the absent Yazidi girls and women with a certain uneasiness in dealing with saved ones. In the car, fleeing from al-Hol, one rescued woman sobs, articulates her fears and begins to testify to ISIS's violence. Mahmud seems tense, checking his mobile or looking out of the window, but not at her. She is silenced twice: 'Calm down and breathe' (24:40). In another scene, after the liberation of seven-year-old Mitra, the girl is lying outside the Center before being cared for by the women. Mahmud does not take on the roles of hero, substitute father or uncle, but distances himself, already busy on the phone (1:07:30). Later, when some escaped women leave the Center and say their goodbyes, the men focus on efficiency and rush a couple of hugging, crying women: 'Please, we have to go' (1.19:44). At the border, where the escapees return to their families and new infiltrators are picked up, they again stress them to hurry. After a quick exchange, the men remain sober: 'Our job here is done. We have to leave' (1:21:23). Later the women in the car sleep. Instead of an emotional climax, relief or a glimpse of happiness, Shejk Ziyad's description of his psychophysical state is toned down: 'The problem is that I'm so tired I can't drive. I have blisters under my feet from driving' (1:22:10). The need to keep driving is a fitting metaphor for this restless state which hardly allows for the articulation of emotions or their connection to the unfolding genocide. In Hirori's portrayal, the survival of genocide seems to have ruptured the ontological equilibrium of presence and absence, here and elsewhere: the dead and abducted, the missing and displaced occupy body and mind of those left behind with an intensity that disables other relations. Even with those displaced persons that have returned. This seems to be the meaning of Mahmud's comment that they do not need to care about danger because they are already dead.

Hirori's lens shows this dynamic and the work of the Yazidi Home Center as deeply gendered.[6] It is the women who comfort each other, who nourish their survival and who thus unearth subtle dimensions of the genocide. In one

[6] The need for a more-nuanced and gender-based discussion of genocide is an important desideratum. For a policy-based introduction, see Rosenberg (2021). For an introduction into aspects of intersectional, especially gendered memory of genocide, gender-based victimisation, the roles of women as perpetrators as well as questions of women's empowerment during and after genocide, see Bemporad and Warren (2018).

scene, Mitra is sitting outside the Home. She kisses one woman on the cheek, they are holding hands, bedtimes are negotiated, tender relations between a child and responsible, caring adults are hinted at. Mitra is asked who combed her hair in al-Hol[7] and if she understands Kurdish, but she does not reply to the latter. While Mahmud is on the phone and discusses the geopolitics of an upcoming Turkish attack on Syria, his wife uses her smartphone to show Mitra a children's song. In the next scene, Zahra combs the girl's hair and tells her story: having been abducted from Sinjar as a one-year-old baby, her parents are still missing, siblings and an uncle might still be alive. She does not speak Kurdish but Arabic. The care work is an inventory of what the genocide destroyed: routines, familial bonds, a shared mother tongue.[8] What sounds abstract in the UN's definition of genocide, 'forcibly transferring children of the group to another group' (UN II e), is here documented in small gestures of care and interest. By caring for Mitra, the women implicitly gather evidence – as does Hirori's camera. Caring is not only a form of survival, but an epistemic practice: it maintains and preservers, it empowers those vulnerable to make themselves visible again in the public space and to tell their stories. Caring can transform a traumatic experience, that was once unutterable, to an object of aesthetic and political contestation.

Hirori's interest in the post-genocide politics of family and ethnicity do not stop with Mitra. He documents an anonymous young woman, recognisable by her green headscarf. She and her baby son have also been saved by the Yazidi Home Center. Her command of Kurdish seems to have suffered (1:17:20). While she is returned to her family, she has to give her son away – as a 'temporary solution . . . [until] you have convinced your family' (1:17:25). Even though the former Baba Sheikh Khurto Hajji Ismail, the Yazidi religious authority, demanded the reintegration of formerly enslaved

---

[7] Mitra answers 'Mama Fatima' which the subtitles translate as '"Mommy" Fatima'. The quotation marks are a significant intervention. While Mitra as a child unknowingly affirms the genocidal family politics of ISIS, the inserted quotation marks shift the meaning of Mitra's answer. While her original answer is a testimony to ISIS's indoctrination, the subtitle is its deconstruction. The woman called Fatima has appropriated the role of mother without being one.

[8] Due to the gender politics depicted in the film, this gendered term might be literally adequate here.

Yazidi women into the community, it remains difficult – especially for those women with children fathered by ISIS militants who are – according to Iraqi law – *de jure* Muslims (Schmidinger 2019: 98–9). The young mother seems to not (want to) understand the political implications and insists on ontological evidence: 'My child is innocent' (1:18:00). Through fathering and indoctrinating children, ISIS's genocidal politics leave behind generational chasms in Yazidi families that continue to challenge familial-ethnic cohesion. This is aggravated by endogamous Yazidi marriage conventions in traditional areas that do not allow for inter-religious or inter-ethnic marriage (Schmidinger 2019: 27).

Through the genocidal pressure, the intersectional and precarious connection between family and ethnicity can come to breaking point. While Mahmud uses his phone to reconnect with the abducted women, some former ṣabāyā – as *The New York Times* reports – are forbidden by Yazidi elders to call their children fathered by ISIS militants in Syrian orphanages (Arraf 2021). One woman explained the intergenerational paradoxes engendered by the violence: After leaving her elderly mother to reunite with her five-year-old daughter, she said: 'I've been crying for three days . . . I feel like this would kill my mother. She is a mother. She would die for me just like I would die for my daughter' (Arraf 2021). Being a mother means to cease being (present as) a daughter. The othering of the children inscribes complex ethnic, juridical and social fault lines into the intergenerational relations of the families. Ali Elyas, the new Baba Sheikh since late 2020, has broken with the welcoming view of his predecessor: bringing the children fathered by ISIS militants to Sinjar 'would destroy the Yazidi community . . . The fathers of these children killed the parents of these survivors. How can we accept them?' Irritated by a perceived international focus on those children, Ali Elyas pronounced: 'Yazidis are all orphans. No one is taking care of us' (ibid.). Deferring from specific (semi-)orphans to an ethnic identity as orphan, Ali Elyas does not want to accept the fault lines, the estrangement, the heterogeneity of a community after genocide as a possible identity of difference.[9]

[9] In contrast to this inter-familial conflictual division, some communities have shown solidarity-across-difference and found modes of collaborative survival. At least some Yazidi and Christian communities, both targeted by ISIS and betrayed by their Sunni neighbours, have come together 'to rebuild places of worship and reassert their identity and belonging' (Isakhan and Gourlay 2022: 10).

Sabaya's documentary aesthetic, on the other hand, remains with the minutiae of separation between mother and son. They have a last portrait photograph taken. It is the mirror image of the collages by Mahmud and Shejk Ziyad. While the purpose of those images is to help finding the missing, this image's purpose is to stay connected to a child that is – temporarily – abandoned. The intergenerational violence of fathering a child through rape will remain existential because it is indelible from the child's, the family's, the community's identity. Yet, the photograph, the tears, the comforting hugs for the mother, a group of women and boys witnessing the heartfelt handover of the child might constitute a *rite de passage* strong enough to keep the child that is being given away as a part of the imagined community (Anderson [1983] 2006). When genocide is – among other things – constituted by 'the forcible transfer of a child to another group', this group's affection means that the genocide – in the case of at least this one child – has not been successful. Through their cultures of survival, the Yazidis retroactively contest the absoluteness of the genocide and change its meaning. And through his cinematic testimony, Hirori maintains as well as creates an image of a Yazidi home that may not exist at the moment.[10]

Consent and the Murad Code

Hogir Hirori, born in the Kurdish city of Duhok in 1980, came as a refugee to Sweden in 1999. *Sabaya* is his third documentary about ISIS's war

---

[10] In this regard, Hirori's trilogy is related to what Julia Bee following Gilles Deleuze discusses as 'fabulation' (translated as storytelling). Deleuze and Bee analyse the work ethnographic of filmmakers such as Rouch and Perrault with regards to their efforts to constitute a (manifold) people by (re-)inventing its founding fabulations. The work of the Home Center, the scenes of separation and reunion, witnessed by Hirori's camera, might function as such a 'fabulation'. As Bee describes it: 'when . . . [people] practice the cultural roots of the group in a diffractive movement of reinvention, when future and past are not immediately consecutive and no origin story can be found' ['wenn die Menschen . . . die kulturellen Wurzeln der Gruppe in einer diffraktiven Bewegung der Neuerfindung praktizieren, wenn Zukunft und Vergangenheit nicht mehr linear aufeinanderfolgen und sich keine Ursprungserzählung des Kollektivs finden lässt'] (Bee 2018: 109, see Deleuze 1989: 147–55). Genocide as rupture between past and future, as reorganisation of the ethnicity of its victims through systematic rape can make such a diffractive movement of reinvention necessary. Yet, to not damage their status as testimonies, it would be important to further clarify notions such as 'invention' and 'making up legends'. While a criticism of colonial and hegemonial epistemology is important, it should not undermine minoritarian claims to truth.

of aggression, following *The Girl Who Saved My Life* (2016) about refugees in Iraqi Kurdistan fleeing the militants and *The Deminer* (2017) about the Kurdish colonel Fakhir Berwari who single handedly demined hundreds of explosive devices in the region. Hirori's cinematic engagement is emblematic for a Kurdish cinema that transcends the borders of typical nation-state conceptions of cinema, is shaped by diasporic and transnational approaches to filmmaking, nurtured by many Kurdish initiatives and often addresses the long-standing political and violent conflicts of the Kurdish people (Smets 2015: 2436–7). Regarding *Sabaya*, Hirori describes his approach as a filmmaker in social terms, stressing the 'extended relationships, immersion, deep engagement with people's trust' in the film's production. Working with protagonists in distress required Hirori 'to interact with them for a long time, live with them, get involved with their lives for extended periods of time'. Due to Western media being well informed, 'but often missing a deeper understanding and different perspective that those like me who belong to the region carry in ourselves', Hirori claims his 'right to take part in writing history' (Hirori 2021a). He emphasises the situatedness of knowledge (Haraway 1988) and thus the indispensability of those affected in social discourse. Hereby, situatedness is not a definitive identity or trait acquired by birth, but a consequence of the work to build relations and to take someone's side in conflict. By blending filmmaking with building long-term relations, Hirori subscribes not only to a relational aesthetics that is aware of power dynamics and political violence (Brunner and Kleesattel 2019), but also – especially in *Sabaya* – to an aesthetics of care. This resonates with what film scholar Erika Balsom has described as a recent trend in documentary cinema to the observational form: 'The appearances of the world need our care more than our suspicion' (Balsom 2017). In this sense, *Sabaya* is not about ISIS and not even immediately about its practices of sexual enslavement, but about attending, affirming, caring for and depicting survival.[11]

Nonetheless, Hirori came under attack after the film's release. A *New York Times* article claimed in October 2021 that some women had not given informed consent to being filmed. Especially since the MeToo movement,

---

[11] Yet, as part of a cinema of survival, Hirori's film is not awarded the measures of control and relative safety that an observational gaze is predicated upon.

scrutinising consent practices in documentary as well as fictional cinema has become a major point of contestation regarding the ethics of filmmaking, encompassing far more than sexual relations.[12] According to journalists Jane Arraf and Sanger Khaleel, three Yazidi women in the film claimed that they did not understand the film's scope and exposure in Syria and Iraq; a fourth woman had actually declined to appear in the documentary. They accused Hirori of submitting consent forms to the participants only after the film's premiere and in English, a language most of them do not command. One woman was supposedly pressured by Yazidi officials to sign the form, another supposedly complained to Hirori that her face was visible in the film against her will (Arraf and Khaleel 2021). The gendered relations of female complainants to a male director may gesture towards the heightened vulnerability for women in zones of conflict and war.

Hirori responded a few weeks later, stressing that everybody had consented during filming and that those who changed their mind had been anonymised accordingly. Prompted by the article, Hirori returned to Syria to re-watch the film with its protagonists and their kin. Afterwards, he uploaded seven translated transcriptions of voice messages of the female protagonists and a worker on the film, emphasising their consent, their sympathy for the filmmaker and his high ethical standards.

While the exact definitions of best practice documentary filmmaking with regard to survivors of political violence lie beyond the scope of this article, it is important to point to at least one structural limitation of the model of informed consent. Human Rights Watch decided not to invite *Sabaya* to their film festival due to the depictions of seven-year-old Mitra. While Mitra's legal guardian did consent to her depiction, this model of legal representation is questionable. While the uncle might act in good faith, he has no way of knowing how future Mitra might position herself to her depiction – or her omission. The title quote on Schmidinger's book on the genocide – 'The world has forgotton us' – reminds us that not depicting the survivors, even

---

[12] In the same month as the *New York Times* article, the *International Documentary Association* and the *Documentary Accountability Working Group* hosted a panel discussion on trauma-informed approaches to documentary, stressing the representational power of filmmaking, consent as an evolving process and the importance of trust and transparency (Bursic 2021).

when done for their own good, can also be a way to violently erase them from history. While codes of conduct must be established, refined and followed, Hirori's choice to include Mitra seems to be a consequence of his approach to filmmaking as a situated and highly mediated form of writing history from within the scenes of violence.

In his open letter, Hirori, emphasising his will to improve, referenced the Murad Code as a new standard in working with survivors or victims of systematic and conflict-related sexual violence. The Murad Code received its name from Yazidi survivor and Nobel Peace Prize Laureate Nadia Murad, whose NGO Nadia's Initiative was deeply involved in its development. Thus, not unlike *Sabaya*, the Code is an immediate reaction to the genocide in Sinjar. How do *Sabaya* and the jurido-political Code of Conduct negotiate consent and the dignity of survivors? Can the Code also be read as an aesthetic manifesto?

The Murad Code's writing was in itself a process striving for transparency, valuing situated and transdisciplinary knowledge. In the first phase, the authors analysed existing codes of conduct. Between July 2019 and February 2020, preliminary discussions were held with 166 individuals and organisations, among them survivors themselves, regarding the standards of the Code. In June 2020, six months before the premiere of *Sabaya* at Sundance Film Festival, a draft was published to invite criticism (Murad Code 2020). In this process, 1,310 individuals and organisations across 112 countries gave feedback to the Code. This feedback was published in detailed as well as condensed form and used to rework the Code (Murad Code 2022b; Murad Code 2022c). The so-called 'working' version of the Code was published in April 2022 (Murad Code 2022a). For the coming years, the initiators plan to compose an additional survivors' charter as well as to prepare the implementation of the Code in organisations.

The Murad Code is an important achievement for survivors of political violence and those striving to work with them ethically. While carefully explaining that following the Code is neither 'a license or encouragement' nor a 'shortcut' to working ethically with survivors, it proclaims to articulate 'universal, non-negotiable core standards'. It provides overarching, preparatory and implementation-orientated principles for 'the safe, effective and ethical gathering and use of victim or survivor . . . information in relation to systematic and conflict-related sexual violence'. It 'addresses those who document, investigate, report on, research, monitor and otherwise collect . . . and use such information' (Murad Code 2022a: 1). The Code is phrased in the first-person plural to stress the commitment to collaborative work and to hint at the principle 'nothing about us, without us, is for us' (ibid.: 1). While being survivor-centred the Code also addresses the 'over-reliance on survivor information' (ibid.: 2) that might not only re-traumatise those affected but can also lead to epistemological constrictions.[13] Even though the Code does not address the specific ethical and epistemic challenges of aesthetic forms such as in documentary cinema, a film like *Sabaya* that does gather information from survivors falls under its reach.

To discuss Hirori's documentary practices in the framework of the Code the 'Implementation Principles' 8–10 are its most relevant sections. They delineate the necessary material and social conditions for interviewing survivors. Under the headline 'Take the Time, Create the Space' the Code urges interviewers to listen with 'undivided attention', an 'open mind without assumptions' and to not let 'our own reactions impact . . . the interaction'. The survivors should have 'control over the way they tell their story' and should neither be rushed nor pressured by lengthy interactions. The environment should be 'supportive, physically and psychologically safe' and 'gender, age, disability, social, cultural and context sensitive'. In consultation with survivors, a secure setting should be ensured, for example the arrangement of a 'private, discreet, accessible and safe space to meet' that minimises the 'risk of being observed . . . overheard or interrupted'. The survivor's right to privacy 'extends to all communications and contact with them, including before and after any meeting'. This includes a minimisation of the number of people present during the interview: 'We will discuss in advance with a survivor who they would like to be present and who may be taking part from our team (providing information such as their roles, gender, age and affiliation)' (ibid.: 10).

Reading the Code makes palpable how volatile the configurations of documentary films are. After the material is shot, protagonists usually cannot intervene in the post-production. They have no control over who sees the

---

[13] The Code stresses fact-pattern witnesses and expert reports as important alternatives to an overdependence on survivor testimony (Murad Code 2022a: 2).

film, how it is framed and what audience members make of it. Asked about a film called *Sabaya*, Mitra's uncle did not know which film was meant, since in his view he had participated in a 'film about the Yazidi Home Center' (Hirori 2021a). Expectations and understandings from participants can diverge fundamentally from those of the filmmakers and the audience.[14]

On the one hand, films are subject to highly regulated forms of distribution. *Sabaya* was shown at festivals or in subsections with a focus on documentaries, independent cinema or Kurdish films. On the other hand, anybody can see the film, ascribe specific meaning to it or use it in his or her own way. One woman was afraid she would be recognised by her family (ibid.). Others might be afraid of ISIS's revenge. While the Yazidi Home Center gathers portraits to save the abducted, the film's portraits might constitute a target list for militants. The anonymity of the public is not neutral but shaped by the spectre of the militants' retaliation. The worries of the film's protagonists show that Yazidis in Syria and Iraq are not only lacking a secure private space, but also a secure public space. The Murad Code emphasises *ex negativo* the fundamental precariousness, vulnerability and exposure of appearing in a documentary film. It is no surprise that Hirori describes his editing process as one of making invisible, that is finding a way 'of showing the infiltration process without endangering the lives of the people involved' and cutting out 'the best scenes' (Hirori 2021b).

Sabaya is a film from within an emergency. After the rescue missions, the team is pursued by ISIS militants; the farmlands are set ablaze, and shooting ensues while the infiltrators are to be smuggled into the camp. While the Yazidi Home Center is a heterotopia (Foucault 1967), a secluded space that does not reproduce the societal logics of its immediate surrounding, the agency of the activists and filmmakers to '[c]reate a space' that is safe, private and has medical and psychological expert teams on hold is lacking. The film documents not survivors, but people in the midst of struggling to survive. It cannot create a space of its own but folds itself into a space of (post-)genocidal mayhem. The survivors, activists and filmmakers are impactful actors but without control over the situation. The Code stresses safety over epistemics: 'We will not proceed if the

---

[14] Observational, investigative or ethnographic documentary forms may also preclude filmmakers from discussing the film's style, agenda or framing with protagonists to not change their behaviour in a specific way.

risks cannot be appropriately mitigated' (Murad Code 2022a: 7). *Sabaya* seems to be torn apart: the filmmakers take responsibility for filming where consent can only be given retroactively: during rescue missions in al-Hol, when survivors are liberated, when children are involved. The editing room seems to be the place where those decisions are mitigated, re-framed, partially taken back through blurs and cuts. Even though – in a very important effort – Hirori tries to prove that he did get informed consent from all participants, *Sabaya* hints at an existential dimension of taking part in conflict: being partial, becoming a secondary witness, speaking from nearby those most vulnerable and violated (Chen 1992: 86–7) means to take responsibility for one's presence and decisions before their consequences can be anticipated.

Testimonies of Survival

Now, I turn to the specific testimonies by those women who survived abduction and enslavement by ISIS to stress the political dimensions of their resistance and survival that *Sabaya* as a film about the here-and-now of the Yazidi Home Center and al-Hol camp does not depict. In *Sabaya* the survivors give explicit and tacit testimony in the present and presence of conflict. They are stuck for the moment and cannot distance themselves to reflect on their testimonies as could Hirori, who edited the film during the COVID-19 pandemic back in Sweden. The form of literary testimony enables the survivors themselves a more controlled environment – often in exile – that protects their immediate affectivity and bodily reactions from the audience's gaze. The more streamlined mode of authorship – in comparison to the complex negotiations of consent in documentary cinema – can help to shift the attention from – important – ethical questions about the form of testimony to its content. Due to the limitations of this article, I will focus on the most famous testimony of Nadia Murad and cannot discuss other testimonies by Şerihan Rajo, Jinan Badel or the anonymous author with the pseudonym Shirin (Schmidinger 2019: 89–96; Badel and Oberlé [2015] 2016; Shirin and Kizilhan 2016).

Those testimonies are historical as well as literary documents that negotiate genre boundaries and draw upon a tradition of feminist narrative politics. As Tanya Serisier has elaborated, survivor memoirs draw on 'long-standing feminist recognition of the cross-pollination of the literary and the political' (Serisier 2021: 43). They negotiate the singularity of their experience and the structural violence inherent to it, anonymity and exposure, individual meaning-making and genre conventions as well as intersectional politics, especially of race. The politics of survivor narratives can enable silenced victims to take on agency, open the cultural space for others to tell their stories and change the social understanding and handling of sexual violence (ibid.: 44).

Nadia Murad grew up in Kocho, south of the Sinjar Mountains. Today, Kocho is known for the massacre committed by ISIS on 15 August 2014, when 600 boys and men were killed, among them members of Murad's family, while the women and children were abducted, among them Nadia Murad herself. Murad was taken to an ISIS centre where she was brutalised and sold as a slave. She was forced to convert to Islam, to dress in abaya and niqab, to marry her captor and to be registered in the para-state's databases. Murad was sold multiple times and had to serve as ṣabiyya at an ISIS checkpoint, vulnerable to whomever would pass by. She was brutalised, raped and gang raped, and was in constant fear for her life and the lives of those dear to her. After three months, she managed to flee. After staying in a refugee camp in Kurdistan, she found refuge in Baden-Württemberg. She joined the human rights organisation Yazda, became Goodwill Ambassador for the Dignity of Survivors of Human Trafficking of the United Nations in 2016, published her memoir in 2017 and was co-winner of the Nobel Peace Prize in 2018.

Murad emphasises the multiple forms of resistance that the ṣabāyā employed. Unable to demonstrate in the streets, to fight back or to start an upheaval, the women had to resort to what cultural theorist Iris Därmann has called 'weak resistance' (flacher Widerstand). These modes of resistance are ephemeral, rarely leave traces and often relate to the body of the subjected. They take place 'in the span between vita activa and vita passiva, survival and suicide, confrontation and flight, public visibility and secrecy, presence and historical belatedness, intentions and effects, singularity and collectivity' (Därmann 2021: 113). Weak resistance can be described as the power of the powerless, the agency of those without access to institutions, the public or their own capabilities: the enslaved, imprisoned or disappeared.

Murad describes that many ṣabāyā tried to sully themselves: by rubbing ashes or dirt on their faces, messing up their hair, vomiting on themselves or avoiding showers (Murad and Krajeski 2017: 120, 127, 134). They lied to their captors, inventing sicknesses to be left alone (ibid.: 159–60). They tried to flee (ibid.: 160, 168). One woman penetrated herself with a bottle so that she would no longer be a virgin (ibid.: 162). Many of the girls and women contemplated or tried to take their own lives: 'Killing ourselves seemed more honorable than submitting to the militants, our only way of fighting back' (ibid.: 131). Murad decidedly conceptualises self-destruction as a way to 'fight back', to bereft the ISIS militants of pleasure, to destroy their property, to devalue their lucrative assets.[15]

Murad and the other women struggled with suicide because their total expropriation also took their means to take their own lives. They contemplated choking themselves, jumping off the roof or provoking militants into killing them (ibid.: 131–2, 138). In this total desolation, the means to take one's life become a relative privilege. The struggle to commit suicide lay also in their testimonial relationships: 'It was impossible that we would watch while one of our neighbors took her own life' (ibid.: 131). Suicide is not only a personal, but a deeply social act. For Murad, it was the thought of her mother, who had taken care and nourished her after an earlier accident, which nullified her death wish. By destroying herself, she would have not only cut off the ties to ISIS, but also her familial bindings.

These acts of resistance have a political significance that transcends their immediate effects of a contestation of violence and power.[16] Murad states that those acts changed the women's later survival and subjectivity:

> Their fight allowed them to feel better after the fact . . . After they were free, they were able to say proudly that they scratched so hard at their captor's arm that they drew blood . . . every gesture, no matter how small, was a message to ISIS that they did not truly own them. (ibid.: 162)

---

[15] This is in synchronisation with cultural historian Thomas Macho's diagnosis that modernity's prohibitions of suicide refer to the claims of ownership of subjects by families, churches, militaries or states (Macho 2017: 45–7).

[16] Därmann describes resistance as a division of powers in the realm of the sensible: 'Even the most inconspicuous and smallest resistance is a challenge of the unbrokenness and absoluteness of power and violence. It leads, at least for the duration of its occurrence and transpiration, to a *diágnosis*, a difference and decision between power and opposing power, sometimes even to radical democratic division of power in *statu nascendi*' (Därmann 2021: 54, see 114). ['Noch der unscheinbarste und geringste Widerstand hat eine diagnostische Wirkung in Bezug auf die Ungebrochenheit und Absolutheit von Macht und Gewalt. Er führt, zumindest für die Dauer seines Auftretens und Sich-Ereignens, eine *diágnosis*, eine Unterscheidung und Entscheidung zwischen Macht und Gegenmacht, mithin eine radikaldemokratische Gewaltenteilung in statu nascendi herbei.'].

Enslavement, rape and the killings aim for an irreversible destruction of an ethnicity, its modes of subjectivation and futurity, manifested in rituals, clothing, languages, holy sites or offspring. These microscopic acts of resistance enable a future reappropriation of the self, they enable different stories of captivity to be told, they facilitate a reconstitution of the social community.

At the end of her memoir, Murad points in a media reflexive gesture to the importance of storytelling: 'My story, told honestly and matter-of-factly, is the best weapon I have against terrorism, and I plan on using it until those terrorists are put to trial'[17] (ibid.: 306). Efforts of bringing perpetrators of systematic and conflict-related sexual violence and slavery to justice are rather a historical novelty. They mostly began with the establishment of international tribunals and courts in former Yugoslavia, Rwanda, Sierra Leone or with the International Criminal Court (El-Masri 2018: 1–5). Bringing ISIS members to justice for their acts of sexual violence and enslavement can take different routes, that is by national truth commissions, national courts, courts of third states or international courts (ibid.: 8–13). While thousands of shortened trials were held in Iraq for members of ISIS, the first one to explicitly address the enslavement of Yazidi women was held in March 2020. It was also the first one in which a survivor, Ashwaq Haji Hamid Talo, was able to come forward to tell her story publically, resulting in the perpetrator's death sentence (Rubin 2020). In December 2021, the Higher Regional Court in Frankfurt sentenced ISIS member Taha Al J. to life imprisonment. This marks the first time globally that a member of ISIS was convicted for genocide. Al J. and his German wife Jennifer W., who was sentenced to ten years in a Munich

---

[17] In a striking montage in her documentary *On Her Shoulders* about Murad, filmmaker Alexandria Bombach shows the violence of the much-repeated and intimate questions in tightly regulated and sensationalised US-media formats: 'How did you manage to escape? / Will you ever go back to your village? / And when you think about the men who raped you, what do you want to happen to them? / Did you at any point try to talk to them, try to reason with them? / Did you try to resist? Could you tell him no? / They killed your mother as well, I think – I imagine there's also moments that you just want to stop and lead a normal life, right? / What happened to the women? What happened to you? How do you deal with all of it? / Do you think about your family a lot? What kinds of things are you thinking about?' (21:00–22:00) Telling one's story can be empowering and subjecting. Testifying can heal or hurt or both at the same time. It can mean to come closer to justice or to despair of the incorrigible injustice.

court, were specifically accused of enslaving a mother and her five-year-old daughter, leading to the death of the latter. This is the first court to confirm that the attempted extermination of the Yazidis constitutes genocide and a precedent-setting universal jurisdiction case in Germany (Kather and Groß 2021; Schütze 2021).

Such juridical approaches to justice are unthinkable without survivor testimonies. Yet, Murad reminds us that she must relive her story each time she speaks, that other Yazidis weep even though they have heard her testimony multiple times, that she remained 'vague' about her ordeal when talking to her surviving brothers to not upset them (Murad and Krajeski 2017: 270). Telling her story seems to root her and the affected listeners deeper in the pain of an unbearable past and, at the same time, to open up a different future. Surviving through storytelling means to not let history end with the genocide.

Conclusion

After the defeat of the self-proclaimed caliphate, a heterogeneous assemblage of artefacts testifies to the survival of the Yazidis under post-genocide pressure. Hirori's documentary *Sabaya* detects a spectral reversal between absence and presence: the male members of the Yazidi Home Center become spectral in their obsession to find the missing girls and women while those who have disappeared seem all the more present in the frantic gestures of coping, in portrait photographs or voice messages. The care and comfort that the female members of the Yazidi Home Center and survivors gift each other has been discussed as a form of shared survival and a care for truth that gathers evidence of genocide by slowly letting wounds and losses come to light. Against the background of ISIS's genocidal politics of rape, procreation and indoctrination of children, the 'Home' in Yazidi Home Center seems to point to social and cultural ways of mending the broken ties between familial and ethnical belonging.

Sabaya is a partial and positioned documentary that is firmly situated in a time and place of immediate survival where the room for manoeuvre is highly limited for all actors. In consequence, Hirori takes on an ambiguous ethical responsibility that will remain debatable even once all consent forms are signed. Yet, uninviting his film and silencing the survivors once more remains a choice as ambivalent. The Murad Code, on the contrary, articulates itself in modes of abstraction. A result of the same landscape after genocide, the Code strives for a non-aesthetic code of conduct to connect multi-directional (Rothberg 2009) lines of dialogue between institutions, survivors and experts and a generalised form of safe, ethical and effective information-gathering from survivors or victims of systematic and conflict-related sexual violence. By following the connections between *Sabaya* and the Code, that Hirori and also Human Rights Watch have hinted at (Abrahams 2021), at least two points have become clear: first, the anonymous structure of the cinematic and other exhibition dispositifs of films hold a specific risk for survivor testimonies who lose control over the framing of their testimony. Second, there is chasm between two different tendencies in gathering survivor testimony: those that intervene into a scene of immediate survival with all the risks involved (like Hirori) and those that prefer a safer, removed, retroactive scenario. Both approaches carry specific ethical and epistemic risks that cannot be resolved.

The discussion of Nadia Murad's memoir *The Last Girl* as a 'cross-pollination of the literary and the political' has enabled a different view on the agency, resistance and survival of the affected girls and women. Their strategies of weak resistance are eminently political, not only because they dispute the absoluteness of ISIS's claim to power, but also because they enable different stories, subjectivities and thus communities to emerge after genocide. Amid a historical crisis that was about to annihilate the future of the Yazidis as a community, the resistance of the enslaved women not only enabled them to survive, but changed the possibilities of future for the whole community.

References

Abrahams, F. (2021), 'Film Controversy Raises Issues of Informed Consent', *Human Rights Watch*, 7 October, <https://www.hrw.org/news/2021/10/07/film-controversy-raises-issues-informed-consent> (last accessed 11 June 2022).

Al-Dayal, N. and A. Mumford (2020), 'ISIS and Their Use of Slavery', *International Centre for Counter-Terrorism*, <https://icct.nl/publication/isis-and-their-use-of-slavery/> (last accessed 11 June 2022).

Anderson, B. ([1983] 2006), *Imagined Communities: Reflections on the Origin and Spread of Nationalism*, Revised Edition, London and New York: Verso.

Arraf, J. (2021), 'ISIS Forced Them into Sexual Slavery. Finally, They've Reunited with Their Children', *The New York Times*, 12 March/28 May, <https://www.nytimes.com/2021/03/12/world/middleeast/yazidi-isis-slaves-children.html> (last accessed 11 June 2022).

Arraf, J. and S. Khaleel (2021), 'Women Enslaved by ISIS Say They Did Not Consent to a Film about Them', *The New York Times*, 26 September/21 October,

<https://www.nytimes.com/2021/09/26/world/middleeast/sabaya-isis.html> (last accessed 11 June 2022).

Badel, J. and T. Oberlé ([2015] 2016), *Ich war Sklavin des IS: Wie ich von Dschihad-isten entführt wurde und den Albtraum meiner Gefangenschaft überlebte*, Munich: mvgverlag.

Balsom, E. (2017), 'The Reality-based Community', *e-flux Journal*, 83 (June), <https://www.e-flux.com/journal/83/142332/the-reality-based-community/> (last accessed 13 February 2023).

Bee, J. (2018), 'Erfahrungsbilder und Fabulationen: im Archiv Visueller Anthro-pologie', in E. Büttner, V. Öhner and L. Stölzl (eds), *Sichtbar machen. Politiken des Dokumentarfilms*, Berlin: Vorwerk 8, pp. 93–110.

Bemporad, E. and J. W. Warren (2018), *Women and Genocide: Survivors, Victims, Perpetrators*, Bloomington, IN: Indiana University Press.

Brunner, C. and I. Kleesattel (2019), 'Earthly Relational Aesthetics. Eine post-koloniale Differenzierung mit Glissant', in C. Brunner, S. Bempenza and I. Kleesattel (eds), *Polyphone Ästhetik. Eine kritische Situierung*, Vienna and Linz: Transversal Texts, pp. 125–48.

Bursic, H. (2021), '6 Tips for Documentary Filmmakers on How to Better Serve Participants with Gender-Based Trauma', *International Documentary Association*, 14 October, <https://www.documentary.org/blog/6-tips-documentary-filmmakers-how-better-serve-participants-gender-based-trauma> (last accessed 11 June 2022).

Busse, L., A. Gehrlach and W. Isak (eds) (2021), *Selbstbehältnisse Orte und Gegenstände der Aufbewahrung von Subjektivität*, Berlin: Neofelis Verlag.

Chen, N. (1992), '"Speaking Nearby": A Conversation with Trinh T. Minh-ha', *Visual Anthropology Review*, 8: 1, 82–91.

Därmann, I. (2021), *Widerstände. Gewaltenteilung in statu nascendi*, Berlin: Matthes & Seitz.

Deleuze, G. ([1985] 1989), *Cinema 2: The Time-Images*, Minneapolis: University of Minnesota Press.

El-Masri, S. (2018), 'Prosecuting ISIS for the Sexual Slavery of the Yazidi Women and Girls', *The International Journal of Human Rights*, 22: 8, 1–20.

European Parliament (2016), *European Parliament Resolution of 4 February 2016 on the Systematic Mass Murder of Religious Minorities by the So-called 'ISIS/Daesh' (2016/2529(RSP))*, <https://www.europarl.europa.eu/doceo/document/TA-8-2016-0051_EN.html> (last accessed 11 June 2022).

Foucault, M. ([1967] 1998), 'Different Spaces', in J. D. Faubion (ed.), *Aesthetics, Method and Epistemology: Essential Works of Foucault*, Vol. 2, New York: The New Press, pp. 175–86.

Haraway, D. (1988), 'Situated Knowledges: The Science Question in Feminism and the Privilege of Partial Perspective', *Feminist Studies*, 14: 3, 575–99.

Hirori, H. (2021a), 'Concerning the *Sabaya* Controversy – Statement by the Director, Hogir Hirori', *Sabaya the Film*, October 14, <http://sabayathefilm.com/index.php/statement> (last accessed 11 June 2022).

Hirori, H. (2021b), '"I had to Put My Own Interests Aside": Editor Hogir Hirori on *Sabaya*', *Filmmaker Magazine*, 30 January, <https://filmmakermagazine.com/111030-i-had-to-put-my-own-interests-aside-editor-hogir-hirori-on-sabaya> (last accessed 11 June 2022).

Institute for International Criminal Investigations, Nadia's Initiative and Foreign & Commonwealth Office (2020), *Background Paper & Draft Global Code of Conduct for Documenting & Investigating Conflict-Related Sexual Violence ("The Murad Code")*,<https://static1.squarespace.com/static/5eba1018487928493de323e7/t/5efa1554a8553428c9395936/1593447765159/English+DraftMuradCode%2BBackgroundPaper+June2020+Website.pdf> (last accessed 11 June 2022).

Isakhan, B. and W. Gourlay (2022), 'State–Society Relations and Inter-communal Dynamics in Conflict: Non-Muslim Minorities in Post-IS Iraq', *Journal of the Association for the Study of Ethnicity and Nationalism*, 1–15, DOI: 10.1111/nana.12841.

Kather, A. L. and J. Groß (2021), 'Truly Historic: The World's First Conviction for Genocide against the Yazidi', *Völkerrechtsblog*, 17 December, DOI: 10.17176/20220302-103135-0.

Macho, T. (2017), *Das Leben nehmen. Suizid in der Moderne*, Berlin: Suhrkamp Verlag.

Murad Code Project (2022a), *Global Code of Conduct for Gathering and Using Information about Systematic and Conflict-Related Sexual Violence*, 13 April, <https://static1.squarespace.com/static/5eba1018487928493de323e7/t/6255fdf29113fa3f4be3add5/1649802738451/220413_Murad_Code_EN.pdf> (last accessed 11 June 2022).

Murad Code Project and Institute for International Criminal Investigations (2022b), *Collated Main Feedback on the Draft Murad Code of June 2020*, 13 April, <https://static1.squarespace.com/static/5eba1018487928493de323e7/t/6256300c9113fa3f4bea1085/1649815567276/220413+Collation+of+Main+Feedback+on+Draft+Murad+Code+4website.pdf> (last accessed 11 June 2022).

Murad Code Project and Institute for International Criminal Investigations (2022c), *Summary of Feedback Received on the Draft Murad Code* (13 April 2022), <https://static1.squarespace.com/static/5eba1018487928493de323e7/t/625613cd169e554db34c1931/1649808333817/220413+Summary+of+feedback+on+draft+Murad+Code+4website%281%29.pdf> (last accessed 11 June 2022).

Murad, N. and J. Krajeski (2017), *The Last Girl: My Story of Captivity and My Fight against the Islamic State*, New York: Tim Duggan Books.

Ortaç, S. (2016), 'Der Angriff auf die Ezîdî in Şingal im Lichte der Genozidkonvention', in K. Brizić, A. Grond, C. Osztovics, T. Schmidinger and M. Six-Hohenbalken (eds), Şingal 2014: Der Angriff des *"Islamischen Staates"*, *der Genozid an den Ezîdî und die Folgen*, *Wiener Jahrbuch für Kurdische Studien 2016*, Vol. 4, Vienna: Caesarpress, pp. 9–32.

RASHID (2019), *Destroying the Soul of the Yazidis: Cultural Heritage Destruction During the Islamic State's Genocide Against the Yazidis*, <https://doi.org/10.5281/zenodo.3826125> (last accessed 11 June 2022).

REACH (2021), *Camp profile: Al Hol*, <https://www.impact-repository.org/document/reach/e0ca138e/REACH_SYR_Factsheet_NES_CampProfile_AlHol_September 2021-2.pdf> (last accessed 11 June 2022).

Revkin, M. R. and J. Wood (2021), 'The Islamic State's Pattern of Sexual Violence: Ideology and Institutions, Policies and Practices', *The Journal of Global Security Studies*, 6: 2, <https://dx.doi.org/10.2139/ssrn.3654558> (last accessed 11 June 2022).

Rosenberg, E. F. (2021), *Gender and Genocide in the 21st Century: How Understanding Gender Can Improve Genocide Prevention and Response*, Washington, DC: New Lines Institute for Strategy and Policy.

Rothberg, M. (2009), *Multidirectional Memory: Remembering the Holocaust in the Age of Decolonization*, Stanford: Stanford University Press.

Rubin, A. J. (2020), 'She Faced Her ISIS Rapist in Court, Then Watched Him Sentenced to Death', *New York Times*, 2 March, <https://www.nytimes.com/2020/03/02/world/middleeast/isis-iraq-trial.html> (last accessed 11 June 2022).

Saad, N. J. (2020), 'The Al Hol Camp in Northeast Syria: Health and Humanitarian Challenges', *BMJ Global Health*, DOI: 10.1136/bmjgh-2020-002491.

Schmidinger, T. (2019), *'Die Welt hat uns vergessen' Der Genozid des 'Islamischen Staats' an den JesidInnnen und die Folgen*, Berlin: Mandelbaum Verlag.

Schneider, C. (2021), 'The Yazidis: Resilience in Times of Violence', in S. Astourian and R. Kévorkian (eds), *Collective & State Violence in Turkey: The Construction of a National Identity from Empire to Nation-state*, New York and Oxford: Berghahn Books, pp. 400–24.

Schütze, C. F. (2021), 'ISIS Fighter Convicted in Death of Enslaved 5-Year-Old Girl', *New York Times*, 30 November, <https://www.nytimes.com/2021/11/30/world/europe/isis-trial-yazidi-germany.html> (last accessed 11 June 2022).

Serisier, T. (2021), 'Reading Survivor Narratives: Literary Criticism as Feminist Solidarity', in M. K. Holland and H. Hewett (eds), *#MeToo and Literary Studies:*

Reading, Writing and Teaching about Sexual Violence and Rape Culture, New York: Bloomsbury Academic, pp. 43–56.

Shirin, A. C. and J. Kizilhan (2016), *Ich bleibe eine Tochter des Lichts. Meine Flucht aus den Fängen der IS-Terroristen*, Berlin and Munich: Europaverlag.

Smets, K. (2015), 'Cinemas of Conflict: A Framework of Cinematic Engagement with Violent Conflict, Illustrated with Kurdish Cinema', *International Journal of Communication*, 9: 1, 2434–55.

United Nations Human Rights – Office of the High Commissioner (2016), *Statement by the Commission of Inquiry on Syria on the Second Anniversary of 3 August 2014 Attack by ISIS of the Yazidis*, <https://web.archive.org/web/2019100516 4711/https://www.ohchr.org/en/NewsEvents/Pages/DisplayNews.aspx? NewsID=20330&LangID=E> (last accessed 11 June 2022).

Films

On Her Shoulders (2018), directed by Alexandria Bombach, USA: RYOT Films.

Sabaya (2021), directed by Hogir Hirori, Sweden: Lolav Media/Ginestra Film.

PART III

ETHNOGRAPHIC PERSPECTIVES ON IMAGINATIONS AND MATERIALITIES

10

TALKING JIHAD: THE INTERACTIVE CONSTRUCTION OF A RACIALISED THREAT IN THE NETHERLANDS

Martijn de Koning

In 2014, after we presented research for the Dutch National Coordinator for Counter-terrorism and Security (NCTV) on militant activists in Belgium, Germany and the Netherlands, a question was put to my colleagues Ineke Roex, Carmen Becker and I from a member of the audience who, at the time, as far as I am aware, was an official of the NCTV.[1] He asked: 'Why do you call them militant activists? Why not jihadists? Because that is what they are! You should call them jihadists.' Weeks earlier, one of our interlocutors, Mustafa, who rejected all kinds of labels imposed upon him by saying 'I'm just Muslim', said to me 'If you want to give me a label, use *salafiyya jihādiyya*'.

On both occasions the issue of labelling was central, with people telling me what name, what term, I should use for our interlocutors. But these terms do not come out of the blue. They have a complex history set against a

[1] The research was funded, in part, by the NCTV. The University of Amsterdam (through the NWO funded programme 'Forces that bind and/or divide') and the Radboud University Nijmegen also funded the research. See De Koning, Becker and Roex (2020). I would like to thank the editors for their useful work and comments on earlier versions of this chapter.

background of the state's attempts to govern and control the population. Labels, therefore, are not devoid of ideology and power but are constitutive of it. They are, as I will show, a form of interpellating people, of subjecting them to power, but also a way of identifying and recognising them and enabling their subjectivation (Fassin 2011).

The focus of the project we presented was not on whether these individuals were indeed activists, jihadists and so on, but more about how they were seen in the media and politics, and how they engaged with those representations in different contexts (De Koning et al. 2020). Building also on my work with Maria Vliek on 'extremist worldviews' (Vliek and De Koning 2020), this article hopes to further that approach by exploring the construction of jihadism in Dutch policies and the responses this engenders from the people who are labelled in this way. This means, rather than defining what extremism and jihadism are, I want to discuss what these terms do, what institutions do with them, and how people respond to this.

The next section provides a very brief overview of how the construction of jihadism as a technology of social control marking who is in or out of the nation, is entangled with the broader problematisations of Islam and Muslims in Dutch society. Then I outline more specifically how the Dutch approach to national security by foregrounding jihadism as a threat serves as a technology of social control in policy documents, which both homogenises and differentiates the Muslim population. Subsequently, I will analyse several instances of Dutch war volunteers responding to being labelled as jihadists by examining the practice of 'talking back' as a form of counter-conduct. In doing so, I explore the space that is allocated to people (labelled as jihadists) in which they are able to respond. Based upon my findings from the Dutch war volunteers and their activist supporters in the Netherlands, I argue that the main function of the construction of jihadism by politicians and policymakers is to designate some people as being 'out of place' on legal and moral grounds, and to control the narratives about nation and security, which shapes, limits, but also informs and enables modes of talking back by activists who want to claim an outsider status and who, simultaneously, serve as the quintessential 'jihadists'.

Racialisation and Jihadism: Constructing and Imagining a Threat to the Nation

From 2010 onwards, jihadism emerged as the main target of Dutch policies designed to counter/prevent violent extremism (CVE/PVE) and radicalisation.[2]

As Sajjad (2018: 46) argues in regard to people who are labelled 'migrants' or 'refugees', the ordering and classification of social relations can be seen as an exercise of power. Within the dominant centre of society, there are several parties such as politicians, journalists and academics who engage in the categorising and labelling of particular people. Although categorisations and labelling are not, as we know, neutral processes, they are often constructed to appear exactly that: neutral and objective. Labels such as extreme, jihadist, radical or ultra are used by a political centre and policymakers to mark and to accost political activists who are regarded as, in word and/or deed, oppositional and potentially dangerous, deviant and subversive. On this basis, policies are formed to defend the liberal democratic order. Moreover, these policies, in fact, define the liberal democratic order as reasonable, acceptable and good in contrast to these groups (Mondon and Winter 2020: 58–60). Inspired by Browne's (2015) work on the surveillance of black people, I focus on these twin features of the construction of jihadism in anti-terrorism and counter-radicalisation policies as a form of racialising surveillance: 'a technology of social control where surveillance practices, policies, and performances concern the production of norms pertaining to race and exercise a "power to define what is in or out of place"' (Browne 2015: 16). Here I take the term jihadism as a tool to, on the one hand, control particular segments of the population of a nation state and, on the other, to define who is 'in' and who is 'out' of the nation.

The constructions in politics and policies about threats to the nation relate to broader questions such as citizenship and the exclusion and inclusion dimensions of integration policies (Kumar 2020). In the Netherlands an ambivalent and ambiguous belief about a potential Islamic threat to the

---

[2] This section builds on an analysis I published earlier with colleagues: De Koning, Becker and Roex (2020) and Vliek and De Koning (2020).

societal order has long been reflected in Dutch policies on migrants, minorities and Muslims, and the term jihadist is one of many whose use has facilitated the process by which Muslims have become the object of policy and state interventions (De Koning 2016). The rise of the counter-radicalisation perspectives and the focus on jihadism co-emerged with political debates in which Islam, migration and violence were increasingly connected and presented as opposing and endangering security, Dutch identity and the rule of law (De Goede 2008; Van Meeteren and Van Oostendorp 2019; Manjikian 2017). The trope of Islam as a potential threat also circulates in broader political circles and is definitely not confined to far-right groups (Bracke and Hernández Aguilar 2021; Houtum and Bueno Lacy 2017); the trope also combines with, and underlines, other practices of categorisation and surveillance in Dutch policies (Yanow and Van Der Haar 2013; Yanow et al. 2016; Van Schie 2018). The term jihadism is just one of a long and varied line of labels which have been imposed upon Muslims and migrants. These labels reproduce and emphasise narratives of Islam versus the West which are already circulating in the West and through which Islam becomes a racialising marker of hierarchy that regulates access to the labour market, education and civil rights. It is, among other things, through policy papers that these processes of labelling can be considered a mode of racial surveillance precisely as they recode racialising categories as 'normal' terms of debates and policy practices in relation to national security (Browne 2015; Goldberg 2002).

Counterterrorism: Constructing Jihadism as a Technology of Social Control

Threats to the Dutch nation state have been recoded in a number of ways, one of which focuses on Islam as a potential source of danger to social cohesion. In far-right political rhetoric, we see different renderings of the idea of a fifth column. The term jihadism is a more centrist and policy-oriented recoding of such racialising ideas about threat.

Putting people into racialising categories, such as jihadist, creates the illusion of expelling uncertainty, unknowability and lack of precision, as these are regarded as risks in themselves (cf. Goldberg 2017: 32). It does so because, as I will show here, the policy practices that accompany, or follow, the constructions of threat and the labelling of it, reify and normalise the boundaries between 'acceptable' and 'unacceptable' Muslims, and between legitimate and clandestine violence. Yet, as I will illustrate, this attempt to reduce uncertainty and unknowability is also somewhat ambiguous as definitions and policies change. Here we are reminded of Browne's cautionary reminder (2015: 16–17) not to see racialised surveillance as if it was based upon a fixed racial order, but emerging at 'moments when enactments of surveillance reify boundaries and borders along racial lines, and where the outcome is often discriminatory treatment'. In this paper, I treat Dutch policies and policy reports on counterterrorism, radicalisation and jihadism as such moments.

Prior to the 2000s, the Netherlands did not have a comprehensive counterterrorism policy nor any policy to counteract violent extremism. Clandestine political violence was treated as if it was a penal law problem, but the attacks of 9/11 were presented as a wakeup call by politicians, policymakers and journalists (Den Boer 2007). The Madrid attacks in 2004 and the murder of Theo van Gogh put the fear of 'homegrown' radicalism on the agenda and new measures rapidly followed, such as the establishment of the National Coordinator for Counterterrorism (NCTb), after the Madrid attacks (Fadil and De Koning 2019).

The definitions of jihadism change over time and signal a level of uncertainty about how to define the term but also a continuing desire to do so in response to concrete events. This desire is a significant point in itself as it is exemplary of a deeper and historical fear of Islam as the threatening, but also unknown and uncontrollable, stranger from outside and ties in with the process of racial securitisation which states use to try to unmask that 'threatening stranger' (Goldberg 2009).

The terms 'jihadi' and 'jihadism' occasionally appeared in the media after 1996 (Schoof 1999; Stein 1996), but it was only after 2005/6 that the term 'jihadism' really started to become commonplace in the Netherlands in relation to terrorist threats and 'the West's' handling of it (Bakker and Boer 2006).[3] A vague notion of 'the West' appears to be central in the first years of the use of the term. In a 2004 policy paper from the General Intelligence

---

[3] I have used 'jihadis*' as search string in the Lexis Nexis database for articles in Dutch going back to 1990. A similar search in the archives of parliament yielded no results older than the first mention in 2001.

and Security Service (Algemene Inlichtingen- en Veiligheidsdienst; AIVD), we find this description:

> Jihad is actually an end in itself for such groups. The jihadists want to let the apocalyptic battle between good and evil burn in full force so that Islam achieves the final victory and the martyrs enter the eternal paradise. (AIVD 2004: 33)

In a 2007 policy report 'Muslim radicalism' was broken down into 'radical da'wa' (non-violent) and 'violent jihadism': 'the willingness . . . to contribute to the armed struggle against the West and other supposed "enemies of Islam"' (AIVD 2007: 11).

Around 2010, a transitional phase took place. On the one hand, less attention seemed to be paid to radicalisation (partly as a result of budget cuts), de-radicalisation was re-examined and methods of tackling it were discussed. On the other hand, in 2011, concerns were raised about the increase in numbers of militant activist groups but also with uncertainty about how to interpret these networks (De Koning et al. 2020). This initial hesitation and concern changed in late 2012/early 2013 after it became clear that many young people from these networks had travelled to Syria to volunteer in the fight with al-Qa'ida-affiliated factions against Assad's government. Terrorist threats seemed increasingly prescient and government confidence in the resilience of society (in particular Muslim communities) seemed to have disappeared. In early 2013, the threat level was raised from Level Three (Significant: a terrorist attack in the Netherlands is conceivable) to the second highest: Level Four (Substantial: there is a real chance of a terrorist attack in the Netherlands), evidencing just how the phenomenon of war volunteers enabled and facilitated the imagining of such a threat (De Koning 2020b).[4] The focus then became increasingly sharpened on jihadism and, in June 2014, the AIVD signalled that there was a change in jihadist Netherlands, namely that networks which used to be quite separate were becoming more visible and more interconnected.

[4] Five is the highest level. See Government.nl: <https://www.government.nl/topics/counter-terrorism-and-national-security/risk-of-an-attack-threat-level> (last accessed 13 April 2022).

In 2014, a new action programme was announced in response to the phenomenon of the Dutch war volunteers in Syria: 'Action Programme Integrated Approach to Jihadism' (NCTV 2014a). According to the Minister of Justice and Security in his letter to parliament which accompanied the Action Programme: 'The jihadist movement is in every way the opposite of our democratic constitutional state and must be fought with a heavy hand'.[5] While earlier the jihadist movement was defined in response to large-scale violent attacks such as in the US, Spain and the UK, as well as in response to the murder of Theo van Gogh, in this case the phenomenon of the Dutch war volunteers becomes the constitutive element of the political response. This description shows the production of moral boundaries between 'us' and 'them', 'the democratic constitutional state' and 'the jihadist movement' rendering the latter out of place and a threat that needs to be countered.

In the Action Programme itself we find the following description of (global) jihadism:

> **(Global) jihadism**: an ideological current within political Islam that, on the basis of a specific interpretation of Salafist teachings and, on the basis of the ideas of Sayyid Qutb, strives for the global rule of Islam and the re-establishment of the Islamic State (caliphate) by means of an armed struggle (jihad). (NCTV 2014a: 31)

Here, as is the case in most other policy reports of the AIVD or NCTV, the phenomenon of jihadism is not demarcated from other perceived extremist threats such as those presented by far-left and far-right organisations; it appears to stand on its own and severely connect to global phenomena such as (political) Islam and Salafism.[6]

Slightly different definitions are found elsewhere. In the 'National Counterterrorism Strategy 2016–2020', jihadism is described as transgressing the

[5] Letter to parliament, 29 754, Terrorismebestrijding, Nr. 253, p. 2.
[6] These definitions are reasonably similar yet also more precise compared to those we find on the AIVD website (AIVD 2020).

moral boundaries and threatening the security of the nation as the 'main threat . . . to our national security'. The NCTV there refers to jihadism as

> an extreme political ideology that seeks to fulfil the divinely perceived duty to spread Islam around the world. This must be achieved by waging a 'holy war' against all infidels: anything that deviates from the 'pure doctrine' from the perspective of jihadists must, in their opinion, be fought with violence. (NCTV 2016)

Elsewhere, the NCTV refers to jihadism 'as a global violent ideological movement with cult-like characteristics' (NCTV 2014b: 9). In all definitions (including those of other policy papers, for example from the AIVD), ideology and violent action are linked to Islam as a religion, but also with a familiar distinction drawn between Islam and radical Islam. This distinction serves a tendency in policies to be very careful not to brand Muslim communities as a whole as terrorism suspects to avoid stigmatisation and to be able to include Muslim authorities in the fight against radicalism.

By focusing on the term 'jihad' and reducing it to a clandestine violent struggle, the issue becomes, almost by definition, a problem of Islam and Muslimness; instrumental in reifying the boundaries between Islam and the West and/or Islam and Dutch society. The point is, however, that groups like al-Qaʿida and IS claim that their struggle is Islamically legitimised. The term jihad (apart from a vast range of potential meanings) is an expression of it and, at the same time, a rhetorical move to convince supporters and opponents that they are fighting a legitimate war. It is, therefore, a religious-political claim for, and a practice of, violent struggle and both are heavily contested by other Muslims (including Salafi Muslims) (see, for example, Huda 2017; Pektas and Leman 2019).

The reification and essentialism are exacerbated because, as with other terms (such as radical and extremist), the label jihadism also results in reducing those who are classified under this label to individuals and groups who are, allegedly, ideologically, and in practice, only concerned with armed struggle and its legitimacy (Li 2019: 24–5; see also Sedgwick 2015, 2007). Moreover, the term jihadism also reduces a variety of practices which can be seen as jihad from different Islamic traditions, to an association with clandestine political violence, fanaticism and barbarity (Renton 2018; Edmunds 2012; De Koning

2020b). In sum, we can say that the terms jihadism and jihadist emerged at specific moments in time, and both homogenise particular subsections of the population as well as differentiate these from other subsections. In so doing the practice of labelling individuals as jihadists builds on, and contributes to, distinctions made between the 'acceptable' and the 'unacceptable' Muslim which go back centuries, and which are very much tied to local and global political interests (De Koning 2020a). As such, the term jihadism can be seen as part of the production of racialising categories partly through different combinations of differentiation and association. Precisely these qualities are crucial to understand how people labelled jihadists engage with and disengage from these terms.

Confirming and Reappropriating 'Enmity': Counter-conduct by Talking Back and Performing Unruliness

Whereas the above-mentioned Action Programme against Jihadism was presented as a response to the growing radicalisation evidenced by the increasing number of Dutch war volunteers, some people within the ranks of the Dutch war volunteers responded in turn to the Action Programme. One prime example of this response was the dissemination of two videos which

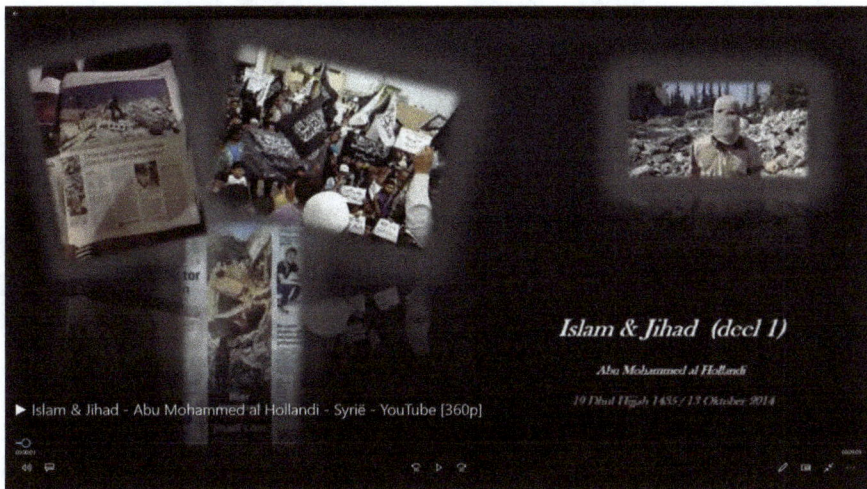

Figure 10.1 Still from the video *Islam & Jihad (Part 1)*.
Source: Abu Muhammed al-Hollandi.

appeared online shortly after the publication of the Action Programme in 2014: *Islam & Jihad, Part 1* (9:11 minutes) and *Part 2* (8:31 minutes). Both videos, consisting of the spoken word only, were made and distributed by Muhajiri Shààm, one of the many names Abdelkarim el Atrach from the city of Arnhem which he had adopted. El Atrach had already left for Syria in 2013 and was known for a video message he sent in 2014 in which he criticised the Dutch government and called on his 'brothers' to act against the Dutch and American governments in response to the American bombing of a centre of Jabhat al-Nusra where three of his friends were killed.[7] Articles about his threats appear in the main image in the video.

Shortly before the release of both videos, el Atrach was placed on the national terrorism list. In the videos he claims that Islam and jihad are inextricably linked (Part 1) and he focuses on the Action Programme (Part 2). In Part 1 he presents the programme as part of a diabolical plan to stop jihad. According to him, this Action Programme had criminalised 'an act of worship imposed on every Muslim and coming from God': 'This is to strike Islam in the heart' and 'This is the enmity that has been warned about' (Part 1). He then tries to show, on the basis of a reading of Islamic traditions, that the (armed) jihad does indeed belong to Islam and is an important act of worship and duty, unstoppable and growing. He argues that all plans to thwart armed jihad act as an incentive to make people even more steadfast.

It might be good to pause here to explain my perspective on videos such as this. In this contribution I suggest that we can analyse particular interactions such as these with (mediatised) political debates, as an example of counter-conduct through talking back. In the next section I will focus more on explaining the modes of talking back; here I will elaborate on the matter of counter-conduct. Foucault (2007a) (in Death 2011: 428) put forward the term 'counter-conduct' to describe forms of protest and resistance that are less large-scale than uprisings and revolts, but are attempts to 'not to be governed like that, by that, in the name of those principles, with such and such objective in mind and by means of such procedures, not like that, not for that, not by them'. By conducting themselves as Muslims, activists, and

---

[7] In the possession of M. de Koning.

creating a public presence through such frames, our interlocutors conducted themselves in, and through, the ways that they are addressed by the frames of the Dutch liberal secular security state. At the same time, as I will show below, they question its assumptions: is democracy living up to its promises, are we indeed all equal and free under the law and the public's perception, is the Dutch state consistent about international human rights, is the Dutch state able to provide security and inclusion?

The general idea behind this type of resistance is that the same mechanisms used by the state to control the conduct of individuals also creates space for the development of forms of resistance that enable dissidents to behave in a 'deviant' way and claim the 'right to be different' (Foucault 1982: 781; 2007b). The videos by Abdelkarim el Atrach are examples of performing deviancy in order to resist the prescribed conduct of Muslims (the Action Programme) and to make a plea for another sort of conduct (his version of Islam). His message builds upon and responds to the Action Programme but should not be understood only as a protest against the regulation of Muslims based upon ideas about national security, integration and liberal-secular rule, but also as a protest for an alternative that is more just and satisfying according to him.

Figure 10.2 Still from the video *Islam & Jihad (Part 2)*.
Source: Abu Muhammed al-Hollandi.

We can also see this move between protest 'against' and protest 'for' in the second part. In this video Adelkarim el Atrach states that the 'crusaders of today' present themselves as wolves in sheep clothes and protectors of 'false democracy' who fear jihad and Islam. That is why, according to him, the Netherlands has not only joined the fight against Islam (in Syria) but has also launched an 'offensive against jihad' at the national level by introducing the Action Programme. The deployment of civilians who have to help track down and report possible war volunteers, the experts in educational institutions who profile people with deviant ideas, and the establishment of new centres for the 'fight against jihad' are presented by him as parts of a cunning plan. 'They even go so far as to use the Muslim community in fighting jihad.' This is what particularly inflames el Atrach: 'This is where the red line is drawn.' And:

> That infidels help each other in fighting jihad is still understandable. After all, their *kufr* has blinded them to the truth . . . But that they even want to go so far as to use Muslims in this false cunning crusade is disgraceful. And dangerously misleading.

In this way, Muslims are 'used as a human shield against other Muslims'. According to him, the fight against jihad is cleverly packaged as a fight against 'an extremist group'. According to el Atrach, this dangerous development could be very destructive for those same Muslims, not only 'because of the loss of their true identity in this world' but also because of the loss of access to Paradise. He addresses this message specifically to Muslims in the Netherlands:

> Do not be used and abused by the Dutch government . . . do not be misled by the so-called Western and free character that they have linked to this, or by the false claims that the *mujāhidūn* [jihad fighters] have hijacked and abused Islam.

Muslims are called upon to take sides (for the *mujāhidūn* and against a Dutch government that sends fighter jets to bomb Muslims and restricts their freedom). His advice to Muslims is to completely distance themselves from any cooperation with the Dutch government because, based on Islamic sources: 'Whoever takes them as an ally is one of them.'[8]

El Atrach's video message shows how government policies directed against jihadists can be taken as an incentive to 'persevere' and remain 'steadfast' and to respond with the correct ways of behaving. Going against the policy in public videos and taking a public stand was, in addition to a form of recruitment, also intended as a demonstration of one's own steadfastness. But it's also more than that. El Atrach points here to an important part of the Dutch Action Programme, namely the cooperation with Muslims and Islamic organisations. In addition to being seen as a weapon in the fight against violent jihad, el Atrach presents the programme as a tool in the fight against Islam because it encourages society to disrespect Muslims engaged in a legitimate and obligatory struggle. And this fight is for their own good; Muslims should take up that struggle and not let themselves to be divided. In this way he presents jihad and Islam almost as the mirror image of the Action Programme, which presents the fight against jihadism as a struggle for everyone's good.

Counter-conduct through Talking Back

El Atrach not only speaks out against the Dutch government, but he also claims to speak on behalf of, and to, Dutch Muslims. And whereas jihadism is presented as a threat to the Netherlands, he presents the Action Programme as a threat to the purity of the Muslim faith. It is useful, I suggest, to analyse this as a specific form of counter-conduct employed by an early and very small but vocal contingent of Dutch war volunteers: talking back. In an analysis of her experiences of growing up in a southern black community in the US, bell hooks (1986, 1989) emphasises the distinction between speaking and being heard. Defining 'talking back' as 'speaking as an equal to an authority figure' (hooks 1986: 123) 'talking back' refers to making 'a speech that compels listeners, one that is heard' (ibid.: 124). A different approach can be found in Bracke's work on Dutch women who were affiliated with an Islamist organisation and their ways of talking back to the dominant discourses (Bracke 2011). She shows how women may embrace, resist or ignore the terms through which they are

---

[8] El Atrach refers to Qur'an 5:51. See Nasr et al. (2015).

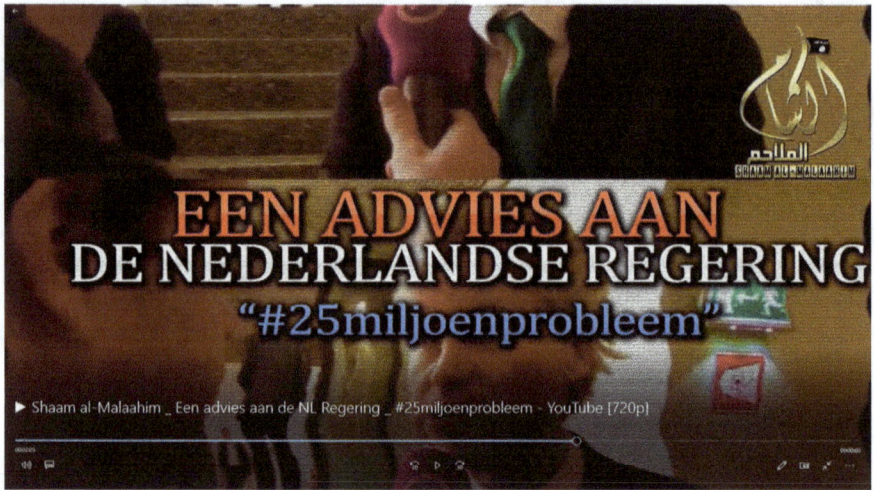

Figure 10.3 Still from the video *Advice to the Dutch Government*.
Source: Shaam al-Malaahim.

interpellated, but may also use aspects of different styles simultaneously. Bracke aligns different modes of talking back with different ways of becoming an unruly subject who 'fails' to align herself with the terms through which she is interpellated. Abdelkarim el Atrach was only one of the people who presented himself as, (from the viewpoint of the conduct of Muslims by the Dutch state), an unruly subject 'staging the moment of talking back' (ibid.: 38) through his video statements. His statement was clearly fashioned as a rejection of the Dutch plans. Many public performances, however, reveal a mixture of the different styles outlined by Bracke and, while the speech may be designed to be compelling, one may also wonder who was actually listening. An example of this mixture of styles is illustrated in a video statement by Abu Muhammed.[9]

In his video called *Advice to the Dutch Government #25 million problem* (2:05 minutes), which he presented shortly after arriving in Syria (made under the pseudonym Shaam al-Malaahim), Abu Muhammed claims to present an answer to the oft heard cry 'Go back to your own country' and

[9] I have written about Abu Muhammed and about Abdelkarim el Atrach before. See De Koning (2021).

to the debates about removing Dutch nationality from war volunteers who have dual nationality. Presenting such videos from Syria in response to Dutch policies against war volunteers can be seen as an example of counter-conduct by adopting a critical attitude, and performing it by talking back. As Lemke (2011: 24) explains, Foucault identifies counter-conduct as activities that refer to people constituting and articulating themselves as being intrinsically critical, as they include problematisation, voluntary insubordination and exposing oneself as a subject. Adopting a critical attitude is then an intellectual and ethical practice of subjectivation that is vital to people's endeavours to conduct themselves differently.

Abu Muhammed's video aims to adopt such a critical attitude by claiming to expose the deception and hypocrisy of the Dutch authorities. After images of Dutch politicians from Dutch news programmes are shown, Abu Muhammed and his friend both come into the picture masked.

> A message to the Dutch government. If you are so eager to get rid of the jihadists and the radical youth in the country, why are you holding them back? . . . And when they come back to the Netherlands, you complain.

According to Abu Muhammed, these young people had no problem handing in their Dutch passports. 'Never come back that's the solution – Have a conversation with them' reads the final message followed by '25 million problem' (all three sentences in red – white – blue). The twenty-five million is a reference to the costs of dealing with the war volunteers.[10]

The accusation of hypocrisy here is partly related to the fact that 'the government' claimed not to want Dutch war volunteers to go to Syria but at the same time preferred that they actually went. In the video, politicians from the House of Representatives and from the government are identified under the heading 'government'. The government policy which authorises the Dutch nationality of war volunteers with dual nationality to be withdrawn can, and could, count on mixed reactions in these circles. At the time, we saw Dutch war volunteers burning their Dutch passports, but for alleged jihadists in the Netherlands, the threat of passport withdrawal means that one could actually

---

[10] *Advice to the Dutch Government* – in the possession of M. de Koning.

be deported. The double message that was disseminated, as was evident from explanations at the time from Abu Muhammed, is related to the racialising slogan 'Go back to your own country' which offers Abu Muhammed exactly the space to build and spread his message, yet also embraces the terms through which he feels addressed, as is also the case with the term jihadist. The latter, in particular, brings us to the politics of labelling in relation to talking back as counter-conduct.

Talking Back through the Politics of Labelling

Whereas the above-mentioned examples show not only bold ways of talking back but also how the space given to the war volunteers is produced, informed and shaped by government policies, the labelling of these people as jihadists has severe consequences in relation to the perceived legitimacy of their statements. In both cases above, the hold of the governmental labels was weak for both Abu Muhammed and el Atrach as they were already in Syria. This is different for those who were, and still are, residing in the Netherlands. The activists in the Netherlands were keenly aware of this. Take the following war volunteer: according to him terms such as radical or extremist are used to justify how war volunteers are treated, and a way of imagining them but also excluding them:

> For example, I'm on the terrorism list. My parents could go to jail if they sent me money. Do I want radical change? Yes, I want radical change. In my head I am a radical, but that does not mean that I want to shed the blood of innocents. It gives people a false image of who we are, and it gives the idea that . . . they are extremists, who are fixed in their beliefs and there is always something of that. No matter how much they became like us again. Labels can be used to push people aside. You're a terrorist, so we don't have to listen to your arguments. People think, when a terrorist speaks, he's lying. People are biased.

Here we see how this person plays with the label 'radical' and how he tries to distinguish it from the interpretation that the government and/or others would give to it. Below we also see a critical attitude among activists towards the terms used. But one that mainly shows how those terms can have their own, for them, oppressive effect:

If you stand up for your brothers and sisters who are in prison, you will be labelled a jihadist.

If you stand up for your sisters who wear a niqab, you will be labelled a jihadist.[11]

The term for labelling used in Dutch here is *bestempelen* or *stamping* which could be roughly translated as branding or marking; this fairly accurately reflects the idea that the notion of danger sticks to individuals perceived to be jihadist because of the negative ascription from above and from the outside. According to them, their statements are distrusted because they are perceived to be jihadists, their grievances are thus associated with jihadism and thereby delegitimised. These fragments clearly show how the issue of labelling by the government is actually seen as a combination of the state boxing people into certain categories and pushing others out of them, and thus providing an opportunity for the state to present itself as virtuous, and enabling moral condemnation based upon the perceived ideological and normative charge behind the labels. The response above relates to government policy in general, but more specifically to the 'Dutch Terrorism Threat Assessment 52' which stated, among other things:

> Online, Dutch jihadists and Dutch jihadist initiatives are (still) mainly engaged in propaganda, fundraising and strengthening solidarity among jihadists. For example, online attention is drawn to the fate of jihadist supporters, in particular detained jihadists. (NCTV 2020: 13)

The activists we have spoken to were very alert to the homogenising and differentiating effect of labels. For example, one of the war volunteers told me:

> I understand that they want to make it clear that they have a zero-tolerance policy towards people who leave for jihad, but it is very demonising. But certainly, terms like radicals and extremists . . . It is not up to them to determine what is radical and extremist. Socrates was also critical of democracy. Also an extremist?

[11] Excerpt of a social media post by one of our interlocutors. Screenshot is archived.

Many activists seemed to assume the criminalising and stigmatising effect of labels and preferred to foreground other terms: lions, fighters, *mujāhidūn*, martyrs, and so on. Others who are thought to have been abandoned by the government, but also by Muslims, are often referred to, or refer to themselves, as 'Forgotten'. Another popular self-identification is 'Revolutionary' (used by one to also distinguish himself from who he considered extremists: the people from IS). Also, the term Syria travellers (*Syriëgangers*) is often used. This is also an imposed term but regarded as neutral by most of my interlocutors. Such counter-identifications only have limited success, but as a form of talking back we can see such play as a way of turning back the gaze, and importantly for the activists, resisting the damaging dimensions of labelling. Two examples will illustrate this.

After the publication of research by Koopmans on fundamentalism and out-group hostility (Koopmans 2013), and amid the political and media debates about radicalisation in December 2013, the website *De Ware Religie* (The true religion) published a new article, 'True, we are radical'. According to them, radicalism meant holding on to the foundations of Islam and not giving in to the idea that Muslims have to dilute their faith in order to be accepted as citizens (which, according to the website writer, would not work anyway). Here we can see the writers of *De Ware Religie* employing a paradoxical performance of unruliness and of being critical through talking back: they used Koopmans' research which highlighted patterns of intolerance and hostility among Muslims to (at first sight) confirm and submit themselves to one of the labels that they are addressed with: radicals. But they did this by reappropriating the label and using it to focus on what they felt was crucial to leading a good life: holding on to what they saw as the fundamentals of Islam and not submitting to the pressures of 'infidels'. The use of the term 'radical' here serves here to confirm an outsider status on their own terms.

Another example was already mentioned in the introduction. During an informal conversation with Mustafa, one of my regular interlocutors in the militant activists' scene, we were discussing the different labels attributed to him and his friends: 'I'm just Muslim', he declared over and over again. In that same conversation, however, he also said: 'If you want to give me a label, use *salafiyya jihādiyya*.' Like in the previous example, conduct and counter-conduct are entangled and co-emerge. The conduct is affirmed by 'allowing' me to use a label *jihādiyya* at all. Yet, the counter-conduct is also in evidence as he rejects all the other labels attributed to him. He does not so much reject labelling itself but brings forward an alternative which exemplifies how he ought to be seen. However, this alternative label is also an example of the complex entanglement of conduct and counter-conduct. One of the first times the term '*salafiyya jihādiyya*' was used in public was in reference to the arrest of alleged militant activists in Morocco in 2002, who were said to be members of a network called '*salafiyya jihādiyya*'. But Pargeter argues that, in the case of those arrests, the term '*salafiyya jihādiyya*' was a label that the Moroccan authorities put on this group of people, who in reality were members of various networks who advocated clandestine political violence. The people in question rejected the label (Pargeter 2005). Mustafa's mode of talking back is based upon a critical reflection of labelling and a reappropriation of the labels by first opposing them, then using a different label (which is not lighter) that is also, partly, an imposed label. Like with the example 'radical', this serious play on labels is used to present themselves as warriors, as steadfast Muslims, without undoing the negative meanings of the labels (in fact incorporating them). After Mustafa was arrested in 2014 and put on trial in 2015, he returned to his original statement 'I'm just a Muslim' when during the trial the Public Prosecutor accused him of being a jihadist and equated that with being a terrorist. The Public Prosecutor, however, saw Mustafa's statement as a form of ideological deception typical of 'jihadists', basically shutting down the space of talking back through rhetorical closure (De Koning 2018).

Conclusion

Imagining and governing particular groups of Muslims as if they represented a potential risk and/or threat to the nation state is hardly a new thing. It has been an integral part of the figure of the Muslim as a racialised configuration which has circulated across time and space and acquired new and different meanings with each new context (but also solidifying the tropes on the way). Terms like radical, jihadi/jihadism and extremist are used to define, profile and criminalise a particular group of people who are seen by politicians from the political centre and policymakers (and presented as such by the use of these terms) as immoral, dangerous and out of place. While the analysis in policy reports is often presented as focusing on the dangerous and immoral actions of a group of people, the way they are defined as jihadis reveals a concern with Islam and Muslimness as an indicator of threat. As this occurs against a background of the securitisation and racialisation of Muslims and migrants which already turns these people into people 'out of place', the construction of jihadism cannot be seen apart from it.

The practice of defining jihadism by politicians and policymakers then becomes a tool for reifying moral boundaries by putting some people in a category of threat based upon features ascribed to them, which is then used to mark, profile and surveil large sections of the population in order to determine to what extent they constitute an unacceptable risk in an undetermined future. The definitions of jihadism by the state come with legislative powers, and intelligence and security measures which enable the state to perform its role as the protector of national security and of the identity of the nation state by pointing to an immoral and dangerous Other.

Yet, the construction of jihadism through policy can also be challenged and reappropriated by the very people who are the object of it. Whereas the activists are used, in their capacity as war volunteers, to imagine and construct the jihadist, the activist themselves have used the label to re-imagine and present themselves as steadfast fighters. By using talking back as part of their repertoire of counter-conduct, they take over and confirm the terms of the debate but also instrumentalise them and give them new meanings to serve their purpose of legitimating themselves and recruiting others. This talking back is productive in that it illustrates an enmeshment of the exercise of power by the state (the conduct which subjects citizens) and of resistance (the counter-conduct that enables and produces their subjectivation). The fact that they do respond to policies and labels and sometimes lament the consequences of them, shows how these policy reports and labels are forms of interpellation by which people feel accosted in public. As such, they feel the need to respond and to reappropriate the terms as ways of fashioning and performing their counter-subjectivity as steadfast and unruly Muslims; rejecting the state's policies and opting for a different kind of conduct based upon their reading of Islam.

Furthermore, as the Action Programme shows, the actual counter-radicalisation policies are heavily determined by the phenomenon of the Syria war volunteers of which my interlocutors were a very visible example. At the same time the activists realise that by being assigned the label jihadist by the state, they may have become discredited and their claims pathologised and depoliticised. This shows that designating particular phenomena as 'jihadism' shouldn't simply be seen as a tool to determine who is out of place, or should be out of place, but also as a method of controlling the narratives of security and of what an acceptable religion is. Although the state presents jihadism as being outside the rule of law, partly based upon the war volunteers as the exemplary jihadist threat, both the state and the war volunteers were heavily enmeshed in the ongoing construction of jihadism.

References

AIVD (2004), 'Van dawa tot jihad. De diverse dreigingen van de radicale islam tegen de democratische rechtsorde', <https://www.aivd.nl/documenten/publicaties/2004/12/23/van-dawa-tot-jihad> (last accessed 26 July 2022).

AIVD (2007), 'Radicale dawa in verandering. De opkomst van islamitisch neoradicalisme in Nederland', <https://www.aivd.nl/documenten/publicaties/2007/10/09/aivd-rapport-%E2%80%98radicale-dawa-in-verandering-de-opkomst-van-islamitisch-neoradicalisme-in-nederland%E2%80%99> (last accessed 26 July 2022).

AIVD (2020), 'Inlichtingenwoordenboek', <https://www.aivd.nl/onderwerpen/over-de-aivd/inlichtingenwoordenboek> (last accessed 6 May 2022).

Al-Malaahim, S. (2014), 'Een advies aan de Nederlandse regering. #25miljoenprobleem', not available anymore, in the archive of the author.

Bakker, E. and L. Boer (2006), 'Al-Qaida vijf jaar na "9/11": Vulkaan of veenbrand?', *Internationale spectator*, 60: 9, 419–24.

Bracke, S. (2011), 'Subjects of Debate: Secular and Sexual Exceptionalism, and Muslim Women in the Netherlands', *Feminist Review*, 98: 1, 28–46.

Bracke, S. and L. M. Hernández Aguilar (2021), 'Thinking Europe's "Muslim Question": On Trojan Horses and the Problematization of Muslims', *Critical Research on Religion*, 10: 2, 1–21.

Browne, S. (2015), *Dark Matters: On the Surveillance of Blackness*, Durham, NC: Duke University Press.

De Goede, M. (2008), 'The Politics of Preemption and the War on Terror in Europe', *European Journal of International Relations*, 14: 1, 161–85.

De Koning, M. (2016), '"You Need to Present a Counter-Message": The Racialisation of Dutch Muslims and Anti-Islamophobia Initiatives', *Journal of Muslims in Europe*, 5: 2, 170–89.

De Koning, M. (2018), 'Ethnographie und der Sicherheitsblick: Akademische Forschung mit "salafistischen" Muslimen in den Niederlanden', in S. Amir-Moazami
(ed.), *Der inspizierte Muslim: Zur Politisierung der Islamforschung in Europa*,
Bielefeld: Transcript Verlag, pp. 335–66.

De Koning, M. (2020a), 'From Turks and Renegades to Citizens and Radicals: The
Historical Trajectories of "Good" and "Bad" Muslims in the Netherlands', *Trajecta:
Religion, Culture and Society in the Low Countries*, 29: 1, 3–26.

De Koning, M. (2020b), 'The Racialization of Danger: Patterns and Ambiguities in
the Relation between Islam, Security and Secularism in the Netherlands', *Patterns
of Prejudice*, 54: 1–2, 123–35.

De Koning, M. (2021), '"Reaching the Land of Jihad" – Dutch Syria Volunteers,
Hijra and Counter-conduct', *Contemporary Islam*, 15: 1, 107–22.

De Koning, M., C. Becker and I. Roex (2020), *Islamic Militant Activism in Belgium,
the Netherlands and Germany – 'Islands in a Sea of Disbelief'*, London: Palgrave
Macmillan.

Death, C. (2011), 'Counter-conducts in South Africa: Power, Government and
Dissent at the World Summit', *Globalizations*, 8: 4, 425–38.

Den Boer, M. (2007), 'Wake-up Call for the Lowlands: Dutch Counterterrorism
from a Comparative Perspective', *Cambridge Review of International Affairs*, 20:
2, 285–302.

Edmunds, J. (2012), 'The "New" Barbarians: Governmentality, Securitization and
Islam in Western Europe', *Contemporary Islam*, 6: 1, 67–84.

Fadil, N. and M. de Koning (2019), 'Turning "Radicalization" into Science: Ambivalent
Translations into the Dutch (speaking) Academic Field', in N. Fadil, M. de Koning
and F. Ragazzi (eds), *Radicalization in Belgium and the Netherlands: Critical Perspectives on Violence and Security*, London: I. B. Tauris, pp. 53–81.

Fassin, D. (2011), 'Racialization – How to Do Races with Bodies', in F. E. Mascia-
Lees (ed.), *A Companion to the Anthropology of the Body and Embodiment*, Oxford:
Wiley-Blackwell, pp. 419–34.

Foucault, M. (1982), 'The Subject and Power', *Critical Inquiry*, 8: 4, 777–95.

Foucault, M. (2007a), *Security, Territory, Population: Lectures at the Collège de France,
1977–78*, New York: Springer.

Foucault, M. (2007b), 'What Is Critique', in S. Lotringer (ed.), L. Hochroth and
C. Porter (trans.), *M. Foucault, The Politics of Truth*, Los Angeles: Semiotext(e).

Goldberg, D. T. (2002), *The Racial State*, Oxford: Blackwell Publishing.

Goldberg, D. T. (2009), *The Threat of Race: Reflections on Racial Neoliberalism*,
Oxford: John Wiley & Sons.

Goldberg, D. T. (2017), 'Militarizing Race', *Social Text*, 34: 4, 19–40.

Al-Hollandi, Abu M. (2014a), 'Islam & Jihad (deel 1)', not available anymore, in the archive of the author.

Al-Hollandi, Abu M. (2014b), 'Islam & Jihad (deel 2)', not available anymore, in the archive of the author.

hooks, b. (1986), 'Talking Back', *Discourse*, Autumn/Winter 86–7, 123–8.

hooks, b. (1989), *Talking Back: Thinking Feminist, Thinking Black*, Boston: South End Press.

Houtum, H. V. and R. Bueno Lacy (2017), 'The Political Extreme as the New Normal: The Cases of Brexit, the French State of Emergency and Dutch Islamophobia', *Fennia –International Journal of Geography*, 195: 1, 85–101.

Huda, M. K. (2017), 'The Construction of Radicalism Narrations: A Study of Hijra Hadith Quotation', *Advances in Social Science, Education and Humanities Research (ASSEHR)*, 137, 208–14.

Koopmans, R. (2013), 'Fundamentalism and Out-group Hostility: Muslim Immigrants and Christian Natives in Western Europe', <https://wzb.eu/system/files/docs/sv/iuk/koopmans_englisch_ed.pdf> (last accessed 6 May 2022).

Kumar, D. (2020), 'Terrorcraft: Empire and the Making of the Racialised Terrorist Threat', *Race & Class*, 62: 2, 34–60.

Lemke, T. (2011), 'Critique and Experience in Foucault', *Theory, Culture & Society*, 28: 4, 26–48.

Li, D. (2019), *The Universal Enemy: Jihad, Empire, and the Challenge of Solidarity*, Stanford: Stanford University Press.

Manjikian, M. (2017), 'Walking a Thin Line: The Netherland's Counterterrorism Challenge', in S. Romaniuk, F. Grice, D. Irrera and S. Webb (eds), *The Palgrave Handbook of Global Counterterrorism Policy*, London: Palgrave Macmillan, pp. 371–92.

Mondon, A. and A. Winter (2020), *Reactionary Democracy: How Racism and the Populist Far Right Became Mainstream*, London: Verso Books.

Nasr, S. H., M. Dakake, C. Dagli, J. Lumbard and M. Rustom (eds) (2015), *The Study Quran*, New York and San Francisco: HarperOne.

NCTV (2014a), 'Actieprogramma Integrale Aanpak Jihadisme – Overzicht maatregelen en acties', <https://open.overheid.nl/repository/ronl-archief-34fd2206-62da-446e-90b0-1fe2743cba8e/1/pdf/a5-nctvjihadismedef3-lr.pdf> (last accessed 26 July 2022).

NCTV (2014b), 'Het mondiaal jihadisme. Een fenomeenanalyse en een reflectie op radicalisering', <https://www.nctv.nl/documenten/rapporten/2014/11/12/het-mondiaal-jihadisme---een-fenomeenanalyse-en-een-reflectie-op-radicalisering> (last accessed 26 July 2022).

NCTV (2016), 'Nationale Contraterrorismestrategie 2016–2020', <https://www.nctv.nl/documenten/rapporten/2016/07/11/nationale-contraterrorismestrategie-2016-2020> (last accessed 26 July 2022).

NCTV (2020), 'Terrorist Threat Assessment Netherlands 52', <https://english.nctv.nl/documents/publications/2020/06/09/terrorist-threat-assessment-netherlands-52> (last accessed 26 July 2022).

Pargeter, A. (2005), 'The Islamist Movement in Morocco', *Jamestown Foundation Terrorism Monitor*, 3: 10, 23–32.

Pektas, S. and J. Leman (2019), 'Prospects for Counter-theology against Militant Jihadism', in S. Pektas and J. Leman (eds), *Militant Jihadism: Today and Tomorrow*, Leuven: Leuven University Press, pp. 187–216.

Renton, J. (2018), 'The Figure of the Fanatic: A Rebel against Christian Sovereignty', *Ethnic and Racial Studies*, 41: 12, 2161–78.

Sajjad, T. (2018), 'What's in a Name? "Refugees", "Migrants" and the Politics of Labelling', *Race & Class*, 60: 2, 40–62.

Schoof, R. (1999), 'Ook Musharraf stuit op fundamentalisten', *NRC Handelsblad*, 26 October, <https://www.nrc.nl/nieuws/1999/10/26/ook-musharraf-stuit-op-fundamentalisten-7467829-a546491> (last accessed 26 July 2022).

Sedgwick, M. (2007), 'Jihad, Modernity, and Sectarianism', *Nova Religio*, 11: 2, 6–27.

Sedgwick, M. (2015), 'Jihadism, Narrow and Wide: The Dangers of Loose Use of an Important Term', *Perspectives on Politics*, 9: 2, 34–41.

Stein, M. (1996), 'Hezbollah betrokken bij aanslag S-Arabie', *NRC Handelsblad*, 27 June, <https://www.nrc.nl/nieuws/1996/06/28/hezbollah-betrokken-bij-aanslag-s-arabie-7315418-a758604> (last accessed 22 July 2022).

Van Meeteren, M. J. and L. N. van Oostendorp (2019), 'Are Muslims in the Netherlands Constructed as a "Suspect Community"? An Analysis of Dutch Political Discourse on Terrorism in 2004–2015', *Crime, Law and Social Change*, 71: 5, 525–40.

Van Schie, G. (2018), 'Origins: A History of Race-Ethnic Classification in the Dutch Governmental Data Ontology', *Journal for Media History*, 21: 2, 67–88.

Vliek, M. and M. de Koning (2020), *Beleidsinstrumenten en extremistische wereldbeelden – Een verkennend rapport*, Nijmegen: Radboud Universiteit, The Hague: WODC.

Yanow, D. and M. van Der Haar (2013), 'People out of Place: Allochthony and Autochthony in the Netherlands' Identity Discourse – Metaphors and Categories in Action', *Journal of International Relations and Development*, 16: 2, 227–61.

Yanow, D., M. van Der Haar and K. Völke (2016), 'Troubled Taxonomies and the Calculating State: Everyday Categorizing and "Race-Ethnicity" – the Netherlands Case', *The Journal of Race, Ethnicity, and Politics*, 1: 2, 187–226.

11

FRAGMENTS OF UTOPIA:
POLITICAL AND RELIGIOUS EMIGRATIONS
FROM FRANCE TO SYRIA

Hamza Esmili

Let me tell you that my childhood as well as my whole life before the events of 2011 in my country have no connection with my departure to the (Islamic) State. Many people think that there are causes related to childhood and life before the departure. This is not true, at least for me and for many people I knew there. Before the events in 2011, there was nothing. The issue (of leaving for the Islamic State) has to do with thought. From 2011 onwards, new words and concepts emerged: *al-ṭāghūt* (tyranny), *al-sharī'a* (the way), *a'wān al-ẓalama* (the servants of the oppressors), *al-ḥākim bi ghayr sharī'at Allah* (the ruler without the way of God), and so on. Some people have begun the search for the truth. It is true that few people left Benghazi, for example, while from the poor areas of Tripoli, many left. But even in the working-class neighbourhoods, there are several types of departures.

The reason for my emigration is faith. It is faith, beyond the questions of the nature of the society of origin, unemployment, or other problems. The question has a pure link with faith. It is the question of thought. For me, it was a journey of searching for the *ḥaqq* (the right, the true). The very reason that led me to *tanẓīm* (the organisation, that is, the Islamic State) ended up taking me out of *tanẓīm*.

The person speaking – I will refer to him generically as Abdellah – is sought by various belligerent sides. He has fled the Islamic State after

261

initially joining its fighters in 2013. However, it is not the vengeance of his former brothers in arms that he fears the most. While hiding under a made-up name in Iraq, he is first and foremost trying to avoid the punishment that is universally addressed to those who consented to the caliphate's call. Therefore, in the small house that he rents in Kirkuk's poor suburbs, the man is keen to explain his actions beyond the objectifying lens that two researchers – Montassir Sakhi and myself – were keen to be applying to his biographical trajectory. Abdellah recognises that 'few people left Benghazi' – a relatively prosperous city in Libya – while 'from the poor areas of Tripoli, many left'. But he immediately adds his disdain for such a mechanical explanation: 'Even in the working-class neighbourhoods, there are several types of departures.'

Starting in 2011, thousands of *muhājirūn* (emigrants) came from all around the world to Syria and the rebellion that arose against the regime of Bashar al-Assad. There, '*sur zone*',[1] the fluidity that characterises the revolution in which they arrived (Kassab and Shami 2018), remained for a few years. Emigrants engaged in a variety of movements and activities, whether civil or military. In 2014, a breach: the Islamic State, until then one fighting group among others in the same 'freed zones' (*manāṭiq muḥarrara*) where the regime had no control, was recast as a territorial government in vast regions of eastern Syria and Iraq. A modern government was founded, encompassing eight million Syrians and Iraqis, and complete with borders and a spatially stratified administration, centralised taxation, a monopoly on physical violence, and a theology of national belonging, which further developed along with the proclamation of caliphate. The two historical phenomena overlapped: though they were neither at the origin or at the heart of the newly established Islamic State, most of the emigrants still responded to its call.

I propose to address the convolutions of the politico-religious quest of emigrants through a perspective inspired by Karl Mannheim's sociology of knowledge. Relying on an in-depth description of emigrants' experiences, from their departure from their home country to their integration into Syrian 'freed zones', and eventually, the restoration of governmental power within

---

[1] *Sur zone* – on the zone – is the common expression used by French intelligence to indicate that one has gone to Syria or Iraq.

the Islamic State, I aim to highlight several 'fragments of utopia' that appeared along their sinuous path. Through this notion, I try to depict emigrants' various experiences of intense and even eschatological nature that followed one another during a relatively short period (from 2011 to 2017), without making assumptions regarding their internal coherence. Their utopian nature is understood in Mannheim's sense of a state of mind more than an ideology or a projection towards a future that is yet to come. Indeed, according to Mannheim, 'utopian mentality' is immediately transformative of its own reality (*hic et nunc*) and its reach is beyond 'history of ideas' as it proceeds from 'deeper-lying vital and elemental levels of the psyche' (Mannheim [1929] 1954: 193). More than a defined political project to be realised, fragments of utopia are to be understood as a notion reconciling the intensity of emigrants' existential quest to go to Syria (and participate in jihad) and the increased uncertainties and competing forms of politics that appeared along the way.

Hence, my paper breaks with the common linear and processual approach within radicalisation studies (see, for instance, Crettiez and Seze 2017) in three different ways. While radicalisation studies are defined by competing scholarly attempts to locate what led individuals to become 'radicalised', I will try to demonstrate that the distinctiveness resides in the act of emigration itself and its underlying politics, which must be understood with respect to the historical ways in which Muslim communities – and subjectivities – established themselves in France and more broadly in Europe. Second, while it is often presumed that emigrants to Syria were directly headed to the Islamic State, I aim at showing that they first joined the freed zones of cities such as Aleppo, Homs or Hama, where an experiment of a radical dismissal of governmental politics was taking place. In return, they were accepted in various ways by the Syrian people engaged in a deep and long-term revolution against an oppressive regime. Lastly, while it appears that most of emigrants did join the Islamic State after 2014 (and still, not all of them), the ways in which they engaged with the caliphate's religious, political and military life were far from homogeneous. Some of them were soon to be considered as *ghulāt* (extremists) by the nascent state, as their politico-religious understanding of Allah's path (*shar' Allah*) differed from the newly established governmental orthodoxy.

My paper is based on a long-term investigation with families of French and Maghrebi emigrants to revolutionary Syria and supplemented by fieldwork conducted with Montassir Sakhi at the Turkish–Syrian border and in northern Iraq. We have been following French, Belgian and Maghrebi emigrants (as well as their relatives who did not go to Syria) for many years, as we tried to reconcile our inquiry into their lived experience in their home countries with a broader investigation into the historical sequence that started with the Arab revolutions. Thus, during our fieldwork at the Turkish–Syrian border (in cities such as Gaziantep, Reyhanlı, Kilis or Antioch) and northern Iraq (Erbil, Kirkuk, Sulaymaniyah and the Mosul area), we aimed at understanding the nature of the political experiments that were (and still are) taking place during the Syrian revolution and in war-torn Iraq, as well as the positions that were held by emigrants during these historical sequences.

For this paper, I will rely mainly (but not exclusively) on the trajectory of Laurent, who left France for Syria in 2012. Montassir Sakhi and I began by working with his mother in France before pursuing our exploration with his Syrian in-laws who had taken refuge in Iraq, and then, with the Libyan emigrant who married his widow after Laurent died in 2013.

Children of Post-colonial Immigration: Emigration within a Collective Condition

Between 2011 and 2017, tens of thousands of men and women (van Ginkel and Entenmann 2016) went on the laborious journey into the heart one of the deadliest conflicts of our time, that is to say the Syrian revolution and its ongoing repression by the regime of Bashar al-Assad and his allies. Although this movement was massive, this was hardly the first occurrence of Muslim departures from Europe. In Bosnia, during the Balkan wars (Li 2020), in Afghanistan, and throughout the American occupation of Iraq, Muslim men and women from France – and elsewhere in Europe – joined the fight for various reasons. More prosaically, the phenomenon of hijra – which is the act of leaving one's country to different destinations – while quantitatively rare, exists among Muslim communities in Europe. In the midst of existential precariousness and political constraint, it often signifies the attempt of a 'return' that undoes the generations of post-colonial immigration or, in the case of converts to Islam, of a settlement in 'Muslim' lands (Fadil et al. 2021). But the term hijra – although reproducing the seminal act of Islamic history – is only informed by what is left behind: unlike the sense of 'elevation' embodied in the Hebrew *aliyah*[2] for instance, hijra is primarily defined – and experienced – as a way out.

According to my interlocutors, emigrations to Syria are not to be understood with regard to what is left behind, since the gesture was filled with a positive content that needs to be apprehended for itself. As Abdellah said, 'My childhood as well as my whole life before the events of 2011 in my country have no connection with my departure.' Joining jihad against the oppressive regime of Bashar al-Assad was deemed by emigrants and their relatives as a way of actualising a 'thought' that is supposed to be defined by a 'pure link to faith'. Was it the biographical illusion that is commonly described by the scholarly literature as a vain resistance to sociological approach? In the wake of Pierre Bourdieu's work, self-explanation is understood as *post festum* rationalisation that breaks with the actual 'logic of practice' (Bourdieu 1990). According to Bourdieu, the sum of personal beliefs is the *illusio* necessary for the continuation of the social game (Bourdieu [1997] 2000). Thus, it is no surprise that, when tackling radicalisation, social sciences have focused on the search for a unifying and necessarily hidden motive which nevertheless explains the phenomenon. Hence, a profusion of contending explanations has been put forward, such as delinquency, failure at school, colonial racism or existential precariousness. While functioning as competing models, these scholarly attempts share an identical utilitarian epistemological premise of an ideological supply that is supposed to meet social demand. Thus, radicalisation is deemed to describe an extreme doctrine produced elsewhere (Kepel 1987; Roy 2002) that flourishes in the fertile social or individual soil of Europe (Ollion 2017) and eventually results in emigration to Syria (Khosrokhavar 2014).

While it is accurate that emigration to Syria is primarily associated with the working class and, in the case of France, with the specific condition of post-colonial immigration, such a correlation does not amount to a causality: not all have left within the urban projects – *la cité* – where immigrants and their children live. Such an obvious paradox is nonetheless easily resolved within radicalisation studies: if some go on the path of jihad in Syria and

---

[2] The Hebrew meaning of *aliyah*, which signifies for a Jewish person to go the Holy Land, means the rise to a higher altitude.

others do not, then it is a matter of questioning what it is about the paths of émigrés that distinguishes them from their peers who share a common socio-historical condition. Each of the competing motives (racism, failure at school, the impossibility of leaving the 'second zone' of delinquency, and so on) is correspondingly understood as the 'biographical accident' that deviates emi-grants' trajectories from the cluster of similar ones (Truong 2017). Therefore, according to radicalisation studies (Khosrokhavar 2014; Benslama 2016; Kepel 2015), emigration to Syria is the outcome par excellence of both a politico-religious doctrine and a series of biographical motives. The process is then said to go as follows: an individual was a child of post-colonial immigration or a convert to Islam – for this latter category, radicalisation is held to be chemi-cally pure since it is unbound by any collective history – then, a biographical accident and an ideological transformation took place – the entry into 'radical-ism' – before being transformed and completed by the departure to war zones.

Inquiry with families whose children have embarked on the journey to revolutionary Syria offers an alternative perspective. According to emigrants' relatives, multiple realities of existential precariousness are widely shared among those who belong to the same condition. Furthermore, the variety of biographical accidents that are deemed to explain 'radicalisation' are only effective as they subjectively actualise a common consciousness. In contrast to studies explaining radicalisation through splits within the condition of post-colonial and working-class immigration (Khosrokhavar 2014), both emigrants and their relatives affirm that departures are a potentiality that is inscribed within a shared collective experience.

So it is with Laurent, who left in 2012 for Syria. Born from the short-lived marriage of a French woman to a Moroccan man, Laurent grew up in the poor neighbourhoods of Perpignan's wider area. His mother relates his childhood as follows:

> He couldn't stand racism. I'm sorry to say, but his friends were mostly from Arab origins . . . Laurent was also dark-skinned. And I have to say it: they received constant racist remarks. I'm sorry, but it's the truth. They suffered from racism. It's the reality: in France, there is a lot of racism, and the children suffer a lot from it. It was often other inhabitants of the cité, adults and not so young people who let loose on them. I too, in my work, have been told many times: 'Your children are of mixed race.' Reflections like that, we've had a lot

of them. They grew up like that and it must be said. So there came a time when it didn't work anymore. But I recognise that the other kids have had it rough too. It's not a reason, it doesn't justify, but I'm trying to explain my opinion. In my opinion it's something! They've done some shit in connection with it. They are proposing to build a new state that doesn't exist. A model that doesn't exist. Yes, it can make people want to do that when nothing is left anymore for them. Many people today want to remake the world. It is tempting in a way. Yes, people are tired of living like this in a place where everything is monitored!

At odds with the concept of radicalisation, emigrants' relatives reinscribe their children's experience of life in a common historical condition ('I too', says Laurent's mother). The permanent and protean manifestation of racism is hardly the 'biographical accident' that would explain the radicalisation to come, as racism is common to those who share the experience of post-colonial and working-class immigration within the *cité*. However, Laurent's mother's account is compatible with the objection of Abdellah, the man from Kirkuk who refused the causal relationship improperly drawn between his social milieu and his emigration to Syria. After recalling the shared historical background, Laurent's mother immediately points to the only effective singularity at work in the emigration to revolutionary Syria: the political and religious quest that lies at its core ('They are proposing to build a new state that doesn't exist. A model that doesn't exist').

To what extent is such a form of existential politics indeed a fragment of utopia? According to Mannheim, utopia should be grasped in a dialectical sense: it is the 'existing order' that gives birth to 'unrealized and the unful-filled tendencies' that constitute in turn 'the explosive material for bursting the limits of the existing order' (Mannheim [1929] 1954: 179). As for emigration from France to Syria, its utopian nature has to be understood in regard to the ways through which Muslim communities established themselves in the midst of post-colonial immigration and urban marginality. Facing migratory uprooting (Bourdieu and Sayad [1964] 2020) and the vanishing of the industrial world (Castel [1995] 2017) that was at the heart of their coming to France, and confronted for the first time in the *cité* by the necessity of generational transmission (Sayad 1977), the freshly formed community has renewed its comprehension of the Islamic discursive tradition through the lenses of ritual pietism and care for the self and the others (Esmili 2021). From this perspective, the collective piety that recommenced within the *cité* is first and foremost an alliance between immigrants and their children. All its various actualisations, from building mosques within immigrant and working-class neighbourhoods to the theological stance that Islam is complete wherever Muslims are, point to repairing mutual ties as well as the subjectivities that were damaged by the experience of the *cité* (Castel 2006).

Yet intimate precariousness persists along protean collective marginality, reasserting the community's foundational fragility. Political and religious emigration to revolutionary Syria marks the incompleteness (Laurent's mother says: 'when nothing is left anymore') of collective refoundation in the *cité*. A politics of territorialisation is replaced by its inversion, that is to say a politics of deterritorialisation through the quest for another and radically different society. Mannheim's approach proves to be useful with regard to the passage from one form of politics to another, as he understands utopia as a state of mind that is characterised by *hic et nunc* transformation of immediate realities. Emigration, while sharing some ideological features with the collective condition that lies at its threshold, can be understood as the singular intensification of a shared piety. Departure for distant and revolutionary Syria expresses a first fragment of utopia in the emigrants' quest. It lies in the substitution of one existential perspective to another, from collective and patient reparation in France to the implementation *hic et nunc* of 'a model that does not exist', as Laurent's mother says. Emigration corresponds to the exaggerated actualisation – 'orgiastic' in Mannheim's words – of the renewed experience of piety amongst post-colonial immigrants in France. As Anja Kublitz argues regarding the 'rhythm of ruptures' among Danish jihadists (2019), intergenerational solidarity and emigration intersect in a paradoxical manner. Parents both understand and do not share the horizon of departure. Laurent's mother says: 'It is tempting in a way.'

Arriving to 'Freed Zones': Emigrants within the Syrian Revolution

Laurent's mother narrates her son's departure to Syria:

> This was in 2012. After a month or two, my daughter called me and said she had to go back up to her brother's house because he wanted to sell her his car. He was tired of it and needed money. He sold it to her for 600 euros. It was

an old Renault. She then told me that he wanted her to take him back to the airport in Marseille. Suddenly, he said to his sister: 'Will you take me to the airport in Marseille?' All along the way, his sister asked him questions: 'Where are you going? To whom?' And all along the way, he distracted her. At no time did he answer her questions. When we arrived at the airport, the plane had to take off at 2:00 am. He had never been on a plane, so when he arrived, he had to say to his sister: 'Can you tell me where the ticket office is to go to Istanbul?' At that moment, I thought – for the first time in my life – that I had lost my vocal cords. I just watched and listened. I was completely stunned. At the counter, he put down his nearly empty luggage. As he passed by, the hostess said to him: 'You will get your luggage back in Adana.' He passed by and left. My daughter started to cry. She told me: 'It's over, we won't see him again, we won't see him again.' She cried so much. I didn't want to cry. I told her that no, that he will come back soon when he sees what is going on there. I believed it. Besides I didn't know where Adana was. I went home, plugged in the computer directly to see where Adana was located. I saw how close it was to Syria. But at that time, in 2012, Syria was not talked about at all as it is today. It had started to heat up, but we didn't hear much about Syria. When he arrived, he sent a message to his sister saying that he had arrived.

When departure finally occurs, the families' reflexivity – which we said was forged in a de facto collective condition – fades away along the passage of their children from one historical sequence to another (Laurent's mother says: '[W]e didn't hear much about Syria'). At this point, interlocution with families reaches its natural limit. Relatives of emigrants could describe with rare lucidity what was being left. However, what was to be joined remained unclear, starting from a daunting question: why Syria and not Palestine, a historically powerful motive for mobilisation in the Arab world and elsewhere (Genet [1986] 2003), Tunisia, where the Arab Spring began, or Egypt where a post-revolutionary Islamic-orientated government was overthrown by a blood-soaked coup in 2013? In answer to this question, radicalisation studies state the following: Syria was the seat of Islamic State's power, which was the emigrants' exclusive objective (Kepel 2015). Despite its palpable discrepancies,[3] such a narrative offers a mechanical explanation: radicalised

---

[3] For instance, the Islamic State was established in Iraq several years before the beginning of massive emigrations to Syria. Thus, why did emigrants not go to Iraq?

individuals were headed to the most radical Islamic political organisation of the time. Teleological, and therefore ahistorical, that the radicalisation thesis is unsurprisingly oblivious to 2011's 'miracle' (Kublitz *op. cit.*), the historical sequence of Arab revolutions that took place at the start of emigration to Syria.

In Tunisia, a man sets himself on fire: slapped by a policewoman, the incident epitomises a life marked by *hujra* – the ordeal of injustice. Collective suffering resonates in Mohamed el-Bouazizi's tragedy: first in Sidi Bouzid, the scene of the self-immolation, then in the rest of the country, and eventually throughout and beyond the Arab world. The initial paradox of emigration from France to Syria reveals itself: didn't the revolution first take place in the Maghreb, from which most of post-colonial immigration to France came as well? But, in the Maghreb, the only convergence between locals and emigrants is the insertion of 'binational' actors into the new associative and political life following the revolution (Geisser 2012). Conversion of economic and cultural capital became possible through the institutional translation that was given to the deflagration of 2011: new constitutions were drafted, elections held, and the mantra of the Arab revolutions, 'bring down the regime' (*isqāt an-niẓām*) was progressively delegated to civil society. Abdellah, the man from Kirkuk, states:

> I was twenty-six years old when I left. There were demonstrations in my country, but I was against them. Demonstrations don't serve any purpose. In itself, I was against different practices of people in different areas. Later on, I became opposed to the whole world apparently (laughs). No, seriously, I was against the police and against the army. It's like these institutions were weighing me down.

While the desperate gesture of the man from Sidi Bouzid is the canonical starting point of the Arab revolutions, the fracas quickly moves eastwards: first to Libya, Egypt and Yemen, where protests topple regimes that were thought to be everlasting, then to Syria. There, another canonical story is heard: in February of the fateful year 2011, children in Deraa declared themselves to be revolutionaries (*thawwār*). On one of the walls of the city, they wrote in dialect 'It's your turn, doctor.' The response of the ophthalmologist-president is brutal, as will be each subsequent manifestation of the repression. A dozen teenagers are kidnapped by Military Security, imprisoned and cruelly tortured. But in this region, where tribal customs still have a collective meaning, a delegation of wise men (*wujahā'*) appealed to the state for their children's freedom. In the revolutionary memory, the scene remains vivid: the notables put down their turbans, a sign of appeasement and a request for negotiation, but the local governor, while correctly deciphering the action, decided to send the headgear to the garbage dump. Oddly enough, violent repression does not discourage protests: more and more martyrs (*shuhadā'*) fall, but their burial is the scene of a constantly renewed and amplified revolt. Participation in the first demonstrations that start to erupt in the whole country are a rite of passage: it dismisses everyday life in favour of what is deemed to be revolutionary times. As early as June 2011, the regime starts to retreat from various localities in Homs, in Hama, and in eastern Damascus, as well as from vast rural regions, henceforth designated as 'freed zones' (*manāṭiq muḥarrara*).

Unanimity around the nascent protest is immediately remarkable: if the sequence of the Arab Spring has strengthened the idea of exceptional times among the demonstrators, nowhere else in the Arab world was revolution as massive and lasting as it was in Syria. The same sequence of events is constantly repeated: immediate state repression paradoxically leads to suspension of the monopoly of physical and symbolic violence, leading to an exponential extension of the perimeter and depth of the revolt. Reciprocally, 'freed zones' are organised by dismissing any power external to the community and to the solidarity experienced within the revolutionary society (Kassab and Shami 2018). Revolutionary slogans such as 'one, one, one, the Syrian people is one' (*wāḥid wāḥid wāḥid, al-sha'b al-sūrī wāḥid*) assert the existence of collective conventions that are more sacred than the economic or ethnic organisation of society.

Far from being the territory of a reconstructed sovereignty, 'freed zones' were established through local communities' materialities. Absence of territorial continuity or stabilised political structures favoured major differences between the various practical configurations while at the same time interweaving contestation with the bonds of solidarity organic to each situation. However, despite the heterogenous nature of 'freed zones', the existence of a unique revolutionary society is nonetheless asserted by the flag of the Free

Army (*al-jaysh al-ḥurr*), which is systemically flown during the continuing demonstrations. The Free Army is itself only a constellation of brigades that are military counterparts of localised communities, founded as a response to the extremely violent repression, but its existence forms a discursive totality, which allows, in turn, the reflexive discussion of the historical options that are offered to the revolutionary society.

However, the possibility of death remained omnipresent. Mortality tolls during the first six months – when the demonstrators were still chanting '*silmiyya, silmiyya*' (peaceful, peaceful) – were heavy: thousands, including children, were killed during what were still peaceful demonstrations. Consequently, while protests initially evolved around traditional liberal concerns (criticism of economic corruption, social inequalities, regime's opacity, lack of freedom of expression and pluralism, the pan-Arab ideology that stifled the cultural rights of minorities, and so on), massive massacres by regime's military forces and loyalist militias (*shabbīḥa*) quickly transfigured the sensible reality of the protest toward existential commitments where death – possible and probable – would be understood as the price to pay for a life finally freed from injustice.

Early liberalism progressively grew into a form of pacific pessimism, as many of the civil revolution's figures were assassinated (Bassel Shehadeh, Basil al-Sayed, Khaled al-Isa, and so on), kidnapped (Samira al-Khalil, Razan Zaitouneh, Father Paolo Dall'Oglio, and so on) or forced into exile (Yassin Haj-Saleh, Rayan Rayan, Fadwa Souleiman, and so on). Alternatively, another utopia emerges through the *hic et nunc* actualisation of divine justice within 'freed zones'. The name of Allah infuses its universality into the protest, slogans such as '*mā lanā ghīrak ya Allah*' (we have only you, O Allah) accordingly opposes divine truth to violent repression and the silence of the so-called international community. A famous revolutionary song by Abdelbassit Sarout states, after having affirmed the sole presence of God, that 'your protocol is killing us', referring to the United Nations Security Council. Khalil, Laurent's Syrian father-in-law, narrates:

> At the beginning of demonstrations, we chanted for the regime's fall. But when the regime started shooting at the crowds, killing women and children in the streets, bombing the neighbourhoods, and so on, the story changed. We went from regime's fall to the struggle for the triumph of religion, the

triumph of the oppressed and the elevation of the word 'there is no God but Allah and Muḥammad is his prophet'. We have moved from demanding a change in the constitution to the triumph of religion.

As protest evolves towards jihad, revolution gains in millenarian depth. However, proclamation of jihad (Littell 2012) is neither a civilisational and global project, nor is it a simple translation of the struggle from a secular language to a religious one (Asad 2018). It pertains to a historical potentiality intrinsically linked to the conflict's escalation. Syria's appeal to emigrants thus appears more intelligible: millenarist consciousness – in the sense of suspension of governmental times – within the revolutionary society facing a systemic massacre matches the intensity of an existential quest that began in Europe. Remarkably, the growing presence of emigrants among the revolutionaries in Syria starting in 2012 provokes no suprise within the host society: emigrants are deemed to be the *muhājirūn* who have come to help Syrians confronted with the extreme violence from the regime of Bashar al-Assad. This idea is based on the inversion of a formative moment in Islamic history with deep theological implications, the hijra, in which the Prophet's followers, emigrating to Medina, were supported by the local population, the *anṣār*. Abu Obeida, a revolutionary brigade commander in Aleppo, relates:

> As Muslims, we had the idea that this was a jihad on the path of Allah from the beginning (of the outbreak of the war). But our jihad was confined to our land, against tyranny. Often, in interviews, I would say that I was not surprised that an American, a British or a Frenchman would fight with me, but at the same time, if one day the revolution broke out in their countries, I would be ready to fight with them. There is something called injustice. No matter what your religion, your ethnicity, and so on. The French Revolution, when it broke out, there was nothing called jihad, but it is a form of jihad for me. For us, as Muslims, we do indeed go into battle with the intention of dying on the path of Allah against a tyrant.

Reciprocally, most emigrants justify their coming to Syria through the idea of 'helping the oppressed Muslims'. Even on a more intimate level, emigration becomes immigration – in accordance with a regular pattern (Sayad 2004). As soon as he arrived in Syria, Laurent marries a Syrian woman whose family participates – first as demonstrators, then as fighters – in the revolution. His mother tells the story:

> My son went there. At one point he was offered marriage . . . He was communicating with me at the time via Skype. He found a girl with whom he got married and with whom there was a real love story. Of that I am convinced. He chose her. And it was this girl's mother who chose Laurent as a husband for her daughter. When I saw them both on Skype, I was sure that they loved each other: you could see their love. They loved each other very much and when he died, the woman cried a lot. She cried for a long time. I saw her crying live.

Similarly, Khalil, Laurent's father-in-law, says:

> I married my daughter to this Frenchman, and they had a child together. It is true that we belonged to two different groups, but there is no difference in the jihad against the regime and *nusrāt al-dīn*. We are all Muslims, thank God.

'We are all Muslims.' Along with asserting a common sense of belonging, this complicity indicates the affective intensity shared between Syrian revolutionaries and emigrants from all around the world. Solidarity amid *muhājirūn* and *anṣār* is forged through 'jihad against the regime'. The proclamation of this jihad embodies a utopian potentiality that is as contingent as it is singular: faced with astonishing state violence, ordinary reality is transformed into chiliastic times, during which the common passage of time is suspended.

Within the experience of revolutionary zones freed from any coherent form of state sovereignty (Munif 2020), an alliance between the living and the dead is embodied through the permanence of revolutionary jihad against the regime's injustice. Reciprocally, reward in the hereafter of martyrdom is only an individual expression of collective piety through the ordeal of war, so that the *shahīd* is called upon to witness the earthly justice for which he gave his life. Therefore, an expression such as 'going to Syria' reveals its deepest significance: it indicates the existential commitment of emigrants to jihad against the regime that follows immediately after their integration into the revolutionary society of 'freed zones'. As long as reality could be sustained this way, chiliasm was the path through which the relationship to the sensible was deepened within 'freed zones' that were waiting for collective deliverance. Khadija, a shopkeeper from Aleppo whose husband and son died in combat, narrates:

We have learned so much about living in wartime that at the peak of the bombing; we were celebrating a wedding. Of course, we were already living underground at that time, the groom had his hand amputated after a wound at the front against the government forces, but it was a happy celebration, with music, dancing, *dabka*! My God, there must have been 150 of us, there was even a DJ! So, it's true, at one point, we felt that the earth was shaking, but we told ourselves that it was because we were dancing too hard! Only, when we wanted to go out, we realised that the building under which we were had been bombed; we were literally buried under the rubble. So, you know what we did? We kept partying and dancing until the voluntary civil guards got us out. When I lost my son four months ago, I'm not going to lie to you, I was sad. He was tall, handsome and strong as a bull. He was nineteen years old. He had just passed his exams at the University of Gaziantep, and he had come back to Syria to fight on the front in Aleppo, his city. So yes, I buried him, yes, I mourned him, but the struggle does not stop. If my second son told me that he wanted to go too, I would say yes, go, go defend your people. And you know why? Because no matter your international coalitions, your strategies, your strikes and your injustices, we will continue the fight, because we are fighting for our land, for our existence and for our way of life and our religion. Hundreds of innocent people die every day, and we will be sad, and we will mourn them, but we are the people of the Levant, and we will not resign, we will keep fighting.

But the aestheticisation of the world has a terrible reverse effect: when defeat occurs, as a direct result of intervention by Iranian militias and Russian military forces in support of Bashar al-Assad, it indicates the end of a world (De Martino 1977), as well as the radical defeat of the revolutionary society. From within 'freed zones', another form of politics seizes the opportunity: revolutionary jihad is deemed to have been defeated because it did not establish an alternative state. A violent confrontation develops between those who still consider themselves to be revolutionaries and 'soldiers' of the newly established Islamic State. In January 2014, the latter are expelled from the 'freed zone' of Aleppo at a heavy cost for local brigades of the Free Army. In return, revolutionaries, both civil and armed, are imprisoned or exterminated in the vast territories of eastern Syria and northern Iraq that fell under the administration of the Islamic State. For the first time, the alliance between revolutionaries and emigrants is broken, as most of foreign fighters leave for the East and the newly formed state. From Aleppo to Raqqa, their existential quest began by linking itself to revolution, but it is recast in the proclamation of caliphate (June 2014) and the quickly evolving global war waged against it.

From the outset, the Islamic State was instituted as a territorialised government. While the 'freed zones' were the site of an imperfect order, where the general piety of millenarian times was parallel to the proliferation of militias alongside the breakdown of state's monopoly of legitimate violence, the government that was established in Raqqa and Mosul reconstituted a neo-national space. Like any modern state, the Islamic State restored the continuity of space and power as it established borders: externally, with customs fees that were only paid upon entry, and internally, by instituting a strict symbolic order based on the conjunction of extreme violence and an official discourse aimed at 'its' population. For the latter, the new government dismissed all forms of subjective mediations of piety (Asad 1986; Mahmood 2004) in favour of a theology of national belonging: Muslim subjects were defined exclusively by their belonging to the Islamic State and, reciprocally, only those who belonged to it were presumed to be Muslims.

Utopia and Sovereignty within the Islamic State

Laurent never saw any of it. He died in 2013 while fighting Bashar al-Assad's forces, several months before the proclamation of the caliphate. His widow married Abdellah, an emigrant from Libya who reached Syria in early 2012. We met him in 2017 in Kirkuk, not long after he had defected from the Islamic State, for the purpose of a long interview (more than fifteen hours, only interrupted by a short night at his place). After dismissing our early, objectifying approach, Abdellah soon started to formulate both questions and answers, as we entered with him into a realm that was completely unknown to us, that is, the ideological debates within the newly established (at least as a functioning government) Islamic State. Abdellah narrates:

> The reason for my emigration is faith. It is faith, beyond the questions of the nature of the society of origin, unemployment or other problems. The question has a pure link with faith. It is the question of thought. For me, it was a journey of searching for *al-ḥaqq* (the right, the true). And the very reason

that led me to *tanẓīm* (that is, the Islamic State) eventually led me out of *tanẓīm*. Because the only objective of *tanẓīm*, it was that the state must remain! However, the state cannot exist if the people leave it as they wanted to when we started to be bombed by the coalition. But the *tanẓīm* forced them to stay, especially when the bombardments become intensified.

The *tanẓīm* condemned those who said otherwise as *ghulāt* (extremists). But what do the *ghulāt* propose? They propose that everyone should assume their responsibility: they say that there should be an appeal addressed to the Muslims of the whole world. A call that says to Muslims if they believe in the possible existence of a real Islamic state, let them come! And those who disagree can leave, especially when the bombing started to kill everyone. That's when we would understand whether people believe in the state of Islam or not. But the reality is that there were calls for people to come and join the Islamic State, but the immigration of people was small, even insignificant. Few people came. The *muhājirūn* are small in number compared to what we thought. We had to consider that. We left with the idea of an Islamic state that rules by the law of Allah. I personally left for this reason . . . These people did not come to remake Iraq: we emigrated for something else. But it is true that things turned into the situation I mentioned to you: it happened that the policies that survived and dominated were the policies close to that of the Ba'th Party. The organisation rehabilitated the Ba'th. This is how things were organised. Torture, repression, settling of scores, massacres. And most of the *shar'i* (legalists/ leaders of the faith) who are killed are emigrated *shar'i*. We were called to fight without looking at the result. If the result turned out to be a defeat, it does not change anything. But things are quite clear from the beginning: we were leaving because we wanted to leave and because we wanted to try something new.

In his little room in Kirkuk's suburbs, Abdellah was showing us dozens of WhatsApp messages exchanged among *ghulāt*, Islamic State's own extremists. We have progressively come to understand that emigrants, while joining the newly established government, represented one of the lasts fragments of utopia within its ideological debates. For Abdellah, as well as for several of his companions, jihad is not linked to a Clausewitzian war between competing nations as it is understood by the Islamic State's leaders. Neither a stage in the process of becoming a state nor the founding violence of a new society, for Abdellah and his companions jihad is deemed to be a form of life in which one chooses to participate or not, especially in the face of a strong probability of death. The *ghulāt*, the vast majority of whom are emigrants, generally believe that civil populations, known to be unattracted to the Islamic State government, should be excommunicated and free to flee the constant bombings executed by international coalition. The vitalist perspective of this last fragment of utopia is directly at odds with the strategic and modern rationality of the Islamic State. According to the latter, belonging to the Muslim community is entirely defined by acceptance of the newly formed government. Thus, at the background of the theological discussion – the debate is primarily led by religious scholars – the principle at the foundation of the modern theories of sovereignty (Foucault 2009) is reaffirmed: the state resists giving up its population – which is its main wealth – despite the deluge of bombs that decimates it. Abdellah concludes:

> Jihad for me is not about fighting. It is a matter of *ʿaqīda* (creed and transcendental obligation). I am convinced of a number of ideas, and if a group with the same principles of faith is formed, I may join it again, but it will be done without haste and with great understanding. I came [to the Islamic State] for the idea of a land of Islam, of brotherhood. I came to live a dream: you have to know what it means to leave your country to go somewhere else. At first, I had a positive image. I was happy when I arrived in Syria: it is a promised land, a land of the caliphate. For me, it was the fulfilment of a promise. After several trials, and after living with the members of the Islamic State, I knew very well that it is basically just a big lie. I am against any court set up by men. I am a free man. I consider that there will be no *ḥukm* (judgement) other than the judgement of Allah. Allah holds the judgement. There is no worship except of Allah. And this is what it means to be a free man. *Attahākum* (asking for judgement, complaining to an assembly) is *shirk* (idolatry): there is worship only to Allah. This means that there is no worship except for Allah, who has sent us a prophet and rulings that govern and are valid for all places and all times . . . Muḥammad was sent so that he would bring people out of the worship they are worshipping other people: out of the worship of people to the worship of Allah. But laws are what make you worship people and not Allah. This is how the dispute between you and your religion arises. The situation in the Islamic State is far from the image that is being spread to young Muslims. It is not the law of Allah that reigns among them. On the contrary, it is the passion of those who dominate that reigns. The recruitment is often done with young people like me who want to live in the land of Islam because

of the fact that in our countries there is repression. But the Islamic State serves as a purification and physical extermination zone for this type of youth. It also serves to end this spirit and this thought.

The statist perspective won out between Raqqa and Mosul. Against the proponents of a lived and non-governmental utopia, the territorialised power of the Islamic State forces the civilian population to remain in its bombed cities until their final fall. The human cost, which obviously was extremely heavy, is nevertheless deemed by the Islamic State to be negligible in the face of the need for the permanence of government power (*bāqiya wa tatamaddad*, i.e., 'the Islamic State is still there and is extending', a common motto of its soldiers). The debate is as much ideological as it is historical: the oppositions that appear in plain sight are those of radically distinct political figures. However, the success of one over the other is hardly attributable to intellectual discussion alone: is it any wonder that, in a contemporary world durably structured by modern states and the forms of government they establish, even an organisation as little linked to the concert of nations as the Islamic State takes up – admittedly brutally, to the point of fascism – its most salient features?

From a fragment of utopia to another, my interlocutors experimented with various ways of 'dealing with God' (see Anja Kublitz's chapter in this volume) and subsequent forms of politics, as well as reiterating existential stuckedness (Hage 2009). The paradoxical nature of their quest resides in the combination of intensity and uncertainty: at the heart of so many contradictions, the convolutions of emigrants' existence from Europe to revolutionary Syria concentrates the jolts of several fragments of utopia. However, it cannot be described through the teleological lenses of a search for 'radicalisation', as the impasse constituted by the denial of existential depth is both theoretical and political. By rendering the singularity at work unintelligible, such an analytical perspective considerably obscures the categories of the necessary historical discussion of the political figures that emerge in the fabric of the contemporary. Conversely, only the attention to politics that emerge from 'depths of the soul' (Mannheim *op. cit.*) reconstitutes the bumps of shared times, especially when some of the emigrants have fortunately come back to

[4] See Montassir Sakhi's work on returnees from Syria to France and Belgium.

their native society and resumed their previous existence[4] – that is to say, life before 2011 and the various fragments of utopia that ascended since the Arab revolutions.

Yet, what about those who neither died nor returned or are detained in the Kurdish prisons of al-Hasakah or al-Hol? Abdellah, hidden in a poor suburb of Kirkuk, says:

> Today, I feel an air of freedom. I am free because I have no nationality. I cheat the governments that make up this world. I cheat to be able to live outside their laws. I live despite them and despite their laws. Against the world.

References

Asad, T. (1986), 'The Idea of an Anthropology of Islam', Occasional Paper Series: 1–23, Centre for Contemporary Arab Studies, Georgetown University, Washington.

Asad, T. (2009), 'The Idea of an Anthropology of Islam', *Qui Parle*, 17: 2, 1–30.

Asad, T. (2018), *Secular Translations: Nation-state, Modern Self, and Calculative Reason*, New York: Columbia University Press.

Benslama, F. (2016), *Un furieux désir de sacrifice. Le surmusulman*, Paris: Seuil.

Bourdieu, P. (1990), *Logic of Practice*, Redwood: Stanford University Press.

Bourdieu, P. ([1997] 2000), *Pascalian Meditations*, Redwood City: Stanford University Press.

Bourdieu, P. and A. Sayad ([1964] 2020), *Uprooting: The Crisis of Traditional Agriculture in Algeria*, New York: Polity Books.

Castel, R. ([2003] 2017), *From Manual Workers to Wage Laborers: Transformation of the Social Question*, London: Routledge.

Castel, R. (2006), 'La discrimination négative: Le déficit de citoyenneté des jeunes de banlieue', *Annales: Histoire, Sciences Sociales*, 61: 4, 777–808.

Crettiez, X. and R. Seze (2017), 'Saisir les mécanismes de la radicalisation violente : pour une analyse processuelle et biographique des engagements violents', <http://www.gip-recherche-justice.fr/wp-content/uploads/2017/08/Rapport-radicalisation_INHESJ_CESDIP_GIP-Justice_2017.pdf> (last accessed 15 June 2022).

De Martino, E. (1977), *La fine del mondo. Contributo all'analisi delle apocalissi culturali*, Turin: Einaudi.

Esmili, H. (2021), 'Changer l'intention. Adoration et conversion en islam contemporain', in P. Michel and J. Heurtin (eds), *La conversion et ses convertis*, Paris: Centre Maurice Halbwachs, pp. 50–64.

Fadil, N., A. Moors and K. Arnaut (2021), 'Envisioning Hijra: The Ethics of Leaving and Dwelling of European Muslims', *Contemporary Islam*, 15: 1, 1–16.

Foucault, M. (2009), *Security, Territory, Population: Lectures at the College de France 1977–1978*, New York: St Martin's Press.

Geisser, V. (2012), 'Quelle révolution pour les binationaux : Le rôle des Franco-Tunisiens dans la chute de la dictature et dans la transition politique', *Migrations Société*, 143: 5, 155–78.

Genet, J. ([1986] 2003), *Prisoner of Love*, New York: New York Review Books.

Hage, G. (2009), 'Waiting Out the Crisis: On Stuckedness and Governmentality', in G. Hage (ed.), *Waiting*, Melbourne: Melbourne University Press, pp. 97–106.

Kassab, R. and L. Shami (2018), *Burning Country: Syrians in Revolution and War*, London: Pluto Press.

Kepel, G. (1987), *Les banlieues de l'Islam. Naissance d'une religion en France*, Paris: Seuil.

Kepel, G. (2015), *Terreur dans l'Hexagone. Genèse du djihad français*, Paris: Éditions Gallimard.

Khosrokhavar, F. (2014), *Radicalisation*, Paris: Maison des Sciences de l'Homme.

Kublitz, A. (2019), 'The Rhythm of Rupture: Attunement among Danish Jihadists', in M. Holbraad, B. Kapferer and J. F. Sauma (eds), *Ruptures: Anthropologies on Discontinuity in Times of Turmoil*, London: UCL Press, pp. 174–92.

Li, D. (2020), *The Universal Enemy: Jihad, Empire, and the Challenge of Solidarity*, Redwood City: Stanford University Press.

Littell, J. (2012), *Carnets de Homs*, Paris: Éditions Gallimard.

Mahmood, S. (2004), *Politics of Piety*, Princeton: Princeton University Press.

Mannheim, K. ([1929] 1954), *Ideology and Utopia: An Introduction to the Sociology of Knowledge*, London: Routledge.

Munif, Y. (2020), *The Syrian Revolution: Between the Politics of Life and the Geopolitics of Death*, London: Pluto Press.

Ollion, E. (2017), *Raison d'État. Une histoire de la lutte contre les sectes*, Paris: La Découverte.

Roy, O. (2002), *L'Islam mondialisé*, Paris: Seuil.

Sayad, A. (1977), 'Les trois âges de l'immigration algérienne en France', *Actes de la recherche en sciences sociales*, 15: 1, 59–79.

Sayad, A. (2004), *The Suffering of the Immigrant*, Cambridge: Polity Press.

Truong, F. (2017), *Loyautés radicales. L'islam et les 'mauvais garçons' de la nation*, Paris: La Découverte.

Van Ginkel, B. and E. Entenmann (eds) (2016), *The Foreign Fighters Phenomenon in the European Union: Profiles, Threats & Policies*, Hague: International Centre for Counter-terrorism.

12

ACTING WITH GOD: DIVINE INTERRUPTION AND PRACTICES OF JIHAD

Anja Kublitz

Introduction

The day after Hosni Mubarak was removed from power, Khaled decided to quit his criminal activities and move to Egypt.[1] At that time (2011), he declared himself a socialist. Since then, Khaled has not only ceased his criminal activities, changed his political convictions, lived in Egypt for half a year and been part of the revolution – he has also travelled to Syria twice to fight against Bashar al-Assad and has, in his own words, become an Islamist. Like my other interlocutors, who have taken up what they themselves identify as practices of jihad;[2] that is, struggling in the way of Allah, Khaled had been

---

[1] All names used in this chapter are aliases to secure the anonymity of the participants.

[2] Daryl Li argues against using the term 'jihadist' for academic purposes because of its political use and its fraudulent meaning in so-called terrorism studies that lump together different political movements and practices (Li 2019: 23–6). Although I agree with Li's critique of the use of the term in political discourse and terrorism studies, I do not believe that the solution is to refrain from using the concept. Instead – and in accordance with my interlocutors – I believe we should reclaim the concept and explore its emic meanings. When I have chosen to designate the interlocutors' practices as practices of jihad it is first and foremost because my interlocutors refer to their practices of joining Islamic militant movements in Syria as 'striving/struggling in the way of Allah' (in Danish: '*at stræbe/at kæmpe på Allah's vej*'). They also used this term when asked about the relationship between divine determination and their actions. Since the aim of this chapter is to investigate the young Danish men's emic

neither politically active nor religiously observant before the Arab Spring. Rather, he was an established criminal with a good mind and a gift for numbers, who, at an early age, achieved a central position as an accountant for the gang controlling the drug market in his city. 'So, you just stopped from one day to the next?' I asked him. 'Yes', Khaled responded, and continued:

> I did. When I was a criminal, you had this idea that people in the Middle East are idiots, and that you have these corrupt regimes, and nobody does anything about them. And you had no hope of return because who had imagined that Mubarak would be overthrown in fourteen days or that Gaddafi would be killed like that, and that the people would wake up? Nobody had expected that. Nobody had imagined that. It wasn't realistic. I found out that you should not necessarily think about what is realistic. You should not be limited by what is realistic.

When I conducted this interview in 2015, I thought of the Arab Spring as a political event. Only later did I realise that my young interlocutors do not differentiate between worldly events and God. Two years later, therefore, I asked Khaled, 'Do you remember that you said that the Arab Spring was beyond imagination?' 'Yes,' Khaled replied, 'It was a miracle. A miracle.'

It turned out that among my interlocutors, the Arab Spring was experienced as a divine intervention that triggered the beginning of what they refer to as the Last Hour. The miracle of the Arab Spring, the young men claimed, made them wake up to find themselves as part of the *umma*: the Muslim community of the last prophet, Muḥammad – that is, the prophet of the time of the end, but also to find that maybe the end of time (apocalypse) had arrived, and they could choose to join the Great Battle between infidels and believers. As the Arab Spring unfolded and the Syrian people, along with secular and Islamic political movements, started to fight Bashar al-Assad's regime, my interlocutors began discussing whether the apocalypse had begun. To them, the war in Syria offered an opportunity to seize the miracle and join Islamic movements in Syria to hasten the end of the current political order.

understandings and practices of joining Islamic military movements in the Middle East, I have chosen to stick to the terms: 'jihadist' and 'practices of jihad' in my analysis of why they did what they did. Furthermore, the Danish government does not use this term, but rather the term 'foreign fighter'. My interlocutors distance themselves from this latter term because it situates them squarely outside the Danish state.

What surprised me most when I began my ongoing fieldwork in 2015 among returned Danish Muslim men who had joined Islamist militant movements in Syria was the way my interlocutors took for granted that God is an omnipresent factor in the world and the creator of the world. By then I had conducted fieldwork among Middle Eastern Muslim families in Danish housing projects for ten years, and although I had described the families' turn from Marxist to Muslim (Kublitz 2011, 2016), the religious turn had seemed to be more about identity processes than religious beliefs and God as such. It seemed, however, impossible to describe or understand why the young men had taken up practices of jihad without taking God and more specifically divine interruption into account. The question that my fieldwork left me with was: if the young men believe that God is almighty then why would they join militant movements in Syria? Or phrased in more analytical terms: what is the relationship between divine determination and human action? Taking my point of departure in my long-term fieldwork this chapter explores this question by examining how the miracle of the Arab Spring changed my inter-locutors' lives radically. I analyse how the young men responded to what they consider a divine intervention and suggest that their practices of jihad, that is struggling in the way of Allah, can be considered a way of acting 'with' God.[3] Drawing on Giorgio Agamben's distinction between apocalypse (the end of time) and messianic time (the time of the end) (Agamben 2005: 56–62), I suggest more specifically that my interlocutors' practices of jihad can be understood as a way of bridging a divine present and a God-given future.[4]

The chapter is structured in accordance with my interlocutors' spiritual journey from the margin of the Danish state to the centre of the end-times. My hope is that it will allow the reader to gain an ethnographic insight into how God emerged in the lives of my interlocutors and changed their paths. First, however, I outline my argument that practices of jihad are a way

---

[3] In this chapter I treat God as an object equivalent to other objects, such as the welfare state. I do so because it reflects how my interlocutors experience the world. As Jon Bialecki writes in relation to Christian charismatic evangelism, God is rendered an object by the way people refer to him and rely on him (Bialecki 2017: 77), and, I would add, by the effects and affects that my interlocutors believe he causes. See also Amira Mittermaier (2011: 28; 2012: 256) for a similar approach and Bialecki (2014) for a critique of 'methodological atheism'.

[4] For an expanded version of this argument see Kublitz 2023.

of acting with God. I then introduce the field of Danish jihadists and my fieldwork before I analyse how the miracle of the Arab Spring was perceived as a divine interruption and investigate how the young men in my study responded to this intervention by God.

Practices of Jihad as a Way of Acting with God

Theoretically, the chapter contributes to the scholarship of a new generation of anthropologists working on Islam, and religion more broadly. Departing from the groundbreaking work of Talal Asad and his students on Islam as a discursive tradition that forms ethical subjects (Asad 1986; Hirschkind 2006; Mahmood [2005] 2012), these younger scholars have started to investigate God's agency in shaping the lives of religious actors (see, among others, Elliot 2016; Elliot and Menin 2018; Mittermaier 2011, 2012, 2019; Moll 2018, 2020; Schielke 2019). In 'Dreams from Elsewhere', Amira Mittermaier writes that, despite its central role, divine intervention is largely written out of the anthropology of Islam (Mittermaier 2012: 249). Unlike Samuel Schielke, who in an earlier critique of Saba Mahmood argues that there is 'too much Islam in the anthropology of Islam' (Schielke 2010: 2), Mittermaier argues that there is '*too little Islam* – or rather, too little attention to different coexisting forms of being Muslim' (Mittermaier 2012: 249). Mittermaier encourages us to decentralise the subject and the concept of self-cultivation that is central in Mahmood's work and explore 'other modes of religiosity that centre neither on acting against nor on acting within but on being acted upon' (Mittermaier 2012: 252). Interestingly, Talal Asad himself, in a 2012 article on politics and religion after the Arab Spring, writes: 'It is possible for someone to encounter something unpredictably that transforms her, to be gripped through her senses by a force' (Asad 2011: 51). My interlocutors would appreciate this phrasing. Although they grew up in Muslim households, they were not practising Muslims before the Arab Spring, nor did they believe in God. According to the young men, it was the miracle of the Arab Spring that made them wake up to see God's actions and plans. One might say that God took them by surprise (cf. Bialecki 2017: 96; see also Jules-Rosette in Harding 2000: 38; Robbins 2010: 643).

In an article from 2015, Nadia Fadil and Mayanthi Fernando encourages us to take our interlocutors' voices seriously also when it comes to religious subjects we might disagree with (Fadil and Fernando 2015: 82). If we are to take my interlocutors' experience of God seriously, we cannot understand their jihadist practices as individual-driven acts only, nor as a matter of only being acted upon. Unlike the dreams in Mittermaier's book that 'come' to her interlocutors (Mittermaier 2011: 6), jihad literally means to struggle in the way of Allah, and I suggest that my interlocutors' practices of jihad are better described as acting 'with' God.

Alice Elliot explores a similar phenomenon in her article 'The Makeup of Destiny' (2016). Unravelling the paradox of divine predestination and human agency among young Muslim women in Morocco, Elliot describes how her interlocutors' belief that their future husband is God-given does not stop them from the meticulous labour of putting on make-up in the hope of attracting their future husband. Elliot convincingly argues that predestination in Islam is not about religious fatalism, but rather requires a labour of hope to ensure the future to come. In a parallel argument, I suggest that, if we are to understand why European Muslims have chosen to travel to the Middle East and join Islamic militant organisations, we must understand the relationship between living in a world that one believes is determined by God, including when and how the world will end, and still believing that one can affect it.

To explore this relation between divine interruption (Robbins 2019) and my interlocutors' jihadist practices in the aftermath of the miracle of the Arab Spring, I suggest we draw on Giorgio Agamben's distinction between apocalypse (the end of time) and messianic time (the time of the end) (Agamben 2005: 56–62).[5] In *The Time that Remains* Agamben elaborates on the difference between these two temporalities. He describes the apocalypse as the very end of time: the last day (ibid.: 62). In contrast, messianic time, the time of the end, is the period that remains between chronological time and the end of time (ibid.: 56). According to Agamben, messianic time presents itself as the only time

---

[5] When I draw on theories on Christianity as well as Islam, it is because the ethnography in noticeable ways resonates with descriptions of Christian conversions (especially within Pentecostalism), reflecting how my interlocutors are not only influenced by Islam but also by Christianity and popular culture (cf. Larkin 2008). See also Saba Mahmood, who writes that despite the Islamic piety movement's antagonism toward secularism, it presupposes many secular concepts and is far more hybrid than its participants will acknowledge (Mahmood [2005] 2012: xv). See also Kublitz 2023 for an elaboration of this argument.

we have left before the end, as the time of the 'now' (Marshall 2009: 66): 'an incoherent and unhomogenous time, whose truth is in the moment of abrupt interruption, when man, in a sudden act of consciousness, takes possession of his own condition of being resurrected' (Agamben 2007: 111). This is an exact description of my interlocutors' religious awakening in the aftermath of the Arab Spring. The 'abrupt interruption' of the Arab Spring made my interlocutors wake up to find themselves as part of the Muslim community of the last prophet at the time of the end. Consequently, they immediately turned their lives around, stopped their pursuit of money through criminal activities and instead started to pursue *imān* (faith). Furthermore, Agamben writes that the messianic moment, the time of the now, exceeds chronological time by introducing God as an internal surplus that is immanent in secular time (Agamben 2005: 69). The 'abrupt interruption' by God, that is, the miracle of the Arab Spring, made my interlocutors see God's plans as immanent in the development of political events. From then on, they assumed that the cause of the world and the uprisings in the Middle East were part of a divine plan and considered how they best could contribute to it.

The young men's born-again Islam in noticeable ways resonates with anthropological studies on Christian conversions (especially within Pentecostalism), that theoretically builds on Agamben's reading of St Paul's miraculous conversion to Christianity (see, among others, Harding 2000; Robbins 2004, 2007, 2010, 2011; Marshall 2009, 2010; Bialecki 2009, 2017; Haynes 2020). I will draw on this body of literature throughout the analysis of my interlocutors' experiences. Before I return to my interlocutors' religious awakening, however, I will briefly introduce my long-term fieldwork.

Fieldwork among Danish Jihadists

Ethnographically, this chapter contributes to the scarce empirical studies of European so-called foreign fighters who joined Islamic militant movements in Syria (De Koning 2021; De Koning, Becker and Roex 2020; Esmili this volume; Kublitz 2019, 2021, 2023). The Danish jihadists are part of a larger population of European citizens who, since 2011, have set off for the Middle East to take up arms, with the clear aim of overturning oppressive secular regimes and substituting them with Islamic ones. Denmark affords a unique fertile vantage point for a study of returned European foreign fighters. Since 2012, approximately

160 foreign fighters have left Denmark and joined military movements in Syria and Iraq (Center for Terroranalyse 2018: 14) out of a total of approximately 4,000 foreign fighters from the EU (Van Ginkel and Entenmann 2016: 3). Relative to the size of its population, this means that Denmark produces the second largest number of foreign fighters in Europe (Neuman 2015) and the highest percentage (approximately 50 per cent) of returned foreign fighters (Van Ginkel and Entenmann 2016: 29). Furthermore, Denmark only began to prosecute foreign fighters in 2016, so it has therefore been possible to conduct fieldwork among many of those who returned.

My fieldwork among returned Danish jihadists is an extension of my ongoing research since 2005 among refugee families from the Middle East in Danish housing projects. What started out as one and a half years of fieldwork among nine extended families in seven housing projects for my PhD has, over time, evolved into an intimate engagement with these families, consisting of regular visits, conversations and informal interviews. It has also introduced me to a broader range of residents in the projects. From 2012, some of the young-sters that I had known since they were children started to leave for Syria, and in 2015 I received funding to study how and why Danish youth become for-eign fighters. My ethnography of returned Danish jihadists, therefore, consists of youngsters I have known for fifteen years and others whom I have known since 2015. The material encompasses the communication that the families had with their children while they were in Syria, along with participant obser-vation among and interviews with those who returned. This chapter takes its point of departure from the stories and lives of three returned Danish jihad-ists, with the aim of investigating how they struggle in the way of Allah (that is, their practices of jihad) at the end of time.[6] Khaled, Amr and Yassin all grew up at the margin of the Danish state, in housing projects that are identified by the Danish government as 'hard ghettoes', because of their high percentage of immigrants, unemployment and crime (see also Kublitz 2013, 2015, 2019, 2021). Khaled's parents fled Syria in the early 1980s when Hafez al-Assad cracked down on the Muslim Brotherhood. Amr's and Yassin's families have fled twice: first in 1948, when they were expelled by the newly declared Jewish state, and then again in the 1980s, after the Palestinian revolution and the War

---

[6] In Kublitz 2019, I present excerpts of Khaled's and Amr's and their parents' stories in order to explore how history repeats itself with a difference.

of the Camps in Lebanon when the Syrian-backed Amal militias attacked the Palestinian refugee camps (Peteet 2005: 151).[7]

Khaled ended up joining an Islamic faction that, at the time, was part of the Free Syrian Army (FSA), whereas Amr and Yassin joined Islamic State (IS). I have chosen these specific cases to highlight the similarities of the ideas and practices across the spectrum of different political organisations. Although the ideologies of the FSA and IS are very different and even antagonistic, my ethnography shows that the choice of which political and military groups my interlocutors joined was more dependent on chance and their social networks than based on ideology (see also Sageman 2004). In these specific cases, Khaled, who joined FSA, an organisation that from its outset was defined by its goal of bringing down the government of Bashar al-Assad, was more engaged in Islamic religious ideas than Amr and Yassin, who joined Islamic State.

The Arab Spring as a Divine Interruption

It was the Arab Spring that sparked my young interlocutors' spiritual journey. Confronted with what they conceive of as a miracle – a divine intervention and as the beginning of the end – the young men decided to turn their lives around.

Amr and Yassin, who both left for the Islamic State when the caliphate was announced in 2014, tell stories akin to Khaled's. Like him, they grew up in housing projects and were engaged in criminal activities before their religious awakening in 2011. When I asked Amr what he meant by 'miracle', he responded:

A miracle is something that happens without the human capacity to organise or plan it. It wasn't us. It wasn't the Muslims who planned the Arab Spring. The Egyptians only had to take one step, then God opened the possibilities . . . It was obvious.

My Danish interlocutors were not alone in believing that the uprisings in Egypt were driven by a divine force. Mittermaier describes how her Egyptian Sufi interlocutors believed that it was God who moved the people to dispose of Hosni Mubarak (Mittermaier 2017), and the famous Muslim televangelist

---

[7] The Palestinian revolution (*al-thawra*) lasted from 1969 to 1982. It consisted of a number of Palestinian popular uprisings that succeeded in liberating the refugee camps in Lebanon and paved the way for the Cairo Agreement, which handed over control of the camps from the Lebanese government to the Palestine Liberation Organisation.

Amr Khaled, appearing on state television shortly after the fall of Mubarak, told the programme host: 'I saw God in Tahrir. When you entered Tahrir Square you immediately noticed a different spirit' (Mittermaier 2015: 379). This resonates closely with Khaled's description. Before his religious awakening, Khaled had never been to the Middle East. Nevertheless, when he decided to quit his criminal career, he immediately took up a job in a Danish human rights organisation and started to save his money. Ten months later, he arrived at Tahrir Square:

> Tahrir Square in 2011 was a miracle. Christians stood between the water cannon and the Muslims and prayed for them. There were capitalists and anarchists. People hugged and kissed. It was like heaven on earth. I lived next to a stall by one from the Muslim Brotherhood whom I did not know. It was crazy. I got food and cigarettes. People shared their bread with each other.

The fall of Mubarak also initiated Amr's spiritual journey. Unlike Khaled, however, he did not set off for Tahrir Square but rather to the local mosque in Denmark, which he started visiting regularly. Here he befriended a group of other young Danish Muslims, who, besides praying, also followed the political developments in the Middle East closely, including the uprisings in Syria. 'As a Palestinian,' he explained, 'when I started practising Islam, I also brought that, you know, *hamās* along – you know, enthusiasm, the idea that we want to make a difference. Not just talk but do something.' Echoing Ghassan Hage's article on Palestinian suicide bombers entitled 'Comes a Time We Are All Enthusiasm' (2003), neither Khaled, Amr nor Yassin got stuck in talking. Khaled ended up joining an Islamic militant organisation that, at the time, was part of the Free Syrian Army, and both Amr and Yassin decided to check out the newly resurrected Islamic *khilāfa* (caliphate) for themselves.

Despite the different contexts, my interlocutors' responses to the miracle of the Arab Spring resembles, in remarkable ways, the descriptions of miracles within Christianity that portrays them as radical ruptures that change people's lives and time itself. Inspired by St Paul's allegedly miraculous conversion to Christianity (Badiou 2003, 2007; Agamben 2005), anthropologists have for a long time considered Christian conversions as disruptive events that, through the grace of God, 'make the continuum of history explode'

(Robbins 2011: 185; see also, among others, Bialecki 2009, 2017; Engelke 2004, 2010; Harding 2000; Marshall 2009, 2010; Meyer 1998; Robbins 2004, 2007, 2010). In a similar fashion, the miracle of the Arab Spring intro-duced a radically different temporality to the young men in my study. Instead of being caught up in what they perceived to be a capitalistic accumulative time of infinite needs that they attempted to satisfy through petty criminal activities (cf. Sahlins 1966), they woke up to find themselves in the centre of the time of the end, which is characterised by that time is running out as it is approaching apocalypse (cf. Agamben 2005: 63). However, unlike Agam-ben's interpretation of the Christian miracle of St Paul, the Danish jihadists did not conceptualise the miracle of the Arab Spring as a singular event, but rather as a series of events that would eventually lead to the end of the current political order and the world as we know it. In this way they reflect an Islamic apocalyptic narrative in which small signs of the Last Hour is succeeded by great signs that set in motion a sequence of events that ultimately leads to universal resurrection (Filiu 2011: xix).

Four years after Khaled returned from Egypt, and one year after he returned from Syria, he described the political developments as a spiritual avalanche:

> I believe that the whole world is amid a spiritual evolution. What happens in the Middle East is because of this. *Ya 'ni*, I dare, I do not fear anymore, I can. I believe in justice. It's an avalanche and it's not gonna stop. Most Muslims are convinced that we will rule the new world order.

In a similar fashion, Yassin, who left for the Islamic State, describes it as an irreversible growing development:

> It's like climate change. It's irreversible. It won't go away. God says: 'If you take one step towards God, God will take ten steps towards you.' It's not like we (Muslims) planned this. It's more like suddenly you wake up and you take one step, and then the other take one step, and suddenly it's Afghanistan, Chechnya, Somalia, Mali and Europe.

Joel Robbins argues that religious ruptures constitute a 'life-altering force' (Robbins 2019: 22), that involves radical changes in people's values (Robbins 2004). According to my interlocutors, their decision to take up practices of jihad (to struggle in the way of Allah) was not motivated by the desire to kill themselves or others (Roy 2017: 56), but rather that they wanted to live their lives in a radically different way. When they woke up to find themselves in the time of the end – where time was running out – they stopped their pursuit of money overnight and instead started pursuing *imān* (faith).

From Money to Faith

One afternoon, Amr and I had spent the entire day in the dim basement of the housing project watching jihadi *anashīd*: YouTube videos that call upon Muslims to take up arms to save their Muslim sisters and brothers from atrocities committed by secular forces around the world (such as Afghanistan, Chechnya, Syria and Palestine). Over and over again, we had witnessed Muslim children and women being killed while we listened to different imams discussing the concept of justice and doing good. When we emerged from the basement, the sun was setting behind the grey blocks and we decided to head into town to buy dinner. Entering the local bus, which was crammed with people carrying enormous shopping bags, we realised that it was Black Friday. 'Holy day for consumer capitalism', as Amr remarked. When we reached the centre, it appeared as an uncanny reverse reflection of the jihadi *anashīd*. The town had been turned into a battlefield of people fighting over goods on sale or celebrating their newly appropriated material items by drinking and eating voraciously at the many restaurants. As we gave up trying to find an available table at a café and settled for a schawarma on a bench, Amr continued our discussion. What kind of civilisation was this, he asked, where people only worshipped money and had no moral values. Of course, they would lose the 'Great Battle'. Unlike Muslims who believed in God, these people wouldn't last one day. That had also been the case in Syria, where those who fought for a salary didn't last long, whereas those who fought for justice never stopped.

Our discussion reflected an ongoing theme in my conversations with returned Danish jihadists – namely, the contrast between secular capitalism and Islamic values.[8] Reflecting on their criminal past, Yassin, Amr and Khaled all explained their immoral deeds as the result of growing up in a

---

[8] This is, of course, not an idea that preoccupies jihadists only, but is a central theme in many Islamic movements (see for instance Mahmood 2012; Mittermaier 2013).

capitalist society that primarily values the pursuit of money. In stark contrast, they emphasised the lack of pursuit of money in the Islamic State and the Islamic movement that Khaled was a part of. Amr described how everybody in the Islamic State left their shops unlocked when they went to the central square to receive the latest bulletins, or when they went to the mosque to pray, because no one was fearful of thieves. And just as Khaled described Tahrir Square as a paradise where people shared their bread and cigarettes, he would also describe how in Syria – before the establishment of the Islamic State – the mujahidin (fighters in the way of Allah) of different Islamic political movements would join each other's military posts and share their bread and cigarettes with one another. Furthermore, he emphasised how the position of the commander of his military unit was not privileged in any way. The commander was the only one who received a small salary, but he had to spend it on food and cigarettes for his men. The commander would bring the men back to his village, where his mother would wash their clothes, bake bread and serve them food.

Unlike many European states and scholars on so-called radicalisation (for example Basra et al. 2016), my interlocutors did not consider their journey from criminal to jihadist as a continuation of criminal activities; on the contrary, they viewed it as a radical rupture. To them, the miracle of the Arab Spring introduced a fundamental break with what they describe as 'consumer capitalism', which allowed them to imagine a radically different political order that was centred not on money, but on faith. Reversing Marx's famous dictum of religion as 'the opium of the people', they believe that capitalism has sedated people in Denmark and elsewhere into living what they refer to as a disenchanted *robot liv* (robot life). According to the jihadist interlocutors, the miracle of the Arab Spring made them wake up from this numb condition. Until then, they had found themselves marginalised at the end of the world; now they woke up to find themselves as 'strangers' at the end of time.

At the Centre of End-times

The third time I visited Yassin in the housing project where he grew up, he played the *nashīd Ghuraba* (strangers) for me on YouTube.[9] Only later

---

[9] Available at <https://www.youtube.com/watch?v=TjzxYdbiLk4> (last accessed 15 February 2023).

did I realise that the beautiful a cappella song is a classic among jihadists' Islamic vocal songs. Yassin explained that the concept of *ghurāba* has several meanings. It refers to adherents of Islam who are considered strangers among those who do not believe; it also refers to Muslims who, as foreigners, travel to join the Great Battle at the end of time. Finally, Yassin related the lyrics to his own life. It made perfect sense, he explained, that the new world order would emerge from the margins inhabited by strangers (one of the ways ethnic Danes refer to immigrants is as '*fremmede*', that is, strangers). In the housing project where he grew up, all nationalities were present. He grew up among Arabs, Somalis, Afghanis and people from the Balkan countries. They had learned each other's languages and traditions and were much better equipped to bring about a new world order than the provincial young Danes who only spoke two languages (Danish and English) and had no clue about what went on in the world.

> When the Great Battle arrives here, Danes don't stand a chance. People in the ghettoes know how to fight. All the parents here can easily make a bomb. They learned that in Afghanistan, Lebanon, Syria. Even the women can assemble a Kalashnikov blindfolded. The young Danes have no clue of what is going on in the world. They are clueless.

What might come across as a young man bragging about his parents' violent deeds reflects Yassin's (and his generation's) understanding of their parents' experiences of war and fight.

During one visit, Yassin told me that when he was younger, his best friend had come across a photo of his mother in a Danish textbook they were reading in school. The image was part of a chapter on the Danish left wing and the Palestinian revolutionaries (*fidā'iyūn*) in Lebanon. A beautiful young woman dressed in green army clothes, a Palestinian scarf around her neck and a Kalashnikov in hand had stared back at his friend. Shocked to see his mother with a machine gun, his friend had confronted her with the photo when he got back home. Bent over pots and pans in the kitchen, his mother, who still wore a scarf although by now a Muslim headscarf, had taken a quick look at the photo, confirmed that it was her, and continued cooking.[10] Although the young jihadist interlocutors in general considered that the residents of the ghettos – owing to their violent past and present (Kublitz 2019) – were much better equipped to face the Great Battle when it arrived in Denmark, they also believed that they did not necessarily have to wait. Maybe the Great Battle had already begun in Bilad al-Sham (Greater Syria)?

The miracle of the Arab Spring did not only pave the way for an Islamic interpretation of time among my interlocutors but also for an Islamic interpretation of space. When the interlocutors woke up to find themselves as 'strangers' at the end of time, they also awoke to find themselves as 'strangers' in terms of a religious geography. When the uprisings in Syria evolved into a regular battlefield, with Russia supporting Bashar al-Assad and the emergence of many different Islamic militant movements fighting Assad, Muslims in the housing projects started to discuss whether the Last Hour had begun. They explained to me that it is written in the prophecies that the Great Battle between believers and infidels will take place in Bilad al-Sham (spanning the contemporary countries of Syria, Lebanon, Jordan, Palestine and parts of Turkey) (see also McCants 2015: 99). 'Go to Sham and those who cannot go to Sham, go to Yemen,' Yassin recited to explain why the war in Syria might not be just any war – and the potential role of 'strangers' in this battle. Showing me the list in Wikipedia and a number of YouTube videos with Middle Eastern shaykhs, Khaled explained to me that the arrival of the Last Hour is accompanied by a range of greater and smaller signs. Scanning the (divine) natural and political terrain for such signs, the interlocutors would discuss a wide range of phenomena from bad weather ('Even the sky is crying'), to waves of fires caused by drought in Israel ('No one knows the soldiers of God, except God'), to local and international political events.[11] Two events stood out, though. In 2013, Assad killed hundreds of civilians with sarin gas in Ghouta, and the footage depicting rows of pale, dead

[10] In Kublitz 2011 and 2016, I describe the movement from Marxists to Muslims among Palestinians in Denmark. See Kublitz 2011 and 2019 for an analysis of the intergenerational relations in the families.

[11] See Filiu (2011: 59) for a description of the natural catastrophes that are believed to foretell the final state of the world.

children lying on a concrete floor went viral. Years later, several of the returned jihadists would show me these images and highlight that it was this event in particular which had made them realise that they had to help their Muslim sisters and brothers. What made this violent incident stand out as a significant event that imposed a moral and divine demand on the interlocutors was not only the use of sarin gas, the scale of atrocities or the horrible images, but also that the massacre took place in Ghouta. In the prophecies it was written, I was told, that Muslims would assemble in Ghouta for the Great Battle. The second event that was highly debated in the housing projects was, of course, the establishment of the Islamic State in 2014. When the Islamic State announced the resurrection of the *khilāfa* in Bilad al-Sham and raised the black flags, it was breaking news. Everybody in the projects was discussing whether this was it. Whereas the majority, by far, of the parental generation of Muslims decided for themselves that the caliphate was false and had this interpretation confirmed by the local Danish imams, the young generation did not know whom to believe. They considered the Danish and Western media generally unreliable and had access to different news and imams via the Internet. Counting the flags of the countries of the coalition against the Islamic State, to see whether by now it matched the prophecy that predicted that the infidel forces would gather under eighty flags for the Great Battle, Amr explained:

> You know, there is so much propaganda. So, I thought I would rather take the chance and go there myself and see what is happening than stay in Denmark and sit and doubt what is wrong and what is right.

Bridging the 'Time of the End' and the 'End of Time'

The miracle of the Arab Spring did not introduce God only, but also a new temporality to the young men in my study. From then on, they started interpreting present events from the divine vantage point of the future apocalypse, scanning the present for signs of the Last Hour that potentially could arrive any minute and intensively discussing how to understand current events.

My interlocutors set off for Syria not only because they identified themselves as 'strangers' and wanted to hasten God's plan, but also because they did not know whether the end of time had begun and, in the words of Amr, wanted to 'check out' whether the Islamic State was the real caliphate and whether the battle in Syria was the Great Battle. My interlocutors' journeys to the Middle East thus cannot be interpreted as a kind of religious fatalism but rather reflect internal debates and doubts within the Muslim communities that are an inherent feature of Islam (Moll 2018; Khan 2012) and my interlocutors' motivation to travel to Egypt and Syria to see for themselves what was happening and if and how they could contribute.

Khaled's recurring journeys to Syria between 2012 and 2014 confirmed to him that the world was about to end: 'When you see all these barrel bombs explode; buildings in ruin; women and children screaming, walking around all disoriented, it really does look like that the Last Hour has arrived.' In 2015, however, he had reached the conclusion that the battle might take years and that he could be of better use if he strived in the way of Allah in Denmark rather than in the battlefield of Syria. Amr's stay in the Islamic State convinced him that it would play a central role in the Great Battle. And although the Islamic State was losing ground in 2018, Amr stated:

> The Islamic State is now in thirty countries. For Somalis, it's easier to travel to Somalia now, where they also fight for a *khilāfa*. The Islamic State also fights in Sinai, in Egypt, and then there are people in Gaza who have sworn an alliance. I follow them like others follow a football club. The Islamic State is the key to all the problems Muslims have today. We will see that in the future. It is these people that will open Palestine, no one else.

To my interlocutors the miracle of the Arab Spring pervaded the present with a 'miraculous energy' (Haynes 2020: 58), that lifted their spirit. It also encouraged an optimistic interpretation of present events from the vantage point of the divine future. Current events were no longer understood as secular phenomena but as potential signs of the times (Haynes 2020: 59; Harding 2000: 233, Filiu 2011: 121ff; Cook 2008: 172ff).

When the Islamic State in Syria and Iraq was dismantled, Yassin argued that it allowed the Islamic State to spread to the rest of the world. When the Danish government decided to forcibly relocate immigrants from the Danish ghettoes (Danish government 2018), Khaled argued that this would make the Muslim residents realise that they never will be treated as equal citizens in a democracy and therefore would contribute to their interest in an

Islamic political order. And when the war in Syria in 2015 led to hundreds of refugees walking along the highways of Europe and crossing the border to Denmark, Amr commented:

> From an Islamic point of view, it is perfect that all the refugees arrive now. In twenty years from now, somebody else will rule Denmark . . . *Venligboerne* [meaning 'the friendly people', a civil movement welcoming refugees in Denmark] are sweet, but what are they going to offer? Nude bathing? Soon the refugees will understand the system here and they will turn towards Islam.

The jihadist interlocutors believe that apocalypse is approaching but they do not know when, and it is exactly this gap between the time of the end and the end of time that allows for human contribution to the fulfilment of God's plan.

Struggling in the Way of Allah: Immediacy and Telos

During one of my many visits to the housing project where Khaled lives, we were back in the worn-down basement. The bleak surroundings did not seem to affect Khaled. He was excited. He was busy accounting for the many signs that the End of Time (*akhīr al-zamān*) was near and that an Islamic political order will arrive eventually. Prompted by my question of why one should bother to fight in Syria or do other good deeds, if an Islamic order was going to come about anyway, Khaled abruptly got up from the white plastic chair and stood up straight. 'If you want to fly,' he explained, 'you can stand like this [both legs solidly planted on the ground], but you can also lift one of your legs, like this. Then you are already halfway there.'

Standing on one leg with his arms reaching for the sky, Khaled was ready for take-off. Khaled's posture of halfway flying illustrates that to him – as well as to my other jihadist interlocutors – there is no contradiction in believing that Allah is almighty and that you can hasten his plans. On the contrary, by acting 'with' God you contribute to his plans. Discussing predestination and action among her Muslim interlocutors, Elliot writes:

> the complex relationship between action and theological imagination is far removed from the kind of inevitable passivity and immobilizing fatalism that Western social theorists, from Weber all the way to Huntington (1993), have repeatedly identified in Islamic conceptions of predestination. (Elliot 2016: 489)

Instead, she suggests that predestination compels people to act in the human world in view of a future that has already been divinely determined (Elliot 2016). My ethnography offers a slightly different case that is more aligned with Agamben's analysis of 'the time that remains' (2005), because the young men's practices of jihad simultaneously are oriented towards a divine present and a God-given future.

Based on my fieldwork, I have come to think of my interlocutors' jihadist practices as guided by both immediacy and telos, what Agamben refers to as messianic time: time of the now (Agamben 2005: 56), and time that is oriented towards apocalypse or eschaton: the end of time (ibid.: 62). On one hand, these youngsters are immediately affected by the violent events in the Middle East, which they think of as urgent potentialities to restore justice and worship God, in accordance with a messianic time of the Now. On the other hand, they understand their current actions through the future apocalypse that will inevitably come. These two perspectives are not exclusive. Standing on one leg with his arms reaching for the sky, Khaled embodies the image of hastening the fulfilment of God's plan (cf. Marshall 2009: 66). This image, however, is complemented by another image that Khaled uploaded to his stories on Instagram. It was a black and white cartoon in Gary Larson's style of drawing. In a relaxed, laid-back position on a black couch, a *mujāhid* – wearing a white tunic, a black beard, and a small smile on his face – was watching the Al Jazeera news channel. In front of him a flat-screen TV displayed scenes of buildings exploding. The text stated: 'Struggling in the way of Allah.'

The two different images illustrate the spectrum of jihadist practices: from hastening God's plan (what I have termed immediacy) to awaiting the inevitable (what I have termed telos). Both poles of practices are responses to the new temporality that the divine interruption of the miracle installed; namely that time is running out: that apocalypse is approaching. I deliberately frame these practices as responses to emphasise my interlocutors' experience of acting 'with' God as they strive to bring about what they believe is God-given. My interlocutors believe that they live in end-times: they know that the world is about to end, but they do not know when. And I suggest that it is this gap that their different practices of jihad strive to bridge.

Conclusion

In the opening vignette to this chapter, Khaled emphasised that the miracle of the Arab Spring had taught him: 'You should not be limited by what is realistic.' Instead, he and my other jihadist interlocutors are struggling to contribute to God's plans. In this chapter I have explored this intersection between divine interruption and my interlocutors' jihadist practices, and I suggest that the young men's endeavours can be understood as ways of acting with God by bridging the gap between a messianic now and a future final hour.

European governments primarily understand practices of jihad as violent practices. Such an interpretation, however, reduces jihadists' practices to random individual acts or psychological deficits. The Danish jihadists are far from mad individuals who have gone astray nor are they violent nihilists (Roy 2017); rather, they are part of a heterogeneous set of global political and religious movements that in different ways strive to bring about an Islamic political order. For my interlocutors, God is the most central actor in that plan. To be more precise, they consider it His plan, but that does not exclude the notion that they themselves can contribute to it. To exclude God from our understanding of why European youngsters joined Islamic military movements in the Middle East is not only empirically incorrect but also analytically hazardous, I argue, because it prevents us from understanding why jihadists act as they do. Leaving out God and the jihadists' contributions to his plans turns the construction of an Islamic state into an irrational endeavour and fails to recognise the radical critique of secular capitalist societies that these practices entail. It also makes us lose sight of what happens when the jihadists return to Europe.

That the Danish state, along with other European states, primarily understand practices of jihad as violent practices implies that, when the young jihadists return to Denmark and stop their violent practices, they are no longer considered jihadists. This is a radical misunderstanding. Upon return to Denmark, my interlocutors are still on the path of God. Though they await the Islamic takeover that eventually will arrive, they do no stay idle. They continuously work on their *imān* by financially supporting their family, assisting the residents in the ghetto, and performing volunteer work. 'Acting with God' the young men are striving to change themselves and the world for the better before it ends.

References

Agamben, G. (2005), *The Time that Remains: A Commentary on the Letter to the Romans*, Stanford: Stanford University Press.

Agamben, G. (2007), *Infancy and History*, London: Verso.

Asad, T. (1986), *The Idea of an Anthropology of Islam*, Occasional Papers Series, Washington, DC: Center for Contemporary Arab Studies, Georgetown University.

Asad, T. (2011), 'Thinking about Religion, Belief and Politics', in R. A. Orsi (ed.), *The Cambridge Companion to Religious Studies*, Cambridge: Cambridge University Press, pp. 36–57.

Badiou, A. (2003), *Saint Paul: The Foundation of Universalism*, Stanford: Stanford University Press.

Badiou, A. (2007), *Being and Event*, London and New York: Continuum.

Basra, R., P. Neumann and C. Brunner (2016), *Criminal Pasts, Terrorist Futures: European Jihadists and the New Crime–Terror Nexus*, London: ICSR Report.

Bialecki, J. (2009), 'Disjuncture, Continental Philosophy's New "Political Paul" and the Question of Progressive Christianity in a Southern California Third Wave Church', *American Ethnologist*, 36: 1, 110–23.

Bialecki, J. (2014), 'Does God Exist in Methodological Atheism? On Tanya Lurhmann's *When God Talks Back* and Bruno Latour', *Anthropology of Consciousness*, 25: 1, 32–52.

Bialecki, J. (2017), *A Diagram for Fire: Miracles and Variation in an American Charismatic Movement*, Berkeley, Los Angeles and London: University of California Press.

Center for Terroranalyse (CTA) (2018), 'Vurdering af terrortruslen mod Danmark', Politiets Efterretningstjeneste (PET).

Cook, D. (2008), *Contemporary Muslim Apocalyptic Literature*, New York: Syracuse University Press.

Danish Government (2018), 'Regeringen vil gøre op med parallelsamfund', <https://www.regeringen.dk/nyheder/2018/ghettoudspil/> (last accessed 25 February 2023).

De Koning, M. (2021), '"Reaching the Land of Jihad" – Dutch Syria Volunteers, *Hijra* and Counter-conduct', *Contemporary Islam*, 15, 107–22.

De Koning, M., C. Becker and I. Roex (2020), *Islamic Militant Activism in Belgium, the Netherlands and Germany – 'Islands in a Sea of Disbelief'*, London: Palgrave Macmillan.

Elliot, A. (2016), 'The Makeup of Destiny: Predestination and the Labour of Hope in a Moroccan Emigrant Town', *American Ethnologist*, 43: 3, 488–99.

Elliot, A. and L. Menin (2018), 'For an Anthropology of Destiny', *Hau: Journal of Ethnographic Theory*, 8: 1/2, 292–9.

Engelke, M. (2004), 'Discontinuity and the Discourse of Conversion', *Religion in Africa*, 34: 1, 82–109.

Engelke, M. (2010), 'Past Pentecostalism: Notes on Rupture, Realignment, and Everyday Life in Pentecostal and African Independent Churches', *Africa: Journal of the International African Institute*, 80: 2, 177–99.

Fadil, N. and M. Fernando (2015), 'Rediscovering the "Everyday" Muslim: Notes on an Anthropological Divide', *Hau: Journal of Ethnographic Theory*, 5: 2, 59–88.

Filiu, J.-P. (2011), *Apocalypse in Islam*, Berkeley, Los Angeles and London: University of California Press.

Hage, G. (2003), '"Comes a Time We Are All Enthusiasm": Understanding Palestinian Suicide Bombers in Times of Exighophobia', *Public Culture*, 15: 1, 65–89.

Harding, S. F. (2000), *The Book of Jerry Falwell: Fundamentalist Language and Politics*, Princeton: Princeton University Press.

Haynes, N. (2020), 'The Expansive Present: A New Model of Christian Time', *Current Anthropology*, 61: 1, 57–76.

Hirschkind, C. (2006), *The Ethical Soundscape: Cassette Sermons and Islamic Counterpublics*, New York: Columbia University Press.

Khan, N. (2012), *Muslim Becoming: Aspiration and Skepticism in Pakistan*: Durham, NC, and London: Duke University Press.

Kublitz, A. (2011), 'The Sound of Silence: The Reproduction and Transformation of Global Conflicts within Palestinian Families in Denmark', in M. Rytter and K. F. Olwig (eds), *Mobile Bodies, Mobile Souls: Family, Religion, Migration in a Global World*, Aarhus: Aarhus University Press, pp. 161–80.

Kublitz, A. (2013), 'Seizing Catastrophes: The Temporality of Nakba among Palestinians in Denmark', in M. Holbraad and M. A. Pedersen (eds), *Times of Security: Ethnographies of Fear, Protest and the Future*, London and New York: Routledge, pp. 103–21.

Kublitz, A. (2015), 'The Ongoing Catastrophe: Erosion of Life in the Danish Camps', *Journal of Refugee Studies*, 29: 2, 229–49.

Kublitz, A. (2016), 'From Revolutionaries to Muslims: Liminal Becomings across Palestinian Generations in Denmark', *International Journal of Middle East Studies*, 48, 67–86.

Kublitz, A. (2019), 'The Rhythm of Rupture: Attunement among Danish Jihadists', in M. Holbraad and B. Kapferer (eds), *Ruptures: Anthropologies of Discontinuity in Times of Turmoil*, London: UCL Press, pp. 253–82.

Kublitz, A. (2021), 'Omar is Dead: Aphasia and the Escalating Radicalization Industry', *History and Anthropology*, 32: 1, 64–77.

Kublitz, A. (2023), 'Optimism at the End of Time: Jihadists' Struggles', *Anthropological Quarterly*, 96: 3.

Larkin, B. (2008), 'Ahmed Deedat and the Form of Islamic Evangelism', *Social Text*, 96, 26: 3, 101–21.

Li, D. (2019), *The Universal Enemy: Jihad, Empire, and the Challenge of Solidarity*, Stanford: Stanford University Press.

Mahmood, S. ([2005] 2012), *Politics of Piety: The Islamic Revival and the Feminist Subject*, Princeton: Princeton University Press.

Marshall, R. (2009), *Political Spiritualities: The Pentecostal Revolution in Nigeria*, Chicago: University of Chicago Press.

Marshall, R. (2010), 'The Sovereignty of Miracles: Pentecostal Political Theology in Nigeria', *Constellations*, 17: 2, 197–223.

McCants, W. (2015), *The ISIS Apocalypse: The History, Strategy, and Doomsday Vision of the Islamic State*, New York: St Martin's Press.

Meyer, B. (1998), 'Make a Complete Break with the Past', *Historische Anthropologie*, 6: 2, 257–83.

Mittermaier, A. (2011), *Dreams That Matter: Egyptian Landscapes of the Imagination*, Berkeley, Los Angeles and London: University of California Press.

Mittermaier, A. (2012), 'Dreams from Elsewhere: Muslim Subjectivities Beyond the Trope of Self-Cultivation', *Journal of the Royal Anthropological Institute*, 18, 247–65.

Mittermaier, A. (2013), 'Trading with God: Islam, Calculation, Excess', in J. Boddy and M. Lambek (eds), *A Companion to the Anthropology of Religion*, Oxford: John Wiley and Sons, pp. 274–93.

Mittermaier, A. (2015), 'Dreams and the Miraculous', in S. Altorki (ed.), *A Companion to the Anthropology of the Middle East*, Oxford: Wiley Blackwell, pp. 107–24.

Mittermaier, A. (2017), 'The Unknown in the Egyptian Uprising: Towards an Anthropology of al-Ghayb', *Contemporary Islam*, 13: 2, 1–15.

Mittermaier, A. (2019), *Giving to God: Islamic Charity in (Post)Revolutionary Egypt*, Oakland: University of California Press.

Moll, Y. (2018), 'Television Is Not Radio: Theologies of Mediation in the Egyptian Islamic Revival', *Cultural Anthropology*, 33: 2, 233–65.

Moll, Y. (2020), 'Living through Thick Concepts in Revolutionary Egypt', *International Journal of Middle East Studies*, 52: 3, 493–97.

Neumann, P. (2015), 'Foreign Fighter Total in Syria/Iraq Now Exceeds 20,000; Surpasses Afghanistan Conflict in the 1980s', *International Centre for the Study of Radicalisation and Political Violence (ICSR)*, last modified 26 January, <http://icsr. info/2015/01/foreign-fighter-total-syriairaq-now-exceeds-20000-surpasses-afghani-stan-conflict-1980s/> (last accessed 1 June 2022).

Peteet, J. (2005), *Landscapes of Hope and Despair: Palestinian Refugee Camps*, Philadelphia: Pennsylvania University Press.

Robbins, J. (2004), *Becoming Sinners: Christianity and Moral Torment in a Papua New Guinea Society*, Berkeley, Los Angeles and London: University of California Press.

Robbins, J. (2007), 'Continuity Thinking and the Problem of Christian Culture: Belief, Time and the Anthropology of Christianity', *Current Anthropology*, 48: 1, 5–38.

Robbins, J. (2010), 'Anthropology, Pentecostalism, and the New Paul: Conversion, Event, and Social Transformation', *South Atlantic Quarterly*, 109: 4, 633–52.

Robbins, J. (2011), 'On Messianic Promise', in D. Lipset and P. Roscoe (eds), *Echoes of the Tambaran: Masculinity, History and the Subject in the Work of Donald F. Tuzin*, Canberra: ANU E Press, pp. 183–96.

Robbins, J. (2019), 'On Knowing Faith: Theology, Everyday Religion and Anthropological Theory', *Religion and Society: Advances in Research*, 10, 14–29.

Roy, O. (2017), *Jihad and Death: The Global Appeal of Islamic State*, London: Hurst.

Sageman, M. (2004), *Understanding Terror Networks*, Philadelphia: University of Pennsylvania Press.

Sahlins, M. (1966), 'The Original Affluent Society', <www.primitivism.com> (last accessed 9 July 2021).

Schielke, S. (2010), *Second Thoughts about the Anthropology of Islam, or How to Make Sense of Grand Schemes in Everyday Life*, ZMO Working Papers No. 2, <http://www.zmo.de/publikationen/ WorkingPapers/schielke_2010.pdf> (last accessed 09 July 2021).

Schielke, S. (2019), *The Power of God: Four Proposals for an Anthropological Engagement*, ZMO Programmatic Texts 13, Berlin: Leibniz-Zentrum Moderner Orient (ZMO), <https://nbn-resolving.org> (last accessed 9 July 2021).

Van Ginkel, B. and E. Entenmann (eds) (2016), *The Foreign Fighters Phenomenon in the European Union: Profiles, Threats & Policies*, Hague: International Centre for Counter-terrorism (ICCT).

13

SECULAR NORMATIVITY IN ANTI-JIHAD DISCOURSE IN FRANCE

Aïcha Bounaga

Introduction

In September 2018, I attended one of the national radicalisation prevention training sessions organised twice a year by the French Ministry of the Interior for public officials and field actors. One of the interventions, entitled 'Key Concepts of Islam', was given by Sofian, a bearded man in his thirties of North African origin, who was introduced as an expert in the history of Islam. His intervention consisted of a brief presentation of the plethora of possible interpretations of Islam, which was mainly oriented towards the idea that certain current conceptions of Islam, such as Salafism, are unnecessarily exclusive and do not allow for the perception of the richness of Islam that appears when one looks more closely at its history. His presentation was interspersed with ironic comments about the absurdity of certain interpretations usually considered to be overly rigid.

At the end of the morning programme, I wanted to talk with Sofian about arranging an interview, since I was interested in the representation of Islam-related issues in the context of radicalisation prevention and his involvement in this training. I waited for him to finish speaking with two women who had attended his presentation, a few steps behind them, but I could overhear their questions: 'Is the call to prayer really a necessity for Muslims?' To which he answered, rolling his eyes: 'No, it is not. These are only communitarian demands (*des revendications communautaristes*).'[1] Another question, coming from a woman who complained about having to deal with difficult young women at work, concerned the obligation to wear the veil, to which he answered that it was once again only some 'obscurantist interpretation'. Satisfied with his answer, the woman turned to me and looked at me from head to toe, defiantly, as if to say, 'you see?'.

I was not surprised, as I was the only person wearing the headscarf in an assembly of several hundred people, and my entrance into the place was met by disconcerted and suspicious looks. I felt that my presence was perceived as a provocation, as there seemed to be a general understanding that the subject of the training was precisely how to deal with such anomalies as the Islamic headscarf.

What surprised me, however, during the meeting we organised afterwards in his office at university, was to discover that Sofian was a practising Muslim, the son of an imam, committed to a traditional religious practice, concerned about Islamophobia and worried about the abuses of the fight against radicalisation – in particular, the ways it affected women wearing a headscarf. His demeanour towards me was very warm and fraternal and, as he walked me back to the exit of the building, he confided about the struggles he had to go through growing up Muslim in France, struggles that were unsurprisingly very similar to mine. As I left the building, I wondered about the contrast between the man I saw in the Ministry of Interior and the man I had just met.

The feeling of contradiction I felt after this encounter stemmed from the a priori incompatibility between Sofian's show of solidarity towards Muslim communities in a time of intensifying Islamophobia, and his seemingly distant attitude towards Muslim French people when he was on the premises of the Ministry of Interior and speaking as an expert in the prevention of radicalisation. The context of the initial encounter helps to clarify this ambivalence, as Sofian was implicitly asked to perform as a

---

[1] The words *communautariste* and *communautarisme* are derogatory and very rarely applied to communities other than Muslims, immigrants and children of immigrants. They generally betray a sense of uneasiness as to what the gathering of such populations might bring about in terms of social unrest. This representation of the threat against the collective is at the root of the measures against 'separatism' in France. See Dhume (2013, 2007).

secular citizen[2] in a secular space, which required him to distance himself from his Muslim *habitus*.

I witnessed the existence of two, seemingly dissonant, facets of a single person's behaviour towards Muslimness several times during this investigation. This phenomenon illustrates how 'when people take up – or are asked to take up – a secular habitus in their capacity as citizens, regardless of what their personal convictions regarding religion may be, the boundary-making of the secular operation runs directly through them' (Scheer et al. 2019: 2).

This internal 'boundary-making' has led me to ponder how a policy that relies heavily on secular normative judgement over Muslim behaviour – the prevention of radicalisation in France – affects Muslim subjectivity. A central element of the prevention of radicalisation apparatus pertains to its effects on all Muslim individuals, not just those who could be perceived as having violent inclinations. The fight against radicalisation, and even more explicitly that which takes place under the name of the 'fight against separatism', is not exclusively a matter of security in the sense of the physical protection of French citizens. It is not only a policy of repression of potentially violent actors, but also a site for the expression and promotion of a particular form of life linked to secular, liberal and nationalist values.

The prevention of radicalisation in France, often described as lagging behind its European counterparts, has been based on professional intelligence gathering – the surveillance of communications, money flows and border controls – but also on the engagement of society as a whole. Indeed, the prevention of radicalisation has consisted mainly of the mobilisation of significant numbers of researchers to produce tables of indicators of radicalisation, which have been disseminated to the whole of French society and its institutions. Indeed, the need for every citizen to be watchful and report any suspicious behaviour has been heavily emphasised as a vital tool for national

---

[2] Rather than the legal political arrangement designated by the French term '*laïcité*', the word 'secular' is used here in the Asadian sense (Asad 2018): it refers to a combination of knowledge, ideas, affects and sensibilities which constitutes an important part of the modern subjectivity. As Asad conceptualises it, the secular is less an identity in itself than an agent of distinction, dichotomy and hierarchy, creating a contrast between the rational and the irrational, the law and the moral, the public and the private.

security. The creation of a toll-free number to receive reports and the organisation of training programmes on the phenomenon of radicalisation were both aimed at facilitating the process of making such reports.

In the specific context of French secularism, although the state has launched its own campaign warning about the dangers and disillusions faced by those who want to leave for Syria, the state's counter-discourse policy has relied heavily on inciting civil society to produce and disseminate discourses promoting *laïcité*, the values of the Republic, and gender equality. Muslim leaders were also called upon to take part in this counter-discourse effort by reinforcing the call to practise Islam in a way that respects the values of the Republic.

The ability to determine right and wrong, good and bad, and what makes a good life and a bad life is omnipresent in the discourses of radicalisation, whether they are promulgated by government officials, social workers, magistrates, teachers, artists or the families of the suspected. It is inseparable, in fact, from the discourse of radicalisation itself, which cannot exist without it (Fadil et al. 2019). Thus, I take as a starting point an observation of the means by which the state, its institutions and its representatives position themselves favourably or unfavourably towards certain forms of life, through a myriad of tools that are deployed at different levels of government and civil society.

This article aims to explore the material discourse of counter-jihad, which, following Talal Asad, can be interpreted as a reaffirmation of the secular form of life (Asad 2003). It seeks to propose a critical look at these policies and practices that is not only directed at their repressive tendencies and their discriminatory consequences for Muslims, but also at the ethical discourses that underlie them and their claims to truth.

To this end, this chapter begins with an analysis of the official literature on the fight against radicalisation, of the academic sources referred to in the official literature, and of the counter-discourse that has been produced in response to the rise of jihadist propaganda. It combines this analysis with the results of long-term fieldwork conducted in France from 2016 to 2021, which included diverse actors involved in radicalisation prevention policies as part of various institutions (social workers, agents of prefectures, penitentiary integration and probation officers, and counsellors for the Juvenile Protection Service (PJJ)).

This article aims to bring to light key aspects of the policies regarding the prevention of radicalisation in France. After explaining how it relates to the idea of the defence of society, I will examine the practice of radicalisation prevention as a secularising process, through which the validity or invalidity of Islamic concepts is decided. The literature of the Centre for the Prevention of Sectarian Abuse Related to Islam (CPDSI) provides rich material with which to inquire into the secularising tendency of prevention of radicalisation policies in France. The latter will then be analysed as a way for the state to uphold its liberal and national standards by brandishing the ideal of Republican values against the 'deindividualising' power of the jihadist project.

'We must defend society'

In a speech presenting a proposed law against 'separatism' (*séparatisme*), later titled the 'Bill Reaffirming Republican Principles' (*projet de loi confortant le respect des principes de la République*), President Emmanuel Macron expressed the need to extend public action against radicalism beyond repressive policies. 'Monitor, prosecute, punish,' he declared. 'But that is not enough. We must combat radical Islamism, brandished as a source of pride, with unabashed Republican patriotism and go even further.'[3] The new directive of the fight against separatism thus constituted the officialisation of a tendency already present in the apparatus set up to counter 'radicalisation': the move away from a focus on security intended to hinder any terrorist tendency, or more generally, any violent act, and towards a more upstream approach, stamping out 'separatism' at its source.

'Monitor, prosecute, punish. But that is not enough.'

The Law Reaffirming the Principles of the Republic[4] is not part of a preventive approach. It intends to combat a phenomenon that is already present. Macron defines separatism in his speech as a 'conscious, theorised, political-religious

[3] 'Fight against Separatism – the Republic in Action: Speech by Emmanuel Macron, President of the Republic, on the Fight against Separatism', 2 October 2020. Available at <https://www.elysee.fr/en/emmanuel-macron/2020/10/02/fight-against-separatism-the-republic-in-action-speech-by-emmanuel-macron-president-of-the-republic-on-the-fight-against-separatism> (last accessed 13 May 2022). In the French version, one can read: 'But prohibiting is not enough. We must act at the root. To political Islamism brandished as pride, we must oppose an assumed republican patriotism.' ('Mais interdire ne suffit pas. Il faut agir à la racine. À l'islamisme politique brandi comme une fierté, nous devons opposer un patriotisme républicain assumé').

[4] Law no. 2021–1109, 24 August 2021.

project [that] is materialising through repeated deviations from the Republic's values, which is often reflected by the formation of a counter-society'. Further on, the president describes what he calls

> a proclaimed, publicised desire, a systematic way of organising things to contravene the Republic's laws and create a parallel order, establish other values, develop another way of organising society which is initially separatist, but whose ultimate goal is to take it over completely.[5]

It echoes the report called 'Islamist Radicalism and the Means to Combat It',[6] which intends to resist 'this small web that has been weaving itself for a long time [and which has] consequences for our unity, our society, our country, and that which is said to make a nation'.[7]

Therefore, the approach that these documents advocate for in the fight against separatism and radicalisation is no longer prophylactic, but rather defensive, in the face of a threat described as gaining ground. In this apparently new paradigm, the threat is not constituted by the possibility of violent action but by the propagation of a phenomenon described as an 'ideology', a 'project', a 'will' or an 'organisation', which is progressively materialising in the form of daily attacks on the values of the Republic.

What is striking about this presentation of the 'separatist peril' is the portrayal of a fragile, precarious Republic intimidated by radical Islamism, which is supposedly spreading insidiously everywhere. The double characterisation of a phenomenon that is both secret and organised, threatening the Republic

---

[5] Ibid.

[6] 'Rapport de la commission d'enquête sur les réponses apportées par les autorités publiques au développement de la radicalisation islamiste et les moyens de la combattre', August 2020. Available at <http://www.senat.fr/commission/enquete/radicalisation_islamiste.html> (last accessed 13 May 2022).

[7] 'Cette petite toile qui se tisse depuis longtemps a aujourd'hui des conséquences dans notre unité, et dans notre société, dans notre pays, et dans ce qu'on appelle: ce qui fait Nation': this is how the senator Eustache-Briniot concludes the commission of inquiry entitled 'Islamist Radicalism and the Means to Combat It' that led to the report. The video of the conclusion is available at <http://www.senat.fr/commission/enquete/radicalisation_islamiste.html> (last accessed 14 September 2022).

from all sides, is able to justify radical measures: it is necessary to 'get to the root of the problem', to defend the Republic, to reinforce 'republican patriotism'. The mission, formulated in this way, echoes Foucault's theorisation of power and state racism, which takes as its object 'the other race, the subrace, the counter-race that we are, despite ourselves, bringing into existence' (Foucault 2020). Reading this report or listening to this speech, one gets the impression of a struggle between the shadows (where the enemies of the Republic are plotting) and the light (emanating from the state institutions that guarantee republican values). This is the meaning behind the recurring expressions of '*stop-djihadisme*', 'counter-djihad' or 'counter-discourse'[8] which designated policies that aim to bolster this effort towards the just and the good (so-called 'republican values') by developing a positive discourse that encourages good forms of life in order to counteract the expansion of jihadist recruitment.

Counter-jihad as a Positive Endeavour

This representation of the threat against the Republic brings to the fore the central issue of the struggle against separatism and against radicalisation: that of an axiological conflict between dominant and minority forms of life. Forms of life, according to Rahel Jaeggi's conceptualisation, are sets of shared social practices, available for critical evaluation as normative phenomena that represent ways of answering, implicitly or explicitly, the ethical question of how one should live (Jaeggi 2018). We can characterise the struggle against separatism and radicalisation in this way, insofar as it tends to evacuate the question of actual security or safety, replacing it with an ethical conflict opposing a republican form of life, which is said to be modern and secular, to the forms of life of the Muslim communities of France, which are viewed as not modern and not secularised.

In this rhetorical frame, the state must therefore reinforce the values that are supposed to be the foundation of national unity in order to stop the 'separatist ideology' that undermines these principles. The fight against radicalisation and

---

[8] See, for instance, the name of the government's website dedicated to the fight against radicalization: stop-djihadisme.gouv.fr. Such an initiative was frequently deemed as counter-jihad, both in the media and during formations to social workers. See, for instance, Mouillard (2015).

separatism, far from being limited to a repressive dimension, thus operates in a positive one as well, attempting to strengthen what is considered to be the cement of French national identity.

This mission implies a set of consequences that I will attempt to analyse, first of all regarding the state's self-proclaimed 'neutrality'. According to the liberal doctrine, the state should not determine what constitutes a good life, that is, a life that deserves to be lived, in the name of plurality and equality of rights and treatment of all citizens (Rawls 2009). This state intrusion into the field of good and evil – corresponding to a perfectionist rather than a neutralist vision of the state[9] – contravenes the imperative of axiological impartiality, which is central to the universalist thinking of the Enlightenment and the exercise of individual freedoms such as the freedom of opinion and the freedom of conscience. The prevention of radicalisation and the fight against separatism thus offer an advantageous point of entry into an analysis of the techniques, contradictions and ambitions of the perfectionist state.

Radicalisation Prevention Discourse and the Sacred

In a small office furnished with a desk and a small library that contains many of the references on Islam recommended by the Ministry of Interior,[10] Clémence, a penitentiary integration and probation officer and the 'prevention of radicalisation' adviser responsible for evaluating the level of radicalisation among prisoners, explains to me the different ways she proceeds. One way is to try to address topics such as the celebration of Christmas, the prisoner's relationship to women, or his beliefs in the power of the invisible. Despite having a very low level of education and training regarding Islam (Beunas 2021) and no personal attachment to it, Clémence shows great confidence in what constitutes or does not constitute a deviant practice or belief.

'Religion must be separate from what they have done. It is not religion: at the end of the day, their radicalisation is based on magical things, but not on

---

[9] On the debate between neutralism and perfectionism in liberal thought, see Escudier and Pélabay (2016: 434).

[10] The references used in theorical parts of the government literature about radicalisation and in the prevention of radicalisation training.

religion.' When asked about the signs of radicalisation, she tackles the subject of jinn:

> Believing in jinn, for example, is not something that a normal believer would think is normal, it's completely magical and crazy. That is the sort of things we look at when we must assess if someone is maybe being radicalised.[11]

Clémence takes for granted that the belief in jinn is deviant, outdated, and thus a sign of radicalisation, despite the fact that the belief in jinn and the possibility of their interaction with the world of human beings is widely shared by a majority of streams of Islam and is an element of the invisible world as described by Islamic cosmogony. Furthermore, this belief has no connection, even indirectly, with any form or project of violence. The characterisation of such belief as unorthodox and superstitious (and thus as a sign of radicalisation) by this 'prevention of radicalisation adviser' stems from a secular axiom that dismisses any belief in invisible creatures as irrational. It is also the product of the early conflation of radicalisation processes with sectarianism (Ollion 2017). The common point that has remained long after the debunking of this equivalence is the decisive criterion of the 'break with society' (Alava et al. 2017). The secular point of view does not admit to the belief in invisible creatures as reasonable, and it thus makes this belief a sign of a break from the dominant rationality.

This interaction is typical of debates among social workers surrounding issues of radicalisation. Social work is the site of massive investment by the state to bolster the detection of radicalisation. The territorial paradigm in which radicalisation prevention mechanisms are embedded (Guibet Lafaye 2017a) necessarily implicates social workers, who interact directly with people who may be suspected of 'radicalisation'. Social workers belonging to various institutions evaluate the speech and habits of these individuals in order to establish degrees of 'radicalisation' as well as an ad hoc mode of care (psychological, penal, social, and so on) (Ragazzi 2017). The public thus

---

[11] Excerpt of an interview with a penitentiary integration and probation officer, a prevention of radicalisation adviser, conducted on 10 December 2019.

314 | AÏCHA BOUNAGA

places significant expectations on the ability of social work professionals to detect radicalisation, and their work is the site of significant theorisation regarding the signs of radicalisation.

Social Work and Detection

The expertise of the Centre for the Prevention of Sectarian Abuse Related to Islam (CPDSI), directed by the educator and anthropologist Dounia Bouzar, is enlightening to analyse in this sense. Despite the extensive criticism it has received (Vincent 2017), it remains an essential reference in the fight against radicalisation and has had a lasting impact on representations of 'jihadism', in particular by conflating it with the phenomena of sectarian influence, involving the notions of brainwashing, confusion and manipulation in the name of Islam. Bouzar's biography gives her a triple legitimacy: professional, scientific and religious. Indeed, as a former educator at the Protection Judiciaire de la Jeunesse (Juvenile Protection Service), holder of a doctorate in anthropology, and a Muslim, her works and articles are omnipresent both in the bibliographies of successive training kits on the prevention of radicalisation elaborated by the French Ministry of the Interior (in the four editions from 2014 to 2018) and in interviews conducted with various professionals invested in the prevention of radicalisation. Dounia Bouzar's work indeed seems to build a bridge between the academic sphere and the professional world of social work. Moreover, Dounia Bouzar's Muslimness plays a similar role as Sofian's, as it gives credibility to her expertise, and is accepted so long as it is framed in a way that validates and enforces secular rationality. Dounia Bouzar's religious affiliation is made explicit in her writings and seems to represent a form of autochthonous capital (Retière 2003) in the logic of radicalisation prevention. The state's use of her expertise makes her take on the role of the 'intellectual of the state' in the Bourdieusian sence (Bourdieu 2018).

The discourse of detection in the CPDSI literature focuses primarily on the religious practices and beliefs of the so-called 'radicalised' people, condemned as deviant forms of Islam. The lexical field of misappropriation is thus often present in the analyses of the religious practices and beliefs mobilised in radical discourse: Islam is thus 'disfigured', 'manipulated', 'instrumentalised', and the jihadists 'use' Islam to achieve their own ends. In fact, the interpretive lens elaborated by Dounia Bouzar offers a characteristic illustration of these processes of delegitimising forms of religiosity associated with radical commitment. It is then a question of rectifying the distorted meaning of the religious vocabulary used by the so-called 'jihadists', by appealing to more acceptable forms of religiosity. Thus, the author takes a stand against the 'inversion among recruiters of the principal verses and the historical verses of the Qur'an'. A clarification is then made in a note: 'A distinction is made in the Qur'ān between principal passages that state constant truths, and circumstantial passages linked to the historical context of revelation' (Bouzar 2015: 32). Here, rectifying this inversion relies on a fixed and simplified representation of exegetical controversies and the Islamic jurisprudential tradition.

This watered-down representation of exegesis and Islamic jurisprudence is accompanied by peremptory assertions about the meaning assigned to concepts in the Muslim tradition, such as *tawḥīd* (divine oneness), *shirk* (associationism or idolatry) or hijra (migration). A distinction is thus made between the use of the term by Muslims (a group that is supposed to be homogeneous and for which the author acts as a spokesperson) and the use of the term by 'Salafists' and 'jihadists'. Indeed, we read: '"*Tawḥid*" and "*shirk*" are rarely used in the conversations of Muslims', whereas 'these two notions are constantly taken up by the Salafists and then by the Jihadists'. Similarly, in *Désamorcer l'islam radical* ('Diffusing radical Islam'), the author surprisingly states that 'there is no link in Islam between spirituality and isolation' (Bouzar 2014), omitting the traditional practices of *iʿtikāf* (spiritual retreat) or *khalwa* (seclusion) (Khoddami 2015).

Secularisation at Work

As its programmatic title indicates (*Détecter le passage à l'acte en repérant la manipulation des termes musulmans par Daesh*) (Bouzar and Valsan 2017), this lexicology is intended, to 'detect the move to action by identifying the manipulation of Muslim terms by Daesh'. This security-oriented understanding of Islamic dogma was common among members of the prefecture where I conducted my research in southern France. Thus, during an interview with an employee of the prefecture who was in charge of the prevention of radicalisation, the employee, eager to show that he knew his way around Islamic doctrine, got up in the middle of a sentence to go and find a French translation of the Qur'an on the shelf of his office. He flipped through the pages with confident gestures to quickly find the passage he wanted to read to me. After reading it with a certain authority, notwithstanding many pronunciation errors, he explained to me how the current interpretations of this verse were misunderstandings resulting from a clumsy translation, and that the meaning given to it by people who made it into a call to jihad was absurd in light of general Islamic doctrine:

> They always rely on the same text: it is the 'Sura [chapter] of Repentance', verse 5, you must have seen it. I'll read it to you, it's this one . . . so it says what? Here it is, so 'After the holy months, atone, kill the associators': among the Salafists, who are always very rigorous, the worst thing is the shir[12] [*sic*], so according to them we must not be 'associating' [the word '*shirk*' designates in Islamic doctrine the sin of associating other creatures to God]. [He continues to read:] 'If they perform the *zalat*[13] [*sic*] and the *zaka*[14] [*sic*], then let them go free for Allah is forgiving and merciful.' This is not a correct translation, because if you kill someone, you can't ask him to repent afterwards. But in the Arabic version of the text, it is the same, except that the root between 'fight' and 'kill' is the same in Arabic. Since the Qur'an is oral, since Qur'an means recitation, they took this sura (as proof).

This explanation of the Qur'anic text by a state representative indicates the direct use of religious scriptural sources in the prevention of radicalisation, which thus draws from these sacred texts arguments for the disqualification of radical commitment in theological terms.

This understanding of radical Islam as faulty and dangerous implies the elaboration of a 'theological counter-discourse',[15] made possible by the investment of Muslim religious actors in the fight against radicalisation, which is given in the 'key concepts of Islam' section of the Interministerial Committee

---

[12] The interviewee refers to *shirk*: in Islamic tradition, the sin of associating other creatures to God, thus contradicting His Oneness (*tawḥīd*).

[13] The interviewee refers to *ṣalāt*, the ritual prayer, one of the five pillars of Islam.

[14] The *zakāt* is the mandatory donation of a proportion of a Muslim's wealth, also a pillar of Islam.

[15] As advised by the report for the National Assembly entitled 'La déradicalisation, outil de lutte contre le terrorisme' ('Deradicalization, tool in the fight against terrorism'), June 2015, by Sébastien Pietrasanta.

for the Prevention of Crime and Radicalisation (CIPDR)'s training handbook. To this end, humour appears to be an indispensable tool, as Muriel Domenech, Secretary General of the CIPDR, indicated in an interview about the National Plan for the Prevention of Radicalisation: 'The counter-discourse to jihadist propaganda is essential and humour is a massive prevention weapon to delegitimise jihadist discourse.'[16] Regarding Selman Reda's play *Ne laisse personne te voler tes mots* ('Don't let anyone steal your words'), financed by the CIPDR and aimed at a young audience, she adds:

> It is an interpretation of the texts that is part of a secular context, it is a secular reading of the texts, which is part of the general culture that must be developed in order to promote a reading that is compatible with the laws of the Republic.

The imperative to bring dogmatic content to the level of the profane is omnipresent among those who deal with the issue of religious extremism, and interviews with professionals responsible for the prevention of radicalization echo this imperative. For example, for Eric, a radicalisation adviser within the Protection Judiciaire de la Jeunesse (Juvenile Protection Service), 'We must bring the question of religion back to a normal level, with no more taboo or tension than that. I am convinced that it is at the same level as sexual, political or ecological identity.'[17]

This dimension of the secularisation of the religious sphere has been theorised by the anthropologist Saba Mahmood, for whom

> the effectiveness of such a globalizing project [as secularism] necessarily depends on transforming the religious domain through a variety of state injunctions. This has often meant that nation-states have had to act as 'de facto theologians' by making certain practices and beliefs indifferent to religious doctrines precisely so that these practices can be brought into the realm of civil law. (Mahmood 2006)

[16] Interview available at https://www.youtube.com/watch?v=JfMzVhI0Yps (last accessed 13 May 2022).
[17] Interview with the 'laïcité and citizenship' adviser of the PJJ of a department of southern France, in charge of the prevention of radicalisation, conducted on 9 April 2018.

For her, secularism is not an erasure of religion but a 'rearrangement of religion to make it more congruent with some modality of liberal political rule'. The strength of secularism lies in the 'production of a particular type of religious subject compatible with the rationality and exercise of the liberal political norm', a phenomenon exemplified by the various debates about the need to reform Islam.[18] The hermeneutic project of secularism aims to create a conception of religion as a 'cluster of symbols to be interpreted flexibly and in accordance with the liberal secular norm' (ibid.).

From this perspective, the analysis of expert discourse on the signs of radicalisation shows the determining character of the normative border between acceptable Islam and forms of Islam considered deviant through an unprecedented insertion of the state into the sphere of individual religious life. While Muslims had previously been the object of police attention and surveillance more as a community, which was seen as foreign to France (state management was mainly exercised on mosques, and on imams, since they were seen as having the power to influence and politicise a community (Jouanneau 2013)), it seems that the paradigm of radicalisation progressively shifts towards preventing an internal ontological threat, targeting the individual's practices and beliefs rather than those of the collective.

Promoting Liberal, Secular and National Values

The normative discourse of the fight against radicalisation is not only about which forms of Islam to prevent and which to encourage. The radicalisation prevention apparatus, which focuses on the notion of radicalisation as a break with society, also provides the occasion for a more general reaffirmation of the secular and liberal form of life and, in particular, of the norms of gender and attachment to the nation that correspond to it.

Bringing Crushed Individualities Back to Life[19]

The grey literature produced in the context of the fight against radicalisation pays particular attention to the notion of 'de-individualisation', which is said to be a method used by Daesh recruiters to dispose of individuals thus

---

[18] See El Karoui (2018).

[19] Expression used in Bouzar (2015).

'depersonalised'. A central theme in the fight against cults, 'lost individuality' is omnipresent in the descriptions of the transformation that is said to take place when the person joins the incriminated group.

The psychopathological analysis of this process of de-individualisation also adopts a gendered approach, emphasising among young women how their loss of individuality manifests in their bodies.[20] Thus, when writing about the 'depersonalisation of girls', Dounia Bouzar pays particular attention to the way they dress, especially the wearing of the *jilbāb* (a garment covering the head and the body). Thus, in the book *Comment sortir de l'emprise djihadiste* ('How to get out of the jihadist mental manipulation') (Bouzar 2015), she writes:

> The girls experience a kind of '*jilbāb* addiction', which leads us to believe that the search for the disappearance of the body in a bubble that underlies the approach of these young girls helps the jihadist discourse to have authority over them.

This change of clothing is described in terms of 'destruction of bodily limits', with the *jilbāb* or niqab physically marking the moment of de-individualisation, as evidenced by several expressions such as 'she put on a huge black *niqāb* that turned her into a ghost', or 'black silhouettes joined her'. It is the parents' point of view that is used here: for them, the adoption of new body and dress norms is an event that marks a personality change initiated by their child. The remarkable frequency of the adjective 'coquette' in the testimonies of parents[21] portraying their child before their 'de-individualisation' echoes the 'radicalisation' indicators of the Centre national d'assistance et de prevention de la radicalisation (CNAPR) in which 'the abandonment of make-up and all coquetry' is listed.[22]

---

[20] See Benslama and Khosrokhavar (2017: 21): 'If Islamist anti-imperialism is an important dimension among men, among a large part of the young women, it is the relationship to the body that prevails, in a form of somatic politics.'

[21] For example: 'She was a coquette girl. But she did not wear make up anymore, and she did not shave either, she did not care about herself anymore', Testimony of a father participating in the Ministry of the Interior's campaign on the prevention of departures. Available at <https://www.europe1.fr/faits-divers/sa-fille-est-partie-en-syrie-on-a-rien-vu-venir-2526011> (last accessed 13 May 2022).

[22] See Institut National des Hautes Études de la Sécurité et de la Justice (INHESJ) (2015).

By highlighting the new bodily habits of these young women, what seems to be implicated in the discourses of the fight against radicalisation is a departure from the norms of femininity dominant in a liberal context and the adoption of the norms of femininity of a group considered as allogenous. This aspect also emerges in the focus on the disappearance of the dichotomy between private and public space. For Dounia Bouzar:

> The jihadist discourse has plunged the young person into a psychic functioning where he no longer has time or private space. It is therefore a question of helping him identify in different registers what belongs to himself and to others, to redefine the frontier between his private sphere and the collective sphere.

And further on: 'The enrolment destroys the notion of private space (there is no longer a difference between public and private space), we have given him back an intimacy, then an individuality' (Bouzar 2015).

This process of disaffiliation and reaffiliation seems to be central to the state's reading of the phenomenon of 'radicalisation', which approaches this process in terms of rupture. Thus, Dounia Bouzar writes: 'The jihadist discourse has established break-up rituals so that the group thinks in the place of the individual, defines him and dictates his behaviour. We therefore ensure the resumption of autonomy rituals' (Bouzar 2015).

This new socialisation with the deviant group, thus conceptualised in terms of loss of individualisation and autonomy, is the object of abundant reflection within official instances. The expression 'love bombing' can be found in the CIPDR training kit (third edition):

> We talk about love bombing to describe the warmth with which the newcomer is integrated [into the so-called 'radical' groups]. The resulting strong sense of belonging, as well as the belief that he or she has found a place where he or she would be fully recognised, is part of the enrolment.

Through this focus on changes to the individual, a condemnation of the group to which this person resocialises seems to emerge. This problematisation of the membership of individuals in groups considered deviant is reminiscent of Étienne Ollion's analysis of the fight against cults in France. For him, what these groups all have in common is that they 'question norms that have long been endorsed by the public authorities' (Ollion 2017), since life in society is one of the dimensions that is the object of 'particularly active state control' in France. Ollion notes that in both the fight against cults and the fight against radicalisation the state condemns the communitarian character of these groups, which are accused of exerting a hold on their members by isolating them from the rest of society. Paradoxically, the condemnation of the process of 'de-individualisation' is accompanied by the reaffirmation of references to collectives such as the Republic or the nation.

Reviving the National Feeling

This specific problematisation of socialisation in deviant groups leads the state to the imperative of strengthening the feeling of belonging to France, to its norms and values, in that the absence of patriotism is presented as one of the causes of the radical commitment of young people. In fact, for the sociologist Sébastian Roché, who was interviewed for the report entitled 'Collectivités territoriales et prévention de la radicalisation' ('Local authorities and the prevention of radicalisation'), there is a

> combination of different elements [required] to understand the hostility of certain young people towards national institutions, a hostility that can go as far as terrorism in some cases: in addition to the importance of the religious and group division, there are two key elements. The first is a rejection of French identity as based on values of equality and not allowing religious affiliation, the second is a form of justification for violence against the police or the school.[23]

With the 'rejection of France' thus identified as a potential cause of violent radicalisation, the state must therefore commit to 'reviving the feeling of national belonging',[24] or 'fostering the feeling of belonging to the Republic and an adherence to its values',[25] thereby, 'preventing any form of communitarianism

---

[23] Informational report made on behalf of the delegation to local authorities, 29 March 2017. Available at <http://www.senat.fr/notice-rapport/2016/r16-483-notice.html> (last accessed 13 May 2022).

[24] See the report 'La déradicalisation, outil de lutte contre le terrorisme', cited above.

[25] See the report 'Guide interministériel de prévention de la radicalisation', March 2016.

in the social organisation of the city'; thus confirming Caroline Guibet Lafaye's analysis that 'the reference to radicalisation serves as a lever to reinstitute a moral and political order' (Guibet Lafaye 2017b).

This dimension of a national order to be defended is remarkable in some of the interviews conducted, notably at the PJJ of a department in the south of France, where the adviser in charge of questions related to radicalisation with PJJ educators, expresses himself about one of the measures of the 2019 counterterrorism plan, 'defending the values of the republican school':

> It bothers me, because if we have to defend it, it means that there is competition, while there should not be any competition: no, in France there are only the values of the Republic. So it's not about defending values, it's about promoting them.
>
> The Republic was built thanks to the Black Hussars of the republic:[26] the teachers, the professors. The ones who used their cane or their ruler to instil the republican identity of France. My grandfather, when he spoke the patois, he was caned: we didn't speak the patois, we didn't speak Breton,[27] we only spoke French. All the previous Catholic identity was replaced by forceps, by cane strokes, by the republican identity. The Catholic Christian morality was replaced by the civic and republican morality.
>
> Before 'defending' them, it is necessary – it is perhaps a little paternalistic or a little Jacobin[28] – but it is necessary to integrate it into the citizens, the individuals, even, perhaps, in my opinion, by force. [He hesitates:] By force? . . . [Then, as if convinced:] yes!

The lexicon of physical coercion ('with canes' three times, 'replaced by forceps', and at the end of the passage 'by force') denotes the non-negotiable dimension of the values of the Republic for which there can be no alternative, and by the same token a form of radicalism, in the sense of an absence of compromise, which can envisage the use of violence.

[26] The Black Hussars is a military nickname given to schoolteachers in the early twentieth century in France.

[27] Breton is a minority language spoken in Brittany that the French government has attempted to eradicate since the nineteenth century in an effort to build a national culture.

[28] The word Jacobin refers to the French Revolution and to the most radical factions in favour of an authoritarian and centralised state.

The prevention of radicalisation thus appears to be much more than a simple security policy aimed at preventing potential violence, but rather a policy of reaffirming the national order. Regarding a response to a PJJ educator's feeling of uncertainty about the possible radicalisation of a young woman, Eric expressed himself as follows:

I tell her: 'Try to see where she's at regarding her relationship to the republican law.' In this case, she was in front of Marianne,[29] consuming cannabis. The educator said to her: 'It's not possible. You can't do that, in front of Marianne!' The young person said: 'Marianne, okay, I don't give a fuck'. But she didn't say 'Marianne has no value', or 'Marianne is shit' in the sense that I don't recognise authority. That is, she was going against it, as a rebel, but she still recognised it. She wasn't denying Marianne was the source of the law. Do you understand the difference? It's fundamental, but you can't put that in the indicators [of radicalisation].

When Eric returns to the theme of the fight against radicalisation, at the end of the quoted passage, through the allusion to the 'indicators' of radicalisation, the vast broadening of the notion of radicalisation appears clearer: a lack of recognition of the republican symbol and the authority of its normativity can thus be interpreted as a sign of radicalisation.

Therefore, the issue of counter-discourses and their normative contents indicates the real stakes in the prevention of radicalisation and the following fight against separatism. Far from being reduced to a security policy aimed at preventing new murderous attacks on French soil, the fight against radicalisation operates by necessarily imposing a certain order of values, at once secular, liberal, and national.

Conclusion

Following Bourdieu's prescription not to be taken over by categories of thought produced by the state while trying to think the state (Bourdieu 2018), the analysis of the discourses of the fight against radicalisation reveals what is at stake behind something that seems to be self-evident (the need to

---

[29] Marianne is an allegory of the French Republic.

prevent the occurrence of new criminal acts): the fight against radicalisation provides the state with the opportunity to reaffirm a strict definition of the secular, liberal and national order summed up by the injunction to respect 'republican value'.

While the fight against radicalisation in France is often condemned because of its repressive and discriminatory methods, the critique should also expand towards the values and forms of life it upholds as being the only valid ones, and the breach to the pluralistic ideal central to the liberal doctrine.

The characterisation of the signs of a 'break from society' as unanimous criterion of radicalisation presupposes a homogenous society that cannot bear differences within itself, pushing away from the liberal ideals of plurality. Failure to respond accordingly to this injunction subjects a person to the risk of a kind of republican excommunication, which produces deep subjective contradictions, like the one I experienced while encountering Sofian in the Ministry of Interior. Insofar as any signs indicating a break from the secular way of life are framed as a potential sign of radicalisation and thus a threat to the nation, the prevention of radicalisation discourse and practices effectively illustrate how the secular claims of neutrality, rationality and reasonableness are central to the national order, illuminating Talal Asad's conception of the secular.

References

Alava, S., N. Najjar and H. Hussein (2017), 'Étude des processus de radicalisation au sein des réseaux sociaux: place des arguments complotistes et des discours de rupture', *Quaderni*, 94, 29–40.

Asad, T. (2003), *Formations of the Secular: Christianity, Islam, Modernity*, Stanford: Stanford University Press.

Asad, T. (2018), *Secular Translations: Nation-State, Modern Self, and Calculative Reason*, New York: Columbia University Press.

Benslama, F. and F. Khosrokhavar (2017), *Le djihadisme des femmes. Pourquoi elles ont choisi Daesh?* Paris: Seuil.

Beunas, C. (2021), 'Que deviennent les référents "radicalisation"? Une étude des référents laïcité citoyenneté de la Protection judiciaire de la jeunesse', *Sociologie*, 12: 4, 371–87.

Bourdieu, P. (2018), *On the State: Lectures at the Collège de France, 1989–1992*, Cambridge: Polity Press.

Bouzar, D. (2014), *Désamorcer l'islam radical: Ces dérives sectaires qui défigurent l'islam*, Paris: Éditions de l'Atelier.

Bouzar, D. (2015), *Comment sortir de l'emprise Djihadiste*, Paris: Éditions de l'Atelier.

Bouzar, D. and S. Valsan (2017), *Détecter le passage à l'acte en repérant la manipulation des termes musulmans par Daesh*, <https://www.bouzar-expertises.fr/livresblancs> (last accessed 10 August 2019).

Dhume, F. (2007), *Racisme, antisémitisme et 'communautarisme'? L'école à l'épreuve des faits*, Paris: l'Harmattan.

Dhume, F. (2013), 'L'émergence d'une figure obsessionnelle: comment le "communautarisme" a envahi les discours médiatico-politiques français', *Asylon(s)*, 8, Radicalisation des frontières et promotion de la diversité.

Dhume, F. and V. Cohen (2018), 'Dire le racisme, taire la race, faire parler la nation. La représentation du problème du racisme à travers la presse locale', *Mots: Les langages du politique*, 116, 55–72.

El Karoui, H (2018), 'La fabrique de l'islamisme', <https://www.institutmontaigne.org/ressources/pdfs/publications/Rapport%20La%20Fabrique%20de%20l'islamisme%20600%20pages.pdf> (last accessed 15 June 2022).

Élysée (2020), 'Fight against Separatism – the Republic in Action: Speech by Emmanuel Macron, President of the Republic, on the Fight against Separatism', <https://www.elysee.fr/en/emmanuel-macron/2020/10/02/fight-against-separatism-the-republic-in-action-speech-by-emmanuel-macron-president-of-the-republic-on-the-fight-against-separatism> (last accessed 13 May 2022).

Escudier, A. and J. Pélabay (2016), *Le perfectionnisme libéral. Anthologie de textes fondamentaux*, Paris: Hermann.

Fadil, N., F. Ragazzi and M. de Koning (eds) (2019), *Radicalization in Belgium and the Netherlands: Critical Perspectives on Violence and Security*, London: Bloomsbury Publishing.

Foucault, M. (2020), *Society Must Be Defended: Lectures at the Collège de France, 1975–76*, London: Penguin Modern Classics.

Guibet Lafaye, C. (2017a), 'De l'ennemi global à l'ennemi intérieur, la territorialisation de la menace terroriste par l'État français dans les années 2000', *Réactions des États français et allemands aux menaces perçues comme terroristes dans les années 1970 et aujourd'hui*, 15 November, Leipzig, <https://hal.archives-ouvertes.fr/hal-01635375> (last accessed 15 June 2022).

Guibet Lafaye, C. (2017b), 'Dénoncer la radicalisation, reconstruire un ordre moral et politique', *Implications philosophiques*, <https://hal.archives-ouvertes.fr/hal-01516579> (last accessed 15 June 2022).

Guide interministériel de prévention de la radicalisation (2016), <https://cache.media.eduscol.education.fr/file/Prevention_radicalisation/07/3/Guide_interministeriel_de_prevention_de_la_radicalisation_581073.pdf> (last accessed 13 May 2022).

Jaeggi, R. (2018), *Critique of Forms of Life*, Cambridge, MA: Harvard University Press.

Institut National des Hautes Études de la Sécurité et de la Justice (2015), 'Radicalisation islamiste et filières djihadistes: prévenir, détecter et traiter', https://www.mairesdemeuse.com/userfile/documents/Radicalisation%20islamiste%20et%20fili%c3%a8res%20djihadistes.pdf (last accessed 13 May 2022).

Jouanneau, S. (2013), *Les imams de France. Une autorité religieuse sous contrôle*, Paris: Agone.

Khoddami, A. (2015), 'Nouvel espace rituel en Iran: le cas de la retraite des jeunes à Chiraz', *Archives de sciences sociales des religions*, 170, 229–45.

Mahmood, S. (2006), 'Secularism, Hermeneutics, and Empire: The Politics of Islamic Reformation', *Public Culture*, 18: 2, 323–47.

Mouillard, S. (2015), 'Le gouvernement renforce son contre-jihad en ligne', *Libération*, 31 December, https://www.liberation.fr/France/2015/12/31/le-gouvernement-renforce-son-contre-jihad-en-ligne_1423779/ (last accessed 13 May 2022).

Ollion, É. (2017), *Raison d'État, Histoire de la lutte contre les sectes en France*, Paris: La Découverte.

Ragazzi, F. (2017), 'Countering Terrorism and Radicalization: Securitising Social Policy?', *Critical Social Policy*, 37: 2, 163–79.

Rawls, J. ([1971] 2009), *A Theory of Justice*, Cambridge, MA: Harvard University Press.

Retière, J.-N. (2003), 'Autour de l'autochtonie. Réflexions sur la notion de capital social populaire', *Politix*, 16: 63, 121–43.

Sénat (2020), 'Rapport de la commission d'enquête sur les réponses apportées par les autorités publiques au développement de la radicalisation islamiste et les moyens de la combattre', <http://www.senat.fr/commission/enquete/radicalisation_islamiste.html> (last accessed 13 May 2022).

Scheer, M., N. Fadil and B. Schepelern Johansen (eds) (2019), *Secular Bodies, Affects and Emotions: European Configurations*, London: Bloomsbury Publishing.

Vincent, É. (2017), 'Vents contraires pour Dounia Bouzar, "Mme Déradicalisation"', *Le Monde.fr*, 24 February, https://www.lemonde.fr/societe/article/2017/02/23/vents-contraires-pour-mme-deradicalisation_5084078_3224.html (last accessed 13 May 2022).

PART IV

AFFECTIVE ARCHIVES – ENDURING SOUNDS AND IMAGES

14

AN EPILOGUE OF IMAGES: ON
THEORISING AND ARCHIVING DAESH'S
VIDEOS OF VIOLENCE

Robert Dörre

Introduction

The release of images showing violence, torture and death always provokes strong reactions and, subsequently, concentrates attention in the media, academia and the public sphere. Accordingly, much of the research focuses on the creation and dissemination of such images, but rarely on what becomes of them after they have reached their peak of attention. This article, instead, is devoted to the afterlife of images of violence. My reflections, therefore, concentrate less on how images of violence enter the digital world, and how they spread there, and more on how these images were afterwards discussed, theorised, and archived. Using Daesh's[1] videos of violence as an example, I would like to examine this nexus by focusing on two aspects that revolve around questions of vision and visibility.

1. 'How are images of violence seen?' Daesh's display of violence is related to the calculated shocks such videos are meant to evoke. Therefore,

---

[1] Daesh is an acronym for *al-Dawla al-Islāmiya fī 'l-ʿIrāq wa-l-Shām*. The sound is reminiscent of the Arabic term for trampling down (*daʿsa*) and accordingly marks the destructive intentions of the group that calls itself 'Islamic State'. The designation is intended to signal a distancing from this self-proclaimed aspiration to be 'the' Islamic state (Zgryziewicz et al. 2015: 12–13).

their production and dissemination are often theorised as a form of warfare in itself. In such military metaphors, the target of the image is declared to be the audience. While this argument seems convincing from a strategic point of view, it obscures the sociopolitical context in which such images are created, as well as the suffering of the people who were tortured and killed to produce them. The first part will, therefore, examine the afterlife of images of violence in discourses that deal with their impacts on spectators. Rather than affirming and perpetuating the metaphorical concepts of 'images as a weapon' or a 'war of images', I will argue for a re-politicisation of the image based on a rereading of Barthes's myth theory. Through this re-politicisation, the politics of representation, the contexts of production and the media environment can become the objects of study.

2. 'How are images of violence presented?' From today's perspective, this question brings attention to the digital archives that store and lock up images of violence, as well as make them accessible, and keep them visually alive. Although at first glance such digital archives may appear to be neutral repositories or databases that simply store documents or files, they too are imbued with politics. This includes the politics of jurisdiction – who is allowed to archive something, and for what purpose? – but also the politics of aesthetics – how are images given to be seen?[2] The aesthetic constitution of the archive accordingly affects how images of violence are received, and what publics they form. In order to analyse those connections between aesthetics and reception, I will use four different archives as examples in which images, videos and sounds of Daesh are still available today, and in which the various effects that the situatedness and aesthetics of the archive entail can be exemplarily demonstrated.

Images and Metaphors

Daesh is infamous for its images of violence. In media and academic discourses, particularly, the videos that show the targeted and staged killing of people have

---

[2] This question is inspired by Johanna Schaffer's conceptualisation of the term 'visibility', for which not only what becomes visible is important, but also 'who gives to see, in what context, and most importantly . . . in what form and structure is something given to seen' (Schaffer 2008: 12). All German quotations were translated by the author.

gained attention (Friis 2018: 248–53; Krona 2020: 123–6). Nevertheless, only some of the numerous videos the groups have produced in the past show such scenes, and almost half of the entire output doesn't focus on violent actions at all (Nanninga 2019: 9–13). The fact that the images containing violence especially generate so much attention seems to have something to do with the rules of visibility that prevail, for example, in journalism and science. In the sense presented by Marie-José Mondzain, those rules of visibility shape the way images are seen and, therefore, what aspects of an image becomes evident for the viewer, and which aspects remain unseen (Mondzain 2009: 30–3). The question 'How are images of violence seen?' is, therefore, much less about the image itself than about the culture of visibility in which it is received.

Against this background, it is illuminating to consider how violence, and the reception of violence, in the videos of Daesh have been discussed so far. Although these images show suffering that was endured beyond its media presence, a shift in focus can be observed: instead of focusing on the violations portrayed, it is often suggested that the viewer should worry more about his or her own vulnerability. Accordingly, many investigations into this topic rely on the rhetoric of an image war. In this regard, the premises in publications launched by Daesh hardly differ from those produced in the context of security agencies, press organs, or academic research of American or European origin. For this reason, I do not want to focus on these as antagonistic spheres, but rather as a common epistemic milieu. While consisting of heterogeneous actors, common figures of knowledge and metaphor, nevertheless, circulate in this milieu, which I would now like to explore further.

Weapons – Images – Wars

The effects of violent moving images are a much-discussed topic in empirical media research. Effects of reduction in violent behaviour, as assumed in the 'catharsis thesis' (Otto 2013), or models of 'negative learning' (Grimm 1999: 461–514), are contrasted by a variety of theories that postulate rather destructive effects. They assume, for example, that images of violence can trigger and reinforce fears and psychoses, or even stimulate violent behaviour themselves (Kunczik 2017: 22–33). What all these hypotheses have in common is that they relate to questions of vision and visibility, insofar as the effects of images are frequently attributed to the assumption that they establish an immediate visual relationship (Althöfer and Buhl 2019: 16; Buss and

Müller 2020: 23–7).[3] In the academic discourse on violent Daesh videos, this notion of immediacy even leads to speaking of 'image as weapons' and 'a war of images'. Such expressions fill the image with intentions and imbue it with a metaphorical dimension. My analysis will therefore focus on the discourse that evolves around these terms. But before I delve into the theoretical considerations and their impact, it is necessary to reconstruct, at least cursorily, where these two conventional metaphors seem to have their origin.

While the notion of images that are, themselves, part of violent acts has become popular primarily through the media politics of Daesh, it draws on topoi that have circulated in academic discourse at least since the attacks of 9/11. The images disseminated of the attacks and their aftermath have not only often been described as invasive (Behrend 2015: 13–15), but in some descriptions the ontologies of image and reality literally collapse into one another.

> Suddenly it was . . . as if images and events had never belonged to completely different categories: like the biblical plague of locusts, the images literally fell out of the sky via Internet and satellite into all monitors and front pages around the globe, leaving behind a disturbed world . . . The horror, initially confined to one country, one city, one building complex, gained a global presence that brought all work and communication processes except image transmission to a hold. (Buttler 2003: 40)[4]

This levelling of image and reality is important for the genesis of the metaphors mentioned above because it always forms the argumentative basis when images are conceptualised as part of violent actions (see Buss and Müller 2020: 23–7). The supposed lack of distance from the violent event makes it possible to understand the image not as a mere representation of violence,

---

[3] From the perspective of media culture studies, this assumption of immediacy is unusual because media are always situated in the in-between – they mediate.

[4] There are similar passages in other texts about 9/11: Gerhard Paul, for example, speaks of 'images that break out of media reality . . . into physical reality' (Paul 2013: 589) and Heike Behrend notes that 'event and image enhanced each other, turning the consumption of the pictures of the event into the event' (Behrend 2015: 14).

but as an act of violence itself. The violence that the images stand for, thus, becomes violence that emanates from the image itself.[5] The image of violence turns into a violent image. Based on such assumptions, more recent studies on 9/11 even speak of the 'image as a weapon' (Althöfer and Buhl 2019: 15), which gives recipients the feeling of being 'directly hit by the images of the attack' (ibid. 16; see also Paul 2013: 567). This topos is strikingly different from the conventional thinking about terrorism as a media strategy. It is no longer about creating fear, a condition that postpones injury into the future. When speaking of the 'image as a weapon', the impact of the image is understood in a much more direct and intervening way: the image already hits and injures at the moment of reception.

As already mentioned, in addition to the 'image as a weapon', there is another metaphorical understanding in which images function as a component of violent actions. If images are understood as weapons, it obviously follows to recognise in them a potential as a military resource. This idea of a so-called 'image war', which seems to exist in the tradition of an 'information war' (Winter 2017), has already increasingly emerged in the course of the analyses of 9/11 as a media event.

> Our time has witnessed, not simply more images, but a war of images in which the real-world stakes could not be higher. This war . . . has been waged against images . . . and it has been fought by means of images deployed to shock and traumatize the enemy, images meant to appall and demoralize . . . (Mitchell 2001: 2–3)

After 9/11, such metaphors are often reactivated whenever images produced by groups like al-Qaʿida or Daesh come into circulation that appear to be a 'caesura'. For example, after the release of the video showing the murder of the American businessman Nicholas Berg, journalistic discussions were fascinated by the concept of a disruptive image. In an article in the German-language daily *Die Welt*, Stefan Leifert, in his role as a communication scholar, is quoted as follows: 'This is precisely the difference between the hostage images and the

---

[5] These dialectical positions can be found in the entire research on media violence (see Buss and Müller 2020: 22ff.).

depictions of war. These scenes only take place because the camera is there. Images have become weapons' (Leifert, quoted in Haustein-Teßmer 2004).[6]

In contrast to 9/11, the motif of the 'image as a weapon' is combined in this new discussion with the motif of 'image warfare'. Iconic examinations of these images make it correspondingly clear that different spheres of images react antagonistically to each other in this context. For example, the orange jumpsuit Berg wears in the video is often read as a direct visual response to the images of torture that became public from Abu Ghraib, where this outfit was the prisoner's clothing (see Gruber 2020; Schmidt 2004). Unlike the pictures that were leaked against the will of the American government, however, the publication of the murder video is, itself, understood as an act of war: 'But the new [video] explicitly wants to start a spiral of horror, it is not a document but visual terror' (Schmidt 2004).

The fact that the use of images is explained via the metaphorical concepts of 'image as a weapon' and of 'image warfare' not only influences the perception of the impact of images, but these discursive formations also shape the media policy regarding the image worlds involved. For example, in 2010 the US Department of State established a Center for Strategic Counterterrorism Communications (CSCC). The motto of this unit, which was tasked with countering the videos of groups such as Daesh with its own productions was, accordingly, 'media is more than half the battle' (Cottee 2015).[7] In 2014, the Center published *Welcome to ISIS Land*, a video that illustrates the influence of metaphors, such as the 'image war'. For this contribution, footage from Daesh videos was used and placed in a new interpretative context. Images of executions and assassinations were shown unedited, with semantic shifts achieved through text inserts. One can then read, for example: 'Run – do not walk to ISIS Land . . . Where you can learn useful new skills for the *umma*. Blowing up mosques! Crucifying and executing Muslims . . . Suicide bombings inside mosques' (TC: 00:00–00:00:46). In both cases, the same images

[6] A few years later, similar production conditions were observed with regard to Daesh videos (see Bredekamp 2016: 24; Klonk 2017: 134).

[7] Surely this is not coincidentally reminiscent of the much-quoted dictum of al-Qaʾida leader Ayman al-Zawahiri: 'I say to you: that we are in a battle, and that more than half of this battle is taking place in the battlefield of the media' (al-Zawahiri 2005: 10).

are played off against and directed at each other: 'In a propaganda war against ISIS, the US tried to play by the enemy's rules' (Miller and Higham 2015), as two journalists put it with reference to the video in *The Washington Post*.[8]

The discourse on 'visual terror' has intensified with the emergence of Daesh, and especially during the peak of its video distribution in 2014 and 2015. In discussions evolving around this phenomena, visual media are often seen as having a unique capacity 'to move the viewer' (Bredekamp 2021: 33). For example, Peter Rásonyi explains in a Swiss daily newspaper article dealing with the ethical dimension of image reproduction: 'Images can transport a special emotionality and hit the viewer with force' (Rásonyi 2017). Similar to the remarks on the 9/11 attacks, the phrasing that viewers can be hit is recognisable as a clear reference to a weapons metaphor. In other publications, though, it becomes even more concrete. The art historian Horst Bredekamp states that the media policy of Daesh is an expression of a transformation of 'image acts': While people used to become images because they were killed, now people are killed 'in order to be able to employ them as images' (Bredekamp 2021: 186; see also Bredekamp 2016: 28). The notion that, in this regard, images are used 'to function, in a direct sense, as weapons' (Bredekamp 2021: 186) leads Petra Bernhardt to speak in relation to Daesh's media politic of 'terror as an image act' (Bernhardt 2018: 309) in the sense that such media politics are grounded in the 'interchangeability of image and body' (ibid.).[9]

The discourse around the image production of Daesh has not freed itself from the escalation logic of the image. Videos such as *Healing the Believers' Chest*, which shows the gruesome execution of the Jordanian Air Force pilot Muath al-Kasasbeh, are particularly frequently cited to describe a climax of the media politics of Daesh, and the use of images as weapons (Beese 2017: 94; Della Ratta 2018: 150–1; Friis 2018: 248–60). This shift of the affective perspective – from the potential for empathy with the victims of violence to a sense of one's own vulnerability – carries the risk that the circumstances and consequences of political violence will be forgotten.

[8] It can hardly come as a surprise that Daesh produced a counter-video in response to the CSCC's piece (Klonk 2017: 203–4).

[9] Bredekamp classifies this as a 'substitutive image acts' (Bredekamp 2021: 137–92).

The cited statements and standpoints are not to be understood as idiosyncratic discourse positions; they are part of an epistemic milieu that is by no means limited to academic, journalistic or governmental spheres.[10] In this milieu, conventional metaphors circulate that, in many respects, make use of the same ideas as those propagated by the producers of Daesh videos. This is paradigmatically illustrated in an article by Marwan Kraidy, who grounds his concept of the 'projectilic image' in writings presented by groups operating in the name of jihad. In the following, this case study will be used to problematise the extent to which speaking of the 'image as a weapon' contributes to depoliticising images of violence and, thus, obscuring the circumstances of their creation, and the related contexts of political violence.

From Myth to Theory

In his widely acclaimed essay, 'The Projectilic Image: Islamic State's Digital Visual Warfare and Global Networked Affect', Marwan M. Kraidy examines the role of image production within the overarching political strategies of Daesh. For this purpose, he analyses two written publications by the group and its predecessors that deal centrally with aspects of media production, as well as the previously mentioned Daesh video *Healing the Believers' Chest*, which, in Kraidy's words, shows 'the spectacular burning of a Jordanian air force pilot' (Kraidy 2017: 1195). In the course of his work, Kraidy refers to both the notion of a destructive image ('projectilic image'), and the use of media productions in a war of images ('image warfare'). More explicitly than in the examples presented above, he derives these metaphorical concepts from positions taken by groups like Daesh.

Kraidy begins his analysis with the two manuals, *Management of Savagery* (2004) and *O' Media Worker, You Are a Mujahid!* (2016), initially paying more attention to the former publication. For him, the manual is to be understood as a 'blueprint for a jihadi spectacle' (Kraidy 2017: 1196) that

[10] The author Clemens Setz, for example, reports that in the aftermath of the dissemination of the video in which James Foley's execution is shown, and which became particularly well-known through its display on YouTube, a whole series of videos circulated on the platform in which people documented their appalled reactions to the Daesh video. Such reaction videos are emblematic of the affective shift that has already been hinted at: from the potential of compassion to feeling one's own vulnerability (see Setz 2016).

follows the claim of making violence excessively and spectacularly visible in order to emerge victorious from an 'image-warfare' (ibid.: 1197), which is not least a battle for attention. The more spectacular the violence appears, the greater the effect seems on the attention economy and the intimidation of the enemy (see ibid.: 1196–8).

To analyse the video showing the execution of Muath al-Kasasbeh, Kraidy relies primarily on the latter publication of Daesh. Central to his argument is the following point, which he takes from the pamphlet's descriptions: 'To IS, images are tantamount to bullets, rockets, missiles – weapons in an arsenal' (ibid.: 1203). However, Kraidy not only wants to convince us that Daesh understands its media campaign as part of a struggle, and the images as weapons, he also suggests that these images have precisely the claimed disruptive effect: 'Here we get the full measure of IS' projectilic affect, where we feel "hit" by the video as if by a hard projectile' (ibid.: 1203). In other words, the author begins by identifying a destructive intention, which he takes from the analysed manuals, in order to prove the functionality of this intention through the video in question and, finally, to transform it into a scientific concept that, thereby, backs up the propagated myth. To understand how this theoretical bridging takes place, it is useful to consider some premises of his argument.

Kraidy distinguishes between representative and operative functions of images. Images contain information and show events (representative function) and images affect the bodies of the recipients by mediating affects (operative function). In the course of discussing the latter function, Kraidy refers to Farocki's concept of the 'operative image',[11] and repeatedly refers to a brief definition of the term by Farocki: 'images that do not represent an object but rather are part of an operation' (Farocki, cited in Kraidy 2017: 1198 and 1203).[12] In this sense, for Kraidy the image no longer primarily

---

[11] This seems surprising, because with this term Farocki describes a technical image that is not necessarily meant to be seen by people but is integrated into processes (for example, in military operations), and on which there are often no people at all (see Farocki 2005: 21–6). In this sense Volker Pantenburg characterises such images as 'visualisations of data that could also take on other, different guises' (Pantenburg 2017: 50).

[12] Already after 9/11, the conditions of visibility were described in a similar way. Also referring to Farocki, Heike Behrend, for example, notes that since the Kuwait War a 'weaponized vision' has emerged in which 'images have become combatants' (Behrend 2015: 14).

serves to document violence, but becomes part of a violent operation. But is the question of representation really so trivial? Despite the valid discussion about staged and orchestrated recordings, people were actually killed for the production of such videos. Moreover, images of torture and killing represent violent relationships and violent conflicts, which indisputably exist. The decision to interpret images in terms of their representational or operational dimension is, thus, also an ethical decision. As argued before, by shifting the affective perspective – from the potential of empathy with the victims of violence to feeling one's own vulnerability – the circumstances and consequences of political violence are obscured. Moreover, the notion of the operative image, in the sense of an image that itself constitutes a violent act, helps to make the myth associated with groups like Daesh more debatable.

Interestingly, Farocki's concept of the operative image is informed in no small part by his reading of Barthes's theory of myth (see Farocki 2005: 26–9; Pantenburg 2017: 50–4), which can also be used to re-analyse the metaphors of the 'image as weapon' and 'an image war'. According to Barthes, the myth is a 'way of meaning', it is 'a speech', and 'is not determined by the object of its message, but by the way it expresses it' (Barthes 2016: 251). In this sense, many forms of expression can be understood as a speech: 'The arrow one delivers, and that signifies a challenge, is also speech' (ibid.: 252). Through such modes of expression, which Barthes calls mythological, delivering an arrow can become a message. But nevertheless, this act remains a threatening speech, it does not itself cause what it threatens. In this example, the arrow is not used to perform an operative function, it is used to perform a representative one. However, for Barthes there are also ways of speaking that resist the myth, because they are not a meta-languages, but object-languages, which are 'transitively linked to their object' (ibid.: 252). Or, in other words, 'a language with which I act upon the object' (ibid.: 299). So even if many researchers insinuate that the dissemination of images of violence is part of an object-language, like in the aforementioned example of the delivered arrow, it stands in the same relation 'as the gesture to the deed' (ibid.: 299).

When speaking of the 'image as a weapon', by contrast, the gesture is declared to be the deed. The act of visual communication is conceived as an object-language, although it is still a meta-language. Through this conceptual confusion, the media politics of groups such as Daesh is not analysed, but the overarching myth is uncritically reused as a thesis. Terms like 'projectile images' deform the connotations of the image in the same way as the doctrines with which they are legitimised, because they are caught by the same myth. On a theoretical level, the problem is the same as that already described by Barthes: 'The myth is a depoliticised speech . . . it organises a world without contradictions' (ibid.: 295–6).

Instead of deconstructing the mythological exaltation of visibility – or, in Barthes's sense, re-politicising the depoliticised image – conventional metaphors, such as the 'image as a weapon', work unreflectively to perpetuate the myth associated with groups like Daesh. To be clear, the point here is not to deny that such images can harm those who consume them. Such images can shock and traumatise, otherwise they would hardly be suitable for mythmaking: 'Mythic meaning is never entirely arbitrary, it is always partially motivated, inevitably contains a piece of analogy' (ibid.: 273).[13] But the problem that arises when talking about the 'image as a weapon' is different. As it takes the form of a myth, it reduces the multiple dimensions of meaning inherent in such images to a single one (see Barthes 2016: 263). In the wake of this reduction of meaning, the conditions of political violence and its mediatisation are obscured, as well as undermining the suffering of the victims: in the myth, '[things] lose the memory of having been produced' (ibid.: 295). Although it would go far beyond the scope of this article to explain these contexts comprehensively, I would, nevertheless, like to elaborate a little on why I consider such a re-politicisation of the image to be important.

Re-politicisation of Images

So far, I have tried to show how the reception of images of violence in the case of Daesh videos is theorised, and how this discourse benefits a myth. I would now like to take a further look into the conditions and effects of this myth, assuming that this knowledge makes it possible to alter the rules of this discourse and re-politicise the images. What is necessary for this? A re-politicisation of images and videos of violence disseminated by groups such as Daesh would have to

---

[13] It would, therefore, also be important to question the aesthetics of Daesh videos – in Barthes's sense the form of their speech – for their part in myth-making. After all, videos of executions and assassinations are designed to create a myth.

take a closer look at minimum at these three aspects: (1) the policies of depiction, (2) the political contexts and (3) and at the rules of visibility.

1. First, one would have to ask how it is even possible to shift the focus from the suffering of the victims, who were tortured and killed for such images and videos, to the effects that people may experience when they receive this content. Therefore, it would be necessary to analyse the policies of depiction within which the videos operate, for example the means by which the exercise of violence is glorified to appear as a legitimate act, and the visual and rhetorical strategies that undermine the suffering of the victims. Execution videos of Daesh are always concerned with highlighting the 'sins' of the delinquents, so that the violence appears as righteous punishment, as compensation in the sense of a talion principle (Krona 2020: 226 and 129–43). According to this interpretation, counter-violence does not add a new wound, but heals the wounds of previously suffered violence. Video titles like *Healing the Believers' Chests* are an expression of such an understanding.

   The victim not only has to pay for his own 'sins' but is also a temporary substitute for the 'sins' of the addressed audience (ibid.: 130–1). The threatening gesture suggests that those addressed will also atone for their 'sins' and, thus, proposes the aforementioned shift in attention. The policies of depiction are, therefore, by no means only aimed at disturbing, but amount to an interdependence between shocking the viewers and undermining the dignity of the victims (see Dörre et al. 2021: 132–3). The (discursive) fading out of the victims is, in a way, based on the shock of the audience and the glorification of the act, as well as the humiliation and undermining of the victims, creating the possibility of perceiving an image as a weapon in the first place. Thus, in their article on images of violence, Buss and Müller emphasise that there is a connection between the degree of contextualisation and the effect of an image of violence (Buss and Müller 2020: 37). When such images are fed into an affective escalation spiral in journalistic reports or academic studies, it is hardly surprising that recipients allow themselves to be captured by the assumed effects. From a lack of context there results 'a lack of important distancing options, which are precisely the prerequisite for turning shocks into reflection' (ibid.: 39). This already leads to the second requirement for deconstructing the myth.

2. A re-politicisation of the image would also have to be combined, in the literal sense, with a political analysis of these contexts. The focus on images of violence, and the destructive effect of these images, virtually blocks the recognition of the dynamic contexts of power relations and political violence from which these images emerge, and to which they refer. In this sense, many Daesh videos are already political, and address problems of capitalist states and imperialist foreign policy (see Akil 2016: 367–73). By focusing on the barbarity of some videos, whose discussion promises the most publicity, the conditions of political conflict, and the assertion of monopolies of power and violence, are faded out. Felix Koltermann, for example, draws attention to the fact that speaking of a war of images disguises the fact that images are simply used 'as justification for military intervention' (Koltermann 2015). Correspondingly, in political conflicts, images are often used to create an image of an enemy (Klonk 2017: 218).

   Parallel to the individual suffering of the persons shown in the media productions of Daesh, it is, therefore, also important to emphasise that these are created in the context of political conflicts that cause and determine violence, and are, thus, to be understood as symptomatic in their ontology and aesthetics. As Ariella Azoulay noted: 'Picturing atrocity . . . is not an activity external and subsequent to the horror itself . . . It is rather an activity that takes place as part of the atrocity and of the conditions that enable its appearance, its very being' (Azoulay 2011: 249). Such images do not primarily represent singular events, as the logic of media attention would suggest (see ibid.: 250), but a history of violent political conflicts and corresponding sociopolitical circumstances in which violence has become regular. The media irregularity of the spectacular images only displaces the actual regularity of violence in the myth.

3. The question 'how are images of violence seen?' cannot be answered without taking into account the rules of visibility that influence the use and understanding of media. A re-politisation of the image would, therefore, also have to consider that there is no such thing as a pure

denotation. With Marie-José Mondzain, one could, accordingly, argue for a conceptual separation of image and visibility. Visibility describes the system that is directing the gaze and, thus, forces which aspects of an image are seen, and which remain unseen (see Mondzain 2009: 30–3). Particularly in European and US news media, the tendency can be observed to privilege a gaze that is much more interested in the spectacular, and even atrocious, qualities of images than in their value for understanding the complex historical, social and cultural conditions of political violence. As long as the dominant rules of visibility favour the first over the latter mode of viewing, it will be possible to bolster an epistemic milieu where the notion of images that act antagonistically against each other (see Klonk 2017: 211; Gruber 2020: 139–48; Paul 2013: 92–3) and their viewers can persist.[14]

However, the hegemonic rules of visibility are not only influencing what aspects of images of violence are seen, but also which images of violence become part of the news attention circle. For instance, videos documenting murders of white, non-Muslim men receive much more attention in European and US news media than the countless Daesh videos in which violence is inflicted on people from, for example, Syria or Iraq. A clear bias is evident here, because the group has arguably been able to enforce its claimed monopoly on violence far better in the region than outside the so-called caliphate. Accordingly, the representation of what is seen is heavily guided by aspects of race, religion and gender. This supports Mondzain's thesis that the rules of visibility, themselves, exercise a form of force: 'The violence of the visible results in the intentional abolition of thought and judgment' (Mondzain 2009: 34). The distorted representation of violence as reproduced by the media attention economy is an expression of a regime of visibility.[15] To deconstruct this regime, it would be

---

[14] From this perspective, the effects of such videos depend less on the general attention they generate (see Müller 2018: 87f.; Paul 2013: 567ff.) than on the specific modes of attention applied to them.

[15] In a similar way Günther and Pfeifer speak of 'sensory regimes to refer to socially acquired, culturally learned, technologically extended and highly dynamic techniques of observation. . . . As such, sensory regimes shape the ways in which we do or do not listen to and see ourselves, others and the world around us, and hence our capacity to perceive, appreciate, classify and interpret certain sounds and images' (Günther and Pfeifer 2020: 10).

important not only to ask 'how' but also 'what' images of violence are seen. What I have tried to show so far is that there exists a common myth that neither challenges how nor what images are seen but facilitates the existence of those rules of visibility.

In conclusion, rather than delegating responsibility for violence to images, it is necessary to examine the role of images in the formation of a myth that attempts to obscure the realities in which these images are created. The myth insists that violence is a singular and individualisable problem, but it is a decidedly political one, and must, therefore, be considered in its recipro-cal conditions. But the question of the political is by no means limited to the discourse outlined here. It continues in the archives that preserve these images and keep them available. Archives position themselves in relation to the stored contributions through the modalities of their access, visibility and functionality. In this way, they sometimes respond supportively or defensively to the notion of 'images as weapons' or 'wars' waged with images. Images are conceived in specific ways in different archives, because archives are consti-tuted by discourses of visibility.

Images and Archives

Having focused on the question 'how are images of violence seen?', I will now focus on the question 'how are images of violence presented?' As indi-cated before, the context in which media are received plays a decisive role in the way they can be approached. Thus, archives, in Derrida's sense, come into focus as authoritative instances (Derrida 1997: 9–17), and as privileged places where distribution of documents is regulated, controlled, inspected, suspended, or even stopped. In the following, I will identify archives that store violent material of Daesh as part of the contextual conditions of their reception and examine how their constitution relates to the previously dis-cussed metaphors. By focusing on the aesthetic and epistemic conditions of archives, it will become clear that the raised questions are inevitably inter-twined. Referencing Foucault, the archive is not only 'the law of what can be said' (Foucault 1989: 145), but also the law of what can be seen.

Although the production of new videos by Daesh has nearly come to a standstill by now (see Nanninga 2019: 9–13), the existing content is still accessible under specific conditions of networked databases (see Fischer et al. 2019: 8–21). The various archives in which the videos of Daesh can still be found make them visible in different ways, and each under specific media-aesthetic, information-technical, and legal conditions. In order to make this observation analytically useful, four different archives will be examined here: (1) the Internet Archive, which plays a central role in the dissemination of unconstitutional media content, because videos of Daesh are still available there, and links to corresponding contributions are distributed via Telegram channels and other messenger services, (2) the site jihadology.net by American researcher Aaron Y. Zelin, who frames it as an academic project to make primary sources accessible to researchers, (3) a website, presumably run by supporters of Daesh, which makes a large part of the better-known productions available as streams and downloads and (4) the archive of the Time-based Image Area Annotation Tool (TIMAAT), which was developed as part of the research group 'Jihadism on the Internet', where I was a postdoctoral researcher from August 2020 until the end of the project in May 2022. With the help of these heterogeneous examples, which show the diversity of contexts, I would like to provide evidence for the thesis that archives regulate visibility.

Internet Archive

The Internet Archive was started in 1996 as a project that stores dated versions of websites. At the same time, however, its own website, archive.org, also contains countless libraries that preserve a wide variety of files (texts, images, software, and so on). Unlike most social networks, blogging sites and messaging services, the digital library insists on a strictly libertarian approach. The operators do not systematically take action against violent or illegal content, nor do users have the option to report such content directly on the site. The Internet Archive has, therefore, long been used as a repository for Daesh videos by various actors (Daesh supporters, researchers, and so on) interested in this material (see Della Ratta 2018: 177). Above all, it follows an accumulation logic – hardly anything is unimportant or sensitive enough not to be integrated into its collections. The contents and formats that the archive holds are correspondingly heterogeneous. However, there is nothing in the site's interface that indicates that the Internet Archive provides violent content, and it is only in the terms of use that this possibility is even mentioned:

the Collections may contain information that might be deemed offensive, disturbing, pornographic, racist, sexist, bizarre, misleading, fraudulent, or otherwise objectionable. The Archive does not endorse or sponsor any content in the Collections, nor does it guarantee or warrant that the content available in the Collections is accurate, complete, noninfringing, or legally accessible in your jurisdiction, and you agree that you are solely responsible for abiding by all laws and regulations that may be applicable to the viewing of the content.[16]

Despite the easy and reliable availability, access to such videos is also possible elsewhere (see, for example, the archives discussed below). This already draws attention to the fact that the choice of a particular archive may not only be about the mere availability of contributions – for this, the Internet Archive would suffice – but also about certain ways of making content visible, and about the associated modulation of its visibilities. From this point of view, the Internet Archive enables a form of clandestine visibility. Daesh videos do not achieve salient attention there (for example, on a front page), but they can be found via the search function, and can be accessed under relatively reliable links, making them very suitable for a further dissemination via messenger services.[17] The sheer mass of contributions simultaneously hides and exposes the videos of Daesh. This fact has contributed to the project's popularity as a repository for images of violence produced by groups like Daesh, although it is not generally perceived as an archive that supports such content. In other words, the website is not guiding a specific vision but allows distribution visibility to different actors in a different way.

---

[16] Available at <https://archive.org/about/terms.php> (last accessed 15 February 2023).

[17] In this respect, the Internet Archive holds a special position among the examples represented here. It is the only archive that does not directly position itself to videos that were created in the name of a jihad. There exist other platforms that meet this criterion, but unlike archives such as justpaste.it, which is also a popular repository for such videos (see Shehabat and Mitew 2018: 87–91), the Internet Archive is searchable. Even without knowing a URL, specific contributions can, therefore, be found there. Via hashtags and channels associated with a video, it is even possible to find other contributions of similar provenance.

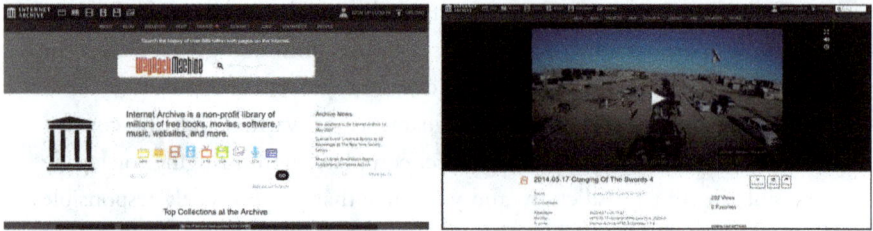

Figure 14.1 Left: search mask and interface of archive.org. Right: example of Daesh video on the Internet Archive.
Source: Image in the public domain.

Furthermore, in the course of a video upload, visual material, such as stills and gifs, are created by default, which can be used on social media platforms to promote a video, or as a preview of its content. This makes clear why the Internet Archive is not limited by the traditional role of an archive to store documents for the purpose of preservation (Rothöhler 2020: 561): it also serves as a starting point for new dissemination. Outside of specific academic studies, however, the Internet Archive is rarely criticised for such content. So far, the website has been under suspicion mainly for possible copyright infringements. The availability of images of violence is seen more as part of an accumulated pile of files that can be found via the search function but seem to be removed from their context. Since the Internet Archive does not fulfil the condition of intentional distribution of videos of violence, the images, even if they come from groups like Daesh, are not perceived as weapons. There is no 'image war' raging in the Internet Archive. The uninhibited nature of the archive dispels the question of responsibility and intentionality. Here there are no 'archons' (Derrida 1997: 11) to watch over what is stored by whom, and who has access to it. The situation is different with the website of the American researcher Aron Y. Zelin, which has been frequently criticised for making such videos available.

jihadology.net

The website jihadology.net presents itself as a 'clearinghouse for jihādī primary source material, original analysis, and translation service'. In addition, it emphasises that it is an 'academic website', and that content is made available for 'research purposes'.[18] Jihadology thus situates itself as an academic project – the

---

[18] Available at <https://jihadology.net/> (last accessed 15 February 2023).

name literally suggests its own discipline – that makes specific content digitally accessible for a specific purpose. It is not only in this respect that the website differs from the Internet Archive. The site is also less reminiscent of a classic archive than of a blog, on which, in reverse chronological order, mainly news about, and contributions from groups acting in the name of jihad, are published. Although the site can certainly be used as an archive and, for example, specific videos can be found via categories, the blog format focuses more on the topicality of contributions.[19] As can be seen in Figure 14.2, it is, therefore, usually indicated that the video is a 'new' one. Even though the origin of the images is not clearly attributed by Zelin, many of the videos seem to be from channels of popular instant messaging services, which are frequently listed as their source. By being published on a website, the visibility of this content is modulated (the framing on Jihadology differs strikingly from those in the channels) and redistributed (the videos become visible for other kinds of audiences).

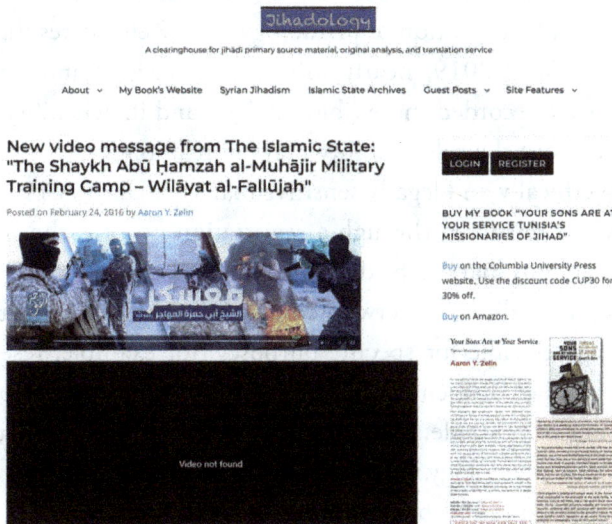

Figure 14.2 Visitor view on jihadology.net when not registered and not logged in. Videos cannot be viewed with these settings.
Source: Image in the public domain.

[19] Unlike the Internet Archive, the site is not freely searchable, but categories make it possible to find material on specific topics. For example, there are categories that refer to individual groups (such as 'The Islamic State'), assign contributions to specific regions or administrative districts (such as 'Syria' or 'Wilayat al-Raqqah') or allow the assignment to the media offices responsible for the production of a video (such as 'al-Furqan Media').

Founder Aron Y. Zelin has attempted to document the creation of the site, and the changes it has undergone over time, in a kind of autoethnographic report. In this subjective description, he highlights various motives for establishing the archive. It becomes clear that during his Master's thesis he was confronted with the problem of acquiring primary sources: 'Therefore, the idea of a dedicated website (*Jihadology*) emerged, that could provide a stable environment where researchers could find older materials that in time might no longer be accessible online . . .' (Zelin 2021: 226). What Zelin has labelled as the ambition of scientific accessibility and verifiability has, at the same time, triggered fears that the website could just as well be used by supporters of the same groups whose productions Zelin archives there.[20] Accordingly, the archive's website has often been the subject of challenges: for example, Wordpress – which acts as the blog host of jihadology.net – has repeatedly received takedown requests for individual posts. The site has also been completely blocked in some countries and paralysed by hacker DoS attacks a few times (see ibid.: 231–2).

The widespread recognition of jihadology.net – Zelin states that between May 2010 and April 2019, nearly thirty million views and nearly seven million visits were recorded there (ibid.: 227) – and its reliability fostered a critical debate about the role visibility plays in relation to archives that provide access to ethically and legally sensitive material. Until 2019, the year in which access was restricted through a registration process, the site fulfilled ambivalent functions that can be described as two sides of the same coin. On the one hand, such digitally networked archives store documents in order to make them accessible for specific purposes (for example, research). On the other hand, they also enable uses that runs counter to the propagated visibility claim (for example, as a repository in Academia). Remarkably, the discussion about jihadology.net intensified at the very moment when the visibility of corresponding contributions began to decline:

> It is likely the UK government started to focus on me and Jihadology because beginning around 2015–2016, mainstream tech companies began to take

---

[20] The Terms of Service of the site, on the other hand, emphasise: 'In no way are you allowed to use the contents of Jihadology.net with the intent to promote, glorify, and/or express support for terrorist activities, or to incite others to commit terrorist offences' (see <https://jihadology.net/about/legal-notice/> (last accessed 15 February 2023)).

down jihadi content from their platforms to varying degrees. As a result, my website became one of the few likely stable places online where there was jihadi primary sources. (ibid.: 233–4)

Jacques Derrida has pointed out that there is 'no political power without control of the archive' (Derrida 1997: 14). The efforts of various state institutions to restrict the content of the site, or access to the site, are, accordingly, an expression of the attempt to establish the archive as a space under their supervision, but at the same time also reveal Zelin as an authority (see Derrida 1997: 9–17), who for his part claims sovereignty over visibility for himself:

with the onset of IS's video campaign and increasing levels of explicit excessive violence, for the first time I began to censor certain content . . . I did not feel it was appropriate to show it; it is my website after all! (Zelin 2021: 230)

In the tradition of the archon described by Derrida, he claims the task and competence of interpreting and evaluating the stored documents (see Derrida 1997: 11). While signalling the ambition to be 'the' academic site for content related to jihad, it exclusively covers images and videos that are linked to a militant interpretation of the concept. Jihadology leaves no room for contributions from groups that operate on the basis of peaceful interpretations of the concept, as we discussed in the introduction. It programs a certain gaze that influences what can be seen, and what cannot be seen. The archive, thus, defines the subject area that it claims only to cover.

In 2019, the interventions of state authorities led to the restriction of access to the site. Since then, access to certain content – for example, videos containing violence – is only possible if users register in advance, and are logged in with the corresponding account (see Zelin 2021: 236). The blog, as such, is still accessible, the publication of contributions can be tracked, and some contributions – such as news or Zelin's analyses – can still be viewed without restriction, but such content that was suspected of all too easily becoming part of the 'jihadist information ecosystem' (Fischer 2019) remains inaccessible. Registration is, in turn, linked to conditions that are intended to ensure that the visibility of sensitive content is distributed for a specific purpose. For this reason, it is only possible via specific email addresses that are on a whitelist, and that suggest a 'legitimate institutional affiliation' – for example, to 'academia, journalism, the humanitarian sector, government, etc.' (Zelin 2021: 236).

How something is made visible is, thus, not only an aesthetic question, but also relates to the question of accessibility, especially in such cases where visibility is contested. With this measure, Zelin reacted to the aforementioned dual character of the archive and restructures the visibility relations in such a way that the exclusive use as a scholarly repository becomes plausible. The policies of various authoritative instances (both state and academic) are thus embedded in the archive's current visibility structure. Not least, it is intended to prevent images from becoming weapons. But the assumption that such images are only received as destructive is, in any case, too short-sighted, as the example of a Daesh-owned site suggests.

Daesh Videos on Demand

Daesh videos are not available on conventional streaming portals, but there are digital archives that make such contributions available and come very close to the appearance of Netflix or comparable providers. The screenshot on the left in Figure 14.3 comes from such a site and, in comparison with the screen capture from Netflix on the right, makes it clear that similar reception aesthetic formulas are served in both cases. At the top, for example, a current production is prominently advertised and, below that, a number of other films are displayed that can be selected directly via the interface. Already on the user interface, both pages visually indicate that an extensive selection of contributions is available, thus inviting the user to view a diverse range of films. So, it is not about the one-time exposure of a contribution,

Figure 14.3 Left: interface of a website that makes Daesh videos available for streaming or download. Right: overview page of the Movies category on Netflix. Source: Image in the public domain.

it is not even about its mere distribution, but is about the compilation of a whole selection of contributions. For this reason, not every shadowy video document of battles or attacks is collected indiscriminately. The archive concentrates on high-quality productions where attention has been paid to audiovisual and narrative design.

If the digital reception environment of entertainment-oriented streaming providers is emulated for the distribution of Daesh productions, then it seems obvious that such videos do not serve to provoke and disturb in every context but, rather, seek to attract quite heterogeneous audiences. Even if it seems difficult to imagine a pleasant movie night with this programme, such forms of visibility formally demand an affirmative relationship of reception and, thus, insist to a certain extent on the entertainment and information value of the archive. As suggested earlier, meaning is not reducible to the image itself, but is shaped depending on the particular gaze. Images that emerge in the context of political violence, especially, are viewed under very different cultural and discursive conditions and, accordingly, shape different target audiences (see Klonk 2017: 219)

Thus, the violent videos of Daesh can be read as a message to, and weapon against, an 'enemy', but they can also be understood as a message to supporters or to their 'own' citizens, who should not feel threatened by the images. For example, the 'punishment' of the pilot in the aforementioned *Healing the Believers' Chests* also sends a message to the population of the former caliphate, who were themselves affected by the airstrikes that are the subject of the video, and who may be affected differently by what is shown than people who are not directly affected by this politico-military violence. Ultimately, the website shows that this reading is not a mere assumption, but that concrete contexts of reception are created that suggest or even presuppose such readings.

Despite design similarities, the Daesh site is, of course, not a congenial counterpart to popular streaming providers. Differences can already be identified in terms of aesthetics and interactivity: the Netflix interface, for example, is much more reactive, and plays previews of films and series. Nevertheless, it is, above all, the distribution conditions that separate the two archives. The Daesh site does not offer regulated access, it is not even accessible via a fixed address, but is constantly being posted anew. Without being able to trace this process in detail, it is reasonable to assume that the page is affected by deletions and, therefore, has to be reactivated more frequently with small changes to the URL. In order to stabilise access, variants of the site can now be found online as blockchain domains, which are websites that cannot be blocked in principle because they do not have to be registered via ICANN, and are owned by the respective operators. Since such pages are not yet supported by all common browsers, tutorials are circulating in associated messenger channels that explain how to access the website, for instance, with the help of browser add-ons. In the form of a screencast, what they wish not to be visible to everyone is made visible for insiders with the help of such tutorials.

Furthermore, there are no references to any terms of use that attempt to regulate how the site is to be used. Unlike Netflix, where not even screen recording is possible without technical know-how, the Daesh site not only allows downloads, but actively advertises them. The site preserves the contributions, but does not lock them, and rather actively works to ensure that the contributions can be distributed further and remain visible beyond their own radius. Functions are also integrated that are familiar from social media and refer to community dimensions. Thus, it is possible to 'like' contributions, as well as to exchange information about them in comments. Whether images of violence are said to have a dangerous effect has to do with the context of reception, both the dispositive in which something is given to be seen (for example, a specific archive), and the personal circumstances from which something is seen (for example, as a resident of the former caliphate). Both contexts make this example strikingly different from the last one because, on the one hand, there is an attempt to contain the image aesthetically via the archive and, on the other hand, the archive comprises completely different contexts of use.

TIMAAT

The last archive is integrated into the annotation tool TIMAAT, which can be used to annotate videos from groups such as Daesh (Figure 14.4). The tool is being developed as part of the work of a junior research group funded by the Federal Ministry of Education and Research's security research programme and, thus, operates in the gravitational field of state authority. The archive that the software currently draws upon in this research context is constituted from various collections of videos that are related in one way or other to jihad. Much of the footage came from the archives of the researchers involved, which were collected in earlier research projects, but there were also many contributions taken from accessible websites, such as the Internet

Archive or Jihadology. In addition, videos were extracted from services such as Telegram during the online field research, and there were grants from security authorities who shared collected material.

The aim of the software development is to create a tool that can be used to annotate such videos for scientific analysis. While jihadology.net, for example, makes videos available for research purposes, TIMAAT is intended to be used to do research on these videos, for example, to examine the aesthetic aspects of visibility. The functions are, accordingly, extensive. In addition to annotation, however, the archival and reception-related functions come to the fore in this context. In contrast to the archives described above, TIMAAT is much more closely connected to the logic of a database. Contributions are not simply stored, but are provided with extensive metadata, according to which the contributions can be grouped and searched. This enables a curation of the material that does not necessarily require a sifting of images of violence.

But though the archive by no means contains only violent videos, the interface responds aesthetically to a certain extent to assumptions of effects, such as those already discussed above. It programs a gaze that accounts for contact with potentially violent content and is aimed at a small group of people who need to engage with the material quite extensively for research reasons. TIMAAT's grey-on-white functional interface allows for a detached view of materials that can affectively challenge and traumatise. The functional logic of the interface, therefore, suggests not viewing videos in full screen mode, thus maintaining the protective environment of tabs and other control elements. The interface, thus, reacts to the fact that in archives one cannot only get lost in the quantity of data (see Farge 2011: 8–9), but can also be affectively taken over by the collected materials.

It is no coincidence that in the course of using TIMAAT, reception practices have emerged within the research group that are intended to contain the affective potential of archival work. Some colleagues have avoided watching the videos in full screen, so that the media dispositive remains reflexively present, others only watched videos that potentially contained violence during specific times of the day. One colleague developed a whole ritual that included specific clothing that he could take off afterwards. Based on this, I chose to wear specific glasses when watching such videos. They became my media of vision for this specific application and could be replaced by (affectively speaking) clean glasses thereafter. Such measures bear witness to the 'form of stickiness' (Ahmed 2014: 92) that Sara Ahmed notes for affects in another context.

Figure 14.4 Archive and analysis tool of the junior research group Jihadism on the Internet.
Source: 'Jihadism on the Internet: Images and Videos, their Appropriation, and Dissemination'.

However, the function of state-legitimised archives, such as TIMAAT, certainly goes beyond research purposes. The ongoing circulation of material is 'marked by such projects as a problem to be dealt with – and thus declared an ongoing task'. Metadated, categorised, ordered and protected from access, the material 'appears as something that [still] needs to be governed' (Hagener et al. 2020: 12). The positions of the users and developers of such tools needs to be reflected just as clearly as the funding lines from which they emerged (see the introduction to this volume). Metaphorical concepts, such as the 'image as a weapon' or the 'image war' have, after all, also been shaped by a securitised research landscape in which civilian security research plays a greater role. Archival tools, such as TIMAAT, respond to these notions of impact, but perhaps also have the potential to play a role in the re-politicisation of the image by helping to analyse it, because how images can affect viewers (for example, affective or reflexive) depends largely on the context of their reception and use.

Conclusion

Images of violence retain relevance long after their production and publication because, among other things, they are the subject of scholarly debate, and because access to them remains possible through various digital databases. If these contributions are understood as weapons or as part of image-wars, the characteristics and conditions of their production, representation and media culture become blurred. Instead of paying attention to the violations portrayed, the viewer begins to worry about his or her own vulnerability. Rather than framing those images in an antagonistic way, one should take into account the epistemic conditions under which they are perceived. Speaking of the 'image as a weapon' or an 'image war' cannot be understood independently from a rhetorical logic of escalation that links the media politics of journalism to that of groups like Daesh. Archives and their relationship to the system of visibility play a decisive role in the reception of videos of violence. Not only do they direct a particular gaze that reveals certain aspects of the image and obscures others, but their diversity also draws attention to the variety of reception possibilities and audiences. As controversial as the images are, so, too, are their archives and the forms of visibility they enable.

References

Ahmed, S. (2014), *The Cultural Politics of Emotion*, Edinburgh: Edinburgh University Press.

Akil, H. N. (2016), 'Cinematic Terrorism: Deleuze, ISIS and Delirium', *Journal for Cultural Research*, 20: 4, 366–79.

Al-Zawahiri, A. (2005), 'Letter from al-Zawahiri to al-Zarqawi', <https://ctc.westpoint. edu/wp-content/uploads/2013/10/Zawahiris-Letter-to-Zarqawi-Translation.pdf> (last accessed 7 July 2022).

Althöfer, M. and B. Buhl (2019), 'Das Bild als Waffe: Eine Gegenüberstellung von terroristischen Kommunikationsstrategien und medialen Bewältigungstaktiken am Beispiel von 9/11', in R. Biesinger, K. Sachs-Hombach, J. R. J. Schirra, A. Ulrich and L. R. A. Wilde (eds), *Digitaler Dschihad. Vom Attentäter zum Medienagenten*, Tübingen: Stauffenburg Verlag, 11–29.

Ayad, M., A. Amarasingam and A. Alexander (2021), 'The Cloud Caliphate: Archiving the Islamic State in Real-Time', Combating Terrorism Center at West Point; Institute for Strategic Dialogue, <https://ctc.usma.edu/wp-content/ uploads/2021/05/Cloud-Caliphate.pdf> (last accessed 7 July 2022).

Azoulay, A. (2011), 'The Execution Portrait', in G. Batchen, M. Gidley, N. K. Miller and J. Prosser (eds), *Picturing Atrocity: Photography in Crisis*, London: Reaktion Books, 249–59.

Barthes, R. (2016), *Mythen des Alltags*, Berlin: Suhrkamp.

Beese, Y. (2017), 'Exekutionsvideos des Islamischen Staates Filmsprache, Zielpublika und rhetorische Potenziale', *Zeitschrift für Semiotik*, 39: 3–4, 71–105.

Bernhardt, P. (2018), 'Terror als Bildakt. Die strategische Nutzung der Kraft von Bildern durch den "Islamischen Staat"', in S. Seitz, A. Graneß and G. Stenger (eds), *Facetten gegenwärtiger Bildtheorie. Interkulturelle und interdisziplinäre Perspektiven*, Wiesbaden and Heidelberg: Springer VS, 305–18.

Behrend, H. (2015), 'Introduction', in H. Behrend and T. Wendl (eds), *9/11 and Its Remediations in Popular Culture and Arts in Africa*, Berlin and Münster: LIT, pp. 8–37.

Bredekamp, H. (2016), *Das Beispiel Palmyra*, Cologne: Walther König.

Bredekamp, H. (2021), *Image Acts: A Systematic Approach to Visual Agency*, Berlin and Boston: De Gruyter.

Buss, F. and P. Müller, P. (2020), 'Hin- und Wegsehen. Formen und Kräfte von Gewaltbildern', in F. Buss and P. Müller (eds), *Hin- und Wegsehen. Formen und Kräfte von Gewaltbildern*, Berlin and Boston: De Gruyter, pp. 11–44.

Buttler, J. (2003), 'Ästhetik des Terrors – Die Bilder des 11. Septembers 2001', in M. Beuthner, J. Buttler, S. Fröhlich, I. Neverla and S. A. Weichert (eds), *Bilder des Terrors – Terror der Bilder? Krisenberichterstattung am und nach dem 11. September*, Cologne: Halem, pp. 26–41.

Cottee, S. (2015), 'Why It's So Hard to Stop ISIS Propaganda', *The Atlantic*, 2 March, <https://www.theatlantic.com/international/archive/2015/03/why-its-so-hard-to-stop-isis-propaganda/386216/> (last accessed 7 July 2022).

Della Ratta, D. (2018), *Shooting a Revolution: Visual Media an Warfare in Syria*, London: Pluto Press.

Derrida, J. (1997): *Dem Archiv verschrieben. Eine Freudsche Impression*, Berlin: Brinkmann & Bose.

Dörre, R., C. Günther and S. Pfeifer (2021), 'Journalism and Images of Violence – Ethical Perspectives', in S. Baden, L.-D. Fuhrmann, J. Holten and K. Jörder (eds), *MINDBOMBS. Visuelle Kulturen politischer Gewalt*, Berlin: Kerber Verlag, pp. 127–36.

Farge, A. (2011), *Der Geschmack des Archivs*, Göttingen: Wallstein.

Farocki, H. (2005), 'Der Krieg findet immer einen Ausweg', *Cinema*, 50: 1, 21–31.

Fischer, A. (2019), 'How Jihadist Groups Exploit Western Researchers to Promote Their Theology', *Online Jihad*, 18 February, <https://onlinejihad.net/2019/02/18/how-jihadist-groups-exploit-western-researchers-to-promote-their-theology/> (last accessed 7 July 2022).

Fischer, A., N. Prucha and E. Winterbotham (2019), 'Mapping the Jihadist Infor-mation Ecosystem: Towards the Next Generation of Disruption Capability', Global Research Network on Terrorism and Technology, 16 July, <https://www.

rusi.org/explore-our-research/publications/special-resources/mapping-jihadist-information-ecosystem-towards-next-generation-disruption-capability> (last accessed 7 July 2022).

Foucault, M. (1989), *The Archaeology of Knowledge*, New York: Routledge.

Friis, S. M. (2018), 'Behead, Burn, Crucify, Crush: Theorizing the Islamic State's Public Displays of Violence', *European Journal of International Relations*, 24: 2, 243–67.

Grimm, J. (1999), *Fernsehgewalt. Zuwendungsattraktivität, Erregungsverläufe, sozialer Effekt*, Opladen and Wiesbaden: Westdt. Verlag.

Gruber, C. (2020), 'The Visual Culture of ISIS: Truculent Iconophilia as Antagonistic Co-evolution', in I. Busch, U. Fleckner and J. Waldmann (eds), *Nähe auf Distanz. Eigendynamik und mobilisierende Kraft politischer Bilder im Internet*, Berlin and Boston: De Gruyter, pp. 123–54.

Günther, C. and S. Pfeifer (2020), 'Introduction – Jihadi Audiovisuality and Its Entanglements: A Conceptual Framework', in C. Günther and S. Pfeifer (eds), *Jihadi Audiovisuality and Its Entanglements: Meanings, Aesthetics, Appropriations*, Edinburgh: Edinburgh University Press, pp. 1–24.

Hagener, M., S. Opitz and U. Tellmann (2020), 'Zirkulation. Einleitung in den Schwerpunkt', *Zeitschrift für Medienwissenschaft*, 12: 2, 10–18.

Haustein-Teßmer, O. (2004), 'Der inszenierte Schauder', *Welt*, 30 September, <https://www.welt.de/wirtschaft/webwelt/article343670/Der-inszenierte-Schauder.html?icid=search.product.onsitesearch> (last accessed 7 July 2022).

Klonk, C. (2017), *Terror. Wenn Bilder zu Waffen werden*, Frankfurt am Main: S. Fischer.

Koltermann, F. (2015), 'Terror im Rampenlicht. Mediale Inszenierung und Bildpolitik des IS', *Qantara.de*, 22 April, <https://de.qantara.de/inhalt/mediale-inszenierung-und-bildpolitik-des-is-terror-im-rampenlicht> (last accessed 7 July 2022).

Kraidy, M. M. (2017), 'The Projectilic Image: Islamic State's Digital Visual Warfare and Global Networked Affect', *Media, Culture & Society*, 39: 8, 1194–209.

Krona, M. (2020), 'Visual Performativity of Violence: Power and Retaliatory Humiliation in Islamic State (IS) Beheading Videos between 2014 and 2017', in C. Günther and S. Pfeifer (eds), *Jihadi Audiovisuality and Its Entanglements: Meanings, Aesthetics, Appropriations*, Edinburgh: Edinburgh University Press, pp. 123–47.

Kunczik, M. (2017), *Medien und Gewalt. Überblick über den aktuellen Stand der Forschung und der Theoriediskussion*, Wiesbaden: Springer VS.

Miller, G. and S. Higham (2015), 'In a Propaganda War against ISIS, the US Tried to Play by the Enemy's Rules', *The Washington Post*, 8 May, <https://www.washingtonpost.com/world/national-security/in-a-propaganda-war-us-tried-to-play-by-the-enemys-rules/2015/05/08/6eb6b732-e52f-11e4-81ea-0649268f729e_story.html> (last accessed 7 July 2022).

Mitchell, W. J. T. (2011), *Cloning Terror: The War of Images, 9/11 to the Present*, Chicago: University of Chicago Press.

Mondzain, M.-J. (2009), 'Can Images Kill?', *Critical Inquiry*, 36: 1, 20–51.

Müller, P. (2018), 'Realitätskollaps? Zum Status von Bild und Betrachter bei Gewaltvideos', in K. Fromm, S. Greiff and A. Stemmler (eds), *Images in Conflict*, Kromsdorf, Weimar: Jonas Verlag, pp. 80–101.

Nanninga, P. (2019), 'Branding a Caliphate in Decline: The Islamic State's Video Output (2015–2018)', International Centre for Counter-Terrorism – The Hague, <https://icct.nl/app/uploads/2019/04/ICCT-Nanninga-Branding-a-Caliphate-in-Decline-April2019.pdf> (last accessed 7 July 2022).

Nessouli, A. (2015), 'Showing the Burning Video', *Ramel Media*, 4 February, <https://medium.com/ramel-media/showing-the-burning-video-affd58573af0> (last accessed 7 July 2022).

Otto, I. (2013), 'Mediengewalt und rituelle Reinigung. Zur Katharsis-Hypothese', *Zeitschrift für Kulturwissenschaften*, 7: 1, 121–31.

Paul, G. (2013), 'Reality 9/11. Das Bild als Tat, der Aufmerksamkeitsterror und die modernen Bilderkriege', in G. Paul (ed.), *BilderMACHT. Studien zur Visual History des 20. und 21. Jahrhunderts*, Göttingen: Wallstein, 567–99.

Pantenburg, V. (2017), 'Working Images: Harun Farocki and the Operational Image', in J. Eder and C. Klonk (eds), *Image operations: Visual Media and Political Conflict*, Manchester: Manchester University Press, pp. 49–62.

Rásonyi, P. (2017), 'Warum wir Terrorbilder trotzdem zeigen', *Neue Zürcher Zeitung*, 21 June, <https://www.nzz.ch/international/die-haltung-der-redaktion-der-nzz-warum-wir-terrorbilder-trotzdem-zeigen-ld.1302013> (last accessed 7 July 2022).

Rothöhler, S. (2020), 'Virtuelle Archive', in D. Kasprowicz and S. Rieger (eds), *Handbuch Virtualität*, Wiesbaden: Springer VS, pp. 557–69.

Schaffer, J. (2008), *Ambivalenzen der Sichtbarkeit. Über die visuellen Strukturen der Anerkennung*, Bielefeld: transcript.

Schmidt, T. E. (2004), 'Die Rache der Bilder', *Zeit Online*, 19 May, <https://www.zeit.de/2004/22/Die_Rache_der_Bilder> (last accessed 7 July 2022).

Setz, C. (2016), '"Islamischer Staat": Das grelle Herz der Finsternis', *Zeit Online*, 24 March, <https://www.zeit.de/2014/40/is-enthauptungsvideo-verbreitung-internet/komplettansicht> (last accessed 7 July 2022).

Shehabat, A. and T. Mitew (2018), 'Black-boxing the Black Flag: Anonymous Sharing Platforms and ISIS Content Distribution Tactics', *Perspectives on Terrorism*, 12: 1, 81–99.

Winter, C. (2017), 'Media Jihad: The Islamic State's Doctrine for Information Warfare', International Centre for the Study of Radicalisation and Political Violence, <https:// icsr.info/wp-content/uploads/2017/02/ICSR-Report-Media-Jihad-The-Islamic-State%E2%80%99s-Doctrine-for-Information-Warfare.pdf> (last accessed 7 July 2022).

Zelin, A. Y. (2021), 'The Case of Jihadology and the Securitization of Academia', *Terrorism and Political Violence*, 33: 2, 225–41.

Zgryziewicz, R., T. Grzyb, S. Fahmy and J. Shaheen (2015), 'Daesh Information Campaign and its Influence', *NATO StratCom*, <https://stratcomcoe.org/pdfjs/?file=/ publications/download/daesh_public_use_19-08-2016.pdf?zoom=page-fit> (last accessed 7 July 2022).

15

REMEDIATING IMAGES OF WAR: CULTURAL PRACTICES BEHIND SYRIAN DIGITAL ARCHIVES AFTER 2011

Enrico De Angelis and Yazan Badran

Introduction

The Syrian uprising-turned-conflict constitutes an unprecedented case when it comes to visual documentation. The production of audiovisual material by journalists, media activists and ordinary citizens is overwhelming, probably making the Syrian issue one of the most documented international events of all time. Even if there are no precise figures, the videos on YouTube alone are estimated to be in the hundreds of thousands (Atassi 2020). As a recent article by AFP describes, the verification and contextualisation of the available material is prohibitive for any media organisation (Chaise 2018).

Syrian image-makers, citizen journalists and media activists used predominantly social media (Facebook, YouTube and Twitter) as the main repository for the images they produced. Social media had different crucial advantages. They offer a practically unlimited space to stock digital visual content, and they offer a public space through which this content can be immediately shared and distributed. This last element was especially important in the context of a particularly dangerous situation such as the war in Syria. A photo or a video of a bombing could be lost if their producers are killed in the aftermath. An archive situated in a hard disk could be lost if its owner is arrested. Therefore, during the protests and then the conflict social media became the privileged place around which Syrians not only uploaded the content, but also consumed, reacted to, interacted with and discussed it.

The visual material was produced mostly by unknown people, often participating directly in the events (demonstrations, battles). Many of these people were not trained photographers or video-makers, nor were they familiar with journalistic professional values as regards how to handle the visual content in relation to the filmed/photographed people, or ownership rights of the material.

Because of the conditions of shooting, it has been noted and discussed how the material tended to present a specific aesthetic: pixelated, blurred, out of focus, shaky images, which seem to disregard institutional notions of 'quality' in cinema and photojournalism. In this respect, the production was referred to as 'emergency cinema' (Elias 2017), a 'pixelated revolution' (Mroué et al. 2012), 'networked images' (Della Ratta 2018), and as a revival of 'imperfect cinema' (Elias and Omareen 2014).

Keeping these elements in mind, this chapter will examine the production, circulation and interaction with these images as practices that can be thought of under the conceptual frame of archival work. We believe that the post-2011 Syrian context constitutes a particularly interesting laboratory when it comes to discussing the nature, aims, opportunities and limits of contemporary digital archives. The concept of archive can contribute not only to illuminate certain dynamics of how we approach digital images in the networked public sphere, but also to elaborate strategies in order to improve our interaction with them.

In this chapter we will focus in particular on images of horror: visual content representing scenes of war and torture, and their impact on people, infrastructures and objects. Photography will be given predominance as a medium, due to the wider dissemination of photos in digital archives. At the same time, the cultural practices we will identify, in terms of interaction and consumption of the content and specifically the debates around it, often include or can be extended to video material.

Building on earlier work (see De Angelis 2020), we aim to analyse the various communities of practice that develop around these archives: a fluid constellation of groups of media activists, intellectuals, artists, journalists and image-makers (photographers and video-makers) who were involved, in different manners, in the uprising against the Syrian regime. As such, they are often the first-hand producers, or the users for propaganda aims, of the visual documentation of the horrors that the Syrian state, but also armed rebels and international actors, provoked in Syria since 2011. Through interviews and conversations with these actors, as well as a critical reading of the public debates (in different media fora) that regularly re-emerge around this archive, this chapter aims to map the various understandings of, and orientations towards, this archive, and think through the theoretical and conceptual corollaries of these positions, as well as their implications.

These orientations range from a complete rejection of this archive to its affirmation as an act of resistance against hegemonic and default practices that tend to dominate the field of vision and deactivate horror images as a tool to challenge the relationships of power at the base of the violence. In elucidating these positions, these actors depart from and leverage different anxieties and interpretive lenses with regard to the archive (corporal dignity versus memory), its social, economic and political conditions of production (the hegemonic gaze versus the lens of the 'unknown photographer') and circulation (control versus diasporicity). The tension between these two poles produces a continuous process of negotiation and contestation between different communities of practice – which we argue are essentially enacting the 'controversial archive' – as well as multifarious attempts at synthesis that we explore in the final part of this chapter.

In the following section we attempt to elaborate our understanding of Syria's 'controversial archive' and to ground it within an emerging field of scholarship on (digital) archives that reimagines them as a set of fluid and interlocking 'processes', rather than concrete 'objects'.

Understanding the Controversial Archive

Rather than indicating a corpus of indexed images, the concept of the 'controversial archive' refers to social and cultural practices surrounding images. Indeed, as we argue in this chapter, it is these practices that constantly negotiate which images have the necessary legitimacy to be included in the corpus or be rejected.

These practices, which ultimately shape the controversial archive, constitute a limpid example of what Azoulay calls an 'archival contract' (Azoulay 2017). In analysing this, it is paramount to put the accent on the opposition – as

Azoulay does – between, on the one hand, the logics of traditional archives, which are regulated by 'sentries' and an above-bottom prefixed system, and, on the other hand, the archive conceived as an act of sharing the world with others. In this sense, enacted archival work embodies an act of resistance against the dominant field of vision imposed on them by, among the others, blockbuster social media, international media, local armed actors, and in general the dominant logics that pervades the media field.

Thus, the fact that its borders and logics are subject to a negotiation constantly enacted by its users makes the corpus of images intrinsically and permanently 'controversial' and never fixed.

It is controversial most importantly because the very opportunity of their public disclosure is an object of debate among the core communities that produce and disseminate them. Indeed, some members of the Syrian communities whose work is directly related to these images are of the opinion that they should be archived only for forensic reasons. This points of course to a completely different concept of archive (restricted, not interactive, linear, and so on).

Ali Atassi, a documentary director and cinema expert, criticises the current status of horror images and argues that a 'revolutionary archive' should be created. At the same time, he acknowledges that the making of a unitary archive would intrinsically negate the plurality and diversity that generated it. He concludes that 'the most meaningful step towards an archive would be to define the professional and legal regulations of the collection of such an archive, and to define the themes and sections under which the archive will be indexed' (Atassi 2020: 66). While Atassi considers this only as a first step towards an archive, we maintain that the process itself, through which these rules, categorisations, themes and sections are continually defined and negotiated, already constitutes an archive, albeit never fully realised in its more familiar forms.

A second element that makes this material 'controversial' relates to the technological infrastructure that enables its storage and circulation. Being situated mainly on commercial social media platforms such as Facebook and YouTube, as in the case of the bulk of these images and videos, makes its identification as an archive suspect and open to challenge. Indeed, the fragility of archiving on social media platforms, which constantly erase content or make it unavailable out of ethical reasons, is considered as a reason to create dedicated archives on separate servers (Al Khatib 2020).

Because of the ethically controversial nature of the images, and the socio-technical processes that characterise the practices around them, the 'controversial archive' transgresses many normative and long-held beliefs about what constitutes an archive. In this sense, we need to elaborate the 'controversial', on a conceptual level, as the result of the archive's intersection of a number of different articulations – as a particularly poignant example of a decentred, displaced photographic archive. We will unpack this in the following section.

First, Syrian images of horror constitute what Featherstone (2006) calls a '*decentred* digital archive', blurring the separateness between archive and daily life and privileging processual dynamics and fluidity. The fluidity primarily challenges the linear temporality of archives, which had hitherto fixed them largely in historical time. The simultaneity of the shaping, retrieval and contestation of such digital archives operates contemporaneously in both current and historical time (Moss and Thomas 2017), or as Featherstone put it, 'life increasingly becomes lived in the shadow of the archive' (Featherstone 2006: 591).

Second, they are also a form of a '*displaced* archive' which is largely unmoored from its site of creation and whose provenance and meaning are difficult to ascertain (Lowry 2019). Indeed, Syria's horror images can be seen as a particularly intense example of how such archives are (literally as well as metaphorically) violently decontextualised and always in need of recontextualisation. The de-centredness and displacement of Syria's 'controversial archive' should not be seen simply in relation to its digital nature, but also as overlaying its social and political context of production which is marked by fragmentation, dislocation and displacement of Syrian individuals, communities and their cultural artifacts (amongst which is this archive).

The articulation of de-centredness and displacement creates a condition of deep instability and anxiety (about memory, place and identity) in a process not unlike that of *diasporicity* (Bakare-Yusuf 2008). But diasporicity as a metaphor also opens up the possibilities of an affirmative, transgressive and hybrid relationship that is made possible through the temporal and spatial fluidity of this archive. Indeed, the social practices and contestations that make this an archive reflect the tension between these anxieties and possibilities.

Third, the photographic nature of this archive provides another articulation that both mediates the controversy (that is, mediating the logics of de-centredness and displacement and their articulation), as well as injecting another set of problematics into the mix.

McQuire's discussion of digital photography sheds light on one aspect of how photography articulates with the decentred archive: as imaging technologies have become more widely distributed, as the cost of image capture and circulation has fallen in line with other forms of information processing and as new means of archiving have developed, the cumulative result has been the emergence of a different set of questions around photographic practices and protocols. In this context, the main questions brought about by the advent of digital photography are less about, as it was thought before, the 'demise of referentiality' or the 'loss of evidentiary value', but rather in relation to how photography (and images in general) interacts and is integrated in the network milieu (McQuire 2013: 224).

Moreover, on another level, the displacement of the archive into the network can be seen to offer both opportunities and challenges (see De Angelis and Badran 2021, for the dual nature of networks). Indeed, as Siegenthaler and Bublatzky point out in the case of diasporic and migratory archives, while blockbuster platforms reflect 'hegemonic archives of images' establishing and feeding global structures of economic and cultural domination, they also offer marginalised communities new forms of agencies (Siegenthaler and Bublatzky 2021: 284).

We maintain that it is the constant cultural negotiation activated around the production and circulation of this visual material that makes it an archive, as it enables the communities using it to identify shared, albeit fluid and never fixed, borders, classifications and practices of use of the involved images. This involves a constant negotiation between the decentredness, displacement and photographic understandings of the controversial archive, and the anxieties and possibilities these give rise to.

In the end, this negotiation is about providing legitimacy to the circulating images, among specific communities of practice. Here we assume Mexal's idea that 'the desire for the archive is less a desire for authorial/authoritarian power, than it is for authorial legitimacy' (Mexal 2007: 125).

The archive contract, says Azoulay, 'implies the citizens' right to share not only what is stored in the archive but also have a right to be involved in producing and depositing material in the archive. They all take part in producing and sharing images, knowing that the images one produces always exceed one's capacity to understand their content and meaning, that the interpretation of images is a task that calls for multiple collaborations, and that each of one's images may one day emerge – usually by or through the gaze of others – as 'the missing image' (Azoulay 2012).

Looked at through this prism, the controversial archive as it was created by specific Syrian communities is particularly fluid as it does not have specific boundaries, sentries or fixed categorisation. It is not owned by one specific actor. Rather, as with migrant archives, it is 'situated within this tension and potential of being sighted or not, of being acknowledged as sites of experience and knowledge or not, and of representing societies and communities or not' (Siegenthaler and Bublatzky 2021: 286).

In this sense, through shaping and reshaping the controversial archive, we find acts that oblige us to see the archive in its performance and constant unmaking and remaking. Rethinking Derrida's concept of 'archive fever', Azoulay sees it rather as

> the claim to revolutionize the archive, to a different understanding of the documents it holds, of its supposed purpose, of the right to see them and act accordingly, the claim to the forms and ways of categorizing them, presenting and using them. (Azoulay 2012)

After 2011, the very act of creating the archive became an act of resistance. This act of resistance, however, is not primarily against those who want to control the archive. Indeed, we see three orders – in increasing order of ambiguity and instability – on which this act of resistance can be interpreted. On a first and most basic level, it can be seen as resistance against the imperative of the regime and other armed actors responsible for the enactment of unspeakable violence, which aim at the total erasure of visual documentation of that violence (Della Ratta 2017). On a second level, it can be interpreted as resistance to the specific governmentality of horror instituted by the Syrian regime which, according to Salwa Ismail, uses the 'massacre-as-performance' (the staging and narrativisation of such horrors) to produce abjectified political subjects (see Ismail 2018: Chapter 5). Already, here, the transgressive potential of this resistance is always in danger of entering that narrative circuit rather than shorting it. On a third level, this resistance acts against the tendency of the dominant field of vision to assert its power over the representation of horror. In this last case, there is not a single actor trying to do so (as it is Israel in the cases described by Azoulay), but rather a series of actors with their own, sometimes even conflicting, interests. As we mentioned, blockbuster social media, as the main depositary of this digital content, are at the same time one of the actors imposing a certain field of vision.

These different orders on which the archive is performed as an act of resistance are reflected in the multitude of contestations over the place and meaning of this liquid deposit of images and in the arguments put forth by different actors. The struggle over the iconisation of images and the reduction of photographed people to prefixed categories such as 'victims', 'terrorists', 'fighters', 'jihadists', 'refugees', and so on, can be seen to operate in dialogue with all three orders above.

Logics and Agents behind the Controversial Archive

In light of the above, we examine here the controversial archive as an ongoing negotiation among different Syrian communities and individuals. This negotiation can assume the form of public or private, online or offline, discussions, journalistic and academic articles, and artworks, as well as collective and individual practices (and mobilisations) related to how to approach images of horror in Syria.

This negotiation invests primarily simpler questions related to the personal relationship to a single image and which positioning to assume towards it: should I take this image and why? Should I look at it or not, and how? Should I share it or not? If yes, how to present and frame it? How to use it?

At other times, the debate involves deeper, more theoretical and elaborated questions about the practices around the images, their effects on single individuals and/or international audiences, and how possible future archives should look.

Some communities of practice and single individuals tend to play a central role in these discussions, and thus in creating the controversial archive: Syrian image-makers such as photographers and video-makers, media activists, journalists, artists, intellectuals and, in general, micro-celebrities who have a substantial number of followers on social media. We refer here to communities and individuals who actively participated, or identified themselves, with the 2011 protest movement against the Syrian regime. This is not to say that other types of actors, such as international journalists or Western activists, do not have access to these images and they are not also involved in determining their status. However, their level of engagement with them, and their impact on how they are stored and presented, belongs to a different logic. Moreover, it is more difficult to set any kind of boundary to their relationship with these images.

Here it is important to make a small digression to discuss the relationship of pro-regime actors (and later other violent groups, such as ISIS) to this archive. This is a complex and contradictory relationship, but one that contributes to shaping it in a passive/negative sense. For the most part, much of this photographic archive (and the meanings ascribed to it) are discarded by these publics and actors as mere propaganda or completely manufactured. On the other hand, we should recognise that to a small (but influential) degree, they are themselves generative of this archive as (mostly unintentional) authors themselves. This can be seen in some of the most gruesome videos and photos of horror that are part of this archive, and which were recorded by the perpetrators themselves. Moreover, the archive is also (implicitly) used by regime-loyal image-makers – albeit through inversion and de-contextualisation – to promote their narrative of the conflict (see Abboud 2023).

These practices are analytically outside the scope of the generative negotiation that we propose as the heart of the 'controversial archive', but their influence can be felt in the arguments brought to bear by different oppositional actors in performing the archive.

Indeed, there is a widely spread idea among Syrians participating in the uprising that the regime was the first actor to disseminate violent images, and often with the perpetrators presenting clear sectarian identification traits, in order to escalate the violence (O. al-Muqdad, personal communication, April 2018).

What makes the controversial archive possible is the recognition, among certain specific communities, that there is a corpus of images (horror images produced in the Syrian context after 2011) that can be separated from other images and thus debated as such. This means also that the controversial archive is a historically situated phenomenon, which can be compared, but not extended, to other times and places.

This chapter builds on and continues earlier work (see De Angelis 2020), engaging Syrian photographers and media activists in conversations about their relationship with horror images and their consideration of the media, political and social environment in which such images are immersed. Some photographers are well known and worked or work for international news agencies: Mohamed Abdullah, Hosan Katan and Muzaffar Salman. Others are experienced photographers and video-makers: Maya Abyad, Orwa al-Muqdad and Rafat al-Zakout. Others are less known but have produced many of the images that have come out of Syria in the last few years: Abd al-Kader Habak, Adham al-Hussein, Mohamed Abo Kasem, Amer al-Mouhibani and Yahia Alrejjo. Some interviewees, mainly because they still live in Syria, asked that their names not be revealed. Moreover, these conversations were expanded to include artists whose work and artistic reflection is often based on the use of horror images, such as Khaled Barakeh and Diala Brisly, and people who are involved in the creation of specific archives, such as Hadi Al Khatib. Finally, the analysis also incorporates a number of articles, essays or posts that discuss explicitly the status and the practices around violent images in Syria.

Through these encounters, it emerges that the relationship with the controversial archive is first of all a personal matter.

Each individual has a personal approach to images depending on his or her past experiences, current living conditions and psychological state. The relationship changes not only from individual to individual, but also according to different phases in a single individual's life. Even during the same day, some Syrian photographers point out, there are moments when you feel you can look at the horror, and there are others when you just cannot.

At the same time, distinct patterns shared by different groups can be identified. Around the corpus of images different interpretive communities emerge: fluid groups of individuals who constantly discuss the status of horror images and the practices surrounding them. The negotiation produces shared values and behaviours, even if a definitive agreement can never be achieved. All these communities are quite fluid, and contacts between single individuals enable a continuous exchange between them. In fact, they embody diverse stances towards the images that can often coexist within one single individual.

As mentioned above, this discussion (within one individual and among multiple ones) is aimed primarily at granting (or the opposite: at denying) legitimacy to horror images, or to the practices and the gazing context surrounding them. A photo can be utterly refused as it is, but can be accepted or rejected depending on the context in which it is presented, or how it is presented, by whom, and for which purposes.

In this context, a specific tension has emerged in the last few years in relation to the corpus of images of horror. At one extreme, we find image-savvy communities composed of individuals who carry a more critical approach to images and who mostly live today outside of the country. They are able to follow the entire cycle of life of the images and their effects on different publics. These people are generally over thirty years old and have lengthier experience in cultural production. At the other end of the spectrum, we find groups of younger activists and citizen journalists who live(d) inside the country and who produce(d) most of the material that constitutes the controversial archive. We will refer to these groups as the 'unknown photographers', as their names are usually lesser known or even completely lost in the networks and the flows of information.

Other communities tend to aggregate around specific approaches to the images: journalists, cinema directors, media activists, civil society members – all these groups tend to approach the archive through their professional lenses, but also their own ethics and priorities. This does not mean that they need to share the same stance towards images and, as we already mentioned, the borders between the communities are blurred and the discussions can cross different professional languages and perspectives. In fact, often the debate concerns exactly this element, as the controversial nature of the archive stems also from the different ways horror images can be produced and used. Stefan Tarnowski, for example, describes how horror images can be seen through different, often conflicting, approaches: as evidence, as forms of expression, or as a commodity (Tarnowski 2017).

In the following sections we examine these three main nodes of interpretive communities. In the interplay between these three, we argue, we can locate the core of the performance of the controversial archive.

The Controversial Archive Should Not Exist

The shaping of the controversial archive begins with questioning its own existence as a series of images to which everyone should have access. This position is grounded first of all in the consideration that visual documentation failed, as it was not able to mobilise the expected local and international support, whether in terms of solidarity or as direct military support. This failure made the costs of this abundant, unregulated and unprofessional production of images even more unbearable, particularly in the denial for the photographed people of the rights to their own images. Film collectives such as Abounaddara, documentary producers such as Ali Atassi, and media activists such as Razan Ghazzawi, articulate this rejection of the exhibition of victims' bodies and suffering on social media.

In the aftermath of the chemical attacks against Khan Shaikhoun, when images of dying children were circulating on social media, Razan Ghazzawi, a prominent feminist and dissident activist, for example wrote on her Facebook profile on 7 April 2017: 'Disseminating images of naked children's bodies on social media as means of documentation does not help restore their humanity killed by Assad.'

The archive, seen mainly through its diffuse mediation, is often critiqued as a product of a colonialist and Orientalist gaze. In one statement, entitled 'We are not artists', the film collective Abounaddara contrasted the ubiquity of undignified Syrian corpses functioning as background images to commentators talking of 'religions and sects, of geopolitics and The Thousands and One Nights', with the circumspect, careful and delicate treatment to images of victims of terrorist attacks in Europe and North America (Abounaddara 2017). As a displaced archive, the images, according to another viral post by Abounaddara, 'show a place out of time with only executioners and victims', where Syrian society appears to the world in the same register as that of animals at the slaughterhouse – the 'human slaughterhouse' according to Amnesty International (Abounaddara 2018).

Documentary producer and cultural critic Mohammad Ali Atassi echoes this sentiment:

> Unfortunately, the majority of the images that detail the torturing and defaming (*tashni'*) of Syrian bodies circulate in the Western world, where they are

consumed without any accountability . . . How and why do we accept and contribute willingly to being treated in that world as second-degree citizens?

Atassi asks poignantly:

> How can we persuade a mother or a sister or a wife, or a son, that someone has the right to publish the image of their tortured son or his corpse? How do we allow ourselves to do this, in the name of which right, according to which human principle, heavenly legitimacy, legislation, logic, or art? (Atassi 2015)

The displaced and decentred archive of Syria's horror images according to these critics is not only subservient to this hegemonic gaze, but actively contributes to it by 'flooding the market of vision with pictures and attracting little or no attention'. While the aim should be to 'break this system of watching', through 'a critical presentation that aims at making accountable the pre-existent meanings of the predominant system of watching' (al-Sayyid 2015).

Some authors, however, tend to bring the criticism to another level, as they contest the very possibility that visual documentation can function in the contemporary communication system. Lebanese literary scholar and critic Zeina Halabi, for example, describes that, during the Arab uprising

> the photographs and footage are there but the truth is not. Although lenses captured these tragedies, the narrative surrounding them was constantly challenged, undermined, or erased. Hegemonic narratives continue to tell us that the tragedies we have seen never really took place, that what we have seen is not real. Here, melancholic affect does not feed on an absent archive – for the archive is there, so haunting in its tragedy – but rather on a tragic experience that is not validated. (Halabi 2017)

These considerations echo those of photographers and authors who criticise the effects of horror images on audiences. As art critic John Berger says: 'Any response to that photographed moment is bound to be felt as inadequate' and, as a result, 'the picture becomes evidence of the general human condition. It accuses nobody and everybody' (Berger 2013: 32–3).

The Controversial Archive as a Social Contract

The rejection of the controversial archive, and especially the questioning of the public exposure of Syrian suffering, is part of the archival work itself. It is not a complete rejection of the images, but rather of the ways they are circulated, presented and experienced. The discussion about the archive is therefore also a discussion around the status of the image, and specifically violent images, in the contemporary digital media ecosystem. This cultural negotiation around the archive can be interpreted through the framework of the social contract of photography as developed by Ariela Azoulay (2012).

Azoulay describes the civil contract of photography as a social fiction: a tacit agreement that is never formally set up. It primarily embroils the participants involved in the act of photographing (the photographer and the photographed) as well as the public (the spectator). In her view, the photos can be a powerful, and often the only, tool to express the flawed, non-existent or temporarily suspended nature of the photographed persons' citizenship. The picture can rehabilitate a negated citizenship and testify to the violations perpetrated by human violence or natural disasters against it. It exposes how some citizens are not granted the same rights as others. In the community of photography, everyone is a citizen, independent from state institutions, gender, origin or class.

However, the civil contract of photography requires that a certain field of vision be set up. Azoulay gives the act of staring at the picture a great responsibility in this process. The spectator has to take on a mode of 'cinematic watching': a gaze that includes an intention to investigate beyond the borders of the single frame, and to reconstruct the act of photography. The spectator does not look briefly at the photo, only to identify the icons represented in it. The photo has to be stared at longer, as if it was a film.

A single picture is only 'a projective surface that never discloses anything in itself'. It is a statement among other statements and its content is always partial and obscure. Approaching the photo through cinematic watching implies not reducing it only to what is immediately visible within the frame. Rather, the picture has to be treated as a document that in the first place testifies to the immanent encounter between the photographer and the photographed person. In this sense, a sort of archaeology of images has to be established. As Georges Didi-Huberman (2012) does with four photos taken by the *Sonderkommando* of Auschwitz in his book *Images in Spite of All*, the spectator has to use the photo as a fragment to reconstruct the act of photography, including the positioning of the photographer.

Cinematic watching enables the avoidance of an 'identificatory gaze', reducing the photographed persons to a prefixed meaning that ruling systems of vision try to impose. The photo has to be approached critically, as a space through which new political relations can be constantly renegotiated and the grievances of the photographed person rightly addressed. The criticism towards the horror images in the Syrian context can be therefore interpreted as a criticism of the hegemonic field of vision that surrounds them and prevents the fulfilment of the social contract of photography between image-makers, photographed people and the public.

It is also because of the rupture of the social contract of photography of horror images in Syria that they lose legitimacy and the archive is sometimes completely rejected and stays controversial. At the same time, the controversy is what enables Syrian communities to discuss the reasons behind this failure and re-enact practices that can restore the social contract, give back legitimacy to the images and ultimately transform the scattered corpus of images in an archive.

Capturing Images 'in spite of all'

The critiques outlined above by communities of image-savvy individuals of the current ecosystem surrounding the images, its hegemonic field of vision and the negative effects these have on the photographed victims, the image-makers and the public, pose important questions and can offer creative ways forward. However, their refusal to see these images as a legitimate form of archival work can also be seen as paradoxical. Indeed, it is the very presence of these images that makes this discussion (and these critiques) possible in the first place. As Ariela Azoulay rightly describes, when issues such as rape remain invisible, it is more difficult to debate about the way they are represented and to therefore activate remedies.

This passage illustrates clearly the point we are making here:

> The photographs are part of the tools that enable us to rehabilitate the *sensus communis* and construct around it a common community of negotiation, in

the framework of which we are able to agree on the boundaries of disagreement. When rape images lie outside the sphere of discussion, are removed
from it suddenly or in incisive fashion, we are completely unable to manufacture the boundaries of our agreement or disagreement in regard to them, and
we are prevented from negotiating over turning at least some of them into
emergency claim. (Azoulay 2012: 261)

In other words, horror images circulating on social media, albeit highly problematic, constitute a corpus necessary for the activation of the negotiation.
Without their presence, even their rejection would not function as a statement aimed at denouncing and readjusting the flaws of the wider field of
vision. Horror in Syria would just remain invisible.

At the same time, their complete rejection is also part of a logic that tends
to privilege some of the actors of the photographic acts (the photographed
people, the public) against others (the photographer and the image-maker).

As Syrian leftist intellectual Yassin al-Haj Salih writes: 'The images are there;
somewhere; someone took them, perhaps gratefully, sometimes at his own risk;
and some people saw them. Were they just snooping at something forbidden, if
preventing their exposure is the right thing to do?' (al-Haj Salih 2015).

As previously mentioned, most of the first producers of images during
the Syrian war are young men and women, often at their first experience. We
will call them the 'unknown photographers' as many of them are not well
known, or they want to remain anonymous (as was the case with some of our
interviewees). What is more important, their images are those which mostly
circulate, without names or title, or journalistic context, on social media,
making these images so controversial.

When asked about the criticism that some other Syrians throw at their
work, the reaction is always one of astonishment. The positioning of the
unknown photographers brings another perspective into the negotiation of
the controversial archive. As we will see, reintegrating this perspective within
the discussion about the images is a crucial part in the shaping of the controversial archive and to re-establish a more legitimate relationship between the
photographer, the victim and the public.

In the interviews with the photographers, the act of photography emerges
as desperate and immediate. For them, this instant is the only way to create a

memory of the victims against attempts at erasing them from history and the world. The conditions of photography are often extremely dangerous. Planes often come back to bomb the same site a short while later, in order to prevent both relief operations and documentation. Cameras are often a primary target for snipers. Many photographers have died while they were documenting, and many had been injured several times.

Under these conditions, the relationship the photographer establishes with the photographed is almost inevitably very problematic, and cannot be compared with other, much more controlled, disaster situations in the West, for example in the aftermath of a terrorist attack. In this context, the photographic act becomes the last resource against the danger of oblivion.

Indeed, if the photographic act can be seen as an act of violence, as it is imposed on the photographed person, the photographers do not have a choice: in front of an injustice or an act of brutality, they must record the moment.

Here we can clearly identify the deepest impulse that drives any other archive building: the need to retain memory. As Saeed Al Batal, a documentary maker, writes:

> The camera, as it films, mirrors the plane: it is the exact opposite. The camera strives to protect, clinging on to every reflected shaft of light in order to preserve it forever, while the plane seeks to obliterate everything, to wipe out every memory and the keys to that memory, even smell itself. (Al Batal 2015)

Similarly, when film director Orwa al-Muqdad reflects on taking images of the victims after the bombings, he equates it with the dignity of 'a ritual that replaces the burying of the dead', in contrast to the 'anonymous death' as the deepest indignity imparted on these victims by the regime. The camera in this instance, according to al-Muqdad, is transformed into the place of mourning, the 'ritual through which the victims' beloved want to give meaning so that the dead did not die unknown' (al-Muqdad 2014). The diasporicity of a decentred and displaced archive, rather than being seen as a danger to collective memory, becomes the answer to that anxiety and offering the potential to resist oblivion.

The desperate need to record the event and the criticism towards the digital archives that result from it create what seems to be an unsolvable dilemma.

Maya Abyad, a photojournalist, imagines this tension through a dialogue between two persons:

> The first one says: 'This is not acceptable. Those people are not giving their consent to publish those images with their faces clearly visible . . . Those images and shares are not legal. Rights are not a point of view'. The other argues that without images, the victims would remain but numbers, without moving hearts and minds in the international community. Moreover, pretending to have a lucid consent of the victims or their relatives in a war situation is just impossible and the result would be an invisible conflict. (private message, sent on 16 April 2018)

Re-establishing the Archival Contract

Other individuals and communities appear to mediate between a total rejection of the current status of horror images, and the need to accept and interact with them.

These more nuanced positions are important as they, while they include some criticism of the general field of vision, they also propose in a more practical way different practices of production and presentation of images, or they recycle them in ways that counter the hegemonic flaws of the dominant field. In this sense, they operate a reappropriation and reactivation of those images, and in so doing they are directly involved in an archival work that concretely constitutes the material of the controversial archive.

Some of these actors are photographers who worked in Syria for international news agencies. As such, they have a professional background and an experience on the ground that put them in a privileged position when it comes to mediating between the desperate act of the unknown photographers and the rejection of their images.

Muzaffar Salman, a photographer with a long experience with Reuters, describes his relationship with these images saying that:

> I know that those images are not effective in relation to the West, but my relation with them is not to think about the victims: I think about the photographer, who sees these images each day. He shares this with me so that I can see it. He does not feel the violence [of the images]. So, I developed another kind of empathy: the empathy towards those who see this violence every day, and do not perceive the violence anymore. (M. Salman, personal communication, April 2018)

Salman's approach to the images is particularly relevant as it reflects the need, as described by Azoulay, of reintegrating the photographer into the frame of the photo (in which, of course, she/he does not appear).

We have to remind ourselves that the image does not describe 'what is there', but rather a specific event (the photographic act) which involves the photographed person and the photographer. The photo is just a statement of a series of statements that can help us to arrive to understand 'what was there' (see, Azoulay 2012: 307ff.). The main problem of horror images produced in Syria is that they circulate on social media as if they were 'orphan' (De Angelis 2020), without any reference. We often do not know who took them, why, when, and who are the photographed people nor what is their background story. Omitting the photographer from the frame, therefore, means to absolve the public from watching the photo as a specific event. The photo, deprived of its contextual information, pushes the public to read it through preconceived identifications. In this way, the photographed people, as denounced by Abounaddara, Atassi and others, become ghosts, icons of prefixed categories such as 'victims' and 'refugees', on which the photo imposes only another violence.

Reinstating the photographer into the frame involves a conscious and radical change of approach to the images of horror. While it should be acknowledged that the civil contract of photography is globally hindered by a ruling field of vision, there is also an individual moral responsibility when it comes to establishing a different relationship with the photo. As Maya Abyad points out:

> I look at them because I think it is the bare minimum responsibility we have to undertake. We are not being subjected to the same level of violence. And we are hiding way too much in our bubble if we refuse even to see it. (M. Abyad, personal communication, April 2018)

What Salman and Abyad suggest is that the single individual, and specifically a Syrian, has the responsibility to set up a cinematic watching, in spite of the wider field of vision.

Bringing the responsibility to the viewers and opening to discuss different practices in relation to the photos, means to accept that the existing corpus of horror images can be constantly translated into an archive, if certain conditions are satisfied.

In his series 'The Untitled Images', Syrian artist Khaled Barakeh, for example, takes 'orphan' horror images which contain scenes of loss such as people holding their wounded or dead dear ones in their hands. The victims, however, are erased, and appear as white, blank human shapes. Barakeh writes:

> The act of erasure is, in fact, a protective one: the absence of the bodies makes them more present. The real-time victims are removed and become human silhouettes – they become a symbol of any victim, anywhere in the world, at any given time. Viewers are allowed to identify themselves with a universal feeling of loss and pain, not this specific one that they believe themselves to be far away from. (Barakeh 2018: 143)

In this case, the victim does not become a symbol of a prefixed category that the dominant field of vision already has packaged as a cultural commodity. Rather, the victim is reframed, through its apparent erasure, as a universal one. The blank spot forces the reviewer to stop and reflect on that void and its meaning for the people in the photo, even if they remain unknown.

Syrian artist Diala Brisly also uses photos of horror as inspiration for her paintings. She picks up on Facebook photos taken by non-professional photographers, mainly through mobile phones. Later, she translates these photos into illustrations. She changes little details, giving salience to others. As with Barakeh's work, the artistic reworking on the photos activates another relationship between the represented subjects and the public. The victims cannot be trivialised anymore into mere symbols of human suffering. Brisly suggests through her drawing some possible readings of the scene, on which the spectator is forced to indulge. In so doing, she remediates the role of the photographer, she adds another layer to it. Through her artistic work, the photographer remains unknown, but her framing of the photo is imposed to the viewer, instead of the framing of those of the field of vision (this is just another victim of war).

These cases show how violent images are reframed and presented in a different way, in order to restore a social contract between the photographer, the photographed and the public. These processes, and the discussions around the practices, enable Syrian communities to reappropriate themselves of the images, giving them legitimacy, and use them for the purposes of individual and collective narratives that the dominant field of vision otherwise negates.

References

Abboud, S. (2023), 'Narrating Crisis Through the Loyalist Witness: Victims and Perpetrators in Joud Said's *Matr Homs* and *Darb al-Sama*', *Middle East Journal of Culture and Communication*, 16: 1, 1–19, DOI: <https://doi.org/10.1163/18739865-tat00003>.

Abounaddara (2017), 'Dignity Has Never Been Photographed', *Documenta 14*, 24 March, <http://www.documenta14.de/en/notes-and-works/15348/dignity-has-never-been-photographed> (last accessed 14 July 2022).

Abounaddara (2018), 'Syrie, la révolte des "animaux"', *Libération*, 4 March, <https://www.liberation.fr/debats/2018/03/04/syrie-la-revolte-des-animaux_1633754/> (last accessed 14 July 2022).

Al Batal, S. (2015), 'A Cigarette, and My Anti-aircraft Camera', *Bidayyat*, 27 April, <http://bidayyat.org/opinions_article.php?id=124> (last accessed 14 July 2022).

Al-Haj Salih, Y. (2015), 'Tahdiq fi wajih al-fazi'', *Al-Jumhuriya*, 29 May, <https://www.aljumhuriya.net/ar/33487> (last accessed 14 July 2022).

Al Khatib, H. (2020), 'Corporations Erasing History: The Case of the Syrian Archive', in D. Della Ratta, K. Dickinson and S. Haugbolle (eds), *The Arab Archive: Mediated Memories and Digital Flows*, Amsterdam: Institute of Network Cultures, pp. 89–98.

Al-Muqdad, O. (2014), 'Dafn al-mawta bil swar', *Bidayyat*, 28 February, <http://bidayyat.org/ar/opinions_article.php?id=70#.WtM2cNNuaRt> (last accessed 14 July 2022).

Al-Sayyid, A. (2015), 'Surat al-dahiya wa karamat al-dahiya', *Al-Jumhuriya*, 20 July, <https://www.aljumhuriya.net/ar/33651> (last accessed 14 July 2022).

Atassi, M. A. (2015), 'al-Karama fi hudur al-faza'a', *Al-Jumhuriya*, 2 June, <https://www.aljumhuriya.net/ar/33499> (last accessed 14 July 2022).

Atassi, M. A. (2020), 'The Digital Syrian Archive betweeen Vidoes and Documentary Cinema', in D. Della Ratta, K. Dickinson and S. Haugbolle (eds), *The Arab Archive: Mediated Memories and Digital Flows*, Amsterdam: Institute of Network Cultures, pp. 60–8.

Azoulay, A. (2012), *The Civil Contract of Photography*, New York: Zone Books.

Azoulay, A. (2017), 'Archive', *Political Concepts*, 1, <http://www.politicalconcepts.org/archive-ariella-azoulay/> (last accessed 14 July 2022).

Bakare-Yusuf, B. (2008), 'Rethinking Diasporicity: Embodiment, Emotion, and the Displaced Origin', *African and Black Diaspora: An International Journal*, 1: 2, 147–58, DOI: <https://doi.org/10.1080/17528630802224056>.

Barakeh, K. (2018), 'The Untitled Images (2014)', *Cinema Journal*, 57: 4, 142–6.

Berger, J. (2013), *Understanding a Photograph*, London: Penguin Classics.

Chaise, C. (2018), 'Behind AFP's Syria Coverage', *AFP*, 13 March, <https://correspondent.afp.com/behind-afps-syria-coverage> (last accessed 14 July 2022).

De Angelis, E. (2020), 'The Controversial Archive: Negotiating Horror Images in Syria', in D. Della Ratta, K. Dickinson and S. Haugbolle (eds), *The Arab Archive: Mediated Memories and Digital Flows*, Amsterdam: Institute of Network Cultures, pp. 69–90.

De Angelis, E. and Y. Badran (2021), 'Social Media and Contentious Politics: Revisiting the Debate a Decade after the Beginning of the Arab Uprisings', in A. Salvatore, S. Hanafi and K. Obuse (eds), *The Oxford Handbook of the Sociology of the Middle East*, Oxford: Oxford University Press, DOI: <https://doi.org/10.1093/oxfordhb/9780190087470.013.53>.

Della Ratta, D. (2017), 'The Unbearable Lightness of the Image: Unfinished Thoughts on Filming in Contemporary Syria', *Middle East Journal of Culture and Communication*, 10: 2–3, 109–32.

Della Ratta, D. (2018), *Shooting a Revolution: Visual Media and Warfare in Syria*, London: Pluto Press.

Didi-Huberman, G. (2012), *Images in Spite of All: Four Photographs from Auschwitz*, Chicago: University of Chicago Press.

Elias, C. (2017), 'Emergency Cinema and the Dignified Image: Cell Phone Activism and Filmmaking in Syria', *Film Quarterly*, 71: 1, 18–31, DOI: <https://doi.org/10.1525/fq.2017.71.1.18>.

Elias, C. and Z. Omareen (2014), 'Syria's Imperfect Cinema', in M. Halasa, Z. Omareen and N. Mahfoud (eds), *Syria Speaks: Art and Culture from the Frontline*, London: Saqi Books, pp. 257–68.

Featherstone, M. (2006), 'Archive', *Theory, Culture & Society*, 23: 2–3, 591–6.

Halabi, Z. (2017), 'The Missing Archive of Loss', *Bidayyat*, 28 April, <http://bidayyat.org/opinions_article.php?id=166> (last accessed 14 July 2022).

Ismail, S. (2018), *The Rule of Violence: Subjectivity, Memory and Government in Syria*, Cambridge: Cambridge University Press.

Lowry, J. (2019), '"Displaced archives": Proposing a Research Agenda', *Archival Science*, 19: 4, 349–358, DOI: <https://doi.org/10.1007/s10502-019-09326-8>.

McQuire, S. (2013), 'Photography's Afterlife: Documentary Images and the Operational Archive', *Journal of Material Culture*, 18: 3, 223–41, DOI: <https://doi.org/10.1177/1359183513489930>.

Mexal, S. J. (2007), 'Material Knowledge: Democracy and the Digital Archive', *English Language Notes*, 45: 1, 123–35, DOI: <https://doi.org/10.1215/00138282-45.1.123>.

Moss, M. and D. Thomas (2017), 'Overlapping Temporalities – the Judge, the Historian and the Citizen', *Archives: The Journal of the British Records Association*, 52: 134, 51–67, DOI: <https://doi.org/10.3828/archives.2017.4>.

Mroué, R., Z. Nawfal and C. Martin (2012), 'The Pixelated Revolution', *TDR/ The Drama Review*, 56: 3 (215), 18–35, DOI: <https://doi.org/10.1162/ DRAM_a_00186>.

Siegenthaler, F. and C. Bublatzky (2021), '(Un)Sighted Archives of Migration – Spaces of Encounter and Resistance: An Introduction', *Visual Anthropology*, 34: 4, 283–95.

Tarnowski, S. (2017), 'What Have We Been Watching?', *Bidayyat*, 5 May, <http:// bidayyat.org/opinions_article.php?id=167> (last accessed 14 July 2022).

16

CRITICAL SPECTATORSHIP, VIOLENT CARE

Kevin B. Lee

You are in a giant white room. You have no memory of how you got here, but you sense that this place is not yours. Nothing around you is familiar. All that seems to belong to you is your look. So you look.

You see people walking slowly around you, looking at all that is around you. Filling the center of the room is a large array of publications and images: eighteenth-century posters of Arabs beheading colonial explorers; twenty-first-century Islamist militants presented with menacing dark faces on Western news magazines, and other materials representing how Arabs and Muslims have been depicted in Western printed media. These images face you. They define your space.

Absorbed by these images, the people walk among them as if in a trance. They don't seem to notice you. You notice there is glass encasing you, as if rendering you invisible to them. In the glass, you see yourself reflected. You see that you are a head without a body. You don't resemble any of the images around you. You look like a relic made of stone, except your surface texture seems closer to plastic. You look like an object that one would expect to find in a museum, which seems to be where you are. Maybe it is for this reason that no one pays attention to you.

There are those who try to make you seen. One person leads a group to you. She identifies you as a replica of a Medusa head from the South Ivan region of what is now Iraq. The original Medusa head was created 2000 years ago in the city of Hatra during the Parthian Empire. It watched over the ancient city until 2016, when ISIS militant fighters shot it to pieces and circulated its

Figure 16.1 Morehshin Allahyari, Material Speculation Dead Drops: Medusa Head in the Kunsthalle Mannheim exhibition MINDBOMBS.
Source: Photograph by Kevin B. Lee.

destruction as a viral video, causing a media sensation. Later that year, an artist named Morehshin Allahyari took that footage and used it as the basis to create a 3D model of you. The 3D model was then printed, and it became you. You are here to represent the triumph of artists over the violence of political extremism, and how the iconoclasm of ISIS can be countered.

Moments later, another person leads another group, and provides a more elaborate explanation for what you are doing here. He identifies you as Medusa, so that he can introduce the Medusa Effect: the condition of when a spectator is petrified by their own act of looking, just as in Greek mythological tales when those who saw Medusa would be petrified. This, he states, can also describe what happens to those who encounter terrorist violence in the media, when their gaze produces a state of paralysis. This thematic significance gives a justification for your presence among these more disturbing images.

You are a Medusa, but no one who looks at you is petrified. Quite the opposite, they don't seem disturbed by you in any way, compared to the more sensational images around you. Is it because your presence is too contained in abstract symbolism to register as real? Medusa was defeated when her face was reflected in Perseus' shield, separating her presence from its deadly power. It seems that your existence as a digitally mediated replica of a 2000 year old representation, now hermetically sealed not only in glass, but by the academic attributions of curators and tour guides, has rendered you into a harmless reflection.

And now, is there a way for me to see you beyond my own reflections upon you, in order to behold your power?

I wrote the above text following an October 2021 visit to MINDBOMBS, an exhibition at the Kunsthalle Mannheim. The exhibition presented artworks relating to the history and political iconography of modern extremist violence, from the eighteenth-century French Revolution to contemporary leftist, right-wing and Islamist movements. In a German news radio interview, curator Sebastian Baden expressed his intentions for the exhibition: 'When it comes to political violence, we want to show that the complexities behind it are really multifaceted and you always have to illuminate different perspectives.' Baden elaborated that the exhibition played a uniquely pedagogical role in providing the public with a safe, curated environment to engage critically with extremist images. 'You learn to read in school, but looking at pictures is the job of the museum.'

The question of how to look at extremist media also motivated the production of *Bottled Songs 1–4* (2020), a series of videos that I co-authored with Chloé Galibert-Laîné, that was included in the exhibition. While it was an honour for our work to be included in such a bold curatorial proposition, for some time I had been harbouring doubts concerning a few of the ideological and methodological underpinnings of the project, which the presentation of our work in a museum context brought into view.

We initiated the *Bottled Songs* project in 2016 to employ a method of critical spectatorship towards ISIS propaganda videos. This method was derived from our shared background producing online video essays that reappropriate existing works of media to produce critical insights reflecting upon that same media. Having made video essays mostly on works of cinema, we sought to apply this form to reflect on the phenomenon of ISIS media that was dominating US and European media discourse at the time. At the start of the project, neither of us claimed expertise on ISIS or online extremist media. In a statement that accompanies the series, we account for our position: 'We wanted to dissect the aura around these videos, in the hope that exposing our own spectatorial mechanisms could help others make sense of their own responses to online media terror.'

Figure 16.2 Reconstructing the editing procedures of ISIS. Still from *Bottled Songs: Looking Into the Flames*, dir. Kevin B. Lee.
Source: Photograph by Kevin B. Lee.

Critical to this aim was our use of desktop documentary, a method of film-making in which the film takes place primarily within a computer screen. This method seemed especially suitable for documenting our online encounters with ISIS media as an Internet user without a professional research background in the material might experience. The ubiquity and familiarity of the desktop environment presents a new form of cinematic first-person perspective by linking the viewer's gaze with the author's desktop, leading the viewer through windows, files and other materials on the screen. This phenomenon, which we have elsewhere termed 'desktop subjectivity', immerses the viewer in a desktop space that normally is exclusively accessible to its owner; this sensation of privileged access which can create an intense spectatorial sensation of intimacy and disclosure. In *Bottled Songs*, the narration of subjective experience through the desktop is meant to produce a state of critical spectatorship, interrogating the ways that subjective experience is shaped through the desktop interface. As Galibert-Laîné has written:

> When I say 'I' in the video, it isn't so much about 'Chloé Galibert-Laîné' as a biographical entity as it is about whoever recognize[s] herself in that 'I'.

Adopting the first-person is a way to guide the viewer into thinking reflexively and critically about her own act of watching.[1]

However, over time we realised that our production of critical subjectivity afforded by the desktop documentary approach is problematised by the power relations encoded in desktop subjectivity. We tried to account for them in our statement accompanying *Bottled Songs 1–4*:

> As two Western researchers operating within an online vantage point . . . we are aware of the systemic privilege that enables our perspectives to be considered in the first place. We cannot speak for others affected by these media, but acknowledge that this material affects countless others deserving to be heard. Chief among them are those persons whose harm and suffering are depicted in these videos, which our work cannot possibly redeem.

To what extent were our first-person accounts of watching ISIS propaganda insufficiently addressing or failing to serve those who were most harmed by them? What bearing did our work have on those who had been directly and physically harmed by the violence of ISIS, or those who risked being harmed by the perpetuation of ISIS media and the negative associations it projects upon Muslim peoples and cultures?

These questions were vividly palpable during a tour of the MINDBOMBS exhibition, given to a conference of scholars on political extremism and media violence in the Islamic context, which I and most of the contributors to this volume attended. One of the scholars approached me, visibly disturbed, to tell me that he had watched a section of *Bottled Songs* that examined the social media and online traces of a young French ISIS militant. He informed me that he personally knew the militant's family and was deeply troubled that this video would perpetuate his identity as a militant. One moment that he found particularly disturbing was the appearance of his deceased body on a German right-wing website. We included this moment to show how the militant's image had become instrumentalised to fuel online hatred, but

---

[1] Available at <https://desistfilm.com/interview-chloe-galibert-laine/> (last accessed 16 February 2023).

the scholar's objections now made us reflect on another instrumentalisation taking place in our midst, in which we were implicated. This connected to another of his objections: that he was especially troubled to find these images in a museum, playing on a giant projection in a perpetual loop.

What violence is specifically attributable to a museum's production of visibility? The same video had been available online since 2017, where one of the militant's family members had seen and endorsed it as a just and empathetic representation of the militant. But upon learning of its placement in a museum, this family member expressed her objections to us; in respect to her wishes, we have withdrawn the video from further circulation in any context. The Internet, like a museum, is an archive, a site of preservation for future reference. To consider how a video that was available online for several years without causing objection became offensive as a looped projection in a museum is to consider the politics of the archive: the modes of visibility and status assigned to different contexts of archival access, what value (cultural, economic, ideological) is being produced through their activation, and who possesses agency in determining visibility and value.

What harm was our project unintentionally or inadvertently reinforcing or reproducing, despite, or even because of, our attempts to produce a critical engagement? Such questions arose in the course of making the videos. In the second video from *Bottled Songs*, *Looking Into the Flames*, I deconstruct an hour-long ISIS propaganda video in order to understand the workings of its audiovisual rhetoric. In one sequence, I attempt to reverse engineer the ISIS video by putting it into an editing timeline and cutting it into its individual shots. In doing so, I am re-performing the editing of the film, and am left with a loose replica of the editing timeline of the film, similar to what the original creator of the video would have had. Seeing this timeline on my own desktop put me in a very uneasy position of identification of power associated with media production, specifically extremist propaganda. That these uncomfortable dynamics of identification were then retransmitted to my audience created even more ethical unease.

These questions preoccupy me in pursuing the *Bottled Songs* project beyond its first phase that directly confronted ISIS videos. I am now investigating the ongoing legacy of ISIS propaganda media as digital archival material, and the 'afterlives' of this media as it finds its way into new contexts and uses. I am especially interested in how others have used this media to produce forms of critical spectatorship in the face of online extremist propaganda. Besides artists such as Morehshin Allahyari, there are also researchers, educators and security specialists, whose use of archival materials are examined later.

I lacked words to describe these dilemmas until I encountered the Medusa head in the Kunsthalle Mannheim. Attached to its base is a USB cable to which anyone can connect with a laptop. Upon doing so, the Medusa head is revealed to be a hard drive containing files that document how its creator, artist Morehshin Allahyari, used ISIS videos and research documents to create 3D printed reproductions of artifacts destroyed by ISIS. Allahyari initially intended to make the documentation of all her reconstructed artifacts freely available as a means to overcome the desecration of Middle Eastern cultural heritage enacted by ISIS violence: 'The more people 3D-print these, or even keep them as digital files . . . or read about the history of the artifacts – the more we have collectively resisted the act of forgetting.'

Figure 16.3 Unveiling of a replica of the Palmyra Arch in London, 19 April 2016. Source: Photograph by Reuters.

However, over time Allahyari noticed 'a huge spike in the act of reconstructing artifacts in Europe and the US in parallel with their destruction in Iraq and Syria'. She cites the Palmyra Arch, destroyed by ISIS in 2015, reconstructed using 3D modelling technology and unveiled in London's Trafalgar Square by the then London Mayor, Boris Johnson, who hailed the reconstruction as 'a triumph of technology and determination . . . in defiance of the barbarians who destroyed the original'. Allahyari remarks that Johnson's statement ignores the historical context of colonial and imperial violence inflicted by the West on the Middle East, such as the 2003 US and European invasion of Iraq that contributed to the rise of ISIS. The transference of the Palmyra Arch from its original site in Syria to central London highlights the role of digital technology in transferring cultural heritage from the Middle East to the West, a phenomenon Allahyari has termed 'digital colonialism'. Reflecting further on how an ostensibly humanitarian effort of cultural restoration perpetuates the violence of cultural dispossession, Allahyari offers another term to describe the instrumentalisation of goodwill and empathy. She writes: 'For any Western institution to focus on the reconstruction of the rare and special while other Western institutions have wrought the destruction of the everyday, is violent care.'

Does Allahyari's critique of digital colonialism express concern over the risk of violent care in her own digital restoration of the Medusa and other destroyed artifacts? Allahyari has kept her production files private, waiting for the right circumstances to entrust them to a museum or cultural institution in the Middle East. Realising that the project had entered a state of partial withdrawal, I was both puzzled and grateful that I could stand before the Medusa head in the Kunsthalle Mannheim, a situation made possible with Allahyari's consent. Having access to the history and struggle contained within the head, it addresses me like no other work in the exhibition. I start to imagine a voice associated with this head and ask how this voice could tell its own story. In what language would it speak, what accent would it have? How deep or light, female or non-gendered would it sound? As I speculate on a question impossible to answer, other visitors pass by, unaware of the deeper implications of this head and its presence in this exhibition.

This situation could describe a state of what Edouard Glissant termed opacity, the ethics of unknowability, the right not to be seen. It is a strategy that has become more present in the continuation of the *Bottled Songs* project, as I have fallen away from direct analysis and representation of ISIS media to avoid retransmitting harmful effects associated with its images. To what extent does this opacity support or obstruct the operations of the museum exhibition, to equip its visitors with tools to critically engage with political violence?

For this reason, I secured permission from the museum to film the Medusa head, though I was advised that I could not film any of the museum visitors to preserve their right to privacy. I started to imagine what it would look like to have scenes in the museum with every face rendered into a cloud of illegible pixels. How ironic if the only face exposed in the museum scene would be that of Medusa.

> Like no other work in the exhibition, the Medusa head drew your attention precisely because it was one of the most overlooked works among the museum visitors, its significance to the theme of the exhibition not plainly visible. It reminded you of a scene from *Images of the World and the Inscription of War* (1988), an essay film by Harun Farocki, that reflects extensively on the historical relationship between violence and visibility. The film famously muses upon a photograph taken by a US reconnaissance aircraft during World War II that inadvertently revealed the Auschwitz Nazi concentration camp. Despite this discovery, no action was taken. In his related essay 'Reality Would Have to Begin', Farocki muses, 'The analysts had no orders to look for the camps, and therefore did not find them.'

The most visible image of *Images of the World and the Inscription of War*, the one that appears most prominently in online searches for the film, is one that I've learned to see differently in recent years. It appears in a sequence in which Farocki sits at a desk before the camera, studying *Les Femmes Algeriennes* ('Women of Algeria'), a book of photographs by Marc Garanger, a French conscript stationed during the French occupation of Algeria in the early 1960s. Garanger was ordered to take photos of Algerian women for identification purposes as colonial subjects of France. Women who normally concealed their faces in daily life were photographed against their will. Their faces were exposed in a mode of colonial violence performed by producing visual data to carry on colonial administrative operations. Despite himself being instrumentalised by the French army in these operations, Garanger smuggled the photographs to Switzerland to be published and circulated as images of protest against the French occupation.

This sequence provokes three questions for you. Can these women's images of expressions of protest be separated from their expressions directed at Garanger as he trained his lens (however reluctantly) upon these women? Was Garanger's act of publication a form of violent care, in that it perpetuated and amplified an act of non-consensual image taking? Is it also worth considering that the book's assembly of these faces visualises a collective protest that wouldn't have been possible for those individuals in their actual lived conditions?

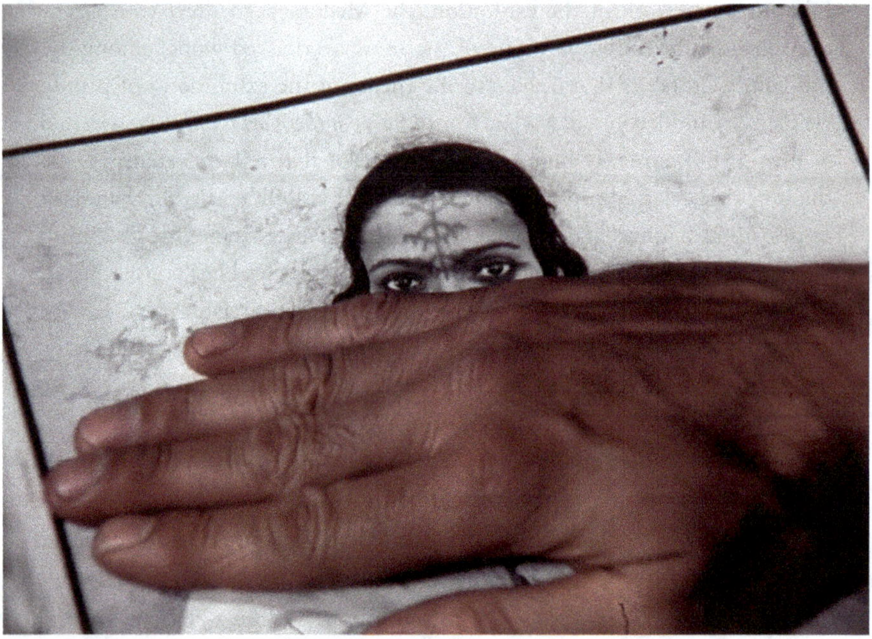

Figure 16.4 Still from *Images of the World and the Inscription of War*, dir. Harun Farocki.
Source: Image by Harun Farocki GbR.

In the film, Farocki turns the pages of Garanger's book, and with every page turned, a different woman's face is exposed. At one moment, he pauses to place his hand over the lower half of a woman's face, so that only her eyes remain visible as they normally would be under a veil. The gesture seems to recover the woman, in multiple senses of the word – to re-cover her face in order to recover her claim to her own image.

> When you first saw this image, you were struck by the brilliance of this gesture as a mode of critical analysis performed by the body. With a simple move of one's hand, one can not only study an image, but transform its meaning. It is a perfect example of the Farockian concept of the counter-image, *das Gegenbild* – an image that opposes another image in order to create a critical awakening. And in this case, one could also attribute this gesture with qualities of empathy and solidarity with the condition of the women in these photos.

When I consider this gesture now, I see a form of violent care. The hand of a male, functioning within the role of a Western researcher, performing a gesture of privilege and power over an image and the human being, the woman, represented by it. In this respect, the poetic gesture re-performs the violence over she who is captured in the image. Even if intended as a poetic gesture of resistance against the Western Colonialist gaze, it cannot quite overcome the institutional framework of the Western gaze and the implicit harm carried within it.

My own Western gaze seeks another view of this scene, not to justify Farocki's method, but to reaffirm the value of a counter-image, if it might even be utilised to critique its own author. In this instance, the counter-image is produced not through an alternative image, but an alternative way of looking at the existing image. Looking at this image now, informed by the visual culture of colonialism and violent care, what changes for me is that I am disinvested in Western agents such as Farocki or Garanger as producers and critical mediators of the image of the Algerian woman. Instead, I reinvest myself in the woman as central to determining the significance of her image. Her agency, her selfhood, becomes more legible to me, even if it remains woefully under-articulated. Above all, the question:

who can really speak on her behalf? The archival value of this image hinges upon this question.

> This came to your mind when encountering the Medusa head at the MINDBOMBS exhibition. You thought of a woman spoken of through an image taken against her will, then interpreted by another's hand. You thought of a head destroyed and digitally recreated in defiance of the forces of destruction, only for that effort to risk feeding back into a cycle of power and violence. You thought of the mythical being represented by the head: Medusa, a woman who was raped by a god whose wife then took vengeance on her, transforming her beauty into monstrosity: selfhood stolen twice over.

This led me to write the passage at the beginning of the chapter. Asking myself how to speak of the Medusa head, I was interested neither in a first-person mode of address that privileged my own subjective position over the head, or in a third person that conveyed a pretense of objective description. To address the Medusa head in the second person, I could simultaneously address my reader through my 'you' as a way to collapse the distance between these two audiences. In this way, I could re-embody the viewer in the subjectivity of the Medusa head.

> At least this is what, in most moments, you would like to believe.

AFTERWORD
ONE PERSON'S TERRORIST IS ANOTHER PERSON'S FREEDOM FIGHTER, ONE PERSON'S JIHAD IS ANOTHER'S CRUSADE: REFLECTIONS ON THE TOKYO REELS FILM FESTIVAL BY SUBVERSIVE FILM AT THE DOCUMENTA 15, 2022

Wendy M. K. Shaw

Near the end of my one long (very long) day in early September spent exploring the venues that staged the fifteenth edition of the quintennial exhibition Documenta held in the city of Kassel, I came through a narrow dark hallway in the former industrial park of the Hübner Company (a venue called the Hübner Areal), where mass transportation vehicles had, until recently, been manufactured. The black back of a film screen initially blocked my view of the cavernous dark space, soon to reveal on its other side a rise of black bleacher-style seating from which to watch the films projected upon it. I was so happy to sit down. Really. So thrilled, in fact, it took me a minute to find my bearings and process what I was seeing. At first, the couple canoodling in the opposite corner of the bleachers distracted me. Their slurpy passion seemed an odd reaction to the melange of recovered footage, replete with burnouts and leader, of children and fighters and Japanese and Palestinian families meeting in Japan, all in a melange, and then right in the mix footage of a very relaxed, perhaps a bit sly, Yasser Arafat explaining in English how much he admires the Japanese people. Then again, is there anything more romantic than revolution? Who has participated in the sustained passion of protest, taken to the streets in spontaneous unison borne of universal outrage and giving birth to hope without also sustaining that passion in the bodily lust for comrades? Perhaps the couple making out in the dark exhibited the most natural reaction. It is, after all, what cinema was made for.

The Tokyo Reels Film Festival on view is the work of Subversive Film, 'a cinema research and production collective that aims to cast new light upon historic works related to Palestine and the region, engender support for film preservation, and investigate archival practices and their effects'.[1] Complementing several longer films screened at the Gloria Kino, the project on view at the Hübner Areal shows a pastiche of films made between 1968 and 1982 under the banner of 'militant cinema' by Palestinian and Japanese filmmakers exploring mutual solidarity. The collective stitched together footage from a multitude of reels in various formats found in a long-forgotten private archive in Tokyo, transported to Belgium where they were restored, digitised and edited. As an effort to publicise 'the overlooked and still undocumented anti-imperialist solidarity between Japan and Palestine', the films exemplified the broader effort of the curatorial team, an Indonesian collective called Ruangrupa, to decentre Europe at the exhibition not simply through a more global inclusion of artists, but also through the recognition of a broad range of aesthetic collective practices that exceed the boundaries of art and implicit expectations of progress and national competition implicit in global art exhibition formats since the inception of the Venice Biennial in 1895.[2]

At an edition of Documenta plagued from the beginning by accusations of anti-Semitism, the only thing surprising about the call to censure the films (on 12 September) was that it did not happen earlier during the exhibition, which ran from 18 June to 25 September 2022. Although accusations of anti-Semitism at the unveiling of a massive work by the Indonesian Collective

---

[1] Available at <https://vimeo.com/706691709#> (last accessed 16 February 2023).

[2] Available at <https://www.theartnewspaper.com/2022/09/15/decision-to-ban-pro-palestine-films-engulfs-documenta-15-exhibition-in-another-censorship-row> (last accessed 16 February 2023).

Taring Padi had already led to scandal and immediate removal of the work following the exhibit opening, the films played for the duration.[3] Echoing the furore at the opening, the renewed accusation of anti-Semitism near the end of the exhibition framed it in a scandal deeply rooted both in the collective German psyche and in contemporary German politics. The discussion thereby overshadowed much other public reflection on the radical concept of the 2022 Documenta to decentre the notion of art as expressive forms reflective of individual and national identity, once designated as 'genius', designed within a framework of capitalist consumption in favour of a concept of art as creativity led by collectivity in service to community. Through a collective curatorial effort that redistributed curatorial power through work with other collectives, largely from the Global South, Ruangrupa cunningly recentred the militancy initially implicit in the term 'avant-garde'. In doing so, it laid bare the knuckles of 'jihad' against 'crusade', terms that waver between physical militarism and moral struggle, reflective of military histories as well as the geographical and spiritual connotations that flow as blood between them. The scandal at the heart of the Documenta 15 is not its anti-Semitism so much as the clash between two legacies of struggle at the heart of both the twentieth-century internationalisation of 'art' and the habit of Western supremacy.

Why consider this controversy in the context of a book on jihad? As the editors indicate in the introduction, the term 'jihad' functions well beyond the limited notion of militant Islam, to distinguish between rightful and wrongful political claims by denigrating the citizen rights of those labelled 'jihadists' or 'terrorists', leading to a unilateral 'perspective on complex systems of power, violence, fear, and domination and sees societal problems not as results of policy . . . but rather as brought about by a threatening "Other"'. Although the Palestinian Liberation Organisation, whose struggle is reflected in these films, never fought through discourses of Islam and renounced the use of violence for political ends in 1988, the legacy of their activities echoes in contemporary public consciousness with more recent, explicitly Islamist armed struggle in the Middle East. One community's freedom struggle, aiming to

---

[3] 'Ruangrupa and the Artistic Team on Dismantling "People's Justice"', 23 June 2022. Available at <https://documenta-fifteen.de/en/press-releases/ruangrupa-on-dismantling-peoples-justice-by-taring-padi/> (last accessed 16 February 2023).

recoup land designated as belonging to the State of Israel in 1948 and resulting in the ethnic cleansing of local populations, and expanded outside of internationally recognised borders as a result of the 1967 six-day war, easily slips
into the designation of 'terrorist' through the association of militancy with
Islamic religious identity implicit in the term 'jihad'. The moral righteousness
of securing political legitimacy against a state understood as having the legitimate right to violence comes to coincide with the moral righteousness associated with religion. The sad irony is that the local population of Palestine that
was 9.5 per cent Christian under British Mandatory Palestine in 1922 largely
fled, rendering the contemporary occupied territories 98–9 per cent Muslim.
Such regional homogeneity, enabling the conflation of political and religious
identity, was unprecedented before the twentieth century.[4]

If the 'terrorist' of the Middle East can all too easily be understood through
the bogeyman trope of the 'jihadist', the righteous voice of the European easily slips into the trope of the 'crusader'. Where the 'jihadist' is understood
as fighting for the wrong god, the false god, the irrational god, the designation of Islam through such tropes of blasphemy reflect a long tradition
defining Europe through a collective Christian identity established during
the Crusades that conveniently forgets the sizable minorities of Christians of
Islamic-hegemonic lands before the sorting of national populations, through
population-exchange, assimilation and ethnic cleansing, during the twentieth
century (Hamilton 1997). Indeed, the association of the term 'jihad' with
the concept of 'holy war' emerges not in the Qur'an or Ḥadīth (sayings of
the Prophet, upon which Islamic law is based), but as a mirror reflection
of the eleventh-century emergence of the term as applied to the Crusades
(Bakircioğlu 2010). Conversely, just as early Islamic sources use jihad to
reflect inner struggle with the temptations of selfhood (*nafs*), the notion of
'crusade' has been frequently demilitarised to designate any collective struggle
against a perceived evil, such as those of alcohol or drugs. Regardless of their
origins, both terms have come to harbour networks of associations, ranging
from the spiritual to the militant and associated, respectively, with Islam in
the twentieth-century fight against European colonialism of Islamic-majority

---

[4] Available at <https://en.wikipedia.org/wiki/Palestinian_Christians> (last accessed 16 February 2023).

regions and against the dominance of 'Western' civilisation through political might, cultural hegemony and/or economic legitimacy in various configurations (Heng 2011).

These shifts parallel the slippage of another articulation of militancy between the cultural and the political embodied in the slippage of the term 'avant-garde', first applied to the social role of artists by Olinde Rodrigues, a follower of the utopian socialist Saint Simon, in 1825. He proposed that

> the power of the arts is in fact most immediate and most rapid when we wish to spread new ideas among men, we inscribe them on marble or on canvas . . . what a magnificent destiny for the arts is that of exercising a positive power over society, a true priestly function, and of marching forcefully in the van of all the intellectual faculties . . . (Egbert 1967: 343)

Adopted in 1838 by Honoré de Balzac who associated it with the bohemian, anti-bourgeois lifestyles such independence fostered, the idea merged with Theophile Gautier's 1835 call for art for art's sake, which asserted that art should be valuable within its own aesthetic function. The application of an evolutionary schema to art through the application of Hegelian philosophy to art history starting in the late nineteenth century enabled modern art to function as a barometer of power, enabling international competitions and prizes in global biennials (Nelson 1997). This legacy of art as a political agent persists as well in the name 'documenta', initially applied to the exhibit of previously prohibited art, designated as 'degenerate' (*entartete*) during the Nazi era, during the Federal Horticultural Show (Bundesgartenschau) of 1955 to articulate the notion of intellectual instruction through art, but also, perhaps less explicitly, to re-establish Germany as a powerful, peaceful actor on the global stage after an era of isolation (Kimpel 1997).

Since that time, the quintennial 100-day exhibition has served as both a reflection on and a challenge for the recognition of what constitutes art, and the drive towards art, at a particular historical moment. Thus the capacity of accusations of anti-Semitism to overshadow a critique of the dominant art-as-commodity system driving Documenta 15 actually reflects the objectives of Documenta as a political agent that might be conceived in two ways: first, echoing Rodrigues's definition, as a reflection of the contemporary order that challenges hegemonic expectations; and second, echoing the bohemian aesthetic favoured under depoliticised, formal definitions of 'art', as a place-marker for the naturalised centrality of Germany in the hegemonic, and there-fore apparently timeless, global world order. While the trope of protection against 'anti-Semitism' has been articulated as an ever-watchful, righteous, protective eye over the Jewish people, it has been deployed as a means of silencing a far more elemental challenge to the capitalist system that has pro-duced much of the imagery of modern anti-Semitism, and upon which the art world is based, and which the Documenta 15 calls into question.

An understanding of this challenge and resistance requires two quick frameworks of contextualisation: first, of the art world sidelined by the meth-ods of Documenta 15; and second, of the discourse of 'anti-Semitism' through which its challenge has been marginalised. To the extent that the first chal-lenge might be championed as offering a path of inner struggle (jihad) against an oppressive global financial-political order, it also comes to be derided as terrorist by a hegemonic resistance framing itself as righteously crusading against a pervasive and insidious evil. One person's terrorist is another per-son's freedom fighter, and also the other way around.

The phenomenon widely known as 'the art world' is a system that has emerged over the course of the twentieth century, often recognised as the second-largest unregulated market in the world (after drugs, to which one might add weapons) (Spiegler 2005). With no means of regulating value, little control over sale and resale, and subject to rapid shifts in market value as governed through complex networks of individual collectors, auction houses, galleries, periodic exhibitions and museums, the art market confers legitimat-ing cultural capital to a wide range of wealthy actors while also enabling the processing of funds from illegitimate to legitimate financial dealings. While art is often romanticised as an individual act, reflective of inspired thought, personal talent, individual genius and reflective of ethnic/national interests, identity and resources, its implication within global financial systems has often rendered its function as a commodity as inseparable from its expressive agency. Artwork that aims at political action often finds itself trapped within the very networks of political, hegemonic and financial power that it seeks to critique.

In this context, and against the backdrop of pending climate cataclysm, rising authoritarianisms and increasing disparities between the wealth and poverty both between and within nation states, at Documenta 15 Ruangrupa slyly critiqued the apparently insurmountable paradigm of art established in the hegemonic art-market system by largely ignoring it. Instead of foregrounding curators as people who select a panoply of known artists joined by a few promising newcomers that is the standard fare of traditional multi-annual exhibitions, such as the crop of international biennials and art fairs that have proliferated after the 1950s and particularly after the 1980s, Ruangrupa invited international collectives to invite artists and collectives whose work engages with community in a wide variety of ways. By focusing on communities rather than art, and on practices of making and gathering rather than on products, the resulting edition of Documenta proved disappointing to those looking for a studied reflection on the art of today. For many, there was no art there. For others, this non-art revealed the beating heart of creativity that survives in the solidarity of collectives who come together through creativity and mutual support. This vision punctures the apparently absolute, universal system of art, which is itself a metonym for the absolute nature of capitalism. The exhibition suggested a vision of what art might be outside of capitalism (Meier 2022; Brown 2022).

Yet the primary critique of the exhibition circled around perceived anti-Semitism. The first controversy focused on figures in an expansive 2002 painting by the Indonesian collective Taring Padi satirising the global support of the autocratic Suharto regime of 1967 to 1998. Stylistically reminiscent of the vibrant, violent, irreverent tradition of caricature, parody and critique embodied in the work of George Grosz (1893–1959), the work brought the Weimar-era style home to a surprisingly less open-minded German audience horrified by the inclusion of overtly anti-Semitic tropes in representation of Israeli officers supporting, alongside others, the Suharto regime (Batycka 2022). Offensive as the tropes are on their own, the context within the larger painting reveals a much more complex history through which Germany was able to export its visual culture through networks of colonialism (Rothberg 2022). Rather than engaging in the meaning of the work as a whole, expressing reactions to a politics largely unknown outside of Indonesia and yet within which so many of us, as citizens of supporting nations, are implicated, the controversy erased the possibility of listening to the expression of non-European actors (Rothberg 2019). Likewise, the broader issues raised by the Archives des Luttes des Femmes en Algérie, an Algerian women's collective, disappeared within the focus on a 1988 brochure focused on political strife in Palestine, including images of Israeli soldiers with Stars of David, one of which is depicted as a monkey being kneed by a woman. In both cases, the only recognisable speech by critics was the quotation from the European visual lexicon.

Taken as art in the sense of aesthetic achievement, these works violate legitimate, even commendable, and perhaps even righteous norms of collective behaviour censoring hate speech in all its forms. One would not want these works to decorate living rooms or concert halls, or to be placed in museums as exemplars of artistic genius. But in these contexts of political strife, the capacity to recycle visual tropes born in Europe and disseminated globally reflects an earlier cycle of the same power dynamic that now crusades against it. In crusading against anti-Semitism at the exhibit, German commentators reasserted their power to establish global norms, now in a manner perceived as philo- rather than anti-Semitic. By establishing the German voice as that of global arbiter, however, critics of Documenta as anti-Semitic regulate the possibility of speech from non-Western actors concerning not Judaism per se, but the State of Israel understood as representing all Jews – the widely critiqued framework put forth by the International Holocaust Remembrance Alliance (IHRA) and opposed by the Jerusalem Declaration's distinction between anti-Zionism and anti-Semitism.[5] The controversy reiterated previous instances of the censorship of non-German actors, particularly from the Global South, for failing to align their speech within German norms of support for the State of Israel (Michaels 2020). Conversely, critique of German participants in the art market with direct connections to Nazi histories and wealth have been far less controversial (Rothberg and Hauenstein 2021).

The righteousness behind the critique stems from the moral work engaged by large swathes of the German people to process and set right the historic wrongs of the National Socialist Era through unwavering support of the State of Israel, a solution established through the *Vergangenheitsaufarbeitung*

---

[5] Available at <https://www.holocaustremembrance.com/resources/working-definitions-charters/working-definition-antisemitism> (last accessed 16 February 2023); <https://jerusalemdeclaration.org> (last accessed 16 February 2023).

(working out of the past) dominating German public discourses since the reunification of Germany in 1990. The focus on works critiquing Israel in its domination of Palestine through the trope of 'anti-Semitism' focuses on three regions – Indonesia, Algeria and Palestine – with large Muslim populations. As such, it reflects a common apprehension of Islam as inherently anti-Western and anti-Jewish, raising the spectre of jihadism behind the memories of 1970s militancy conceived as 'terrorism'. Yet, in Germany, the driving force behind this critique has been an internal working-through and coming to terms with the self. *Vergangenheitsaufarbeitung* might be conceived as a jihad in its original sense, which has less to do with Islam as a belief system than with making peace with the unresolved self through which to become able to engage with (in the case of Islam) the Divine or, in the case of Germany, with the rest of the world.

The controversy over the films underscores the losses when the internal jihad of German political memory overrides the possibility of the speech of others. For what makes the Tokyo–Palestine reels special is not their capacity to induce militancy in contemporary viewers, so much of their reflection of the global solidarity network that enabled the films to survive to the present, in the absence of government institutions as well as input from Western forces. The pastiche of films may have made that couple enjoy a welcome respite from the exhibition, but it hardly set them to joining a cause. It included footage of Palestinians as producers of their own image, less as victims and refugees than as people resisting the ethnic cleansing of their land. Unlike in the case of the Taring Padi painting and the pamphlet, here there were no quoted tropes to be interpreted as anti-Semitic, but perhaps something far more subversive: the capacity of one people to listen to the suffering of another. The films do not simply screen militant Palestinian propaganda, but they demonstrate the support of an unrelated collective of people in Tokyo to value that speech. If there is to be an inner jihad born of the horrors of the past, it would be articulated not through a crusade honouring the infinite historical tragedies that will always remain irredeemable, but to achieve the humility necessary to engage with the Other in the fullness of their unfamiliar, sometimes uncomfortable, and frequently challenging speech without stepping in the way.

The distinction between legitimate and illegitimate speech, like that between legitimate and illegitimate violence, rests on the fulcrum of power.

In the effort to critique the system of power embodied in capitalism, Ruangrupa relinquished the curatorial imperative to control. In doing so, it suggested how collectives enable a complexity of speech that may often challenge the desire for a curated, frictionless world, one often supposed to exist in the realm of art. By resisting this possibility of conflict and friction, the accusations of anti-Semitism surrounding the exhibit of Documenta 15 recognised this challenge not as a working out of the problems of the past as inherited by the present, but as a threat to the solutions of a global order that depends on ignoring our immanent collective peril. East v. West, Muslim v. Christian, Jihadist v. Crusader, Terrorist v. Peacemaker: if the answer to conflict remains its censorship, then how sustainable is the peace achieved?

References

Bakircioğlu, Ö. (2010), 'A Socio-legal Analysis of the Concept of Jihad', *The International and Comparative Law Quarterly*, 59: 2, 413–40.

Batycka, D. (2022), 'All the Red Lines Have been Crossed', *Artnet*, 21 June, <https://news.artnet.com/art-world/documenta-conceal-artwork-antisemitism-2133662> (last accessed 16 February 2023).

Brown, K. (2022), 'Documenta Presents an Invigorating Alternative to a Market-driven Art World: Maybe That's Why the Industry's Establishment Has Largely Dismissed It', *Artnet*, 1 July, <https://news.artnet.com/market/documenta-art-market-2135862> (last accessed 16 February 2023).

Egbert, D. D. (1967), 'The Idea of "Avant-Garde" in Art and Politics', *The American Historical Review*, 73: 2, 339–66.

Hamilton, B. (1997), 'Knowing the Enemy: Western Understanding of Islam at the Time of the Crusades', *Journal of the Royal Asiatic Society*, 7: 3, 373–87.

Heng, G. (2011), 'Holy War Redux: The Crusades, Futures of the Past, and Strategic Logic in the "Clash" of Religions', *PMLA*, 126: 2, 422–31.

Kimpel, H. (1997), *Documenta, Mythos und Wirklichkeit*, Cologne: Jonas Verlag.

Meier, P. (2022), 'Documenta in Kassel: Eine Ausstellung ohne Künstler. Gekommen sind vor allem unbekannte Aktivisten', *Neue Zürcher Zeitung*, 17 June, <https://www.nzz.ch/feuilleton/die-documenta-in-kassel-eine-kunstausstellung-ohne-kuenstler-ld.1688894> (last accessed 16 February 2023).

Michaels, R. (2020), 'On the Mbembe Anti-Semitism Debate in Germany: A Decolonial Critique of German Universalism', *Max Plank Law*, 4 August, <https://law.mpg.de/wp-content/uploads/Perspectives-Ralf-Michaels-On-the-Mbembe-Anti-Semitism-Debate-in-Germany.pdf> (last accessed 16 February 2023).

Nelson, R. S. (1997), 'The Map of Art History', *The Art Bulletin*, 79: 1, 28–40.

Rothberg, M. (2019), *The Implicated Subject: Beyond Victims and Perpetrators*, Stanford: Stanford University Press 2019.

Rothberg, M. (2022), 'Learning and Unlearning with Taring Padi: Reflections on Documenta', in *New Fascism Syllabus*, 2 July, <http://newfascismsyllabus.com/opinions/documenta/learning-and-unlearning-with-taring-padi-reflections-on-documenta/> (last accessed 16 February 2023).

Rothberg, M. and H. Hauenstein (2021), 'Nazi-Hintergrund, NS-Erbe und materielle Kontinuiität', *Berliner Zeitung*, 10 April, <https://www.berliner-zeitung.de/wochenende/nazi-hintergrund-ns-erbe-und-materielle-kontinuitaet-das-schweigen-brechen-li.150838> (last accessed 16 February 2023).

Spiegler, M. (2005), 'The Art Trade is the Last Major Unregulated Market', *The Art Newspaper*, 1 June, <https://www.theartnewspaper.com/2005/06/01/the-art-trade-is-the-last-major-unregulated-market> (last accessed 16 February 2023).

INDEX

EU representative:
Easy Access System Europe
Mustamäe tee 50, 10621 Tallinn, Estonia
Gpsr.requests@easproject.com

www.ingramcontent.com/pod-product-compliance
Lightning Source LLC
Chambersburg PA
CBHW050623280326
41932CB00015B/2497